LINGUISTICS AND LANGUAGE

JULIA S. FALK

Michigan State University

LINGUISTICS AND LANGUAGE

A SURVEY OF BASIC CONCEPTS AND IMPLICATIONS

Second Edition

JOHN WILEY & SONS

New York • Chichester • Brisbane • Toronto

Library of Congress Cataloging in Publication Data

Falk, Julia S
  Linguistics and language.

  Bibliography: p.
  Includes indexes.
    1. Linguistics.   2.   Language and languages.
I. Title.
P121.F28   1978   410   77-22927
  ISBN 0-471-02529-1

Printed in the United States of America

10 9 8 7 6 5 4 3 2

ADAPTED FROM THE PREFACE TO THE FIRST EDITION

Although linguistics is the field of inquiry most fully concerned with the investigation of human language, scholars and students in other disciplines are also interested in language. It is to such readers—interested in language but not specialists in linguistics—that this introductory survey is directed. In general, the topics included are essential for an understanding of the nature of language and provide insights into language that are useful to those concerned with such areas as elementary and secondary education, foreign language teaching, speech and speech therapy, psychology, and sociology.

As an introductory survey of linguistics and its implications for other disciplines, this book is not designed to teach the reader how to carry out linguistic analyses of language. Narrower, but more detailed, works exist for that purpose. Nor will the reader find here a full and explicit discussion of English or of any other language. Examples are provided, of course, but their purpose is to illustrate general principles of linguistic theory and application. All examples come from real languages, although the use of real examples has occasionally required that data be simplified for the sake of clarity of presentation. The majority of the examples are taken from English, but, in discussions of such topics as foreign language teaching, an effort has been made to draw from those languages most commonly taught in the United States. Other, less familiar, languages are also discussed in order to illustrate the diversity that exists among human languages, as well as to demonstrate that there are many similarities among all languages, even those often assumed to be greatly different from English.

This survey basically follows the assumptions, goals, and terminology of an approach to linguistics known as transformational grammar. Some linguists investigate language within somewhat different frameworks, but the transformational approach is the most widely utilized and also the most relevant to other disciplines. It is, therefore, the most useful approach for the beginner in linguistics, as well as for the nonspecialist.

The basic concepts and some of the results of contemporary linguistic research are presented in Parts 2, 3, 5, and 6, while Parts 4, 7, 8, and 9 are devoted to those linguistic issues of more immediate concern to specialists in other fields. Technical terminology is found in any scientific discipline, and linguistics is no exception. The terms are necessary if linguists are to share a clear, concise, objective way of discussing language. The nonlinguist must master the basic terminology of the field in order to comprehend not only purely linguistic works but also the ever increasing number of linguistically oriented books and articles relevant to his own special area of interest, whether it is the acquisition of language by children, the teaching of reading and writing, the mastery of foreign languages, the analysis of literary style, or the investigation of dialect differences. The majority of special terms are introduced along with the basic linguistic material in Parts 2, 3, 5, and 6.

In an initial overview of a subject as broad as human language, some aspects must be omitted or presented in less detail than they might otherwise deserve. Those who wish to become more fully acquainted with the issues and questions about language presented here should go on to other, more advanced studies. To that end, each chapter of this survey concludes with an annotated list of articles and books containing more detailed information about the topics that have been introduced. Complete bibliographic information is provided in the Bibliography for all selections discussed in "Further Exploration" at the end of each chapter.

I gratefully acknowledge the influence of those scholars whose works are cited at the conclusion of each chapter and in the cumulative bibliography of this book. Some were my teachers, others are friends and colleagues, and still others I know only through their writings. All have made important contributions to linguistics—contributions that are the foundation of this work.

J.S.F.

PREFACE TO
THE SECOND EDITION

In this new edition, every chapter has undergone at least some minor revision, but the basic orientation, organization, and approach remain the same as in the first edition. The most noticeable addition is a section, at the end of each chapter, on "Further Exploration," containing material that an instructor may use as a basis for class discussions, supplementary lectures, or homework assignments. Students will find that much of this material may be pursued independently. The "Further Exploration" sections contain: (1) annotated recommendations for additional reading at appropriate levels of difficulty, (2) flexible activities and topics for discussion and exploration, (3) applications and extensions of the concepts introduced within the chapter, and (4) exercises for practice with the techniques, tools, and terminology of descriptive linguistics. In many cases, these supplementary materials go beyond the typical, mechanical exercises of introductory texts and, instead, require readers to think about new concepts, explore and test them, and relate them to their own language experiences. Thus, in some instances, the explorations will result in open-ended discussions, with no single "right" response. This appropriately reflects the reality of certain aspects of current linguistic research.

The major textual revisions occur in Parts 6, 8, and 9. Part 6, now entitled "Syntax, Semantics, and Pragmatics," has been considerably expanded to include recent developments in linguistics. For the interdisciplinary areas of child language acquisition, foreign language learning, and reading in the elementary school, Parts 8 and 9 have been revised and expanded in order to incorporate the significant advances of the past five years. Several other chapters also include new material.

Length has increased because of these expansions, but instructors will still find it feasible to use the text in shorter courses (e.g., 30 class hours), as well as in the traditional half-year semester. Each chapter is sufficiently self-contained, with important terms and concepts adequately defined and illustrated, so that students can achieve satisfactory understanding through independent reading. Therefore, it is possible to use the text either for courses that emphasize linguistic theory and description or for courses that focus on the interdisciplinary aspects and implications of linguistics for related fields; material not directly relevant to the primary aim of a course may be assigned as outside reading or even omitted entirely. Terms and concepts introduced in unassigned chapters may be located through the detailed Subject Index whenever necessary for other chapters in which such terms occur.

In addition to the Subject Index and the Language Index, this edition contains an Author Index identifying all references in the text to books and articles by the scholars whose work provides background information or recommended supplementary reading. As in the first edition, full bibliographic information appears in the Bibliography.

J. S. F.

CONTENTS

PART 11111111111111111

INTRODUCTION

CHAPTER 11111111111111111111111111

THE STUDY OF LANGUAGE

Our everyday encounters with language are so natural and so extensive that we rarely consider language as an object of sufficient interest to warrant study. Language is always there, and we make use of it automatically, often without any conscious effort. All human beings have known and used a language since childhood. On the surface, there is nothing particularly interesting about so commonplace a phenomenon as human language. In fact, it is widely believed that, because everyone knows a language, everything about language is known. Yet, this is far from true.

Since the use of language is so natural to all people, it may seem that language itself must be quite simple, perhaps consisting of many words but involving only a few principles that serve to control pronunciation and the organization of these words into sentences. However, investigation of any human language demonstrates that a language is an extremely complex, highly abstract, and infinitely productive system linking meanings with sounds. We all know the system of our native language, but this knowledge, although constantly in use, lies far below our consciousness. We may be able to describe particular sentences that we hear and we are certainly able to produce and understand an unending variety of sentences, but the foundation of these abilities is a body of knowledge about our language that we cannot readily explain. Observing an activity, even participating in it, is not equivalent to understanding it. Many people, for example, are able to work out arithmetic problems with large numbers, without being able to describe the mental processes they have used in arriving at the answer. It is possible to be a skillful driver and yet be unable to describe the mechanical functioning of an automobile or the neurophysiological bases for one's own physical actions (such as steering or braking) and mental decisions (such as when to steer or brake). Similarly, we speak and comprehend sentences with little or no awareness of the mental and physical processes involved in language.

The goal of linguistics—the scientific study of language—is to describe languages and to explain the unconscious knowledge all speakers have of their language. Science does not consist merely of the observation and description of phenomena, although these are the two activities of the scientist that are most obvious to the outsider. Every science, including linguistics, seeks to discover the general principles which underlie the variety of observable facts. In human language, the factual data are almost overwhelming, although linguistics has made substantial progress in describing and explaining many of the characteristics of language.

Every human being is capable of producing or understanding an infinite number of possible sentences in his or her language. Each day, we encounter sentences we have never seen or heard before, and yet we understand them and don't even notice that they are new. We speak, but usually we are not aware of the movements of our tongue, lips, or other parts of the mouth or throat involved in the production of sounds. Given a set of sentences, our knowledge of English leads us to a judgment about which sentences follow the normal patterns of our language and which do not; we can determine when a sentence has more than one meaning or when several sentences all have the same meaning. These and many other facts about language require an explanation. What is it that speakers of a language know? What kind of knowledge underlies our daily use of language? When we hear speech, all that really reaches our ears is noise; what do we know that enables us to interpret this noise as the expression of meaning? Such questions form the basis of the linguist's investigation of human language.

MODERN CONCERNS

Linguists are not the only scholars who are concerned with the study of language. In many other fields, an understanding of language is highly important. In studying language, educators, philosophers, psychologists, anthropologists, and students of literature all find important insights into their own areas of specialization.

Elementary school teachers, whose task it is to help children learn to read and write, can carry out their responsibilities effectively only if they understand the relationship between writing and speech, the level of language acquisition that the child has achieved at the time of school entrance, and the role that dialect differences may play in children's reading difficulties. The secondary school teacher also needs some understanding of language for the analysis of literary style, as well as for such matters as the effective teaching of composition and classes in the grammar of English. In foreign language teaching, it is not enough to provide students with examples of the foreign language. The teacher must be aware of the rules and forms that make up the language system, and, if students are ever to achieve complete command of the foreign language, the teacher must understand the kind of linguistic knowledge possessed by native speakers of that language.

The philosopher finds in language one of the chief factors that distinguishes man from other animals. What language is and how it contributes to man's special place in the universe are matters of important philosophical concern. Furthermore, the philosopher is interested in determining relationships between language and logic and between language and thought. To do so requires a sophisticated understanding of language. For the psychologist, language provides a wealth of material for the investigation of learning. Any theory of how people learn must be able to account for the acquisition of language since all human beings, except for those with serious mental or physical problems, do learn their native language completely and perfectly during childhood. Indeed, the learning of our first language is generally considered to be our most complex intellectual achievement. Linguists and psychologists share so many interests in the study of language that a new interdisciplinary study—psycholinguistics—evolved during the 1960s. In the past decade, psycholinguistic research has involved such issues as the relationship between language and cognition, the development of language in children, and the interpretation of meaning in sentences.

Anthropology and linguistics have long been closely related fields in the United States. Much of the work in linguistics during the early part of this century was carried out by anthropologists investigating the language and culture of various American Indian communities. Even today, the anthropologist must deal with language as an integral part of the culture of any society. For the sociologist, an understanding of language is also important, especially insofar as particular varieties of language are associated with particular social groups. Another interdisciplinary field—sociolinguistics—reflects the interrelationship between sociology and linguistics. Extensive recent work in sociolinguistics has treated the matter of social dialects—differences in language and language use that correlate with differences in social class.

Authors and poets, as well as literary critics, are interested in language as the medium in which ideas are expressed. To understand the use of language in prose or poetry, one must also understand the possibilities for expression offered by the language. Even to those individuals with no special professional needs regarding language, there are significant advantages in knowing the assumptions and results of linguistic research. Only through an awareness of language can one truly appreciate its use, not only in literature but also in everyday life. The appreciation and understanding of language and language use are not purely an aesthetic matter; sometimes, language is used to confuse or mislead. Vagueness or ambiguity in advertising, highly legalistic contracts, evasive responses made to reporters or in the courtroom—these are only a few examples of common instances where linguistic awareness may have important practical consequences for both speaker and listener, writer and reader.

Of all of the modern concerns regarding language, only those of the linguist deal directly and immediately with language itself. Other scholars are interested in the relationship between language and other aspects of man or the world. But before such scholars can develop adequate theories and explanations of language in relation to other factors, it is necessary that they understand the nature of language. Linguistics provides this understanding and thus serves as a basic source of information for the development of theories, explanations, and methods in many other fields of inquiry.

HISTORICAL PERSPECTIVES

Concern with language is not new. From the earliest recorded history, there is evidence that people investigated language. Many of the assumptions, theories, and goals of modern linguistics find their origin in past centuries. In addition, nonlinguistic studies of language have also been influenced by the ideas of the past, as have the views about language held by many people in our society. A brief overview of the history of linguistics provides a base for understanding the contributions of the past, as well as the misconceptions about language that developed in earlier times and have continued among nonlinguists until today.

Much of the terminology used in the modern study of language dates back to ancient Greece, when philosophers and literary critics devised terms to use in their study of language. The earliest records of Greek interest in language relate to the Sophists in the fifth century B.C. The Sophists' concerns were practical in nature, for they were teachers of rhetoric, the art of public debate. Not greatly interested in understanding the principles underlying language, the Sophists carefully studied the speeches of the masters and counted the various elements in such speeches. They then advised their students to use the same number of sentences, words, and syllables in their own language, modeling their utterances on those of the masters. The meaning of a speech was of little interest to these rhetoricians; they were interested primarily in the linguistic form. This practical and purely descriptive approach to the study of language, however, was of relatively little interest to the Greek philosophers, who were more concerned with the nature of language, people, the world, and the relationships among them. One of the earliest philosophical questions about language is still with us today—what is the relationship between the pronunciation of a word and its meaning? Some scholars argued that the relationship was a natural one in which pronunciation was related to meaning, while others maintained that the relationship was conventional and arbitrary with no direct connection to reality. In support of the "natural" position, Greek scholars cited the Greek equivalents to such English words as *moo, bow-wow, crunch,* and *tinkle,* in which the pronunciation seems to bear some resemblance to the actual sounds involved in the activity represented by the words. Supporters of the "convention" position pointed to the fact that a large majority of words in language bear no such relationship to natural sounds. There is, for example, no reason why a table should be called *table;* it could just as well be called *mesa,* as it is in Spanish. It should be pointed out that the Greeks studied mainly their own language. Not having evidence of words with the same meaning but completely different pronunciations in other languages, it was relatively easy for the naturalists to maintain their position. But, today, with the linguistic descriptions of many languages available, the "natural" view is clearly untrue for the great majority of words found in all languages. Of course, there are instances of apparent connections between sound and meaning, but in insufficient number to assume the "natural" view for language in general. For the most part, then, the "convention" view that the relationship between sound and meaning is arbitrary provides the most valid and accurate position.

A second matter of philosophical concern in Greek linguistics that is still of interest today revolves around the issue of regularity in language. Some scholars maintained that language was basically systematic and regular and set about demonstrating their view by describing the consistent patterns found in Greek word formation. Examples of such patterns in English are the plural forms, such as *maps, characteristics, interests,* and *effects,* in which the plural is created by adding *s* to the singular form. Other Greek philosophers, while not denying that regularity was present in language, emphasized that there were many aspects of Greek that appeared to be irregular. In English, words that do not follow the general pattern for plural formation include *men, sheep,* and *children.* Those who stressed the regularity in language were known as analogists, while those who emphasized the presence of irregularity were called anomalists. It is clear today that language is essentially systematic and regular. If it were not, there would be no way in which human beings could learn such a complex system. The Greek interest in regularity and irregularity led grammarians to describe both aspects of the Greek language, thereby establishing a form of language description which survives today. Modern linguists seek to describe the regularities in language and account for the irregularities. It is often the case that what initially appears to be irregular is, upon careful investigation, actually a regular, systematic form.

Not all Greek interest in language centered on philosophical matters. The Alexandrians of the third and second centuries B.C. were interested in the literature of the past. Since all languages change over a period of time, the literature written in the fifth century B.C. contained words and expressions that differed from those used by the Alexandrians themselves. It was necessary, then, for literary scholars to produce commentaries on the differences between the language of literature and the language spoken by the people. These commentaries served as guides for understanding the literature, much as do the explanatory notes often found in modern publications of Shakespeare's plays. An unfortunate side effect of the Alexandrian study of language in relation to literature has continued down to our own times. Admiration for the literature led to the totally unwarranted assumption that the use of language in great literature is somehow "better" or "more pure" than everyday language use. Common speech was assumed to be a "corrupt" form of language. From an objective point of view, there is no truth to such claims. A language is a system for the communication of meaning, and every language meets the communicative needs of its users. If the fifth century B.C. writers of Athens had lived instead in third and second century B.C. Alexandria, they would have used the language of Alexandria in their works. Yet, the Alexandrian scholars' emphasis on an older, written form of the Greek language influenced the study of language for many centuries.

The most influential and well-known Roman grammarians followed the Alexandrian tradition. Writing about Latin, rather than Greek, they nevertheless concentrated on the language of literature instead of describing the Latin used by their contemporaries. Although Latin and Greek are different languages, many Roman scholars used the same terms and forms of description as the Greeks had several centuries before. To some extent, this method of analysis worked fairly well, for there are a number of similarities between the two languages. But, when the same tradition of grammatical description was later applied to other languages such as English, the result was a distortion of English—an attempt to fit it into the same mold which had been designed for quite different languages. Even today it is possible to encounter notions, totally out of place for English, but nevertheless set forth as "rules" for "correct" usage. Consider, for example, the claim sometimes made in "grammar" books, that it is wrong to split an infinitive. That is, sentences like the following are said to be incorrect:

(1) For this assignment, you are expected *to clearly describe* the major factors that resulted in the decline of Roman civilization.

(2) *To fully understand* the effect of gamma rays, a person must have some background in science.

The idea that adverbs such as *clearly* or *fully* should not be placed between *to* and a verb can be traced back to Latin. In Latin, the infinitive form of a verb consisted of only one word, as in *describere* 'to describe'. It was, therefore, impossible in Latin to split an infinitive, for to do so would require the insertion of an adverb into the middle of another word. There is no similar reason to prohibit split infinitives in modern English. Such prohibitions arise in part because the rules of Latin are incorrectly applied to English. Languages often share a number of characteristics, but in describing a language one should take care not to impose on it the characteristics of some other language.

The descriptive work of the Roman grammarians, based on written language, continued for approximately a thousand years, supported in part by the fact that Latin was the language used by European scholars until the fifteenth century. Other scholars were more interested in philosophy than in language description and literary criticism, and, beginning in the thirteenth century, a different tradition of linguistic research began to emerge.

Scholastic philosophy, dominant during the thirteenth and fourteenth centuries, attempted to form a unified theory of human knowledge. The scholastic philosophers concerned with the study of language were known as Modistae. They sought not merely to describe language but also to explain why languages consist of systems of rules and forms. Their explanations were based on a series of assumptions about the relationship between language, thought, and the universe: thoughts and knowledge are determined by the universe (since both refer to, or are about, the universe), and language is a reflection of thought. The Modistae concluded that because the universe is governed by a system of rules, thought and the attainment of knowledge are also rule-governed, and, therefore, language is also rule-governed. Furthermore, according to the Modistae, the universe, including the people in it, is everywhere the same, and language, as a concrete means for expressing this knowledge, must also be universal. Despite the superficial differences among human languages, there are basic, underlying similarities—a core of linguistic universals shared by all human languages. The Modistae's interest in explanation, linguistic universals, and a theory of language was continued by the rationalist philosophers of the sixteenth, seventeenth, and eighteenth centuries. Although there were important philosophical differences between the Modistae and the later rationalists, both groups were concerned with the meaning of linguistic utterances as well as with their form. The questions that they asked about the nature of language, as well as many of the answers that they proposed, are strikingly similar to those of concern to modern scientific linguists.

Between the rationalist approach to the study of language and the modern linguistic view intervened a period of more than one hundred and fifty years when different interests prevailed among scholars of language. Late in the eighteenth century, European students of language were exposed to another tradition of linguistic description—that of India —and to the Sanskrit language, which had been spoken in India long before the time of Christ. Studies of ancient Indian descriptions of Sanskrit revealed many similarities between this language and Greek and Latin. European scholars turned their attention away from the philosophical investigation of language and began to concentrate on the study of language change, using Sanskrit, Greek, and Latin as a base. Even the oldest written records of language are far too recent in terms of man's total history to reveal the origin of human language, but the nineteenth-century linguists did succeed in determining various relationships among existing languages. Some languages that are currently distinct can, upon careful investigation, be shown to have many common characteristics, indicating that, at some earlier time, these languages had gradually developed from a single language which no longer exists. With the exception of a few languages, such as Basque, Finnish, Hungarian, and Turkish, most of the languages of Europe and many of those spoken now or formerly in India and nearby areas can be traced back to a truly ancient language, Indo-European.

While we have no direct records of Indo-European, we can explain the similarities among the existing European and Indian languages only by hypothesizing that, at one time, these modern languages were a single language. This language underwent different changes in different areas over a period of thousands of years, and today there are numerous languages in a region where there was once a single language. Languages that are believed to have developed from a single language, because of similarities in vocabulary, sounds, and grammar, are said to belong to the same **language family.** Indo-European is only one of the language families studied from a historical perspective in the nineteenth century, as well as more recently.

Examples of major language families in the world include Sino-Tibetan (the most well-known languages of which are Chinese, Tibetan, and Thai) and the Semitic family (including Hebrew and Arabic and other languages that are no longer spoken, such as Akkadian, Phoenician, and Punic). For many languages the lack of old written records makes it difficult to determine with certainty the historical development that has taken place. Scholars disagree on the correct family classification for some of the languages of Africa and the Pacific area, as well as for the native languages of North and South America. Representative families from Africa include the Chadic languages in the area of Nigeria, including the Hausa language; the Bantu languages of eastern and southern Africa, the most familiar of which is Swahili; and the Khoisan family, consisting primarily of Bushman and Hottentot, in southern Africa. In the Pacific area, the largest family is Malayo-Polynesian, which includes Indonesian, Javanese, Fiji, Hawaiian, and Tahitian. So little is known about the native Indian languages of South America that most linguists hesitate to classify them into families, but there is general agreement that the Mayan family is distinct from the variety of languages in Central America. Linguists have been most active in working with North American Indian languages, but there are so many of these languages that it is not always clear how they should be grouped in terms of historical development. Some well-known North American Indian language families are Eskimo-Aleut, extending from the Aleutian islands all the way across northern Canada to Greenland; the Athabaskan family, concentrated in Alaska and northwestern Canada but also represented by Navaho and Apache in the southwestern United States; the Uto-Aztecan family, in the Southwest and Mexico, which includes Nahuatl, Hopi, Shoshoni, and Comanche, among other languages.

As linguists in the United States became involved in the study of American Indian languages during the late nineteenth and early twentieth centuries, it became increasingly clear that the historical orientation of nineteenth-century European linguistics was not very practical for work with languages that lacked extensive written materials from the past. Furthermore, as noted earlier, many American linguists of this period were also anthropologists. These factors led to a shift in the emphasis of linguistic studies in the United States. Scholars turned their attention once again to the form of languages, emphasizing descriptions, rather than the history, of these languages. Unlike the Modistae and the rationalists, who were fluent speakers of the languages they studied, American linguists frequently approached American Indian languages without the advantage of knowing even the basic sound system, let alone the principles of sentence formation or meaning. Thus, they had to start their studies with what was most immediately observable in the languages—the sounds. Syntax (the grammatical principles of sentence formation) and meaning are the most complex aspects of language and to understand them fully requires a fluent knowledge of the language similar to that possessed by native speakers. Since few linguists ever achieved this degree of fluency in American Indian languages, American linguistics of the first half of this century was characterized by an intensive investigation of sounds and the principles of word formation, and little attention was paid to syntax or meaning.

Despite the limitations of this early work on American Indian languages, the detailed, objective investigations of linguists during the first half of the twentieth century provided concrete evidence about the diversity that exists among human languages. This evidence served to dispel erroneous nineteenth-century myths regarding language and race. Partly influenced by Darwin's theory of evolution and partly by the period of romanticism, some nineteenth-century students of language had suggested that the type of language used by a people was determined in part by their race and their culture. The notion of "primitive" languages was popular, and those people who lived in societies with different values, customs, and technologies from western Europe were considered, by some Europeans, to be primitive. But the twentieth-century studies of the languages of such people failed to confirm such notions. It was found that there is no relationship between language and race. The same types of languages can be found among different races and, at the same time, within any given race, many differences in language can and do exist. Furthermore, all languages, whether spoken by western Europeans or people from other parts of the world with different cultures, are of great complexity. Reports of "primitive" languages are sometimes received from travelers to other cultures, but on careful, objective investigation, such languages are found to be far from primitive. Their syntax and their sound systems are as complex, productive, and suitable for their users as are those of other, more familiar languages, such as English, Russian, French, or German.

Because of its attention to the form, or structure, of languages, American linguistics in the first half of the twentieth century came to be known as **structural linguistics.** Attempting to describe languages that they themselves often did not speak, structural linguists were forced to concentrate on those aspects of language that were most directly observable. In their work, they gradually evolved a set of procedures considered useful in determining the sound system of languages. Later known as **discovery procedures,** these techniques of linguistic analysis were eventually extended from sound systems to the principles of word formation in various languages. When structural linguists began to investigate syntax, however, the discovery procedures, which had seemed to work for sounds and words, no longer produced results. The study of sentence formation, being so much more complex than that of sounds and word formation, required more sophisticated principles and techniques of investigation and analysis.

Structural linguistics contributed little to our understanding of meaning. Furthermore, the insights into syntax achieved by this approach to the study of language were extremely limited. Partially in response to these facts, and with a renewed interest in the rationalist approach to language, some American linguists, led predominately by the distinguished scholar Noam Chomsky, developed a new approach to the study of language now known as **transformational linguistics.** Although the subject of much debate among linguists in the late 1950s, the basic goals, assumptions, and principles of transformational linguistics are now accepted by the majority of American linguists, as well as by linguists in many other countries. In the following chapters, we shall examine language and linguistics from a transformational point of view, but we should note that other existing approaches to the study of language share with transformational linguistics a great number of fundamental concepts.

SUMMARY

Language, the most commonplace of all human possessions, is possibly the most complex and the most interesting. All people learn a language and use it throughout their lives, often without ever realizing that the system of rules and forms they utilize under the most ordinary of circumstances has been a subject of study for more than two thousand years. In the past, as well as today, language has been investigated for a variety of practical reasons, but there have always been those who have seen in language a means for understanding people and their minds in relation to the world. A brief survey of the history of linguistic studies reveals the source of some common misconceptions about language, and, at the same time, provides a basis for understanding the areas of concern to the modern linguist.

FURTHER EXPLORATION

A Short History of Linguistics by R. H. Robins provides a comprehensive overview of linguistic studies from the time of the ancient Greeks to the present; although presupposing some knowledge of linguistics, most of the material presented is clear and of general interest to nonlinguists. A less detailed presentation, assuming no linguistics background, can be found in the first chapter of *Introduction to Theoretical Linguistics* by John Lyons. In "Linguistic Contributions to the Study of Mind: Past" (Chomsky 1972a), Noam Chomsky offers a brief survey of the study of language in the rationalist period, along with comments on structural and transformational linguistics. In a book entitled *Noam Chomsky,* John Lyons sketches the development of twentieth-century American linguistics and the contributions made by Chomsky; the biographical note and first three chapters provide an introduction to these topics.

CHAPTER 2222222222222222222222222

MODERN LINGUISTICS

Although the word *linguist* is sometimes used to refer to a person who speaks several languages, the modern scientific linguist is not particularly interested in actually using languages for communication. A scientific linguist is not necessarily a polyglot but may, in fact, speak only the native tongue. Since the linguist is interested in describing the syntax and meanings of a language, as well as the sounds and principles of word formation, it is often necessary to concentrate on either the native language or, if possible, on some other language that is equally well known. The result is that much American research during the past two decades has been devoted to English, although languages as diverse as Japanese, Turkish, Swahili, and the languages of western Europe have also been investigated in great detail.

Language and *speech* are not synonyms. **Speech** is a concrete, physical act—the production of specific utterances containing particular words arranged in particular ways and expressed by means of certain sounds. **Language** is a mental phenomenon, a body of knowledge about sounds, meanings, and syntax which resides in the mind. This knowledge can be put to use, of course, but the speech, or writing, that results is merely a representation of the language—it is not the language itself. Linguists are concerned with determining the knowledge of the speakers of a language—the knowledge that enables them to produce and comprehend all of the actual utterances possible in their language.

LINGUISTIC COMPETENCE AND LINGUISTIC PERFORMANCE

The knowledge of language is rarely conscious. Speakers of a language are not aware of what they know; they cannot provide a complete description of the sounds they use when they speak, nor can they state all of the rules they follow in converting their thoughts into speech or writing. Furthermore, our use of this unconscious knowledge is often subject to error. We all occasionally make slips of the tongue, fail to complete a sentence we started to say, are distracted while listening or reading and subsequently misunderstand, or produce an ungrammatical sentence. But such errors do not mean that we do not know our language. The knowledge is present in our minds, but some factor has interfered with our ability to use that knowledge. Thus, someone may say sentence (1) rather than (2).

(1) I took the hook bome.
(2) I took the book home.

No one would claim that (1) reflects a lack of knowledge about the pronunciation of the words *book* and *home*. Instead, it would simply be assumed that the speaker's knowledge was not reflected by what was said because the speaker was tired, drunk, or affected by some similar factor that interfered with speech production.

The knowledge of language, therefore, is not always accurately reflected by the use of language. Because of this, linguists have found it useful to distinguish between **competence** and **performance.** Linguistic competence is the unconscious knowledge about sounds, meanings, and syntax possessed by the speakers of a language. Linguistic performance is actual language behavior—the use of language in daily life. The distinction between competence and performance is important, for it represents a major difference between the linguist's approach to the study of language and the approach of other scholars in education, psychology, sociology, foreign language teaching, and similar disciplines. The linguist is primarily interested in competence—the body of knowledge that makes linguistic performance possible. Scholars in other fields are usually concerned with performance—the use of language.

Any instance of linguistic performance naturally requires that the speaker or hearer involved possess a knowledge of the language. But performance involves other, nonlinguistic factors as well. A person's health, emotional state, memory and attention span, the topic and the context—all of these factors, as well as many others, will affect that person's use of language. The study of linguistic performance is, therefore, an exceedingly complex task. The investigator must determine a wide variety of facts about the situation before he or she can explain why someone used the language in the way that it was used. By isolating linguistic competence from the other factors involved in linguistic performance, the linguist hopes to be able to explain the chief basis of performance without having to cope with all of the external factors that also affect language use.

Linguistic competence is an abstraction from reality. Since it is knowledge, it is not directly observable. Since reality includes other factors as well, linguistic competence is an idealized version of language as it exists in the minds of individuals. In attempting to study linguistic competence apart from actual performance, the linguist is following a method of investigation long familiar in other sciences. The chemist, for example, does not go into the kitchen to carry out research on the properties and composition of a substance. The chemist takes the substance into a laboratory and investigates it under ideal conditions, using sterilized equipment so that no external factors will prevent him or her from noting the real properties of the substance itself. Under more normal conditions, in the real world, the substance will interact with others, but before one can explain the reactions and interactions among elements, it is first necessary to understand the properties of each element. And so it is with the study of language. Before we can hope to understand the interactions of all those factors involved in linguistic performance, we must first study each factor separately. Modern linguistics, as one of its primary goals, seeks to describe the properties of language and thereby to determine the nature of linguistic competence.

The linguist's domain of study is language itself. Various errors in language performance often are caused by factors that have nothing to do with our knowledge of language. The linguist, therefore, must sort out linguistic competence from all of the other factors involved in performance. Only in this way can we arrive at some understanding of the linguistic system that constitutes a human language. In sentences (1) and (2) above, for example, it is necessary to distinguish the first, which does not accurately reflect what the speaker knows of the language, from the second, which is a more accurate reflection of the speaker's linguistic knowledge.

Since linguistic competence is a mental reality, not a physical one, the isolation of competence from performance is a difficult task. Only performance is directly observable. Therefore, the linguist begins to investigate language by noting instances of actual language behavior. The linguist observes the sentences produced by speakers and writers, as well as those comprehended by listeners and readers, and attempts to determine the kinds of linguistic knowledge that people must possess in order to use language as they do. Not all sentences actually produced or understood, however, constitute valid data for the study of competence. Some must be rejected as failing to reflect competence because of nonlinguistic factors, such as those discussed above.

In addition to normal language use, there is another type of performance that provides the investigator with information about the speaker-hearer's knowledge of his or her language. Speakers of a language can make judgments about sentences; they can tell when a sentence is ambiguous (has more than one meaning), when it is ungrammatical (fails to follow the rules of the language), or when two or more sentences are paraphrases (have the same meaning). To make such judgments requires an underlying knowledge of the language, and thus speakers' judgments about sentences provide the linguist with further insight into that knowledge. These judgments, of course, are subject to the same errors as normal language use. Speakers may, for example, simply fail to perceive the ambiguity in a sentence, such as (3), if it is produced in a context where the meaning is clear.

(3) The President fired the Secretary of the Interior with enthusiasm.

In fact, (3) has three different meanings, represented by the paraphrases (4), (5), and (6); but, in a particular situation, only one of these meanings might be appropriate.

(4) The President fired the Secretary of the Interior who possessed enthusiasm.
(5) The President enthusiastically fired the Secretary of the Interior.
(6) The President instilled the Secretary of the Interior with enthusiasm.

Although speakers of English may fail to immediately detect the ambiguity of (3), they will normally agree that it has the meanings (4), (5), and (6) once these are pointed out. In attempting to determine linguistic competence by investigating actual language use and language judgments, the linguist is seeking to discover the kind of knowledge about language that speakers must possess in order to perform as they do.

THE GRAMMAR

The end product of the linguistic investigation of competence is a systematic description of linguistic knowledge, called the **grammar** of the language. In this sense, the word *grammar* means more than simply a description of the rules for combining words into sentences (syntax). The grammar of a language includes an account of the speaker's knowledge of sounds and meanings, as well as syntax.

A grammar is a hypothesis regarding the mental reality that serves as the basis for linguistic performance. As a hypothesis, any particular grammar proposed by linguists for a language may be disconfirmed. In other words, as a model of the representation of language in the minds of speakers, the grammar either correctly describes this knowledge or it does not. The adequacy of a grammar can be evaluated. To the extent that the grammar accounts for the data of language use and language judgments, it is supported, but if there are linguistic aspects of language use and judgments not included in the grammar, it is incomplete and possibly also incorrect as a representation of linguistic competence. An alternative hypothesis—a different grammar—must be proposed and then subjected to empirical investigation.

All speakers of a language function in a dual role as speakers and hearers; in some societies, many speakers also function as writers and readers. Underlying all four of these uses of language is a single body of linguistic knowledge. The grammar describes this knowledge. It is not, therefore, a model of how people produce sentences or of how they interpret them, for these are matters of performance and require information, not only about linguistic competence but also about other factors that play a role in actual language use. A grammar is neutral; it does not describe the processes of production or comprehension (almost nothing is known about such performance processes) but simply the underlying knowledge that forms part of all language use.

The traditional grammarians of the scholastic and rationalist philosophies (discussed in Chapter 1) were also concerned with the description of linguistic knowledge. One of the main problems with their descriptions was a lack of explicitness. Traditional grammars covered certain aspects of language, but, in many cases, they failed to discuss properties of the language being described, leaving to the reader the task of supplying the missing information. It is, of course, extremely difficult to evaluate the adequacy of a description that lacks explicitness, for what is vague or has been left unsaid cannot be tested. Modern scientific linguists, therefore, have made every effort to provide explicit descriptions of all aspects of linguistic competence. To do so, they often have had to develop special terminology that is precise and unambiguous. Furthermore, an explicit grammar is a highly detailed grammar, for it must represent every aspect of the speakers' knowledge of the language. Such explicit formalization of linguistic facts may seem excessively complex to the nonlinguist, but the nonlinguist who is initiated into the terminology and the formalism will find that these formal statements provide clear, testable hypotheses. The layman's description of German, for example, as a "guttural" language is really quite uninformative; the linguists' description of the sounds of this language (in terms of the various movements of the lips, jaw, tongue, and throat required to produce the sounds) is far more explicit and informative.

One of the fundamental aspects of language that must be accounted for by a grammar is its **creativity.** Every human language is a creative system in that the system enables its users to regularly produce and comprehend new sentences—sentences that a particular speaker may have neither heard nor produced in the past. And, a linguistic system is infinitely productive, for the range of possible sentences in a language is truly infinite. Any given sentence, for example, can be extended simply by adding to it a conjunction, such as *and,* followed by another sentence. There are many other ways of extending the length of a sentence. The use of multiple relative clauses is illustrated in sentence (8), which is an extension of sentence (7).

(7) I never suspected that the crime was committed by that man.
(8) I never suspected that the crime was committed by that man who occasionally dated the girl who is the sister of the contractor who built my parents' house.

How is it, then, that speakers are capable of dealing with a potentially infinite number of sentences? What do they know about their language that enables them to do this? Since the human mind is finite, it is clear that we could not have memorized all of the sentences in our language. Instead, we must know some finite set of principles, or rules, which produce the infinite number of sentences of our language. Linguistic competence, therefore, must consist of a finite body of knowledge, in the form of a set of rules, about a language. The grammar of a language is simply the formal, explicit description of these rules.

Linguistic rules are rules of a very special type. The rules of a language actually constitute that language. Without these rules, there would be no language. Given a set of words, for example, we cannot combine them haphazardly and expect to produce a sentence in the English language. We must follow the rules that constitute the principles of sentence formation if we are to produce a linguistic utterance rather than a series of unrelated words. Many of our activities are governed by such rules. In games, for example, the playing boards, cards, dice, and other equipment are merely objects. They become a particular game only when used according to a set of rules. The rules and any necessary equipment ARE the game. Rules that are essential for the very existence of an activity or phenomenon may be called **constitutive** rules. They are basically different from rules that regulate an already existing activity. Such **regulative** rules are very common in our society. Laws are regulative rules, as, for example, a law prohibiting smoking in theaters or requiring a license to drive a car. Smoking is possible whether or not laws are written to control it; one can drive a car without a license (although such action would be illegal, of course). Linguists are concerned with the constitutive rules of human language. It may be noted that regulative rules of language also exist, particularly in "grammar" textbooks and in the "grammar" classes of high schools and colleges, where teachers may insist that certain forms of language be used. We will return later to the distinction between constitutive and regulative rules of language.

THE THEORY

Linguists are concerned not only with writing grammars of particular languages but also with determining the general principles of human language—universal characteristics present in every language. The determination of features shared by all languages leads to a definition of the concept "human language." Linguistic universals provide the basis of linguistic theory. Linguistic theory, in turn, provides the basis for the writing of grammars of individual languages. Thus, the search for universals of language and the writing of particular grammars are interrelated aspects of modern linguistics. On the one hand, each particular grammar reveals properties in a language that may be universal. On the other hand, the development of a tentative list of universals serves as a guide to the investigation of specific languages.

There are many conceivable ways in which one could describe a language. The linguist is concerned with describing languages in such a way that the resulting grammars are in accord with the linguistic competence of speakers and not merely with a few of the observable facts about language use. It is necessary, therefore, that linguists develop a general theory that explains the nature of all human languages. Such a general theory includes an account of language universals. Since these universals are, by definition, a part of every human language, it would be redundant to include them in the grammars of particular languages. This fact leads to an important conclusion: in writing the grammar of a language, the linguist is constrained in making hypotheses, for nothing in the grammar can come into conflict with the universals that are part of a general theory of language. Thus, although there are many ways in which a language could be described, not all of these are actually possible if the resulting grammar is to be in accord with the general principles that apply to all human languages.

General linguistic theory provides further constraints on what constitutes an adequate grammar for a particular language. A grammar must be natural, in the sense that it does not unnecessarily propose rules or forms which conflict with the kinds of phenomena normally found in other languages. And, like all scientists, linguists seek to discover and describe generalizations about a language. That is, a general statement, covering a wide range of facts, is always to be preferred to several, more specific statements about the same range of data.

By incorporating into general linguistic theory a set of linguistic universals, an insistence on naturalness, and the necessity for generalizations, linguists attempt to characterize all human languages. The descriptions of particular languages must conform to this general characterization.

OBJECTIVITY

As the scientific study of language, linguistics is objective. There is no place in science for emotionally based or culturally determined views. Yet, in a basically literate society, where the majority of people have had some formal education, many ideas about language are accepted solely because they were learned in school. Most readers have undoubtedly experienced a class in English "grammar" where they were taught that certain words, pronunciations, or sentence structures are "incorrect," "careless," or "bad" English. Since few elementary or high school students question the validity of comments about language made by teachers and textbooks, the views about language learned in school are often simply accepted and retained by society without further objective investigation. The serious student of language must learn to distinguish subjective views from objective, documentable facts about language.

A grammar of a language, in the linguistic sense, is a description of the underlying, mental linguistic competence of its speakers. Such a grammar is **descriptive;** it describes the knowledge that underlies actual language use; the rules in such a grammar are constitutive—they describe what the language is. But the grammars that one usually encounters in school are not descriptive at all; rather, they are **prescriptive** grammars, which usually contain regulative rules—rules of what the language "should be." These grammars attempt to change actual language use by prohibiting certain forms. Such prescriptive efforts occasionally succeed in creating attitudes about language that are difficult to change. There are many who cringe at sentences (9), (10), and (11), particularly when these sentences appear in print.

    (9) I don't have none.
  (10) You was wrong about that.
  (11) Charlie is taller than me.

From a purely objective and strictly linguistic point of view, there is nothing wrong with any of these sentences. Each conveys its meaning clearly, and the expression of meaning is, after all, the chief purpose of language. In fact, until the end of the eighteenth century, sentences (9), (10), and (11) were completely acceptable; even the best writers used them without any hesitation. Why, then, do many people today reject such utterances as "bad" English? The answer lies in British prescriptive grammars such as one written by Bishop Lowth in 1762, *A Short Introduction to English Grammar; with Critical Notes*. Partly influenced by the Latin language and partly because of personal preference, Bishop Lowth decreed that "two negatives make an affirmative"; that *you* should be followed by *were,* whether it referred to only one person or to more than one; and that in comparative constructions the subject form of a pronoun should follow *than*. Lowth had no inside information about English that should have been accepted as the truth by others, nor did he have any authority to make changes in the language. The crucial factor was that his grammar was widely used in the schools, and people gradually came to accept this man's personal opinions about language use. Today, many people use (12), (13), and (14) rather than (9), (10), and (11), but it should be noted that the latter often still are found in the speech of those who have not been subjected to the prescriptive grammar of the classroom.

19

(12) I don't have any.
(13) You were wrong about that.
(14) Charlie is taller than I.

Lowth's success in imposing his view of English on others was unusual. Many other aspects of prescriptive grammar have been taught to children for years, and yet people continue to use the "prohibited" forms, especially in casual conversation. In fact, Lowth's prohibition against (11) has not been totally effective even among educated people. The fact that prohibitions of this type must be taught demonstrates that they are not really part of the language.

Linguists are not interested in prescriptive grammar. They attempt to describe the knowledge that underlies what people actually say and are not concerned with the subjective, often emotional views of the self-styled "authorities" who insist on obedience to the regulative rules of prescriptive grammar. The linguist's lack of interest in prescriptive grammar, however, should not be interpreted as a denial of the existence of differences in language use. Linguists fully recognize that some usages are restricted to members of particular social classes or regions of the country. In fact, the field of sociolinguistics is devoted to the study of such social differences in language, and the investigation of regional dialect differences has been a major concern of American linguistics for at least fifty years. Linguists recognize and study differences in language use, but unlike the prescriptivists, they carefully refrain from attaching to such differences subjective labels such as "incorrect," "sloppy," or "bad."

Although there are no linguistic reasons for accepting some uses of language and rejecting others, there may well be legitimate grounds for teaching a particular dialect or pattern of language usage in the schools. In a socially stratified society, for example, it is often necessary that people learn the patterns of language used by members of some particular social class if they wish to be accepted into that social class. In a country like India, where a number of different languages are spoken, it may be necessary to select one language as the official language for government business or education. Whatever language is selected for official use is no "better" than those that are not selected; it is merely more convenient to print documents, textbooks, and other materials in one language than it would be to publish several editions in different languages. The factors involved in the selection of an official language or dialect are not linguistic; they are political, cultural, social, and historical. Precisely the same types of concerns are involved in the subjective evaluations that some individuals make about the language and language use of other people.

APPLICATIONS

Modern linguistics is a theoretical discipline, similar to the "pure" sciences. Scholars have always considered the pursuit of knowledge to be worthwhile even in those cases where there are no immediate, practical applications for the knowledge they acquire. The development of a general linguistic theory and the descriptions of particular languages are the primary goals of linguistics, and both aspects of the field provide important information about people, their minds, and their languages. Neither of these goals, however, has been fully and satisfactorily achieved. Many languages have not yet been studied, and much about the nature of human language is not known. Therefore, despite the significant achievements of linguistics, many linguists hesitate to apply the results of their research to practical matters, such as the teaching of reading, the analysis of literary style, or foreign language instruction. Such hesitations reflect the conscientious, scientific approach characteristic of contemporary linguistics. In the past, linguists, sometimes under pressure from educators and scholars in other disciplines, have not been as careful about withholding suggestions for the application of the results of their research. Consequently, various "linguistic" methods of teaching reading or foreign languages and of analyzing poetry and prose were proposed by linguists and used by those people who looked to linguistics for a scientific method of teaching. As more recent developments have demonstrated, however, some of the assumptions and conclusions of earlier linguistics were invalid, and, therefore, the applications of these assumptions and conclusions were also invalid.

Yet, much of what modern linguists have learned about language is clearly relevant for other fields of inquiry. It would be highly unfortunate if psychologists, sociologists, literary critics, speech therapists, educators, and others who are involved professionally with language were totally unaware of the results of linguistic studies. In the sections that follow, the basic principles and some results of contemporary linguistic research are presented, accompanied by suggestions regarding the possible relevance of this material for other areas of study. In some cases, the reader will find objective confirmation of the beliefs, attitudes, and methods arrived at before engaging in the study of linguistics. In other cases, however, linguistic evidence may conflict with established concepts or point in new directions, never before considered, and it is then that the reader faces the most challenging task—to cast aside preconceptions about language and examine this evidence in a totally objective manner.

SUMMARY

The primary aims of modern linguistics are the development of a general theory of language and the description of the variety of languages known by man. In both of these tasks, linguists distinguish between speech and language, for speech is actual language behavior, subject to interference from many nonlinguistic factors. Language, on the other hand, is a body of knowledge that resides in the minds of human beings—the linguistic competence of the speakers of a language. The grammar of a language is a formal, explicit hypothesis about the set of constitutive rules, unconsciously known to the users of that language. A grammar in this descriptive sense should be distinguished from the prescriptive grammars, which for centuries have been designed and used in attempts to alter actual language usage.

FURTHER EXPLORATION

Many of the issues discussed in this chapter are also presented in Chapter Four of John Lyons' book *Noam Chomsky*. More technical is the treatment provided by Chomsky himself in the first chapter, "Methodological Preliminaries," of his book *Aspects of the*

Theory of Syntax. The concepts of constitutive and regulative rules are introduced by John Searle in his book *Speech Acts: An Essay in the Philosophy of Language.* The related distinction between descriptive and prescriptive grammar is the subject of pages 151–166 of *An Introduction to General Linguistics* by Francis P. Dinneen; here the reader will find examples of prescriptive English grammar drawn from several eighteenth-century works.

1. Nonlinguists, when discussing language, frequently confuse (or fail to distinguish between) concepts such as linguistic competence and linguistic performance, knowledge of language and the actual use of language, descriptive and prescriptive grammar, and constitutive and regulative rules. The following are statements about language made by people who have never considered such issues. In terms of the concepts discussed in this and the preceding chapter, comment on each statement.

   a. The English spoken today is not as pure as that used in Shakespeare's time.
   b. The study of Latin provides a necessary foundation for understanding English grammar.
   c. Most college graduates in the United States today do not have a firm knowledge of English grammar.
   d. It is a waste of time to try to write a description of a language; if you want to know how a language works, just ask someone who speaks it.
   e. People who use *can* where they ought to use *may* are ruining our language.
   f. It is really bad English to say "Who did you give that to?"

2. Relate the concepts of Chapters 1 and 2 to your own experiences with language study. Try to recall at least two "rules" for English that you were taught in high school. Are they constitutive, descriptive rules or regulative, prescriptive rules? Have you ever failed to communicate or been misunderstood because you did not follow these rules? Do you follow them when you are talking casually with a friend? When you write a term paper or a formal letter requesting a job? What conclusions can you draw about your own attitudes toward language and about the attitudes of our society?

PART 22222222222222222
WORDS

Languages differ from one another in many ways, including their writing systems, the sounds they utilize, the order in which elements are arranged in sentences, and the ways in which various meanings are expressed. Of all these aspects of language, however, people are usually most conscious of words as linguistic units. What would you do, for example, if you were asked to translate the following sentence into a language you know nothing about?

The spirit is willing, but the flesh is weak.

Most people would prepare for such a task by obtaining a bilingual dictionary and translating each word in the sentence. Such a response is clearly insufficient, even leaving aside problems of writing systems or word order. A translator may still have problems, especially when puns, proverbs, or metaphors are involved. For example, when the sentence above was translated word-by-word into Russian and then retranslated into English in the same way, the result was as follows:

The whiskey is agreeable, but the meat is decrepit.

Obviously, words alone do not constitute language. Yet, we are all probably more aware of words than of sounds, syntax, or even meaning itself. Exactly what is a word? Are words the smallest unit of meaning in languages? How do the speakers of a language produce words? Where do new words come from? Are slang words different from other words? These and other questions about one of the most well-known units of language are discussed in this section.

CHAPTER 3333333333333333333333333333

WORDS AND MORPHEMES

Any human being, given the time, could list thousands of words in his or her native language. If this list were then passed on to another speaker, the second person would undoubtedly agree that at least 99 percent of the items on the list were, indeed, words. But what is a word? Can this concept be defined in such a way that the definition accounts for every item identified as a word by speakers of a language?

Linguists and dictionary makers have tried to describe the concept ''word,'' but all of their attempts have failed in some way. And yet, speakers of every language know what a word is; they demonstrate this knowledge through their ability to list words, segment utterances into words, or identify words, as opposed to phrases, when they encounter them in a list. If the linguist, whose goal is the description of the knowledge speakers have of their language, and the dictionary compiler, who would like at least to provide clear, complete definitions of common terms, have not succeeded in identifying this basic concept, the problem must be extremely complex. We all know what a word is, yet no one can explain it. The problem is worth examining in some detail.

DEFINITIONS

One common definition of a word is the following:

> A word is any unit of language that, in writing, appears between spaces or between a space and a hyphen.

Linguists, since they are interested in accounting for the linguistic competence of speakers, examine such definitions and ask whether they are valid, complete descriptions of what speakers know about words. In the definition given above, the answer to the linguists' question is no. Although most literate people would accept the definition, it is not really complete, nor is it explicit. That is, given the statement, we cannot determine in every case whether or not something is a word. Consider the following: *matchbox, match box, match-box*. Each way of writing this form is generally considered to be correct. Yet, it would certainly be awkward to call this unit a single word when it is written without an internal space or hyphen but to call it two words when a space or hyphen occurs between the letters *h* and *b*. To do so implies that the concept ''word'' is not really a unit of language but simply an artifact of our writing system. Some people maintain that this is true, yet even illiterate speakers of a language generally share with their literate counterparts the knowledge of which spoken forms are words and which are not. Words exist, therefore, even for those who do not know where spaces and hyphens are placed in writing. The definition, then, fails to describe the knowledge all speakers of a language share regarding the concept ''word.''

Since all normal people speak their native language, whether or not they are able to read and write, it is worthwhile to investigate actual speech to see if the pronunciation of a sentence contains any information that might lead to a more satisfactory description of ''word.'' Perhaps if careful attention were paid to speech, brief pauses could be detected between the forms we identify as words. This would be a simple solution to the problem. Unfortunately, while pauses often do occur at the end of phrases, clauses, and sentences, it is only in slow, deliberate speech that they are detectable between words, and, even then, pauses are not present between all words. If you attempt to say any sentence aloud with discernable pauses between each word, it will be immediately clear that such production is highly abnormal. The lack of pauses between words is especially noticeable when you listen to a foreign language. For example, in normal conversational Spanish, you might well hear a sentence that sounded like a single word:

(1) *Estosombresondecuador.*

Actually, speakers of Spanish would be able to identify five words in this sentence, which is written as follows:

(2) *Estos hombres son de Ecuador.*
(These men are from Ecuador.)

However it is that Spanish speakers recognize these words, it is definitely not because of any pauses between them, for such pauses only rarely occur. The same is true for all other languages as well.

The investigation of actual linguistic performance—speaking and writing—reveals little about the concept "word," and, therefore, some investigators have attempted to describe this elusive unit in terms of potentials for occurrence, rather than actual occurrence. For example, it is sometimes said that a word is any linguistic unit that is capable of occurring as a minimum free form. A linguistic unit is said to be a **free form** if it may occur as an entire utterance; that is, if it is capable of independent use. Thus, any normal English sentence is a free form, for example, (3):

(3) Some students demonstrated when the president arrived on campus.

It would not be unusual for an individual to produce such a sentence and say nothing more. Units smaller than sentences may also be free forms, such as the sentence fragment (4):

(4) when the president arrived on campus

(4) could occur independently in response to a question like (5):

(5) When did the students demonstrate?

Figure 3.1 illustrates other free forms that might occur as answers to questions in English.

Figure 3.1 _____

Questions	Free Forms That Could Occur in Answers
What did the president do to cause a demonstration?	arrived on campus
Who arrived on campus?	the president
Who demonstrated?	some students
What did the students do?	demonstrated

By constructing similar questions, the reader can undoubtedly find other free forms within the following phrases:

(6) arrived on campus

(7) some students

No matter how great your knowledge of language or your imagination may be, you will probably find it difficult to produce a free form by dividing *demonstrate* into parts. Thus, *demonstrate* is a **minimum free form**; it is capable of independent use but cannot be separated into smaller forms that also occur independently. To label *demonstrate* as a word does conform to the judgments of native speakers of English, and, to this extent, it is correct to define a word as a minimum free form. But, any piece of speech can occur independently. In answer to question (8), one could simply produce the vowel sound in question.

(8) Did you say [ɪ] or [ɛ]?

(The symbol [ɪ] represents the vowel in the word *bit;* [ɛ] is the vowel in *bet*.) Yet, it would be strange to call these isolated sounds words, despite the fact that they can occur alone. Furthermore, some linguistic units commonly recognized as words are not minimum free forms. Consider *textbook, highchair, classroom, blackberry,* and *giveaway.* Each of these can be separated into two forms that can occur freely.

Thus, to say that a word is any unit capable of occurring as a minimum free form only partially succeeds in reflecting the linguistic judgments of speakers of English. On the one hand, some forms not considered to be words can occur independently, and, on the other hand, expressions generally considered to be words are not always minimum free forms.

Other attempts to define the concept "word" involve similar problems. Yet, it is not surprising that, in spite of much investigation, there is no fully acceptable, complete, and explicit definition. What has most frequently been studied is linguistic performance, the very surface of language, which is readily available for inspection. But in order to be able to perform, we must have some knowledge that serves as the basis of our performance. In the case of the concept "word," that knowledge is part of our linguistic competence and is observable only indirectly and imperfectly.

Whenever linguists attempt to account for some aspect of competence, they are confronted with the problem of isolating the nonlinguistic factors that interfere with the competence that the speaker utilizes in performance. When speakers identify a word, for example, they may well be using knowledge other than just their linguistic competence. For example, their knowledge of where the writing system of their language locates spaces may affect their judgment of whether or not a particular item is a word. A writing system is a way of representing language, but it is not language itself. Illiterate individuals know their language just as well as someone who is literate. To describe "word" as a unit of language, we must separate linguistic from nonlinguistic information, but such separation is extremely difficult to achieve. In the present case, our problems in describing "word" may well be due to a confusion of linguistic and nonlinguistic facts, to a confusion of competence and performance. Perhaps "word" is not a single concept at all, but rather at least three related concepts: (1) "word" as a purely linguistic unit of competence, (2) "word" as a unit of performance used in speech, and (3) "word" as a unit of performance used in writing. The definitions examined here concentrated on (2) and (3). But (1) is the most important concept, for it represents the abstract, unconscious knowledge of language that makes (2) and (3) possible.

MORPHEMES

One of the functions of language is to serve as a means for one human being to convey concepts, or meanings, to other human beings. With forms like *dog, text,* and *bad,* it is obvious that one very important property of a word is the meaning it represents. But it is precisely this meaning-bearing function of words that causes difficulty in attempts to arrive at an explicit, complete description of the concept "word." Words are very dissimilar in the ways in which they represent meanings. Thus, *dog, text,* and *bad* each conveys a single, quite specific meaning. A word like *textbook,* however, contains two units of meaning, both of which may occur independently. Now consider the words *dogs* and *badly.* As with *textbook,* each contains two units of meaning: *dogs* means both 'dog' and 'more than one', that is, 'plural'; *badly* means both 'bad' and 'way' (for example, *he did that badly* is similar in meaning to *he did that in a bad way*). Unlike *textbook,* only one of the units of meaning in *dogs,* or in *badly,* can be used independently. *Dog* and *bad* are free forms, but *s* and *ly* are not.

Thus, it is clear that words do not constitute the smallest meaningful units in a language. Instead, words are constructed of smaller parts, called **morphemes** by most linguists. (The term **formative** is also found in some modern discussions of word formation.) Morphemes are the minimal units of syntax in a language—units from which words are formed. Many simple words consist of only a single morpheme; *dog, bad, text,* and *book* are examples. Other words are more complicated; *textbook* is a word, but it is not a single morpheme. Instead, *textbook* contains the two morphemes *text* and *book.* The identification, analysis, and description of morphemes, as well as the study of word formation, is called **morphology.**

A morpheme is not necessarily a word itself. For example, consider the words *dogs, baked, badly,* and *kindness.* Each contains two morphemes; one of those morphemes is also a word, the other is not: *s, d, ly,* and *ness* are not words. Such morphemes that do not occur independently are called **bound** morphemes, while those which can occur independently are called **free** morphemes. Note that every free morpheme is a word, but not every word is necessarily a free morpheme (i.e., some words contain more than one morpheme).

There are a number of differences among bound morphemes concerning their role in the formation of words in human languages. The free morphemes of English provide the basic element in words, but various bound morphemes can be attached to free morphemes to create other words. Morphemes that serve as the basis for words are sometimes called **roots,** while the attached bound morphemes are called **affixes.** Figure 3.2 provides examples of a few of the roots and affixes in English; the affixes are in italics. Note that some of the affixes occur before the root, while others occur after it. Special terms describe affixes according to whether they occur before the root, **prefixes** (*un* in *undo, anti* in *anticlerical*), or after the root, **suffixes** (*ly* in *quickly, s* in *tempts*). In some languages, affixes are inserted within the root; they are then called **infixes.** In Coeur d'Alene, an American Indian language spoken in Idaho, the root morphemes *lup* 'dry' and *nas* 'wet' become *luʔp* 'get dry' and *naʔs* 'get wet' with the insertion of the infix [ʔ] (a sound produced by a momentary blockage of the air stream at the point commonly called the "Adam's apple").

Affixes differ not only in location in the word but also in function. Compare the affixes in column I with those in column II of Figure 3.2. The affixes in column I, called **inflectional** affixes, do not change the part of speech of the root to which they are attached. The affixes in column II, called **derivational** affixes, often do produce such a

Figure 3.2

I. Inflectional Affixes	*II. Derivational Affixes*
piece*s*	*un*do
John*'s*	*anti*clerical
tempt*s*	quick*ly*
jump*ed*	nation*al*
tak*en*	symbol*ize*
read*ing*	*re*name

change (for example, *nation* and *symbol* are nouns, but *national* is an adjective, *symbolize* is a verb). In fact, derivational affixes serve as an important means by which new words may be created in a language, a point that is discussed further in Chapters 4 and 5.

Additional investigation of the affixes in columns I and II will show that, in English, there is usually only one inflectional affix in each word. (The only exception is *s* 'plural' and *s* 'possessive', for we can say *the cats' cheese,* where *cats'* is both plural and possessive in meaning. But note that in pronunciation, *cats'* contains only one *s* sound.) In contrast to the inflectional affixes, many words contain several derivational affixes; consider the word *unkindly,* which consists of the root morpheme *kind* and the derivational affixes *un* and *ly*. Other examples of words with more than one derivational affix are *protectively, consideration, disproportionate,* and *anticlericalism.* The position in which affixes occur relative to the root also provides a criterion by which derivational and inflectional affixes may be distinguished. Derivational affixes occur next to the root or next to another derivational affix. Inflectional affixes, on the other hand, occur in English at the very end of a word, following any derivational affixes that may be present: *considerations, nationalities, democratized.*

Directly related to the number of derivational and inflectional morphemes that may occur in a word are several other criteria useful in distinguishing between these two types of affixes. In English, as well as in most other languages, the number of derivational affixes tends to be much larger than the number of inflectional affixes. It is easy to add to the derivational affixes in Figure 3.2, as illustrated by Figure 3.3. The reader can undoubtedly extend this list. On the other hand, it is difficult to add items to the set of English inflectional morphemes in column I of Figure 3.2.

Although English contains fewer inflectional than derivational morphemes, any particular inflectional affix will be used much more frequently than any particular derivational affix. The reader who examines his own speech will find that the inflectional morpheme 'plural' occurs far more often than does the derivational morpheme *ness*. Finally, it may be noted that in English all inflectional affixes are suffixes, but the set of derivational affixes includes both prefixes and suffixes.

The linguist's use of terms such as *free, bound, root, affix, prefix, suffix, inflectional,* and *derivational* is necessary for a complete, clear, and explicit description of word

Figure 3.3

Affix	As in the Word
ment	fulfill*ment*
ion	construc*tion*
age	spoil*age*
ness	kind*ness*
ism	imperial*ism*
y	pirac*y*
ly	kind*ly*
al	origin*al*
ful	care*ful*
able	commend*able*

formation in human languages. Such terms provide a means through which we can fully appreciate the complexity of the knowledge all speakers have about their language. It should be apparent that every speaker of English knows the widely differing properties of the morphemes of the language. No native speaker of the language would ever attach *ly* before a root morpheme. While the speaker may not have learned a formal label for this type of morpheme, he or she does know that *ly* is a suffix, not a prefix. Similarly, it would require a highly unusual situation for anyone to produce an utterance consisting solely of the morpheme *s* 'plural'. Speakers of English know that *s* is an affix, a bound morpheme. All of the technical terms the linguist uses to discuss morphemes represent an attempt to describe knowledge such as this, which native speakers of English possess.

SUMMARY

Words are among the most noticeable units of a language, yet it is extremely difficult to find a general, explicit description of this concept that agrees with the judgments made by native speakers of English about which forms are words. In part, this difficulty arises from the fact that such judgments are matters of performance, and, therefore, nonlinguistic factors may play a role in the speaker's determination of words. Yet, underlying this performance is knowledge of the concept ''word'' as a purely linguistic unit.

Words are not the smallest units of meaning and syntax in a language. An even more basic unit, the morpheme, serves as the element from which words are built. There are various types of morphemes in human languages, including roots, affixes, prefixes, suffixes, infixes, inflectional affixes, derivational affixes, and free and bound morphemes. The speakers of a language know the properties of such morphemes, even though they may not be aware that there are labels to describe such properties. The linguist's use of these labels is simply an attempt to provide a clear and explicit description of the speakers' knowledge about morphemes and how they are combined to produce words.

1. As a speaker of English, you already know the morpheme structure of words in your language. Try to use that subconscious knowledge to divide the following words into morphemes. Prepare a list of the morphemes that you identify. (*Note.* Not all of the words below are equally easy to divide into morphemes; discuss or make notes of any difficulties that you encounter and reconsider your analysis after you have completed Chapter 6.)

restate	package
somewhere	kids
actively	workbench
uninterrupted	prearrangement
publisher	disentangled

2. For each morpheme on your list from the first exercise, identify the type of morpheme involved (root, prefix, suffix, free, bound, inflectional affix, derivational affix). Note that more than one label may be necessary to describe a morpheme completely.

3. Use the morphemes on your list to create five normal English words (e.g., if your list includes *re* and *work,* you can create *rework*). List five other combinations of these morphemes that would not be normal English words (e.g., *workre*). What does this experience reveal about your knowledge of the morphemes of your language?

4. The identification of morphemes is dependent on the evidence provided by the data of a language. This is particularly clear when one deals with data from a language not known by the analyst. In determining the morphemes of a language, the linguist looks for recurring correlations between form and meaning. For example, in an initial look at some data from Spanish, we might encounter the following words:

muchacha	'girl'	muchacho	'boy'
nieta	'granddaughter'	nieto	'grandson'
tía	'aunt'	tío	'uncle'
abuela	'grandmother'	abuelo	'grandfather'

Notice that the form *a* occurs always and only as a suffix when the word refers to 'female', while the meaning 'male' occurs in conjunction with the suffix *o*. The linguist concludes from these correlations of form and meaning that it is probable, at least for this set of words, that Spanish has the morphemes *a* 'female' and *o* 'male'. Also, there seem to be several root morphemes in the data: *muchach-* 'child', *niet-* 'grandchild', *tí-* 'parent's sibling', and *abuel-* 'grandparent'. (From the data given, we cannot tell whether these are bound roots or not; they do not occur as free forms in the data, but without other information, we cannot be sure that they never occur freely. In fact, they are bound roots in Spanish.)

Now, consider the following words from a hypothetical language. Look for correlations of form and meaning and attempt to list the morphemes involved; assign a meaning to each morpheme. It is helpful to organize the words into separate lists with all similarities of form and meaning placed together. There should be no data left over; your analysis should account for every word in its entirety (with no letters left unassigned to a morpheme).

itap	'man'	aleku	'girls'
mialek	'my girl'	ilekla	'boyish'
ilek	'boy'	atapu	'women'
miitapu	'my men'	itapla	'manly'
alek	'girl'	ileku	'boys'
atapla	'womanly'	atap	'woman'

What is the most likely way of saying 'my boys'? What is the most likely meaning of the form *alekla*? Comment on the English translations of *itapla* and *ilekla*.

miileku , girlish

5. Since a morpheme is essentially a unit of meaning, its spelling and pronunciation are secondary characteristics. In the simple cases discussed up to this point, morphemes have occurred with a consistent spelling. Thus, all examples given for the morpheme *ly* have been spelled *ly: kindly, likely*. However, when we look at additional data, we quickly observe that this is not always so: *kindliness, likelihood*. A morpheme may occur with several different spellings, and as long as the forms always represent the same meaning, we will still identify them as the same morpheme. Similarly, the pronunciation of a morpheme may vary (a matter to which we return in greater detail in Chapter 9). Consider the morpheme meaning 'plural' in English. How many different spellings and pronunciations can you find for this morpheme? (For example, what are the plurals of *book, bag, wish,* and *child*?)

6. The converse of the situation described above in (5) is also found in languages. There are occasions when a common spelling or pronunciation is shared by more than one morpheme. Despite identity in the forms that occur, if more than one meaning is involved, then we must analyze the data as containing more than one morpheme. For example, Figure 3.2 lists three inflectional suffixes of English, all of which may be spelled by the letter *s:* suffixes meaning 'plural', 'possessive', and 'third person singular present tense'. These three suffixes are three separate morphemes since they represent three distinct meanings. Not all cases are as obvious as this one, however. At times, we find a single form of spelling or pronunciation that is correlated with two very similar meanings. For example, consider the spelling *book*. This form can be used as a noun meaning, approximately, 'sheets of paper bound together and containing print'. However, the same form, *book,* can also be used as a verb: *the police planned to* book *the suspected robber as soon as they finished questioning him.* Here the meaning is 'to record charges against someone on a police record'; this meaning, in turn, is related to another use of *book,* meaning 'to record in a book'. How many morphemes are there? We could argue that there is only one morpheme *book* with a range of related meanings. It might be equally easy to defend the alternative position that there are several separate morphemes involved in this case. When such complexities occur in language, the correct analysis is not always clear.

For each of the following words, discuss the number of meanings that can occur; consider, for each set of meanings, how closely related the meanings are (i.e., how similar the meanings are to one another).

(a) kiss   (e) pot
(b) bank   (f) fold
(c) can   (g) cold
(d) sleep   (h) show

CHAPTER 4444444444444444444444444

THE FORMATION OF WORDS

Poets are often particularly sensitive to the productive properties of morphemes, but all human beings possess and utilize creativity by producing new words. Three lines from a poem by E. E. Cummings* represent in a dramatic way this characteristic of human language.

helves surling out of eakspeasies per(reel)hapsingly
proregress heandshe-ingly people
trickle curselaughgroping shrieks bubble

The nonpoet's creativity is not usually considered artistic, but, nevertheless, it does serve as the basis for the production of words the individual has neither produced nor encountered in the past.

*Copyright, 1931, 1959, by E. E. Cummings. Reprinted from his volume *Poems 1923–1954* by permission of Harcourt Brace Jovanovich, Inc.

INFLECTIONAL AFFIXES

The most frequent type of creativity in the formation of English words is also the least noticeable. The word *morpheme* may have been unknown to many readers before they encountered it here, yet no speaker of English, once aware that this word represents a concrete, countable object, would have any difficulty in producing the plural, *morphemes*. The first time someone produces a word that has never before been encountered, that person is, in fact, producing a new word. It is true that the word may not be new to the language, but it is new to that person.

Even when a word is new to the language, all native speakers who come across it will be able to use their linguistic competence to produce other, partially similar words, as in the following case:

(1) Scientists agree that further investigation should be carried out on the gop.

What is the word which means more than one gop? Can you provide the possessive form of *gop* that might occur in the blank that has been left in sentence (2)?

(2) That _____ characteristic behavioral patterns are as yet unknown.

It is beyond doubt that any reader who responds seriously to the questions will supply the words *gops* and *gop's,* respectively.

The creativity illustrated by these examples involves the affixation of the inflectional morphemes *s* 'plural' and *s* 'possessive' to free forms. The great productivity of all inflectional affixes is due to their highly systematic nature. New plurals in English are easily produced because, with the exception of a few forms like *children, fish,* and *oxen,* all plurals are formed by the same rule. The same is true of the inflectional suffixes representing 'possessive' *(professor's, man's, halfback's)*, 'third person singular present tense' *(looks, reconfirms, exemplifies)*, and 'past tense' *(climbed, indicated, selected)*. Of course, as with the plural, there are some exceptions, especially with the past tense *(saw, was, threw),* but these are far fewer in number than the regular forms.

Figure 4.1 _____

Stage	Sample of Words Produced					
1	look	hit	fall	toy	sheep	foot
	looked	hit	fell	toys	sheep	feet
2	look	hit	fall	toy	sheep	foot
	looked	hitted	falled or felled	toys	sheeps	foots or feets
3	look	hit	fall	toy	sheep	foot
	looked	hit	fell	toys	sheep	feet

Given the widespread regularity and productivity of inflectional affixes, it would be unreasonable to claim that every plural form, every possessive form, or any other inflected form had to be memorized individually by the speakers of a language. The simplest possible explanation for this regularity and productivity is that inflectional affixes combine with free forms according to general rules that actually exist in the minds of speakers of English. Children in the process of acquiring their native language may in fact learn their first few plurals by memorizing forms they hear, but they very quickly abandon this inefficient way of learning language. In some way, that is still not really understood by linguists and psychologists, children construct a general rule on the basis of the relatively few forms they do know. Once this generalization has been formulated, the need for memorization is eliminated, except for any exceptions to the generalization that must still be memorized. Support for this theory of how a child learns one aspect of language comes from the way in which many children have been observed to handle irregular forms, as illustrated in Figure 4.1. Children do not necessarily learn the past tense and the plural at the same time, and the age at which particular children reach each stage varies widely. Even so, most children apparently pass through each stage in the same order. Stage 1 represents the early point during which the forms are memorized. The casual observer might easily be misled into believing that a child in stage 1 knows both the generalizations and the exceptions. Stage 2, however, indicates that this is not so. By stage 2, the child has acquired the generalizations and is, in a sense, trying them out. It is as if, once the child makes a generalization, he or she tries to use it everywhere, even with forms that are exceptions for the adult. (The reason stage 2 contains both *falled* and *felled*, both *foots* and *feets*, is probably that the exception involves a change in the vowel of the root, as well as the lack of a suffix.) Eventually, as children obtain more contact with the language use of others, they realize (probably subconsciously) that their generalizations cannot be used everywhere; there are a few exceptions. They learn these and thereby reach stage 3, the point at which the limits to the generalization have been established and the exceptional forms have been recognized as such.

Most linguists and psychologists who have investigated child language acquisition are convinced of the validity of this hypothesis, in spite of the fact that it is impossible either to directly observe the child's brain in operation or to question the child about how, for example, he or she learns to construct English plurals.

It is not clearly understood just how any human being manages to make generalizations on the basis of a highly limited amount of data; and yet, for the inflectional suffixes of English, every normal child does so at a very young age. For some children the process is apparently well underway by the time they are two years old, and it has been substantially completed by age five, with perhaps only a few exceptions not yet recognized.

Like the child learning the native language, adults who are studying a foreign language must also construct the generalizations about inflectional affixes that enable them to produce words they have never heard before. College students learning Spanish may begin by memorizing forms like those in Figure 4.2, but memorization is an arduous task. As quickly as possible, students will, consciously or subconsciously, formulate a generalization about how first person singular present tense verbs are formed in Spanish. In effect, this generalization will be: drop the final *r* and the vowel that precedes it in the infinitive form and add the inflectional suffix *o* after the root. Of course, as students encounter exceptions and further forms, they will modify the generalization. But in any case, once they have arrived at an initial rule, they no longer need to rely on memorization for most forms.

Figure 4.2

cantar	'to sing'	*canto*	'I sing'
pintar	'to paint'	*pinto*	'I paint'
beber	'to drink'	*bebo*	'I drink'
comer	'to eat'	*como*	'I eat'
vivir	'to live'	*vivo*	'I live'
admitir	'to admit'	*admito*	'I admit'

Thus, inflectional affixes play an important role in foreign language learning by adults and native language acquisition by children, as well as in the formation of new words by all members of a language community.

DERIVATIONAL AFFIXES

The process of adding a derivational affix to a root is another important method speakers use to create words in their language. Some derivational affixes combine with free forms according to fairly general rules. Given an adjective, familiar or not, English speakers can usually produce an adverb by adding the derivational suffix *ly,* as illustrated in Figure 4.3. The last two adjectives are "nonsense words" made up to demonstrate the productivity of *ly.*

Unlike *ly,* some other derivational affixes are only partially productive. Nouns can be created from verbs in English by the addition of a derivational suffix to the verb. Such derivation of nouns from verbs, known as **nominalization,** is a common process in the grammar of English. But the particular suffix used with a particular verb is not fully predictable and apparently not subject to the type of broad generalization possible with productive affixes. As examples of this point, consider the variation exhibited in the derivational suffixes of Figure 4.4. A careful investigation of such nominalizing suffixes in English (i.e., suffixes that result in nouns) reveals certain possible generalizations, although these are more limited in scope than those for suffixes like *ly.* For example, the suffix *ion* commonly is attached to verbs that end in the sound *t,* as with *construct/construction, edit/edition, duplicate/duplication.*

Figure 4.3

Adjective	Adverb
firm	firmly
kind	kindly
considerate	considerately
annoying	annoyingly
goppish	goppishly
clange	clangely

Figure 4.4

Verb	Noun
construct	construc*tion*
spoil	spoil*age*
fulfill	fulfill*ment*
refuse	refus*al*
govern	govern*ance*

Nevertheless, children or adults engaged in learning such derived nouns will find it far more difficult to form generalizations about the process of nominalization in English. And, in learning a language, those aspects for which generalizations cannot be found must be memorized.

Some derivational affixes, while not fully productive like *ly,* do seem to be more productive than the nominalizing suffixes. The derivational prefix *re* 'to do again' can be attached to a very long list of verbs in English, only a few of which are given in Figure 4.5. But there are many forms, produced by attaching *re* to other verbs, that sound peculiar or even "un-English," at least in the type of English spoken by the author: *respoil, redestroy, respeak, rerefuse, reunderstand.* It is not immediately obvious why the derived words in Figure 4.5 are common, accepted forms, while those just cited sound odd. What difference is there between *say* and *speak* that allows us to prefix *re* to the former but not to the latter? Other pairs that raise the same question are *construct* and *destroy, consider* and *understand.* One answer sometimes offered is that verbs occurring with *re* represent actions that can be carried on again and again, while verbs not appearing with this prefix involve actions that are completed in some sense. This response seems to hold true for words like *tie* and *read,* but it is not clear how it is any more possible to *reconstruct* a building than to *redestroy* it. In both cases, some action must intervene before the event can take place again, but the former word is common, while the latter is strange. In any case, speakers of English do use the morpheme *re* productively. What is it that they know about this prefix and about the verbs to which it can be attached? The task of the linguist is to determine what this knowledge is, and linguists are continuing to search for a generalization about the use of *re*.

Figure 4.5

retie	resay
reread	reopen
reconsider	reanalyze
reconstruct	repaint

Figure 4.6

propose	repose	depose
progress	regress	
	receive	deceive
protect		detect

Some derivational affixes are almost totally nonproductive, and there may be a question as to whether they should be considered affixes at all. Perhaps they are simply part of a root. For example, the words in each row of Figure 4.6 contain forms that are apparently bound roots, identical in shape and similar in meaning, although the similarity in meaning is not equally obvious in each case. Thus, *gress* might be analyzed as a bound root meaning 'motion' in *progress* and *regress,* but without the aid of information on the history of the words, most speakers of English would find it more difficult to state the meaning of *tect* in *protect* and *detect*. Similarly, the words in each column share a form, *pro, re,* or *de*. But, for any of these forms, it is difficult to assign a single meaning that is accurate for all of the words in the column. We could maintain that *pro,* for example, has the meaning 'forward' or 'in front' in *progress* ('to move forward'), but it is not clear that it has the same meaning in *protect* or *propose*. (These words are discussed again in Chapter 5.)

Morphemes are generally meaningful units. With the verbs under discussion, it is not clear whether the words consist of a single morpheme or whether they should be analyzed as each containing a derivational prefix and a bound root. If the latter solution is adopted, a meaning must be assigned to each morpheme, and both the roots and the prefixes must be regarded as only slightly productive. Cummings' creation of the word *proregress,* combining two of these prefixes and the root *gress,* is an unusual instance; that is precisely why it is effective. Not only does the poet make productive use of morphemes that are only rarely productive, he also combines two morphemes, *re* and *pro,* which do not otherwise occur in the same word in English. Yet, the new word is effective in conveying the meaning 'staggering'.

MORPHEMES AND RULES IN A GRAMMAR

A grammar, as an account of a speaker's knowledge of language, must include a list of the morphemes used in the formation of words. This list is similar to a dictionary. Information is provided about the pronunciation and meaning of each morpheme, along with details about its grammatical features (e.g., whether it is a prefix, suffix, root; what part of speech a root is). The list of morphemes in a grammar is called a **lexicon** in order to avoid confusion with normal dictionaries that list words rather than morphemes. Each morpheme in the lexicon, along with the information about it, is called a **lexical entry.**

Speakers are clearly able to combine morphemes to produce words, and the principles involved in such combinations must be stated in any grammar that is a true representation of the linguistic competence of the speaker. Thus, in addition to a lexicon, a grammar contains a set of rules that describe the ways in which morphemes are combined to produce words.

Figure 4.7 _____

create	mass
creates	masses
created	massed
creative	massive
creatively	massively

Learning a human language is a very complicated task, and there is no evidence to contradict the hypothesis that human beings carry out this task and store what they have learned in the simplest possible way. Linguists seek to account for word formation in the simplest possible way because they hypothesize that people do so. This hypothesis is in complete accord with the principles that guide all scientific investigation: the simplest solution, or description, is the preferred one. Simplicity is achieved through maximum use of generalizations. Thus, the grammar a linguist writes will contain as many rules and as few separate lexical entries as possible. There is no reason to suppose that speakers of English store in their minds a separate lexical entry for each of the words listed in Figure 4.7. Instead, the linguist works on the assumption that the lexicon of the speaker, and therefore of the grammar, contains the morphemes *create, mass, s, d, ive* and *ly.* The grammar also contains general rules to account for the ways in which these six morphemes combine to produce the ten words given. With the addition to the lexicon of even one more item, such as *destroy,* five additional words can be derived by the rules. If both *destroy* and *respect* are added to the lexicon, the grammar will contain the same rules and eight morphemes instead of six, and will produce twenty words rather than ten. For speakers, this means that when they learn a new root morpheme, they need only to add it to their lexicon and an entire set of new words, derived from that root, will automatically be produced by the generalizations they already know. In a parallel manner, each generalization the linguist is able to discover and include in the grammar decreases the number of lexical entries, while simultaneously increasing the number of words that can be produced. The grammar thus becomes a description of the speaker's knowledge and an explanation of creative use of language.

COMPOUNDING AND IDIOMATIC EXPRESSIONS

Another common process through which words are formed in many languages is known as **compounding:** the combination of two roots (usually free forms in English). The resulting words are just those which presented problems for definitions of the concept "word," such as *textbook, classroom,* and *matchbox (match-box* or *match box*—compounds are not necessarily written as one word). Each of these examples consists of two nouns, but compounds in English may also be made up of an adjective and a noun *(Englishman, greenhouse),* two prepositions *(upon, into),* a verb and a preposition *(puton, takeover),* and a noun and a verb *(sunbathe, earthquake).* The reader can undoubtedly list other possibilities.

Although English contains many compound words, the process of compounding has not willingly submitted to the linguist's search for generalizations. Compounding appears to be irregular in several respects. Consider first the seemingly unsystematic way in which morphemes combine: we say *Englishman* and *Irishman,* but not *Germanman* and *Spanishman;* we have the word *into,* but not *inthrough;* a person can be known for his *putons,* but not for his *jumpintos;* we can *sunbathe,* but no one goes outside to *rainstand.*

There is also no immediately apparent way of predicting the part of speech a compound will be: *earthquake* is a noun formed from a noun and a verb; *sunbathe,* which also contains a noun *(sun)* and a verb *(bathe),* is a verb; and *takeover* can occur as a noun, yet it consists of a verb and a preposition. Most compounds formed from an adjective followed by a noun are nouns, but the meanings of such compounds are often unpredictable: an *Englishman* is a man who is English; a *strongbox* is a box that is strong; a *highchair* is a chair that is high; but a *greenhouse* is not a house that is green; a *blackboard* is not necessarily black; and *hot dog* certainly does not normally mean a dog who is hot. Detailed linguistic investigation has led to a number of descriptions that account for various compounding processes in English, but the results of such studies are beyond the scope of this introductory survey. Readers who are interested in learning more about the subject may consult the material listed in "Further Exploration."

Compounds like *greenhouse, blackboard,* and *hot dog* might even be labeled idioms. An **idiom** is any string of words for which the meaning of the whole expression cannot be determined from the meanings of the individual morphemes that make up the string. Some idioms are well known and immediately recognized as idioms, like those which are italicized in the following sentences. Compounds like *greenhouse* are not usually thought of as idioms, but it should be quite apparent that, in both cases, knowing the meanings of the morphemes involved does not help very much in understanding the meaning of the full expression.

(3) Hal sent Mary flowers every day, but he still couldn't *get to first base* with her.

(4) After their fight, Sam and Joe decided *to bury the hatchet.*

(5) John doesn't know much but he has managed to *pull the wool over their eyes.*

We know that Hal was not really trying to get Mary to walk with him to the first base on a baseball diamond, nor did Sam and Joe dig a hole and bury an object that resembles an axe; likewise, no one had any wool physically placed over his or her eyes.

For almost all idioms, a language usually contains a seemingly identical string of words which has a literal nonidiomatic meaning. Compare the idioms in (3), (4), and (5) with their literal counterparts in (6), (7), and (8):

(6) Hal's batting average was so bad that we were sure he could *get to first base* only on a walk.

(7) After chopping firewood for four hours, Sam and Joe decided *to bury the hatchet* under the oak tree.

(8) We were shearing the sheep last spring and John playfully put some wool on her head; then he *pulled the wool over her eyes.*

Proverbs are similar to idioms. Although a proverb may be interpreted literally, more often its meaning is understood as something more than the sum of the meanings of the morphemes it contains. We can say *a stitch in time saves nine* even if we are not sewing; *every cloud has a silver lining* although there may be no clouds at all in the sky; and *there is no use crying over spilled milk* when you break a window.

Now consider the italicized portions of the sentences:

(9) The riot was reported in the newspapers with *screaming headlines.*

(10) Your daughter is a *playful little lamb,* Mrs. Johnson.

Each of these expressions is similar to an idiom in that the phrases cannot be understood simply as the combined meaning of their parts. They are **metaphors,** expressions that attribute qualities to an object not normally associated with those qualities. Headlines do not scream, and Mrs. Johnson's daughter is a human child, not really a lamb.

Idiom, proverb, and *metaphor* are all terms that describe expressions with unexpected meanings, and it should not be surprising that there is often some overlap among these terms. For example, when speaking of a *lame duck congressman,* are we using a metaphor or an idiom? The expression seems to be a metaphor, since congressmen are people, not ducks, and yet in this case, the qualities of a lame duck are being associated with a congressman. But the expression could also be labeled an idiom, for its meaning cannot be determined simply from a knowledge of the meaning of its morphemes.

Compounds like *greenhouse,* idioms like *get to first base,* and proverbs like *every cloud has a silver lining* are all items that the learner of a language must memorize as a complete unit. There are no generalizations you could learn about English that would enable you to correctly understand such expressions if you had never heard them before, nor do speakers of English create such forms in their normal use of language.

Metaphors, however, are produced more often, and every author, journalist, and newscaster strives to create interesting new metaphors. What might be the reason for this difference between metaphors, on the one hand, and idioms, proverbs, and some compounds on the other? Language is essentially a way of expressing meaning. With a metaphor, it is always obvious that the expression is not intended in its literal meaning. In fact, the literal meaning of a metaphor is usually complete nonsense. But idioms, proverbs, and compounds may have both a literal and a nonliteral meaning. If one attempted to create a new idiom, listeners would probably understand the expression as having the normal meaning of the morphemes it contained. In any case where the speaker means one thing and listeners automatically assume that the speaker means something else, communication breaks down. Such situations will usually be avoided, and, therefore, new idioms will seldom be created.

Children acquiring their native language and adults learning a foreign language must memorize the idioms, proverbs, and some of the compounds in that language. Such expressions are idiosyncratic; that is, their meaning cannot be predicted by means of generalizations. All idiosyncratic information about morphemes, words, and expressions is presented in the lexicon of a grammar.

Any expression that must be memorized will constitute a single lexical entry, no matter how many morphemes the expression contains. For example, the lexicon in the grammar of English contains the morphemes *throw, in, the,* and *sponge.* The grammar also contains a number of rules describing how these and other morphemes combine to produce a variety of sentences, one of which might be as follows:

(11) Noticing a pail of water nearby, he decided to *throw in the sponge* rather than walk to the faucet to wet it.

The meaning of this phrase is predictable from the meanings of the morphemes in the lexicon. But the lexicon also contains the single entry *throw in the sponge* with the meaning 'stop because overwhelmed'.

(12) After studying for the exam until 4 A.M., he decided to *throw in the sponge* and go to bed.

There are no generalizations in the grammar that would lead to this particular combination of morphemes with this particular meaning. The expression is an idiom, and it must be represented in the lexicon as a single entry, distinct from the entries for the morphemes *throw, in, the,* and *sponge.*

Since idioms, proverbs, and certain nonproductive compounds must be entered in the lexicon of a grammar as single units as if they were single morphemes, it is not surprising that these items pose difficulties when translation from one language to another is involved. The difficulty was illustrated but not explained in the example cited in the opening to this part:

(13) The spirit is willing, but the flesh is weak.

The word-by-word translations failed to lead to a final sentence with the same meaning as the original proverb because proverbs, idioms, and some compounds are single units as far as meaning is concerned. To illustrate this fact, let us consider examples of idiomatic English expressions and the way that their meanings are expressed in other languages.

Figure 4.8 presents two English compounds, with words for the same meanings in Spanish and German; a rough translation into English of the morphemes that occur in the foreign language form is given in quotation marks. If one attempted to translate the morphemes in the English compounds directly into German and Spanish, the result would be a word like *Schwarztafel* 'black board' or *verdecasa* 'green house', which a speaker of German in the first case or Spanish in the second would not understand. Traditional bilingual dictionaries have recognized this problem and, therefore, list all such compounds as entries separate from the individual words *black, board, green,* and *house.* The lexicon of the grammar written by the linguist is quite similar to more familiar dictionaries in this respect.

Figure 4.8

English	Spanish	German
blackboard	*pizarra* 'slate'	*Tafel* 'board'
greenhouse	*invernadero* 'winter place' (thus, a place where plants are grown in the winter)	*Treibhaus* 'force house' (thus, a place where plants are forced to grow)

Perhaps because many idioms are almost as long as whole sentences, traditional bilingual dictionaries rarely include them, but, for many of the well-known languages of the world, bilingual dictionaries of idioms exist. Without such lists, translation of idioms is all but impossible for the beginning student of a language who has not had the time to memorize them.

In English we may use the idiom *to be crazy about somebody*. German also has an idiom to express the same concept, but the words that make up the German idiom are completely different from those in English.

(14) *einen Narren an jemandem fressen*
     'a   fool   on somebody   to devour'

A word-by-word translation of the German idiom makes no sense to a speaker of English, just as an equivalent word-by-word translation of the English idiom into German would sound like nonsense to a German speaker.

Sometimes two languages will have similar idioms for the same concept, but no language learner should depend on this. *To bury the hatchet* in German is as follows:

(15) *das   Kriegsbeil   begraben*
    'the   waraxe   to bury'

    (to bury the waraxe)

But in Spanish one merely says:

(16) *dejar   de   pelear*
    'to stop   of   to fight'

    (to stop fighting)

Not all English idioms are translated as idioms in German. *To bite off more than one can chew* is expressed as follows:

(17) *sich   übernehmen*
    'oneself   to   overexert'

    (to overexert oneself)

On the other hand, many idioms in other languages have no idiomatic parallel in English; the same concept must be expressed in a different way. For example, in the Spanish spoken in many areas of South America, one can say:

(18) *Juan   <u>se</u>   <u>colgó</u>*
    'John   himself   hung'

    (John hung himself.)

The underlined expression is an idiom used about students, meaning 'to fail', so to express the same concept in English, we would say *John failed,* or, more informally, *John flunked.*

    When one language is compared with another, there are always a number of differences in how concepts are expressed. It has already been shown that what is an idiom in one language is not always an idiom in another. It is also the case that a concept expressed by a single morpheme in one language may be expressed by several morphemes in some other language, as illustrated in Figure 4.9. In spite of these differences among languages,

Figure 4.9

English	German
crib	*Kinderbett—Kinder* 'children', *bett* 'bed'
truck	*Lastkraftwagen—Last* 'load', *kraft* 'powered', *wagen* 'wagon'
curtain	*Vorhang—Vor* 'before, in front of', *hang* 'hang'

it is important to recognize that translation, even of idioms, is always possible. Although there may not be a word-by-word or morpheme-by-morpheme parallel between two languages, the concepts expressed in one can also be expressed in some way in the other.

SUMMARY

The basic processes of word formation used by all speakers of English are inflection, derivation, and compounding. These processes are essentially regular and systematic, and the linguist represents them in terms of general rules describing how the morphemes in the lexicon combine to produce words. The generalizations that account for words formed by means of inflectional affixes are quite clear, for inflectional affixes are highly productive. Derivational affixes in English are also often fully productive, but many are subject to certain restrictions in terms of the roots with which they combine. The grammar of a language must include both the productive and the restrictive aspects of derivational affixes. Although many English words are the result of compounding, this process is at times somewhat obscure, and, in fact, a number of compound words are similar to idioms in that their meaning cannot be automatically determined from the combined meaning of their root morphemes. Languages differ in the extent to which they utilize inflection, derivation, and compounding, as well as in the concepts that they express idiomatically.

FURTHER EXPLORATION

Readers will find much of relevance in the classic textbook *Morphology: The Descriptive Analysis of Words* by Eugene A. Nida. It is technical, detailed, and demanding for the beginning student of linguistics; nevertheless, it is a valuable source of information. Chapter 2, ''The Identification of Morphemes,'' contains samples of word formation in many languages, such as Arabic, Hausa, Navaho, Spanish, Turkish, and English, while Chapter 5, ''The Distribution of Morphemes,'' discusses different types of morphemes. A detailed discussion of compounding and nominalization in English is provided by Robert B. Lees in *The Grammar of English Nominalizations,* especially in Chapter 4. The explicit formal rules presented may be difficult for readers at this stage, but the general discussion and numerous examples provide interesting insights into the English language and the linguist's efforts to describe it. A more comprehensive (but less widely available) source of information is Hans Marchand's *The Categories and Types of Present-Day English Word-Formation.*

    1. Examine the lines from Cummings' poem at the start of this chapter. Name the basic processes of word formation used by the poet to create the words *perhapsingly, heandshe-ingly,* and *curselaughgroping.* Now consider *helves surling.* Do you recognize this as a ''distorted'' version of normal English words? These words represent a **spoonerism,** a normally unintentional interchange of the initial sounds of words. A spoonerism is generally an error in linguistic performance caused by fatigue, distraction, alcoholic beverages, and the like. Why is this appropriate in this poem? Comment on the word *eakspeasies.* What is the poem about?

2. Your internalized mental lexicon and your knowledge of rules of word formation frequently will enable you to determine the meanings of unfamiliar words, even without the meaning clues normally available from the context in which you may first see or hear the word. Provide a possible meaning for each of the following words by considering the morphemes of which they are composed.

photogenic	pesticide
telegenic	mythomania
teletypewriter	photomural
liberticide	telestereoscope

Check your responses by consulting a college desk dictionary.

3. For some other language with which you are familiar, determine how the following English compounds and idioms would be expressed. If you do not know, consult a bilingual dictionary of idioms or a fluent speaker of the language.

easygoing	kick the bucket ('die')
lighthouse	jump the gun ('start too soon')
handmade	talk a blue streak ('talk at length')
takeover	hit the sack ('go to bed')

CHAPTER 55555555555555555555555

LANGUAGE CHANGES: THE LEXICON

Through the basic processes of word formation, all people are capable of producing words—not only those words they have used or encountered in the past but also "new" words, such as the plural of a noun they have just learned or the past tense of a newly acquired verb. Such words result from the combination of morphemes (which the speaker knows) according to general principles of word formation (which the speaker also knows). Since the morphemes and the principles are familiar, the speaker is seldom aware that he or she has used language creatively. Such individual creation is the result of the fact that language, by its very nature, is productive. Words produced in this way by a particular speaker have no consequences whatsoever for other speakers of the language. Every speaker of the language can produce similar words in exactly the same way.

Throughout the history of any language, however, there are cases when truly new words appear, words that no speaker of the language has ever produced before. The study of the origin and development of words is **etymology.** In this chapter we examine the chief sources of words that were new to English at one time, discuss some of the effects the introduction of new words has had on the language, and investigate certain popular attitudes toward word creation.

BORROWING

All languages change over a period of time, often so gradually that speakers are not even aware of the changes until a century or more has passed. Changes may occur in all aspects of a language—in pronunciation, in syntax, and in the lexicon. Of these three areas, lexical changes are the most noticeable and may be observed almost daily. An important type of lexical change in English is **borrowing,** the addition to the lexicon of a word from another language. English has borrowed so many words from so many languages that today it is almost impossible to say anything without using at least one borrowed word. Modern borrowings are most obvious, such as *kibbutz* from Hebrew, while words borrowed long ago are now often indistinguishable from native English words. One example is the word *cheese,* which our linguistic ancestors borrowed from Latin about 1600 years ago.

When a language borrows a word, as English borrowed *cheese,* the new word is pronounced according to the sound system of the language to which it is being added. Thus, the word for 'cheese' was *caseus* in Latin, but in the English spoken at the time it was borrowed, the word became *cēse* (the letter *c* represented a *k* sound in both Latin and Old English). *Caseus* was assimilated into the English language as *cēse,* became a part of it, and thereafter was subject to the same sound changes as native words. When the sound spelled *c* became that spelled *ch* in English, the change took place in all words in the lexicon at the time—native words like Old English *cēowan* (Modern English *chew*) and borrowed words like Old English *cēse* (Modern English *cheese*). Once such a sound change has taken place, the origin of a borrowed word is no longer apparent. Even if you knew Latin, you might not realize that *cheese* was a word of Latin origin. The Modern German word *Käse,* however, is more obviously of Latin origin because German did not undergo the same sound change as English. Therefore, the *k* sound remains in Modern German much as it was in Latin when the word was borrowed.

Languages do not borrow words from one another in a haphazard fashion, but rather under particular conditions. To trace the history of linguistic borrowing is to trace the history of a people—where they settled, whom they conquered, who conquered them, their patterns of commerce, their religious and intellectual history, and the development of their society. In this way linguistics is closely linked to history. The linguist's accounts of borrowing can confirm the historian's hypotheses, and the historian's description of contacts between nations can guide the linguist to the sources of linguistic borrowing. The anthropologist, of course, also shares many concerns of the historian and the linguist, and borrowing is a phenomenon not only of language but of many aspects of culture. The study of lexical borrowing links these three disciplines, and it is impossible to discuss the matter without including linguistic, anthropological, and historical facts.

In order to trace the patterns of lexical borrowing in English, we must go back to the time when English was, in fact, not English at all, but merely one of several dialects of the Germanic language, a language that over the centuries developed into a number of different modern languages, including not only English and German but also Dutch, Icelandic, Norwegian, and Swedish, among others.

The Angles, the Saxons, and the Jutes were members of Germanic tribes who left their homeland in what is now northern Germany, the Netherlands, and Denmark and migrated to Britain in the fifth century. Prior to the arrival of these Anglo-Saxons, the inhabitants of Britain spoke Celtic, a language quite different from that of the new settlers. There was a great deal of animosity between the Anglo-Saxons and the Celtic peoples, and over a period of time, the stronger Anglo-Saxons came to dominate the area, linguistically and otherwise. Today, of the Celtic languages originally spoken in Britain, only Welsh remains in wide active use there. Breton is still spoken across the English Channel in Brittany by the descendants of those Britons who migrated at about the same time that the Angles, Saxons, and Jutes invaded England; Gaelic is spoken in parts of Ireland, and its use is encouraged by the government. In contrast, English, the modern form of the language of the Anglo-Saxons, is spoken not only in Britain and the United States but also in such widely-separated areas as Australia and India.

The language brought by the Anglo-Saxons to Britain was by no means "pure" Germanic. Borrowing had already taken place, mostly from the Latin spoken by the soldiers who extended the Roman empire through what is now France, Belgium, and parts of Germany. The Romans did not rule the Germanic peoples in northern Europe, but the territories of the two linguistic groups bordered on one another. This, naturally, resulted in **intercommunication,** whereby speakers of one language are in linguistic contact with speakers of another language. Intercommunication is a necessary, if not always sufficient, condition for lexical borrowing. Since the language of the early Anglo-Saxons was quite similar to that of other Germanic groups at this time, many of the early borrowings from Latin now constitute lexical items not only in Modern English but in other modern Germanic languages as well. For example, Latin *vīnum* is the source of Modern English *wine* and Modern German *Wein* (where the letter *w* represents a *v* sound). Like Modern English *cheese* and Modern German *Käse,* the word for 'wine' was borrowed from Latin by Germanic before the Anglo-Saxons were separated from other Germanic-speaking peoples. The differences between the words in the modern languages are due to the fact that different sound changes occurred in German and in English. The geographical separation and consequent lack of intercommunication between the Anglo-Saxons and the Germanic people on the European continent allowed the speech of each group to change in different ways. Since the fifth century, the language of each group has undergone different sound changes, as well as changes in syntax and lexicon, and the result is separate modern languages where once there were only dialects of the same language.

Our earliest written records of the speech of the Anglo-Saxons date from the seventh century and the label **Old English** is frequently used to identify the language as it was from this point until the eleventh century. Of course, the language itself did not undergo any sudden change in the seventh century. The date is merely a convenient point from which to begin a study of the development of the English language. One must start somewhere, and the first written records seem a logical place to begin.

We have already noted that by the start of the Old English period, our language already included a number of borrowed words. Most of those which can still be identified were drawn from Latin. Some entered the language even before the Anglo-Saxon migration across the North Sea, but other words were borrowed after the migration. Britain was a part of the Roman Empire at one time, and the ruling class of the Celtic inhabitants had learned Latin from the Roman soldiers, administrators, and colonists. The Celtic people had been christianized by the Romans. With the Anglo-Saxon invasion, these Christians were driven to the outer reaches of the British Isles. At the beginning of the seventh century, however, various Christian groups sent missionaries into Anglo-Saxon territory in order to convert the pagan invaders.

The missionaries succeeded in their religious work and, in addition, brought with them the Latin language, which from that point on served as the primary language of learning in Britain until the fourteenth century. Some of the earliest written records of Old English were religious texts prepared by the missionaries for the instruction of the Anglo-Saxons. The prestige of Latin increased in direct proportion to the rate at which the Anglo-Saxons converted to Christianity, and the seventh century was a period of substantial borrowing of Latin words. Understandably, many of the borrowed lexical items were words related to the recently acquired religion. The speakers of Old English did not have native words for *mass, creed, bishop,* or *monk,* for example, and so they borrowed these words from Latin, the language of their new church. In the three centuries that followed, Old English borrowed more vocabulary from Latin. Most of these are now considered **learned words** (words used in formal speech and writing, generally borrowed from a classical language such as Latin or Greek).

In the ninth century, much of England was overrun by a new wave of invaders—the Danish Vikings, who spoke a Germanic language quite similar to Old English. The Vikings eventually settled in the northeastern section of England and learned Old English, but they continued to use many words from their native language. Over a period of four centuries, some of these words were borrowed into the Old English spoken by the Anglo-Saxons in the rest of Britain, and words such as *take, sky,* and *they* are no longer recognizable as originally borrowed words. The Viking invasion, however, had only a negligible effect on Old English in comparison with the next major military event in British history.

In 1066, a French-speaking army crossed the English Channel from Normandy under the leadership of William the Conqueror. Unlike the Anglo-Saxons (who came to settle in Britain in large numbers) and the smaller group of Vikings (who also established permanent communities), the Normans were primarily an occupation force. They ruled the land, using French as the official government language, but they did not displace the conquered people. The local population continued to inhabit the land and to speak their native language, although those who had extensive business or social relationships with the Normans gradually became bilingual, using both English and French. Bilingualism is the most complete form of intercommunication, and it was quite natural that many French words were borrowed into English during the period of Norman rule. A large number of the borrowed items were words for upper class concerns and interests, related to feudal society *(castle, court, prince),* law *(crime, jury, prison),* government *(country, state, nation),* and religion *(angel, religion, saint).* Another reflection of the difference in the social status of the Anglo-Saxons and their conquerors was the entrance into English of the French words for certain foods. When we speak of animals, we generally use native

English words such as *calf, cow,* and *swine;* when we speak of food, however, many of the words we use were originally borrowings from French, such as *veal, beef,* and *pork.*

Many thousands of French words were borrowed into English during this period, so many, in fact, that the language gradually became quite different from the Old English spoken in earlier days. It is customary to refer to the type of English that developed from the eleventh to the fifteenth century as **Middle English.** The large number of lexical items borrowed from French during the Middle English period is one of the reasons why it is often easier for a speaker of Modern English to learn French than it is for him to master German. Historically, of course, German and English were the same language, and, therefore, we might expect German to be easier for a speaker of English. But the two languages were separated in the fifth century and have since gone their separate ways, now differing substantially in their sound systems and syntax, as well as in their lexicons. The historical contact between French and English, on the other hand, is much more recent, and of the thousands of French words borrowed into English, most remain in use today.

Three major factors were responsible for the great changes in the lexicon of English during the Middle English period: intercommunication, prestige, and necessity. The most important was the widespread intercommunication among the monolingual English inhabitants and the bilingual members of the ruling and merchant classes, of both Anglo-Saxon and Norman ancestry. But intercommunication does not always result in lexical borrowing; the Normans in England borrowed very few English words into their French. Very likely, there was a prestige factor at work. The language of the masses, English, was of no interest to the conquerors, but the prestige of the rulers was something others might wish to attain. One who used French words might hope to be identified with the upper classes. In other words, French possessed a snob appeal, but not English. Perhaps of even greater importance than prestige, however, was necessity. Even farmers who brought their vegetables to the market may have had to use a few words of French in order to sell their goods. Some of the chief purchasers were speakers of French, and, even if they did know English, they might have been more likely to buy from someone who could use at least a few words of the language of the upper class. Servants probably found that the use of borrowed French words made a better impression on their masters. Defendants in the law court, if they used French terms, may have found the judge to be a little more just. University students were taught in French and Latin. The clergy used French, for the Normans were Christians and brought their own religious leaders with them. Since the upper levels of the Church hierarchy were dominated by speakers of French, use of the language, or at least extensive borrowing from it, extended down to the local priest. And so, it was not only a few prestige-seeking social climbers who borrowed words from the conquerors' language. Men and women of all occupations and social classes found it necessary to do so as well.

It must be noted that the necessity involved in the borrowing of lexical items is social, political, and economic, but not linguistic. Every language has available to it a number of means for creating new lexical items in addition to borrowing. We investigate some of these in the next two sections. Changes in society often result in the need for new words; every language is capable of filling this need. Whether or not the new words come through borrowing or some other source is determined mainly by external, nonlinguistic factors.

Gradually, through the thirteenth and fourteenth centuries, Middle English replaced French and Latin as the language of government and education. Bilingualism subsided and fewer words were borrowed. This change in the linguistic situation in Britain was primarily the result of a growing sense of national unity, itself due to the political and military contests between England and France. Under William the Conqueror and his immediate successors, England was little more than a political possession of France, but the relations between the English and the French kings soon became hostile. As England emerged as an independent nation, Middle English asserted its independence from French. The fifteenth century marks the end of Middle English and the beginning of **Modern English,** but again we must note that the date is simply convenient for discussion; there was no sudden change in the language.

During the sixteenth and seventeenth centuries, a renewed interest in the classics of Greece and Rome led to another wave of borrowing. Many lexical items that serve as the basis for our scientific, technical, and academic vocabulary entered Modern English, among them *accurate, dental, specimen,* and *vacuum.* English has continued to borrow words from Latin, but the extent of such borrowings has decreased in the last two centuries.

When one language borrows so extensively from another, the linguistic system of the borrowing language may be affected by more than just the addition of a number of words. The vocabulary of a language is the sum total of the morphemes in its lexicon and the rules for the combination of these morphemes into words. The first individual to borrow a particular word from another language probably enters it in the lexicon of his or her native language as a single morpheme, even though the word may have consisted of two, or more, morphemes in the language from which it was borrowed. If several words of the same type are borrowed over a period of time, however, their original morpheme structure may become apparent. Recall from Chapter 4 the discussion of the words *propose, repose, depose, progress, regress, protect, detect, receive,* and *deceive.* There is a problem in Modern English as to whether each of these words consists of a single morpheme or whether each contains a derivational prefix *(pro, re,* or *de)* and a bound root *(pose, gress, tect,* or *ceive).* This situation has come about because all of these words were borrowed in the Middle English period from French, which in turn had received them from Latin. In Latin, each word did in fact consist of a prefix and a root. But English and French and Latin are all different languages. Many people who used words borrowed from another language were unaware of the morphemes as they occurred in Latin. As more of these words were borrowed, however, the meanings of the old Latin prefixes and roots became clearer. But it was whole words that had been borrowed—enough to indicate a pattern of word formation, but not quite enough to lead speakers of English to construct a general rule of word formation similar to the one that had originally produced these words in Latin.

Sometimes the set of borrowed words may actually be great enough in number to lead to new rules of word formation, although such rules may be only partially productive, as in the case of the prefix *re,* discussed in Chapter 4, which entered English in borrowed words. Other productive prefixes borrowed into English are *non* (as in *nonacademic, nonconformist, nonmetallic,* and *nonstop*), *pre* (as in *precensor, predispose, pretrial,* and *prewar*), and *anti* (as in *antibacterial, anti-intellectual, antitrust,* and *antivivisectionist*).

For the most part, however, fully productive affixes—those for which there are extremely general rules of word formation—are native morphemes that have been used as far back in time as it is possible to trace the history of the language. In English, the inflectional morphemes 'plural', 'possessive', and 'third person singular present tense', usually represented by the letter *s,* are fully productive, with only a few minor exceptions. These are all native English morphemes. In general, it can be said that inflectional morphemes are normally native to a language and, thus, tend to be productive. Derivational morphemes, on the other hand, are more often the end result of lexical borrowing in English and tend to be only partially productive. Not all derivational morphemes enter a language through borrowing, however. The derivational suffix *ly* in English is a native morpheme; its development can be traced back to Old English *līc* 'like'. In fact, this morpheme also occurred in Germanic, the language that preceded Old English. Modern English *like,* as well as the suffix *ly,* are both developments from *līc.* Recalling the discussion in Chapter 4, notice that the native morpheme *ly* is fully productive, subject to very general rules of word formation in Modern English.

In Modern English, lexical items have been borrowed from a wide variety of sources, but never in quantities great enough to yield fully productive new rules of word formation. English has borrowed words from languages all over the world, including Chinese *(tea),* Japanese *(tycoon),* Russian *(vodka, sputnik),* Spanish *(poncho, ranch),* and the languages of several American Indian groups *(moose. skunk, tepee).* There is scarcely a language with which speakers of English have come into contact that has not served as the source of at least a few words. In almost every case, however, intercommunication has been minimal between speakers of Modern English and those who use the languages from which words have been borrowed. We find that a few words relating to foods (such as Italian *pizza, spaghetti),* culture (such as Russian *samovar, balalaika),* and export products (such as Hindi *dungarees, chintz*) are borrowed because of contacts through trade or with immigrant populations. Immigrants bring to their new country their native language, foods, and customs, but in the United States such new settlers have usually been assimilated into American life after one or two generations. Their foods and some of their customs may remain as family traditions, but the native language is quickly replaced by English.

The great waves of borrowings that took place under the long periods of contact with Latin and French have not recurred in Modern English. In the recent history of English-speaking peoples, no conqueror has come to impose his language on the people as did the Normans, nor has any language, other than perhaps English itself, become the language of scholarship and international communication in the Western world. Without a reliable crystal ball, we cannot tell if such situations will arise in the future, but if they do, we can be sure that extensive lexical borrowing will once again take place.

To conclude our discussion of borrowing, let us investigate the opinion, held by many people, that it is possible to ''improve your English'' by studying Latin or some other factor that contributed to the development of the modern language. This idea is probably based on a recognition of the fact that a large number of English words have been borrowed—many of them either directly from Latin, or from Latin via French. In one sense, it is probably true that someone who knows Latin well may be able to determine the general meaning of some new words that he or she may encounter, especially in scientific vocabulary. But Latin and English are different languages. Borrowed words, like native words, sometimes change in meaning during the course of time. The Latin word *masca* 'witch' appeared in French as *masque,* and from there was borrowed into English as *mask* with a meaning different from the original. It is not clear how knowledge of the Latin word and its meaning would be of any assistance to a speaker of English in such cases. Furthermore, English has its own rules of word formation. As we have seen, even in cases where Latin morphemes have been borrowed extensively, they may not be very productive in English. Any knowledge a person may have of morphemes and rules of word formation in Latin will be of relatively little help in creating words in English.

If individuals wish to improve their use of English, if they want to become a more effective speaker or writer, then their most reasonable course of action would be to study contemporary English—not the history of the language. If you know Latin, then you know Latin; if you can read Old English, then you can read Old English. Neither ability will help you to communicate more effectively in Modern English. Of course, the study of any language, or of an earlier stage of a language, can provide a basis for comparing languages that may make individuals more sensitive to, and aware of, the forms and structure of their own language. These concluding comments are not intended to discourage further study of the history of the English language. To many people, the subject is fascinating. Tracing the development of words, for example, can be an exciting endeavor, a kind of intellectual treasure hunt. But those who enter upon such study solely in order to "improve their English" in some way are doomed to immediate frustration and ultimate failure.

NEW USES FOR OLD MORPHEMES

Every language has available a number of ways to expand or alter its lexicon. While borrowing has been very common in English, for example, German has made extensive use of **loan translation** (or **calque**), a way of creating new vocabulary items by translating the morphemes of foreign words into native morphemes. The word *telephone* in English consists of two morphemes borrowed from Greek: *tele* 'far' and *phone* 'sound'. The same borrowed morphemes occur in a number of other English words, mostly representing various modern inventions, such as *television, telegraph,* and *phonograph.* In German, through the process of loan translation, the word for 'telephone' is *Fernsprecher,* in which the native morphemes *Fern* and *sprecher* mean 'far' and 'talk' respectively. Rather than borrow the word from English, or from Greek, German has simply translated the foreign morphemes to produce a new vocabulary item, without any addition to the morphemes in the German lexicon.

While loan translation utilizes morphemes which are already present in the lexicon, new words can also be created by the use of such morphemes even in the absence of a foreign language to serve as the stimulus. The presence of the morphemes *tele, phone, vision,* and *scope* in English, for example, makes possible the potential formation of new words such as *phonoscope* (perhaps meaning an instrument which permits the observation of sounds) or *telephonovision* (a possible word for a telephone that transmits pictures as well as sounds). In fact, the word *phonoscope* actually has been created. It is a mechanical device used to test the sound quality of stringed instruments. This manner of creating new words by using morphemes already in the lexicon of a language is essentially the same as the processes of word formation discussed in the sections on compounding and inflectional and derivational affixes in Chapter 4.

Creating new words from existing morphemes is not a process restricted to technical terms. In fact, the process is quite popular, especially with advertisers. The following examples of derivation occurred in (1) a billboard advertisement, (2) the yellow pages of the telephone book, (3) the classified ad section of a Sunday newspaper, and (4) a sign in front of a small restaurant:

(1) There's always a *sellabration* at Thrifty Plaza.

(2) Johnson's Moving and Storage Company: our *guesstimates* are guaranteed to be within 10 percent of actual cost.

(3) Opper Realty Company offers this unique *oppertunity.*

(4) Tired of hamburgers? Try something new—our *fruitburger!*

As the third example indicates, proper names can be a source for the creation of new words. New lexical items created from proper names are most often the result of an **extension** in the meaning and use of the name. This is not uncommon with commercial products, when the trade name of a leading brand may be used for all brands of the product. For many people, any tissue is a *kleenex; thermos* is the registered name for a particular brand of vacuum bottle, but most people use the word for any vacuum bottle. The reverse situation also occurs, when an ordinary lexical item takes on a special meaning in addition to its original general meaning. In such cases. we may refer to the creation of words by means of **narrowing.** In recent years, there has been a tendency to use items already present in the lexicon as names for new products, as, for example, the *Pinto* car, *Camel* cigarettes, *Bounty* paper towels, and *Joy* dishwashing liquid.

There are several ways of **shortening** words and phrases to create new words from old ones. **Acronyms** are the result of forming a word from the first letter or letters of each word in a phrase, often the title of an organization. The American Society of Composers, Authors, and Publishers is usually referred to as ASCAP; the United Nations Children's Fund is called UNICEF; a soldier who is *absent without leave* is AWOL; and the Students Opposed to Grading Systems very likely selected the name of their organization carefully, so that it would yield the memorable acronym SOGS. Most acronyms are temporary lexical items, going out of use quickly, as do the organizations or situations that they describe, but a few become permanent entries in the lexicon of a language. *Scuba* is an acronym for self-contained underwater breathing apparatus.

Closely related to acronyms is another type of shortening commonly used in English—the use of the initial letters of the words in a phrase, with the letters pronounced individually, rather than as a single word. These strings of letters are words, not just abbreviations; we often use them without even knowing the phrase that led to their creation. For example, the GOP is the Republican Party, and the source of the letters apparently was Grand Old Party. But many people use the word GOP long before they learn the full phrase. Other examples of this type of word creation are HEW (Health, Education and Welfare), TLC (*tender loving care*), and LSD (in the United States, usually the hallucinogenic drug *lysergic acid diethylamide;* in Great Britain, *librae, solidi, denarii,* a Latin phrase meaning 'pounds, shillings, pence'; and the military phrase *landing ship dock*).

Shortening is also at work in the creation of words by **back formation,** a popular morpheme analysis of long words. In back formation, a short word is created from a longer one on the basis of similarities between the longer word and other words in the language. For example, the word *editor* existed in the lexicon of English long before the word *edit*. Comparing their word *editor* to other words such as *writer, singer,* and *worker,* speakers of English assumed that, just as *writer, singer* and *worker* consisted of two morphemes each, *editor* must also have two morphemes—a suffix *or* (in pronunciation identical to the suffix *er*), meaning 'one who performs the action described by the verb', and a verb *edit*. Thus, the new word *edit* entered the lexicon of English. At first, some speakers objected that ''there was no such word,'' but today *edit* is completely acceptable. In more recent times, back formation has resulted in the creation of *enthused* from an earlier form, *enthusiasm. Enthused* provokes strong negative reactions from some speakers who object that ''it isn't a word.'' In one sense, such people are correct, for *enthused* is a relatively new word. But, on the other hand, back formation is a perfectly proper, normal process for creating words. Making such objections, in an attempt to keep the language from changing, will most likely have no more effect than earlier objections to the word *edit,* or to the words *televise* and *donate,* also created by back formation.

Shortening was also at work in English in the formation of words like *gym* from *gymnasium, math* from *mathematics, piano* from *pianoforte,* and *plane* from *airplane*. Although it is not clear whether there were other words in the language that suggested these shortenings, the process here is obviously similar to back formation, for we have a popular reanalysis of a longer word into a shorter one. Both in back formation and in these similar cases, new words are created through the shortening of old words.

Word creation is never predictable. Through careful study of the history of a language, the linguist can determine the processes speakers have used to form new words in the past, and in this way arrive at a general understanding of the methods of word creation in human language. While such studies result in descriptions of how the modern vocabulary of a language developed, they do not explain why a certain process was utilized to produce a certain form, nor do they enable the linguist to predict the creation of particular new words. We know that *edit* was formed from *editor* by back formation. The same process could have yielded *auth* from *author*. So far, it has not, and we do not know enough about lexical change to be able to tell whether speakers will create a word *auth* in the future.

Similarly, the word *pea* in Modern English was produced by back formation from the word *pease,* originally a singular form now found only in the nursery rhyme

Pease porridge hot,
Pease porridge cold,
Pease porridge in the pot,
Nine days old.

Pease, although singular in meaning, sounded just like a plural word, so speakers reanalyzed it into two morphemes, *pea* and *s*. We can explain the origin of the word *pea,* but consider the word *cheese.* Why did it not undergo back formation and emerge as *chee* in Modern English? We cannot explain that. It certainly has nothing to do with a difference in pronunciation or spelling, for in Middle English the two words were very similar:

Middle English	*Modern English*
chese	cheese
pese	pea

Perhaps the difference here is due to the fact that peas are countable objects, one pea being visibly distinct from a group of peas, whereas cheese is a mass object, occurring in bulk form.

It may be of interest here to note that young children often make use of shortening in their progress toward language acquisition. It is not uncommon, for example, for three year olds who have been talking about their *clothes* to refer to one *clo* in particular, or, for that matter, to hear a child ask for a *chee* rather than a piece of *cheese.* The processes of word creation are available to all human beings and are used even at the earliest stages of language acquisition. When children engage in such creativity, they are usually corrected by adults and their new words disappear. It may be that some changes in the lexicon of a language come about because a few such creations by children are accepted by adults, but the evidence to support this is scanty. Adults utilize the same processes of word formation, however. Sometimes their new words are accepted and become a part of the lexicon. At other times, just as happens with children, the creations are rejected by other speakers, and we never hear them again. An intermediate situation is illustrated by back formations such as *enthused,* which is used by some people, avoided by others. This word is a social outcast for many individuals, but since so many others do accept it, *enthused* probably one day will be as much a part of everyone's speech as *edit* and *pea* are today. We do not know what factors make a new word acceptable, but once a substantial segment of the population does accept a word, it is almost impossible for language purists to prevent a change in the lexicon.

With the present state of our knowledge about lexical change, we can only list general processes and describe particular instances that have already occurred. One goal linguists hope to attain in the future is an understanding of lexical change sufficient to explain and predict the creation of new words.

COINING

Borrowing, inflection, derivation, compounding, extension, narrowing, and various kinds of shortening have all played important roles in the creation of new words in English. All languages make use of at least some of these processes, and some languages also make use of loan translation. The rarest source of new words is **coining,** entirely original creation, utilizing neither words from another language nor morphemes and words already in use in one's own language. Among the few words in English that were probably coined are *jazz, quiz, fun,* and *snob.* Linguists have been unable to find any clear relation between these words and other morphemes in English or any other language. *Jazz* and *quiz* are relatively new words, but *fun* probably dates back at least 500 years to the Middle English word *fonne* 'fool'. Prior to that time, however, there is no record of such a word, and so we must assume that it was coined during the Middle English period. *Snob* may also have its origins in Middle English. Old written texts show *snob* as a popular word for a shoemaker's helper. In Middle English times the meaning of *snob* was extended from 'shoemaker's helper' to 'any member of the lower classes'; in the early Modern English period the meaning narrowed to 'a member of the lower classes who believed he or she was superior to his or her peers'; and today a *snob* is anyone who believes himself or herself superior to others and reveals this belief in behavior. Although we can trace the development of the meaning of this word back over a 500-year span of time, we are not sure of its origin. Perhaps *snob* was not created out of nothing but rather was an alliterative form associated with the Middle English word for 'shoemaker', *cobelere* (Modern English *cobbler*).

Onomatopoeia is a modified type of coining in which a word is formed as an imitation of some natural sound. As in borrowing and the various means of making new words based on old ones, onomatopoeia involves a model that serves as the basis for the new word, but unlike these other processes of word formation, the onomatopoeic model is extralinguistic—it lies outside of language itself. Words like *tinkle, buzz,* and *pop,* as well as those that represent animal noises, like *moo, bow-wow,* and *meow,* were originally attempts to imitate natural sounds.

Since most, if not all, languages have onomatopoeic words, some people believe that early peoples first began to use language by imitating the sounds of nature. There is no evidence to support this **bow-wow theory** of the origin of language, just as there is no way to support the **pooh-pooh theory** (that language started with grunts, groans, and cries of pleasure) or the **ding-dong theory** (that people happened to make noises when they saw certain objects and the noises gradually acquired the status of words naming the objects). All such theories on the origin of human language are pure speculation; they go back beyond the period of recorded history and, because of this, can never be either supported or refuted. While people may indeed have discovered how to communicate by making noises in one of these ways, a few words do not constitute human language. Language consists of a highly sophisticated system of rules and relationships that provide for the combining of morphemes into words and of words into sentences even more complex than the one you are reading now. Even chimpanzees, with a great deal of effort, can learn to produce a few words, but no chimpanzee has ever created words alone or produced sentences as complex as those of most two-year old children. The significant questions concerning the origin of human language, then, are how and when people began to utilize not just a few concrete words, but sentences. As far back in time as our historical records can take us, human languages have always been just what they are today—productive, complex, and abstract systems of communication. There are no primitive languages. If there were, we might be able to trace the emergence of language in the species, as biologists can trace the development of plant life by observing single-celled organisms that still exist. But the linguist cannot follow similar procedures, for there is not even one language in which all communication takes place by means of one-word sentences. In fact, in all human languages the length and complexity of the sentences produced are limited only by physical and psychological factors such as memory span.

SUMMARY

Languages change throughout their existence—new words are introduced, old words drop out of use, meanings shift, and pronunciation is altered. In this chapter we have seen some examples of such changes in the English language. The words discussed here are only a sample; every word in English has a history. No word we use today is exactly the same as it was when our linguistic ancestors, the Anglo-Saxons, used it 2000 years ago. In many cases, they did not even know the items in our lexicon. There is, however, no reason to believe that they were any less able to communicate with one another than we are. No matter how a language changes, it always remains essentially the same—a productive system of communication, completely adequate for the needs of its speakers. The puristic attitude toward language is therefore somewhat mystifying to those who are familiar with the nature of language. Why should anyone object to the creation of new words? Our lexicon is filled with morphemes that were new at one time. Objections to the word *edit* surely existed, but no one objects to it today. Those who cringe at *enthused* or deplore the proliferation of acronyms may find it frustrating to learn that all of their teaching in the schools or letters to the editors of *Time, Newsweek,* or *Saturday Review* will do nothing to halt change in the lexicon of English. Language is democratic; everybody may have their say, but the majority usually wins. If enough people use a new word, it is part of the language, whether it originated through borrowing, compounding, inflection, derivation, extension, narrowing, shortening, or coining.

FURTHER EXPLORATION

"Early American Speech: Adoptions from Foreign Tongues" by Thomas Pyles (Anderson and Stageberg 1975) offers a clear, nontechnical discussion of the sources from which speakers of American English borrowed words from colonial times until the Civil War. The extensive examples are of particular interest, especially those from American Indian languages and the African languages brought to the United States by slaves. In "Word-Making in English" (Anderson and Stageberg 1975), Henry Bradley describes compounding, derivation, shortening, and coining in Old, Middle, and Modern English. Particularly interesting and lively is the book-length treatment of these topics by J. L. Dillard, *American Talk: Where Our Words Come From.* Readers who are interested in tracing the history of particular words in English will find such information in any large dictionary, and even in many smaller desk dictionaries. The chief reference work is *The Oxford English Dictionary,* which includes not only the etymologies of words but also information about their earliest written use. Specific dictionaries that concentrate on etymology also exist, for example, *Origins: A Short Etymological Dictionary of Modern English* by Eric Partridge. Use a major reference dictionary or an etymological dictionary for the first two studies below (some desk dictionaries will provide sufficient information, too).

1. Which of the following words have been borrowed into English? Which are of native English (Anglo-Saxon) origin? For borrowed words, what was the source language? What changes in spelling or meaning have occurred in the native words?

arm	ivy	parade
bleat	krait	stretch
coleslaw	mauve	them

2. Frequently, changes over time in sounds, spelling, and/or meaning obscure a historical relation between words, or, on the other hand, the course of time may result in changes that make words more similar than they were historically. Which of the following pairs of words were at one time based on the same root morphemes? Attempt to determine a relationship in meaning before you check a dictionary for the etymologies.

puddle	—	poodle
shade	—	shadow
batch	—	bake
yoke	—	yolk
evil	—	ill
plain	—	plane
bride	—	bridle
mayor	—	major

3. A service department authorized to do warranty repairs on Frigidaire refrigerators now asks for the model number of the appliance before dispatching a repairman. Formerly, customers were asked only whether they had a Frigidaire, and although servicemen were sent only to those who said they did, the repairman often found that the refrigerator in question was a Gibson, General Electric, or some other brand. Explain the linguistic problem.

4. Make a list of eight brand names for products. For each item, determine the source of the name (e.g., borrowing, compounding, extension, narrowing, coining, or even spoonerism).

CHAPTER 66666666666666666666666666

SLANG, STYLES, AND DICTIONARIES

Sentences (1) and (2) have virtually identical meanings, but they differ in style.

(1) He received a substantial gratuity.

(2) He got a big tip.

The first is quite formal, the second informal, or **colloquial.** Both sentences are "good" English. An educated speaker of the language might use the formal style in a business report and the colloquial style in casual conversation with friends. The question of style in language performance is one of appropriateness in a given situation. In many sentences, the style can be readily identified from the words involved. Certain words, such as *gratuity,* occur primarily in formal language, while others, like *tip,* are usually found in informal speech or writing.

At one time, some people considered colloquial style improper (although they undoubtedly used it themselves in certain situations); only formal style was judged as good. Today, however, few people object to colloquial language, perhaps because society itself is less formal now than it was several generations ago. But

63

there is one style that continues to arouse strong emotional reactions in many people—slang. Parents complain that their children use too many slang words; only a decade ago, editorial writers and reviewers called dictionaries "deplorable" because they contained slang words without labeling them as slang.

What is slang? How does it differ from colloquial speech? Is there any relationship between slang and other types of words, such as professional terminology or obscenity? Should dictionaries include slang? In this chapter we will examine some responses to these questions and to others concerning style in language performance.

SLANG

Every one of you will be able to provide a list of words that you would identify as slang, but if we were to compare several of these lists we might encounter certain discrepancies. What is considered slang by one person may be labeled simply colloquial by another. For example, few students would call the words *math* and *exam* slang, and yet to some older adults these are slang terms. In fact, they appear as examples of slang in one of the suggested readings at the end of this chapter. Obviously, slang and colloquial speech are closely related: one blends into the other, and it is impossible to draw a definite dividing line between the two styles. Over a period of time, a word that originally was slang may come to be identified as merely colloquial, and a new slang word may arise. This is apparently what has happened to the word *cop*. Thirty years ago, *cop* was definitely slang. More recently, however, *fuzz* became the slang word for 'policeman', and later, under new social and cultural conditions, *pig* came into use. When compared to the pejorative word *pig,* the more neutral *cop* is considered colloquial.

No one characteristic of a word is sufficient to place it in the class of slang words. Whether or not any particular item is identified as slang usually depends on a number of factors, such as the existence of other words with the same meaning, the kinds of situations in which the word is normally used, and the social status of the people who use the word. In the following discussion of such factors, examples of slang will be cited. However, you may find it useful to make up your own list of contemporary slang words, and relate the items on your list to the points made here, for one characteristic of many slang words is that they become outdated within a very short period of time. The examples given here may be unfamiliar to you just a few years after this book is written.

Slang words might be considered as a second set of lexical items, parallel to items in the colloquial or formal language. That is, for most, if not all, slang, it is possible to find a word that is not slang but has approximately the same meaning. This point is demonstrated by the fact that we can define slang words by using nonslang vocabulary:

Slang	Nonslang Equivalent
pot	marihuana
rip off	cheat, exploit
smashed	drunk
rap	discuss

If we were to attempt to divide the vocabulary of English into slang and nonslang, we would find that many words play a dual role in the lexicon. In some contexts, they have one meaning and function as slang; in other contexts, they have a different meaning and are part of the colloquial or formal vocabulary. This is true of the four words labeled as slang in the above list: a pot is a cooking utensil in nonslang speech; if something is smashed, it is broken in colloquial language. The dual nature of certain words provides some insight into the origin of slang words. The examples given here were created by an extension of the meaning of ordinary lexical items, a regular process of word formation discussed in Chapter 5. Other slang words have also come about through the usual processes of shortening (as in *coed,* formerly considered slang, from *coeducation),* derivation (*uppers* and *downers,* slang terms for stimulant and depressant drugs, derived from the nonslang morphemes *up, down,* and *er*), and, most rarely, coining (*jazz* was originally a slang word).

It should be noted at this point that it is no more difficult to define a slang word than it is to define any other word in a language. It is occasionally said that slang is somehow more vague and imprecise in meaning than nonslang. This is completely false. The meaning of most words is vague to some extent. If a person says *He is a Republican,* you will understand part of what is meant, but, unless you know not only the general meaning of the word *Republican* but also the speaker's political views, you will not fully understand the sentence. Is it a compliment or an insult? The answer depends on the meaning of *Republican* for the speaker, as well as the politics of the person being talked about. Thus, if the speaker is a Democrat, the remark may well be meant as an insult. Many other examples of vagueness in nonslang vocabulary could be cited; consider the words *warm* and *cold.* Whether to turn the heat up or down is often a continual point of disagreement between roommates; one says *It's too warm in the room,* the other maintains *It's too cold.* Vagueness in meaning results from the fact that the human beings who use a language differ in their beliefs, presuppositions, physical conditions, and prior experiences.

Lack of familiarity with a word also leads to charges that its meaning is vague or imprecise. But, in such cases, it is not really the word that is vague, but rather the knowledge of the individual who makes the charge. Regarding slang, only people who do not use particular slang words feel that they are vague. Those who use the words know what they mean.

People sometimes claim that slang is more vivid, more colorful, than other types of words. Certainly this is true to some extent, but the ''color'' of a slang word, like that of any other word or expression, is present only so long as the word is new. After you have heard it several dozen times, a slang word is no more colorful than its nonslang equivalent. Perhaps this is one reason why so many slang words become outdated. One of the psychological factors at work when people use slang may be a desire to speak effectively—to catch and hold the attention of the listener. With widespread use, a slang word will no longer have this effect, and one reason for its use will have disappeared. The situation is similar to that of clichés, such as *gentle as a lamb, fresh as a daisy,* or *strong as an ox.* These expressions were probably striking the first few times they were used, but overuse has made them trite and now they are avoided by many speakers. Few people object to stylistically uninteresting language, as long as the speaker or writer does not intend the language to be interesting. But people do object when they feel a word is used in order to add interest and yet it fails to do so. This reaction is especially strong regarding slang, but it is not limited to slang. It occurs with colloquial and formal language as well, for colorfulness (or the lack of it) depends on the novelty of a word or expression rather than on style of speech.

In summary, it can be stated that two common reactions people have to slang—it is vague in meaning and colorful in tone—are the result of the same factor: many slang words are used by only a segment of the population and are unfamiliar to a substantial number of people. Slang is generally a group phenomenon, a set of words used by, and identifiable with, some particular part of society. In fact, there are as many kinds of slang as there are separate social groups: the slang used by parents is rarely the same as that of their children; even college students may find that their slang differs from that of high school students; underworld slang and the slang of professional musicians have few words in common.

For some people, the use of slang is a way to achieve identification with a group. If you want to be identified as a college student, use the slang other college students use. If you wish to be recognized as a member of a rock music group, you may use the slang relating to music, instruments, arrangements, and bookings. In other words, slang can bestow prestige. Of course, this depends on one's opinion of the group using the slang. If a person fears or dislikes a group, that person will avoid using the slang and may consider the words themselves disreputable. Many strongly negative reactions to the use of slang are actually reactions to the people with whom the slang is identified. In large part, slang is not respectable because the average American adult considers those who use it not respectable. The situation holds in reverse, too. The special vocabulary items of those who are considered unrespectable are automatically labeled slang, but the special vocabulary of those who are deemed respectable is called "professional terminology."

We have noted that one possible reason for the transient nature of many slang words is that frequent usage tends to blunt their effectiveness. The fact that much slang originates and is utilized by particular social groups may also account for this tendency toward a short life. In many such groups, the membership changes quite frequently. For example, college slang changes from year to year as seniors graduate and new freshmen enter the group. For several decades in the United States, some young people disassociated themselves from the mainstream of American life and formed separate societies. In the 1950s, these people were called *beatniks;* in the early 1960s, *flower children;* in the late 1960s, *hippies.* As the participants in this subculture changed, so did the slang and even the names for the groups.

Not all slang, however, becomes outdated. Many slang words remain in use for years without becoming part of the colloquial vocabulary. As examples, consider the words *booze* 'alcoholic beverage', *weed* 'cigarette', *dough* 'money', and *john* 'toilet'. Such words have lost any group identification they may have once had and thus are exempt from the fate of other slang, which passes from the scene when the group with which it was associated changes.

In conclusion, we may summarize this discussion of slang by observing that, in many respects, slang shares the characteristics of other vocabulary items: it is created through the normal processes of word formation; its meaning is no more vague than that of many nonslang words; whether or not it is colorful and effective depends on its novelty, just as the effectiveness of metaphors and similes depends on their novelty. On the other hand, there are certain properties associated more with slang than with colloquial and formal lexical items: almost anything that can be said using slang can also be expressed with a nonslang word or phrase, but the opposite holds true less often; slang is used by only a limited segment of the population; the groups that use slang are often considered lacking in respectability by the general public, and, therefore, slang itself tends to lack respectability; on the whole, slang words tend to have a shorter life span than nonslang words. None of these properties, however, is unique to the words commonly labeled "slang."

PROFESSIONAL TERMINOLOGY

Every profession has its own set of special vocabulary, terms that designate concepts and phenomena with which the profession is concerned. Such professional terminology shares many of the characteristics normally associated with slang. Like slang, professional terminology is used by only a segment of the population, and it is unfamiliar to most people. Professional terms often have parallels in the nonprofessional vocabulary of a language; for example, linguists sometimes refer to *sounds* as *phones,* and doctors refer to *traumata* when other people would say *injuries*. Professional terminology often provides words for new discoveries or concepts that have no names in a language. For example, linguists introduced the word *morpheme* to refer to the minimal grammatical units from which words are formed. But slang, also, may introduce words for items that, prior to the slang, had no colloquial or formal label. The slang term *funky* has no one-word equivalent in the nonslang vocabulary of English; it means 'youthful, modern, natural'. Of course, the meaning of *funky* can be expressed in ordinary language, but so can the meaning of the professional term *morpheme*. In a number of respects, then, slang and professional terminology are similar.

The most significant difference between professional words and slang words is the difference between the people who use them. Professional terms are used by people who are accepted, or even admired, by society at large. Slang is used primarily by those who often lack respectability. A mathematical topologist, who studies shapes, uses the word *doughnut* as a technical term, referring to objects shaped like a doughnut. No one would claim that this unfamiliar use of a familiar word is slang. On the other hand, when someone whose profession is the illegal sale of drugs uses familiar words with unfamiliar meanings, this usage is immediately called "slang." Consider the word *gofer* (pronounced like *gopher*) meaning 'the person who goes for the drugs and delivers them to the customers'. (*Gofer* somehow seems more acceptable to many speakers when it is used in show business to refer to the person who runs errands.)

Another difference between slang and professional terminology is the way in which new words are produced. Most slang develops through the processes of meaning change (extension or narrowing), shortening, or creation from common morphemes, often of Germanic origin. Professional terminology is more often formed with morphemes of Latin or Greek origin. Speakers of English are aware of this, at least subconsciously, and words without such morphemes do not seem to be technical terms. For example, the word *googol,* used in mathematics to indicate a very large number, sounds more like a slang word than an item of professional terminology.

A consequence of using different kinds of morphemes in professional terminology and slang is that the former tend to be long words, such as *microchronometer,* while the latter are often short, such as *gig* 'booking for a performance' (formerly, 'a one-night-stand') in music, 'a job' in other slang. It may be noted that Americans seem to have developed the attitude that long words are somehow "better" than short words; it is felt that long words have more precise meanings. A person is said to have a "good vocabulary" if he uses a lot of big words, but not if he knows a lot of short words. Yet, insofar as the expression of meaning is concerned, long words are no better than short words; *tip* and *gratuity* mean the same thing. Why, then, should long words have greater prestige? The explanation probably lies in the fact that such words, whether professional terminology or formal language, do not occur frequently in everyday speech or writing. A certain amount of formal education or wide reading is necessary in order to learn them. Knowing the words reflects such experiences; the experiences are viewed with respect by most people; and so the vocabulary items associated with these respected activities have come to be respected. Once again we find that the factors that influence our attitudes toward words are nonlinguistic; that is, they involve a transfer of our attitudes toward particular people and activities to particular words. Linguistically, slang and professional terminology are not very different; however, the attitudinal factors associated with them are quite distinct.

OBSCENITY AND VULGARITY

Obscenity and vulgarity are closely related to slang. They arouse strong negative reactions in many people and are used by only a portion of the population. As with slang, words labeled obscene or vulgar by some people are considered acceptable and colloquial by others. Furthermore, almost every word that might be called obscene or vulgar has, in the colloquial or formal vocabulary of the language, an equivalent that may be used without great social repercussions. Thus, almost anyone may say *intercourse* or *defecate,* but there are other words meaning exactly the same things that some people might be embarrassed to hear, let alone utter. Reactions to obscenity, and even to vulgarity, are so strong in our society that this book might be banned from some stores, libraries, and classrooms if actual examples were cited.

It is clear that societal prohibitions regarding obscenity refer primarily to particular words and not to the actions or things described by the words. For example, it is usually possible to discuss any aspect of sex so long as one avoids certain words. This is a curious phenomenon, but such prohibitions occur in almost every society in matters of religion, sex, ancestry, or bodily functions.

Why particular words are considered obscene or vulgar, when others with the same meaning are not, is far from clear. In our society, the reason appears to be related to psychological fears and the feeling that certain words indicate disdain, disregard, or too casual an attitude toward matters our culture considers highly personal or of great importance. Yet, as with slang, if an obscene or vulgar word is used often enough, it may cease to carry such connotations and become acceptable. A popular example is the word *breast,* at one time considered much too vulgar for use in mixed company. A circumlocution was necessary, and one asked for the *white meat* of the chicken rather than for the *breast,* in spite of the fact that many at the table were undoubtedly aware that the speaker was avoiding the word *breast.* Although we continue to use the expression *white meat,* only a highly conservative, older person or a youngster going through puberty might be embarrassed by, and therefore avoid, the word *breast*.

Obscenity is the use of words that offend the morality of certain people; vulgarity involves words that violate good taste. Since both morality and taste are relative matters, differing according to an individual's background, there are no concrete criteria that can be applied to determine which words are obscene or vulgar. On the other hand, there appears to be no language that lacks words that speakers consider obscene or vulgar. It is doubtful whether people will ever cease to make such judgments.

SITUATIONS AND STYLES

The use of language is frequently a social activity. We rarely speak, listen, read, and write for ourselves alone, but rather in intercommunication with others. The success of our communicative efforts depends not only on the content, or meaning, of what is expressed but also on the form of the expression. In any act of communication, it is necessary to select the vocabulary items, as well as the grammatical patterns, appropriate to the situation.

Language usage varies as situations vary, and there are at least three basic aspects of any situation that must be taken into account in discussing the appropriateness of a given utterance for the situation. First, one must consider the context of the situation: when presenting a formal lecture we use our language differently than we would when discussing a football game at a local bar. Second, the relationships among the people involved in a situation are important: even for the same topic of conversation, a new office worker speaks differently to the president of a company when that person is a stranger than to someone who will share the same office. And third, interacting with these aspects of a situation is the medium of expression—whether speech or writing. In writing, it is often necessary to phrase our thoughts with greater care than in speech. When speaking with someone, we usually can observe immediate reactions to what is said, and, if there is some misunderstanding, we can correct it. In writing, however, those with whom we are communicating are not actually present, and, therefore, we must be sure that there is the least possible opportunity for misinterpretation.

The varieties of language usage associated with different situations are commonly called **styles.** We speakers possess a number of styles, and we choose among them whenever we speak or write. Many aspects of language are common to all styles. Thus, certain morphemes are appropriate in every situation, no matter what the topic, the relationships among people, or the medium of expression. For example, the inflectional suffixes in English, such as *s* 'plural', can be used at any time without causing negative reactions from other people. The same is true of most features of pronunciation and grammar. But there are restrictions on the use of other aspects of language, particularly on the use of certain words. Consider the following sentences:

(3) Rapping is his bag.

(4) He really likes to talk with people.

(5) Verbal intercommunication is his forte.

These sentences represent three different styles of language usage: slang, colloquial, and formal, respectively. Each expresses approximately the same meaning, but they could not be used interchangeably. The slang sentence might be the most appropriate to use when talking casually with people who themselves use the words *rap* and *bag* in this way. To use the formal sentence under such circumstances would not only sound ridiculous, it would be "bad style." Of course, reverse situations also occur. No one would use the slang style in a formal letter of recommendation for someone; in this situation, even the colloquial style might be inappropriate. Each style and its type of vocabulary have a proper place in language usage. Even vulgarity and obscenity may be correct at times. For instance, a college student who worked one summer in a warehouse reported that, until he began to use words he had considered vulgar and obscene, the regular workers were quite unfriendly. When he finally did use the appropriate speech style, however, their attitude changed, and they accepted him as part of their group.

The appropriateness of a style for a situation is determined largely by social convention. Speakers of a language expect to encounter certain styles in certain situations. When such expectations are not fulfilled, there can be interference with the communicative process. In other words, the use of an utterance in an unexpected style often distracts listeners; their attention turns from interpreting the content of the utterance to puzzlement about its form. Normal, effective language usage, therefore, requires of users that they coordinate their utterances with the basic aspects of the situation and with the expectations of those to whom they are speaking or writing.

American linguists have concentrated on those aspects of language occurring in all styles—the core of a language, known to and used by all speakers. There has been relatively little formal investigation into the details of language usage, style, and situation; much remains to be learned. It is clear, for example, that there are as many styles of language as there are differences in situations. The division of usage into slang, colloquial, and formal represents only the most basic, gross distinctions; within each of these styles there are also varieties that deserve study.

The speakers of a language possess an intuitive grasp of style and situation. Based on their prior experiences with language use, speakers know the different styles of language and the situations in which each style is appropriate. Since language experiences vary from one person to another, however, there is sometimes lack of agreement on which style is most appropriate for a particular situation. Generally, situations requiring formal style are as follows: the participants are not well acquainted with one another; there is respect, or at least a desire to indicate respect, for someone else in the group; there is a desire to receive the respect of others. Circumstances such as job interviews, public speeches, or business discussions commonly require formal language. Colloquial style is appropriate to most other situations, where the participants wish to display friendliness or a casual attitude. Slang is normally appropriate only among others who also use the particular slang involved.

It is, of course, possible to violate the conventions of society and deliberately make use of a style that is unexpected or inappropriate for a given situation. In such cases, language users are manipulating the situation—they are expressing more than the content of their utterances. For example, dissatisfied students, presenting a list of complaints to the college president, may use a number of slang words, despite the formality of the situation. Consciously or not, they indicate hostility toward their listener. The president in turn may react by responding in a highly formal style, thereby emphasizing his or her position of power and the respect he or she may normally receive. The communication in such cases is not that of the ideas expressed by the participants, but rather that of their attitudes toward one another.

In contemporary society, many situations that formerly required formal style now accept colloquial language. Sermons, for example, have become friendly chats in many churches; teachers in a college classroom are rarely as formal and unapproachable as they once were. Older people complain that the younger generation seems to be using more slang. This may well be true, for speech styles and situations range along a continuum in terms of degree of formality. As situations once judged formal become informal, those that once required colloquial style tend to move toward slang.

Despite the complexity of the interrelations between style and situation, people manage to arrive at an internalized knowledge of the types of words in their language; that is, each entry in a speaker's lexicon includes information about the style for which it is appropriate. Generally, we construct sentences in which all of the words belong to the same style, which is why the following sentences sound awkward:

(6) He got a big gratuity.

(7) Verbal intercommunication is his bag.

The sentences each contain words from two styles; thus, each sentence, as a whole, is not clearly appropriate for either style. Of course, such utterances do occur. Examples can be found almost daily on televison news programs when a reporter interviews a member of the local community. Knowing that many people will see the interview, the person involved may attempt to speak as formally as possible. If he or she seldom uses this style, colloquial and formal words may both occur in the same sentence. Not everyone knows the same set of words and morphemes; if you have no entry in your lexicon for certain formal expressions, then you must use colloquial ones, even if they are not appropriate to the overall speech style you are using.

Formal vocabulary is sometimes referred to as learned vocabulary, implying that knowledge of such words requires study and learning. Not everyone has the experience and background that lead to the development of a large formal vocabulary. This situation is exploited by the popular press, where magazine and newspaper articles and even entire books are devoted to exercises "guaranteed to increase your vocabulary." The effectiveness of such exercises is open to doubt. Most often they lead to **malapropism,** the confusion of the meaning of two learned words resulting in peculiar sentences. For example, a witness to an accident, not fully in command of the word *extricate,* reported *The car was so badly damaged that the Emergency Rescue Squad had to execute the driver.* Artificial exercises generally consist of little more than lists of words, accompanied by brief definitions. But to master new words, a speaker must encounter them in actual use where their meaning and the style for which they are appropriate can be observed. No one has to be taught slang or colloquial words through artificial exercises; they are learned through exposure. The same is true of formal words.

71

Figure 6.1

DICTIONARIES

The writers of the earliest English dictionaries proclaimed their books to be authoritative
sources of information on spelling and meaning. For example, in 1604, Robert Cawdrey
provided for his dictionary the title in Figure 6.1. Notice the emphasis on "true writing,
and understanding" and on "hard wordes." The public accepted such dictionaries as the
final authority on matters of spelling, pronunciation, meaning, and style—a view still held
by many. Yet, modern dictionaries have abandoned the function of legislating usage, and
many contain statements explicitly denying any such intent. Of course, few users bother
to read the dust jacket or preface of their dictionaries, and, therefore, many continue to
believe that dictionaries are authorities on what usage should be. Writers of contemporary
dictionaries, however, have recognized that the only honest, legitimate function their
work can fulfill is that of an accurate record of usage in spelling, pronunciation, meaning,
and style, whether or not that usage is considered "correct" by some speakers of the
language.

Not even the largest dictionary, however, can include complete information about
the actual usage of all the words known to speakers of a language. Space limitations
always exist, and at some point a process of selection is necessary. The unabridged
Webster's Third New International Dictionary, for example, contains over 450,000
words, yet several times that number could have been included. Words chosen as entries
were those the editors felt people would be most likely to look up. Clearly, then, even if a
word is not in the dictionary, it is still a word—a fact that may displease those who have
relied on dictionaries to settle disputes arising from word games like Scrabble, but a fact
nevertheless.

As with the number of words that can be included, dictionaries must also restrict
the amount of information they provide about each word. In a random sample of the speech
of native speakers of English, ten clearly different pronunciations of the word *because*
occurred. No dictionary lists even half of them. Instead, only the most common pronunciations are given. Similarly, the National Council of Teachers of English has published a
book listing almost 2500 instances of spelling differences found in five commonly used
desk dictionaries of English (see "Further Exploration" at the end of this chapter for the

reference). Frequency of occurrence is a criterion utilized by most editors in choosing the pronunciations and spellings provided in dictionaries.

As records of words and how they are used, some dictionaries also include information about the language style to which certain words belong. Sometimes this is accomplished by labels, such as *colloquial, slang, vulgar,* or *technical.* But labels may be misleading. Many people believe that *colloquial* implies condemnation, whereas, as we have seen, it means merely that a word is appropriate in informal speech or writing. Labels also cause misunderstanding because they are rigid, failing to indicate that judgments about style and appropriateness are variable to some degree. Some dictionary editors have attempted to overcome these problems by using statements to describe style, rather than simple labels. Such statements permit a more accurate description of usage. It should be noted that the inclusion of words such as *ain't* in a dictionary does not constitute a claim that the word is considered "good" English, nor does it represent a condemnation of the word. Instead, words are included in dictionaries because people use those words.

Since a dictionary is a record of usage, there should be no objection to its containing slang. In fact, since slang words are often not widely known, one could argue that they should appear in a dictionary so that people can look up their meaning. But incorporating slang into a dictionary is a task that must be carried out with care. Once a major dictionary is published, it is usually not revised for approximately twenty years. During that time, many slang words will pass out of use and new ones will come into existence. Therefore, a dictionary including slang runs the risk of becoming inaccurate long before a new edition is published. For this reason, most dictionaries contain only the most widely used slang terms, words that may reasonably be expected to survive the life of the book itself. To fill in the gap, special dictionaries devoted to slang are published periodically.

SUMMARY

Slang, vulgarity, obscenity, and professional terminology all represent different points along a continuum of style in language usage. All words in the vocabulary of a language are linguistically equal, although members of every society possess certain judgments and attitudes about the use of certain words. Some of these attitudes are based on generally accepted conventions of usage, such as the situations in which slang, colloquial, or formal words are most appropriate. Other attitudes, however, reflect either a misunderstanding of the nature of language or the personal, aesthetic reactions of an individual. There is, for example, relatively little difference between slang and other types of words in terms of their expression of meaning or the processes of word formation by which they are produced. Modern dictionary editors, as well as modern linguists, attempt to describe style and usage in terms of the conventions that actually exist in our society. Such descriptions neither condemn nor condone the use of any particular style.

FURTHER EXPLORATION

Although some of the examples now seem outdated, "Slang and Its Relatives" by Paul Roberts (Kerr and Aderman 1971) remains an enjoyable discussion of the characteristics and uses of slang, professional terminology, and clichés. One of the best-known slang dictionaries is the *Dictionary of American Slang,* compiled by Harold Wentworth and Stuart Berg Flexner. For descriptions and prescriptions on American English, see *Harper Dictionary of Contemporary Usage,* edited by William and Mary Morris; keep in mind the objective linguistic principles regarding usage as you read the personal opinions of the ''authorities'' quoted. British linguists have conducted fairly extensive, objective research on situations and style; among the best nontechnical discussions of their work is that by Randolph Quirk in *The Use of English,* Chapters 12 and 13, entitled ''Problems of Usage'' and ''Style and Purpose.'' An objective and interesting discussion of criticisms about dictionaries is ''Telling the Truth about Words'' (Kerr and Aderman 1971) by Philip B. Gove, editor of the *Webster's Third New International Dictionary of the English Language Unabridged.* Those readers who wish to pursue the topic in greater detail should consult the interesting collection of articles in *Dictionaries and THAT Dictionary,* edited by James Sledd and Wilma R. Ebbitt. Also relevant is *Variant Spellings in Modern American Dictionaries* by Donald W. Emery.

1. Draw up a list of five slang words that you use frequently and five slang words you never use. Provide a brief definition for each. Is it easier to define the words you use? Do the words that you do not use seem vague or particularly colorful? What do your answers reveal about your own attitudes regarding slang?

2. For your own speech and writing, describe the meaning and usage of the following pairs of words.

bimonthly — semimonthly
imply   — infer
nauseated — nauseous
sensual   — sensuous

Compare your answers to the descriptions provided in a ''usage guide'' (such as the *Harper Dictionary of Contemporary Usage*). Explain any differences you discover.

3. The following passage comes from the program notes supplied to the audience at a performance of Tchaikovsky's Concerto in D for Violin and Orchestra. Find two instances of highly colloquial or slang usage in this otherwise formal writing.

[Tchaikovsky's] brother Modeste had warned him in Switzerland that he found the second movement, an *Andante molto cantabile* (now known as the ''Meditation'' in d minor), far too elegiac and distracting from the whole, and now Tchaikovsky decided to chuck it. In another day, he had written an entirely new second movement, which is the one we hear this evening, the *Canzonetta* in g minor. . . . Tchaikovsky had already once run amuck with his first piano concerto, which he had planned to dedicate to his colleague (and chairman of the Conservatory), Nicholas Rubinstein.*

*This passage is used with permission of the author, Kenneth C. Beachler, Director of the Lecture-Concert Series at Michigan State University.

What type of style would you expect to find in this situation? What is the effect of the shifts in style that occur? Assume that the style shifts were made deliberately; what purposes might be served?

4. Find the answers to as many of the following questions as possible in the preface or foreword of any desk (or college) dictionary of English.

    (a) Do the editors consider the dictionary to be an authoritative legislator of usage or a description of usage?

    (b) What criteria were utilized to select the words that appear as entries?

    (c) Does the dictionary indicate variant pronunciations? What criteria were employed to select the particular variations that are listed?

    (d) What rationale is offered for providing (or not providing) etymologies?

    (e) Does the dictionary include information about the language style of words? In what way is such information presented?

    (f) Is slang included? Why or why not?

PART 33333333333333333333

SOUNDS AND SOUND SYSTEMS

In Part I, language was described as an internalized body of knowledge about meaning, syntax, and pronunciation. Of course, something as abstract as ''a body of knowledge'' is useless for the communication of meaning without some way of converting this abstract information into a concrete form of expression. For all human languages, sound is the concrete means of expression. More than 2000 of the world's languages have no writing system, but all have a sound system.

All human beings beyond infancy know the sound system of their language (unless they have some severe physical abnormality). This knowledge includes more than the ability to produce certain sounds. It also enables us to identify sounds that we hear, even in unfavorable conditions (such as excessive distortion in a tape recording); to distinguish language sounds from other vocal noises (such as sighs or groans); to recognize that two different sequences of sounds represent the same morpheme; and to ignore certain differences among the sounds of our language when we listen, but to make such differences consistently when we speak.

In this part, we look at the sounds and sound system of English, attempting to become aware of the largely unconscious knowledge we have about this aspect of our language. In particular, we will discuss the various instructions that must be sent from the brain to the vocal tract before a language sound can be produced, how these instructions are organized into a system, and why, for example, we interpret the first sound in *pie* as the same as the second sound in *spy,* even though these sounds are really different. There are basic similarities in the sound systems of languages as widespread as English, Spanish, Turkish, and Japanese, and all languages undergo changes in their sound systems. Possible explanations for these facts are offered, and consideration is given to the role children play in language change.

CHAPTER 7777777777777777777777

PHONETICS

Human beings, as well as other animals, are equipped with certain physical characteristics that make possible the activities of breathing, sucking, biting, chewing, and swallowing. Essentially the same parts of the anatomy that participate in these functions also serve as a sound-producing mechanism, called the **vocal tract.** Although the physical properties of the human mouth, nasal passage, throat, and lungs are basically similar to those of certain animals, such as the ape, only human beings produce sounds in the consistent and systematic manner characteristic of language. Why this is so is not fully understood at the present time, but the unique role of sounds in the behavior of all normal human beings is undoubtedly due to special characteristics of the human nervous system, including the brain. A truly comprehensive study of speech sounds should include the results of the research currently being conducted by anatomical investigators, such as biologists and neurophysiologists.

All sounds, whether musical notes, animal noises, or human speech, are simply patterns (or waves) of energy that move through air. Using special mechanical equipment, scientists can record sounds, convert them into pictures of the energy patterns, and thereby examine some of the physical properties of the sounds themselves. The field of study devoted to the investigation of sound waves is known as **acoustic phonetics.** Sounds may also be studied in terms of their origin, that is, how they are produced. When the means of production is the human vocal apparatus, the study is called **articulatory phonetics.** Since both acoustic and articulatory investigations deal directly with physical phenomena (sound waves in the former case, the human vocal tract in the latter), they may be grouped together under the general term **physical phonetics.**

Many aspects of the highly detailed descriptions of speech sounds provided by physical phonetics are of only marginal interest to the linguist. Human beings are capable of producing an infinite variety of sounds, but no language makes systematic use of this variety. In fact, study of many of the languages of the world has indicated that language users, in their dual role of speaker and listener, pay no attention to many of the properties of sounds that can be described in physical phonetics. Certain properties of sounds are important for language and others are not. For example, a child and an adult could both pronounce the English word *fire*. The actual sounds each produces would be quite different in concrete, physical terms; for example, the pitch or tone of the child's sounds would be higher than that produced by the adult, or the child might speak more loudly. Yet to a listener, these very real differences would be irrelevant; the listener would probably not even notice them. In spite of substantial physical differences, the listener would identify the word produced by each speaker as the same.

Individual variations in speech that cannot be controlled by any speaker (such as the size of one's mouth), as well as socially determined variation like loudness or rate of speech, are not relevant to an investigation of linguistic competence. They are matters of performance, superimposed on competence by nonlinguistic considerations, and, as such, they fall within the domain of the physiologist, the psychologist, the anthropologist, or the sociologist. The linguist is interested in features that occur systematically in language, not in aspects of sounds that occur randomly, are never noticed as part of language by language users, or are unnecessary in producing or recognizing an utterance. When linguists study speech sounds, they are concerned with **systematic phonetics,** that is, with just those independently controllable features of sounds that people use in the sound systems of their languages.

THE PHONETIC ALPHABET

In a written discussion, it is awkward to identify sounds in terms of the letters of the alphabet. In English, the same sound may be represented by several different letters, or by combinations of letters, as in the following words:

   do   boo   two   new   you   true

The vowel sound is the same in each word, yet the writing system represents it in six different ways. The same problem exists, although to a lesser extent, for consonants; for example, the sound normally represented by the letter *f* as in *find* is also spelled *gh* or *ph*, as in *enough* and *photo*. On the other hand, our writing system sometimes uses one letter to represent several different sounds. Compare the sounds represented by the letter *a* in the following words:

   *a*gent   f*a*ther   p*a*d   *a*bove

For consonants, notice that the letter *c* represents a different sound in the words *city* and *cow*. Once it is called to your attention, such inconsistency in spelling is obvious, but literate individuals are often so much more conscious of letters than sounds that they will fail to notice very definite differences in pronunciation. Observe carefully the pronunciation of the sounds represented by the letters *th* in the following words:

*th*ing	*th*an
*th*row	*th*ough
*th*igh	*th*y
e*th*er	ei*th*er

The sound of *th* in the first column is different from the sound in the second column.

Because of such variations in normal spelling, linguists have adopted a **phonetic alphabet** in which each letter stands in a one-to-one correspondence with each sound; that is, a particular sound is always written with the same letter, and a particular letter always represents the same sound. Anyone who knows the English alphabet will find most of the letters in the phonetic alphabet familiar, but a few have been borrowed from Greek or combine regular English letters with a special symbol. The letters in the phonetic alphabet that are commonly used for the sounds of English are given in Figure 7.1. From now on, sounds and words will be given in **phonetic transcription,** that is, using the letters of the phonetic alphabet. All phonetic transcriptions are enclosed in square brackets in order to distinguish them from regular spelling. For example, the word *top* will be transcribed [tap].

The phonetic alphabet in Figure 7.1 includes all of the letters of the normal English alphabet except *q* and *x*. In ordinary English writing, the letter *q* always represents the sound [k]. Thus, in phonetic transcription *quit* is [kwɪt] and *unique* is [yunik]; similarly, *kick* is [kɪk] and *cat* is [kæt]. The letter *x* in English writing represents a series of two sounds for which the phonetic alphabet provides symbols: [gz] in *example*—[ɛgzæmpəl], [ks] in *exclaim*—[ɛksklem], and either [ks] or [gz] in a word like *exit,* which is pronounced either [ɛksət] or [ɛgzət].

Every sound that occurs in human languages can be represented, or transcribed, by means of the symbols of the phonetic alphabet. Figure 7.1 contains only some of the sounds and symbols available to the linguist. Even for English, other sounds occur, and when we work with different languages, new sounds and symbols must be utilized. Many such additional details are introduced in the next three chapters as we discuss the capabilities of the vocal tract and the functions of sounds in various languages.

The symbols given in Figure 7.1 are those most often used, but, unfortunately, not all linguists use the same phonetic alphabet, especially for the representation of vowel sounds. As will be shown in the next section, a sound is actually produced through a combination of phonetic features. A phonetic symbol, therefore, is merely an abbreviation for the description of a sound. While it may be somewhat confusing for a reader to learn one set of abbreviations and then encounter a slightly different set in another book, the difficulty is at most temporary and of little importance. In a written discussion of sounds, all that really matters is that the writer utilizes a system of symbols in which each sound is consistently represented by a single symbol and each symbol always represents the same sound.

THE VOCAL TRACT

The symbols of the phonetic alphabet are actually abbreviations for full descriptions of the sounds of a language. The most common means that linguists use to describe sounds involves a set of **phonetic features,** in which each feature describes one of a number of activities carried on in the vocal tract when a speech sound is **articulated,** or produced. Adults learned the sound segments of their language so long ago, and have produced each segment so many times, that they are usually unaware of how many articulation features are involved in the production of a sound. Yet, every speech sound is the result of a number of more or less simultaneous movements in the vocal tract. To produce a sound, speakers must transmit from their brains to their vocal tracts a set of instructions. Although it is the task of the neurophysiologist to determine exactly the nature and form of these instructions, the linguist uses phonetic features to describe, or represent, them. Thus, each phonetic feature represents one of the instructions sent from speakers' brains to their vocal tracts. When a particular set of instructions is carried out, the result is a particular speech sound.

Figure 7.1

Phonetic Symbol	Represents First Sound in	Represents Last Sound in
p	pie	tap
b	buy	tab
t	tie	pat
d	die	pad
k	cap	tack
g	gap	tag
m	might	seem
n	night	seen
ŋ	—	sing
f	ferry	safe
v	very	save
θ	thigh	bath
ð	thy	bathe
s	sue	race
z	zoo	raise
š	shoe	wish
ž	—	rouge
č	chew	birch
ǰ	jury	bridge
l	lead	fill
r	read	fear
h	hit	—
y	yet	—
w	wet	—

Phonetic Symbol	Represents Vowel Sound in		
i	beat	see	eat
I	bit	sit	it
e	bait	say	ate
ɛ	bet	set	Ed
æ	bat	sat	at
ə	but	putt	up
u	boot	suit	ooze
U	book	soot	oops
o	coat	soak	oat
ɔ	caught	sought	ought
a	cot	sot	Oz
ay	cry	bite	eye
aw	cow	bout	out
ɔy	coy	boys	oil

Notes. The last three symbols represent diphthongs, a type of complex sound discussed in Chapter 8. In some dialects of English, speakers do not distinguish between the sounds represented by [ɔ] and [a]; in such dialects, *caught* and *cot* are homonyms; that is, they are pronounced in the same way, usually with the sound represented by the phonetic symbol [a]. There are also dialect differences in the pronunciation of the vowel sound in *cot*; here we represent the sound as [a], but for some dialects, many linguists prefer the symbol [ɑ], which represents a sound made further toward the back of the mouth than [a] (see Chapter 8 for discussion of how vowel sounds are produced). There are also dialect variations in the vowel sound of *cow*, with some speakers using [aw] and others [æw].

The essential ingredient of any act of speech is a moving stream of air. The air stream begins in the lungs and moves up through the vocal tract, the region that consists of the throat, the mouth, and the nasal cavity, as well as the muscles associated with these areas. Whenever we are about to speak, our lungs fill up with air and our vocal tracts assume the position shown in Figure 7.2. This is called the **prespeech position;** it differs from the position of the vocal tract during quiet breathing in several ways, including: the muscles of the vocal tract become tense, the position of the tongue moves up from the floor of the mouth, the air stream is blocked at the larynx, and the velum moves to close off the nasal cavity (see Figure 7.2 and locate these terms). Compare for yourself the differences between the vocal tract in quiet breathing and in prespeech position. First, relax and simply breathe quietly; notice the lack of tenseness and the free flow of air from the lungs through the nasal cavity. Then, pretend you are about to say something (the word *I* will do); observe the changes that occur in your vocal tract.

Once the prespeech position has been taken, the particular sound a person will utter depends on the various movements that then take place in the vocal tract. For example, if you assume the prespeech position of Figure 7.2 and proceed to say the word *mall,* your vocal tract will receive and carry out a number of instructions leading to the articulation of the sound segment [m]; if you issued a different set of instructions, subconsciously of course, a different sound would be produced. Figure 7.3 represents some of the instructions involved in the articulation of the first sound segment of the words *mall, ball,* and *tall.*

Figure 7.2

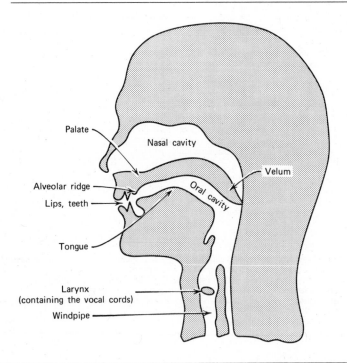

Palate

Nasal cavity

Velum

Alveolar ridge

Lips, teeth

Oral cavity

Tongue

Larynx
(containing the vocal cords)

Windpipe

The four instructions given in Figure 7.3 represent only a few of the approximately three dozen vocal tract activities that all human beings can control. Normally, however, native speakers of a language carry out these activities without any awareness of what is going on in their vocal tract. In fact, they may even assume that only one activity is involved for each sound. But, as Figure 7.3 shows, this assumption is not correct. While two sound segments may differ from one another by only one activity (e.g., the position of the velum in [m] and [b]), there are other cases when sound segments differ in a number of features, as happens with [b] and [t], for which all features mentioned in Figure 7.3 are different, except the position of the velum. When learning a foreign language, a student may encounter sounds that do not occur in English, and, in such cases, the variety of simultaneous vocal tract activities necessary for the production of a sound may be more apparent.

Since the vocal tract of every human being is the same as that of every other human being, all people are capable of producing any sound in any language. To state this important fact another way, linguists assume that there is a universal set of phonetic features that accounts for the sound-producing capabilities of all people. One of the main tasks of modern linguistics is the discovery of all of the phonetic features belonging to this

Figure 7.3

	Sound Segment		
	[m]	[b]	[t]
1	close the lips	close the lips	raise tip of tongue to alveolar ridge
2	drop down velum, allowing air stream to pass through nasal cavity	keep velum against back of throat to prevent air from entering nasal cavity	keep velum against back of throat to prevent air from entering nasal cavity
3	position vocal cords relatively close together, so they will vibrate as air stream passes through them	position vocal cords relatively close together, so they will vibrate as air stream passes through them	position vocal cords relatively far apart, so they will not vibrate as air stream passes through them
4	relax all muscles in oral cavity	relax all muscles in oral cavity	tense all muscles in oral cavity

universal set. On the surface, this may appear to be an easy task, but actually it is not. In order to achieve the goal, thousands of languages must be examined, and the proposed phonetic features must be used to describe all of the sound segments in those languages. If any language is found to have two different sound segments that cannot be described differently, the set of phonetic features must be revised and perhaps a new feature added. In such a case, care must be taken that the new feature does in fact represent a vocal tract activity that can be controlled by all human beings, for, in addition to the description of actual speech sounds, linguists are interested in describing the nature of human language in general. Thus, the universal set of phonetic features serves to identify all sound segments potentially available for use in human language—available because the sound-producing mechanism of all people can produce them.

The universal set of phonetic features has not yet been fully determined. Linguists do agree on a substantial number of features, especially those that play an important role in the sound systems of the well-known languages, such as English, Spanish, German, and Russian. Other phonetic features are still being investigated. We concentrate our attention here on those widely recognized as important for the description and classification of sound segments in English and several other European languages. Readers who are interested in other features that are utilized in languages with different sound systems should consult "Further Exploration" at the conclusion of Chapter 8.

SUMMARY

In the regular writing system of English, the same letter sometimes represents two or more different sounds, and the same sound may be represented by two or more different letters. Linguists, therefore, make use of a phonetic alphabet in describing sounds—an alphabet in which each symbol consistently represents a single sound and in which each sound is always represented by a single symbol. The symbols of the phonetic alphabet, however, are not actually descriptions of sounds, but merely shorthand abbreviations for complete descriptions. To describe a sound fully, linguists make use of a set of phonetic features, each of which represents one vocal tract activity involved in the production of a speech sound.

FURTHER EXPLORATION

A phonetic transcription that utilizes only a basic set of symbols (such as those in Figure 7.1) is called a **broad transcription;** many details of pronunciation are not recorded. With the addition of other symbols and markings, it is possible to provide a **narrow transcription** of speech—one that shows all, or most, of the characteristics of sounds that the transcriber can perceive. Here, and in the following chapters, broad transcriptions are used except where the discussion requires the detail available in a narrow transcription. Some instructors may wish to supplement the symbols of Figure 7.1, either to permit narrow transcriptions or to provide for particular dialect variations. Most phonetics textbooks include too much detail or assume too much knowledge about phonology for readers at this stage. However, an introduction to phonetics and phonetic transcription, emphasizing English, does appear in *Introduction to Phonology* by Clarence Sloat, Sharon Henderson Taylor, and James Hoard. Consonant and vowel transcription is also discussed in Peter Ladefoged's *A Course in Phonetics* following a chapter on articulatory phonetics. In another book, *Elements of Acoustic Phonetics,* Ladefoged offers a brief and straightforward explanation of the basic properties of sound waves and how they are investigated in acoustic phonetics.

1. Provide a broad phonetic transcription of the following English words as you pronounce them in casual speech. Do not base your transcriptions on overly slow, precise pronunciation, and be careful to avoid confusing the sounds of a word with its spelling. If you are not sure of the correct symbol for a sound, compare the sound with those offered as examples for the symbols in Figure 7.1.

(a) easy	(i) garage	(q) trial
(b) that	(j) check	(r) gin
(c) jack	(k) throw	(s) cell
(d) optic	(l) how	(t) bridge
(e) yellow	(m) deal	(u) white
(f) give	(n) rang	(v) joy
(g) look	(o) city	(w) luck
(h) shake	(p) cute	(x) thought

2.   The following broad transcriptions represent the normal pronunciation, in casual speech, of an educated speaker from the northern New Jersey area. In normal English spelling, write the word represented by each transcription.

(a)	[sɛd]	(i)	[ǰali]	(q)	[ɔt]
(b)	[ped]	(j)	[ðɛm]	(r)	[kæč]
(c)	[dɔg]	(k)	[ənəf]	(s)	[myul]
(d)	[θæŋk]	(l)	[kwin]	(t)	[šak]
(e)	[trɪk]	(m)	[kɔy]	(u)	[yuz]
(f)	[trawt]	(n)	[plɛžər]	(v)	[saykaləǰi]
(g)	[it]	(o)	[taməs]	(w)	[ɛkstrə]
(h)	[sok]	(p)	[kʊd]	(x)	[æθlit]

3.   Compare the differences in the configuration of your vocal tract during quiet breathing and in prespeech position; try to notice differences at each of the points in Figure 7.2. Describe the prespeech position as fully as possible (there are more characteristics of prespeech position than the few mentioned in the text). It is possible that the prespeech position may vary slightly from one language to another. If you are a native (or a fluent) speaker of some language other than English, assume the prespeech position for that language and describe the differences, if any, from the English prespeech position.

4.   In Chapter 8, phonetic features are introduced formally, with specific labels and detailed descriptions of the vocal tract activities involved in the articulation of the major sounds of English. Even without such formal labels and definitions, however, you can determine much about your vocal tract as it works to produce sounds. For each of the sounds listed below, begin from prespeech position and produce the sound. (You will find that some sounds, such as [p], are difficult to produce without an accompanying vowel; in such cases, produce the sound with a following [a].) In as much detail as possible, describe the vocal tract activities that occur. (*Hint* Pay attention to all parts of the vocal tract and particularly to any movements of the tongue, noting which part of the tongue moves, where it moves to, and whether it comes into contact with any part of the vocal tract, such as the teeth, alveolar ridge, palate, or velum; consult Figure 7.2 as you make your observations.)

(a)	[θ]	(f)	[t]	(k)	[i]
(b)	[n]	(g)	[f]	(l)	[a]
(c)	[č]	(h)	[ž]	(m)	[u]
(d)	[g]	(i)	[ŋ]	(n)	[æ]
(e)	[l]	(j)	[p]	(o)	[ɔy]

CHAPTER 88888888888888888888888888

PHONETIC FEATURES

The phonetic features discussed in this chapter occur in various combinations, most of these combinations representing different sound segments of English. To readers encountering such features for the first time, this may seem to be a rather cumbersome way of describing sounds, but it is necessary if linguists are to present complete, accurate, and explicit descriptions of the sounds in human language. People who are unfamiliar with phonetic features must resort to subjective terms in describing the sounds of a language. They may say that French is ''nasal'' or that German is ''guttural'' or that, in Spanish, there are sounds that ''break on the teeth.'' But what do these expressions mean? The fact that we cannot produce the sounds of these languages on the basis of such informal descriptions illustrates that these descriptions are not explicit and certainly not complete. However, when the linguist describes the sounds of a language, making use of a carefully defined set of phonetic features, anyone who is familiar with those features can read the description and understand the sounds of the language and how they are produced.

Phonetic features also provide a means for identifying **classes** of sounds, that is, groups of sounds that share one or more features in common and that native speakers of a language may recognize as similar in some sense. For example, among the sound segments listed in Figure 7.1, we may observe that [p, b, t, d, k, g] are similar to one another and different from [f, v, θ, ð, s, z, š, ž]. The phonetic features provide a way of explicitly stating the difference between these two classes of sounds. As we shall see, the former class contains segments that are all [− continuant], while in the latter class, the segments are all [+ continuant].

Classes of sounds play an important role in human languages; therefore, it is necessary that linguists have a set of phonetic features that make it possible to describe such classes. Consider, for example, the formation of plural nouns in English. In spelling, we normally add the letter *s* to a singular form in order to produce its plural, but, in speech, we add the sounds [s], [z], or [əz]. Which sound is used depends on the last sound in the singular form, and the phonetic features enable the linguist to describe and explain this dependency. We return to this subject in Chapter 9, but, for now, the reader should note that phonetic features are of fundamental importance for the description of the sounds of a language and for the explanation of how those sounds are used.

Also note that linguists differ regarding the particular set of features they utilize in their descriptions of sounds. Basically, there are two overlapping sets of features: those of traditional structural linguistics and those of contemporary transformational linguistics. Since both are quite widely used, it is necessary to become familiar with both. Here, we emphasize the features of the transformational approach, but the traditional features are also mentioned whenever they differ from those that are the basis of the discussion.

Each phonetic feature represents an activity that is actually carried out by the vocal tract. Although you may be unaccustomed to consciously noticing what you do when you articulate a sound, you will often be able to determine for yourself the phonetic features involved in the sound segments of English. Examine your vocal tract as you produce sounds; look at your mouth in a mirror; touch parts of the vocal tract with your fingers; observe the variety of movements involved in the production of speech sounds. The phonetic features discussed below are real; they represent abilities possessed by all physically normal human beings.

THE LARYNX

The **larynx** is a cartilaginous structure located low in the throat; it is commonly called the "Adam's apple" and can be felt by placing the finger tips on the middle region of the front of the neck. The larynx is one of the most important parts of the vocal tract, for, as the air stream moves up from the lungs, it must pass through the **vocal cords,** a pair of membranes attached horizontally in the larynx. The vocal cords are made up of elastic tissue and may be spread apart or pulled together. The vocal cords can be pulled together so tightly that there is no way for an air stream to pass through them. But it is also possible to constrict the vocal cords while still leaving a small space between them through which an air stream can pass. Since the space is small, the pressure from the moving air will then cause the vocal cords to vibrate. This is the position assumed by the vocal cords just prior to speech, as well as during the production of many speech sounds. Other speech sounds, however, are articulated with spread vocal cords. In such cases, the air stream moves freely through without causing vibration. Vibration of the vocal cords is characterized by the phonetic feature [**voice**]; sounds produced with vibrating vocal cords have the feature [+ voice]; sounds articulated with the vocal cords spread and not vibrating are [− voice]. The plus sign (+) and the minus sign (−) are utilized consistently with each feature in systematic phonetics; [+] indicates that the vocal tract activity described by the feature is present in the production of a sound segment; [−] indicates that the activity is absent.

The following sound segments of English are [+ voice]: [b, d, g, ǰ, m, n, ŋ, v, ð, z, ž, l, r, y, w, i, ɪ, e, ɛ, æ, ə, u, ʊ, o, ɔ, a, ay, aw, ɔy]. All of the other segments listed in Figure 7.1 are [− voice]. The difference between [+ voice] and [− voice] sounds is easily determined by placing the finger tips on the neck at the position of the larynx. If you then pronounce a pair of words such as [zu]/[su], you will feel vibration during the first sound segment of [zu] but not during the first segment of [su]. The chief difference in the articulation of [z] and [s] is that the former is [+ voice], while the latter is [− voice]; the same is true for other pairs of sounds in English, such as [b]/[p], [d]/[t], [g]/[k], [ǰ]/[č], [v]/[f], [ð]/[θ], and [ž]/[š].

OBSTRUCTIONS AND THE AIR STREAM

Once the air stream has passed the larynx, it may move freely out of the vocal tract, or its movement may be interfered with in some way. The phonetic features [vocalic] and [consonantal] are used to describe this fact.

The feature [**vocalic**] pertains to the position of the vocal cords and the passage of the air stream through the oral cavity. When the vocal tract is positioned in such a way that air moves through vocal cords that are in vibrating position and then passes out of the oral cavity without interference, the sound produced is [+ vocalic]. All of the vowels in English have this feature, and so do the sound segments [l] and [r]. The remaining sound segments of English are all [− vocalic]. In their production, the air stream is blocked completely, but momentarily, from passing through the oral cavity (as with [p, b, t, d, k, g, č, ǰ, m, n, ŋ]); or there is some partial obstacle which, while not completely blocking the air stream, is sufficient to interfere with it (as with [f, v, θ, ð, s, z, š, ž, w, y]); or the vocal cords are not in vibrating position, even though there is no real obstruction in the oral cavity (as with [h]).

The feature [**consonantal**] is present whenever some part of the vocal tract moves substantially away from the prespeech position and forms an obstruction to the air stream in the oral cavity. In many cases, sounds that are [− vocalic] will be [+ consonantal], and sounds that are [− consonantal] will be [+ vocalic]. But since these two phonetic features represent vocal tract activities that may be carried out independently of one another, there is also the possibility that a sound segment may be simultaneously [+ vocalic, + consonantal] or [− vocalic, − consonantal].*

*Normally, in a formal linguistic description, when two or more phonetic features are used in the description of a sound, the features are listed vertically, as follows:

$$\begin{bmatrix} - \text{ vocalic} \\ - \text{ consonantal} \end{bmatrix}$$

However, in order to make the text easier to read, we will list such sets of features horizontally (except in figures and in a few instances where vertical listing is preferable). Thus, a set of features presented horizontally within a single set of square brackets, as in the sentence above, is equivalent in meaning to the same set of features presented vertically within a single set of large square brackets.

Notice that the feature [consonantal] does not necessarily require that the obstruction cause blockage or actual interference with the air stream. It is possible to provide an obstacle to the air stream, while, at the same time, allowing sufficient space for the air to move around that obstacle without any interference. This is what occurs when you produce the sound segments [l] and [r]. For [l], the tip of the tongue is raised up to the alveolar ridge. The tongue is actually touching the roof of the mouth, so there is an obstacle. Thus, [l] is [+ consonantal]. Nevertheless, one side of the tongue is lowered, and the air stream can pass freely out of the mouth by moving over the side of the tongue. Thus, [l] is also [+ vocalic]. Like [l], [r] has the features [+ vocalic, + consonantal]. [r] is distinguished from [l] by the fact that [r] usually is articulated with the tongue tip raised toward the area where the alveolar ridge meets the palate and is curved in such a way that, while the sides of the tongue do touch the roof of the mouth, air passes freely over the center of the tongue. [l] and [r] are distinguished from one another by the feature [**lateral**]. [l] is [+ lateral] because air flows over the side of the tongue; all other sound segments in English, including [r], are [− lateral] since in none of them is the air stream channeled over the side of the tongue.

[h, w, y] are the sound segments of English that are [− vocalic, − consonantal]. These sounds are [− vocalic] for the reasons discussed above, but, since the obstruction to the air stream in the oral cavity is far less than for sounds like [b, s, l], [h, w, y] are [− consonantal].

The phonetic features [vocalic] and [consonantal] thus divide the sound segments of English into the four major classes presented in Figure 8.1. The liquids share one feature in common with the vowels, [+ vocalic], and one with the consonants, [+ consonantal]. This explains why perceptive speakers of English sometimes feel that [l] and [r] are somehow different from sound segments like [b, s, č]. Similarly, some speakers may have noticed that the glides [h, w, y] are as much like the vowels as they are like the consonants. For this reason, glides are sometimes referred to as **semivowels.** The fact is made

Figure 8.1 _____

Phonetic Features	Sound Segments	Common Name of Class
$\begin{bmatrix} + \text{ vocalic} \\ - \text{ consonantal} \end{bmatrix}$	[i, ɪ, e, ɛ, æ, ə, u, ʊ, o, ɔ, a]	**vowels**
$\begin{bmatrix} - \text{ vocalic} \\ + \text{ consonantal} \end{bmatrix}$	[p, b, t, d, k, g, m, n, ŋ, f, v, θ, ð, s, z, š, ž, č, ǰ]	**consonants**
$\begin{bmatrix} + \text{ vocalic} \\ + \text{ consonantal} \end{bmatrix}$	[l, r]	**liquids**
$\begin{bmatrix} - \text{ vocalic} \\ - \text{ consonantal} \end{bmatrix}$	[h, w, y]	**glides**

explicit when sounds are described in terms of features, for glides are [− consonantal] like vowels and [− vocalic] like consonants.

For every [+ consonantal] sound segment, there is an obstruction at some point in the oral cavity. The phonetic feature [**continuant**] is used to describe the degree of obstruction involved in the articulation of a sound. If the obstruction is only partial, with sufficient space left for the air stream to continue moving through the mouth, the sound involved is [+ continuant]. The vowels, liquids, and glides are [+ continuant] since, as was stated earlier, the air stream is able to move freely through the oral cavity. The [+ consonantal, + continuant] sound segments of English are [f, v, θ, ð, s, z, š, ž]; these are commonly called **fricatives,** since the partial obstruction results in frictionlike noise. All other [− vocalic, + consonantal] segments in English are [− continuant]. Every [+ continuant] sound may be "held" for as long as the speaker is able to provide an air stream. For most [− continuant] sounds, however, it is impossible to lengthen the sound because the air stream is completely stopped in the oral cavity. For example, in producing the word *face,* you can make the [f] sound last a long time, but if you try to do this with the first sound segment of *pace,* no sound is produced until the lips forming a complete obstacle are opened and the air stream is released. Thus, [f] is [+ continuant], while [p] is [− continuant].

The only [− continuant] sounds in English that can be lengthened are [m, n, ŋ]. This is because the air stream, although completely blocked in the oral cavity during the articulation of these sounds, continues to move through the nasal cavity. Movement of the air stream through the nasal cavity is described by the feature [**nasal**]. For air to move through the nasal cavity, the **velum,** which is the soft part at the back of the roof of the mouth, must drop down from the position illustrated in Figure 7.2. When the velum is lowered to allow air to pass into the nasal cavity, the sound produced has the feature [+ nasal]. If the velum remains raised, as in Figure 7.2, the sound will be [− nasal]. The [+ nasal] sound segments of English, commonly referred to simply as **nasals,** are [m, n, ŋ]; all other English sound segments are [− nasal]. The importance of the feature [nasal] in our perception of English sounds is indicated by the fact that the sole difference between [b] and [m] is that the former is [− nasal] and the latter [+ nasal]; the same is true for [d] and [n] and for [g] and [ŋ]. It is interesting to note here that it is sometimes said of people with colds that "They sound very nasal." The actual situation is precisely the reverse. When the nasal cavity is congested, air cannot pass freely through it, and someone with a cold may produce no [+ nasal] sound segments at all. Production of the sentence *The man came home,* will be [ðə bæd keb hob], rather than the usual [ðə mæn kem hom]. This misconception about what actually occurs in the speech of individuals with congested nasal cavities simply supports our earlier observation that many people are totally unaware of the movements in their vocal tract.

The feature [nasal] divides the [− continuant] sound segments of English into two classes—those that are [+ nasal], [m, n, ŋ], and those that are [− nasal], [p, b, t, d, k, g, č, ǰ]. This latter class of [− continuant, − nasal] sound segments may be subdivided further into two classes, depending on how quickly the obstacle totally blocking the air stream is removed; the feature [**abrupt release**] describes this phenomenon. If the obstacle, usually the lips or some part of the tongue, is released suddenly, allowing the air to move out of the oral cavity without further interference, the sound has the feature [+ abrupt release], as do the sound segments [p, b, t, d, k, g]. These are sometimes called **stops,** as opposed to **affricates,** which are sounds with the features [− continuant, − nasal, − abrupt release]. In English, there are two affricates, [č] and [ǰ]. These sounds resemble a combination of a stop and a fricative; that is, in the articulation of [č] and [ǰ], the vocal tract begins by totally blocking the air stream (a stop) and then releases the air stream gradually, producing the friction noise associated with fricatives. You may test this by pronouncing the word *church* [čərč]. The stop aspect of [č] is most obvious at the beginning of the word when you can feel the tongue blocking the air stream at the palate; at the end of the word, the friction noise produced with the release of the air stream is usually quite audible. It should be noted that any [+ continuant] sound segment will also be [− abrupt release] since there is no obstruction that could be released suddenly.

The friction noise in fricatives and affricates is accounted for in systematic phonetics by the feature **[strident]**. If you pronounce a series of words like [fɪn], [θɪn], [sɪn], [šɪn], [čɪn] and listen carefully to the first sound segment in each word, you will probably notice that [f, s, š, č] are noisier than [θ]. The same is true of the [+ voice] series [v, ð, z, ž, ǰ], in which [v, z, ž, ǰ] are characterized by greater noise than is [ð]. This noisiness results from the type of obstruction that the air stream must bypass. When the obstruction causes turbulence in the air stream, the sound segment produced is [+ strident]. Thus, among the fricatives of English, only [θ] and [ð] are [− strident]; the other fricatives, as well as the affricates, are [+ strident]. The remaining sound segments of English are all

Figure 8.2

Features \ Segments	p	b	t	d	k	g	m	n	ŋ	f	v	θ	ð	s	z
Vocalic	−	−	−	−	−	−	−	−	−	−	−	−	−	−	−
Consonantal	+	+	+	+	+	+	+	+	+	+	+	+	+	+	+
Continuant	−	−	−	−	−	−	−	−	−	+	+	+	+	+	+
Nasal	−	−	−	−	−	−	+	+	+	−	−	−	−	−	−
Abrupt release	+	+	+	+	+	+	+	+	+	−	−	−	−	−	−
Lateral	−	−	−	−	−	−	−	−	−	−	−	−	−	−	−
Voice	−	+	−	+	−	+	+	+	+	−	+	−	+	−	+
Strident	−	−	−	−	−	−	−	−	−	+	+	−	−	+	+

[− strident] since the particular type of friction noise described by the feature can occur only when turbulence is created at some point in the articulation of a sound by a partial obstruction to the air stream. Since English nasals and stops involve complete obstruction followed by immediate release of the air, there is no opportunity for friction of any kind, nor does the free passage of the air stream in English vowels, liquids, and glides result in friction noise.

MATRIX

Phonetic features serve two primary purposes. On one hand, they describe the various articulatory movements in the production of sounds. At the same time, they provide a cross-classification of sound segments, by means of which each sound segment is identified in terms of its similarities with and differences from each other sound segment in the **phonological system** (the sound system) of the language. The importance of this cross-classification will be demonstrated in the following chapter. For now, we will simply illustrate how it is achieved.

Figure 8.2 is a **matrix** that illustrates the two functions of phonetic features. Each horizontal row represents one phonetic feature, and each vertical column represents a sound segment. By reading down each column, the description of a sound segment is obtained. By reading across the rows, classes of sounds are identified. For example, the class of nasals consists of the segments in all of the columns that contain the feature

š	ž	č	ǰ	l	r	h	w	y	i	ɪ	e	ɛ	æ	ə	u	ʊ	o	ɔ	a
−	−	−	−	+	+	−	−	−	+	+	+	+	+	+	+	+	+	+	+
+	+	+	+	+	+	−	−	−	−	−	−	−	−	−	−	−	−	−	−
+	+	−	−	+	+	+	+	+	+	+	+	+	+	+	+	+	+	+	+
−	−	−	−	−	−	−	−	−	−	−	−	−	−	−	−	−	−	−	−
−	−	−	−	−	−	−	−	−	−	−	−	−	−	−	−	−	−	−	−
−	−	−	−	+	−	−	−	−	−	−	−	−	−	−	−	−	−	−	−
−	+	−	+	+	+	−	+	+	+	+	+	+	+	+	+	+	+	+	+
+	+	+	+	−	−	−	−	−	−	−	−	−	−	−	−	−	−	−	−

[+ nasal]—[m, n, ŋ]. Another class of English sound segments consists of those having the feature [+ vocalic]—[l, r, i, ɪ, e, ɛ, æ, ə, u, ʊ, o, ɔ, a]. Further classes can be identified by reference to more than one feature:

(a) $\begin{bmatrix} +\text{vocalic} \\ +\text{consonantal} \end{bmatrix}$ (b) $\begin{bmatrix} -\text{continuant} \\ -\text{nasal} \\ +\text{ abrupt release} \end{bmatrix}$

Class (a) contains the segments [l, r], while class (b) contains the segments [p, b, t, d, k, g].

The matrix in Figure 8.2 must be expanded if we are to have a full description of each sound segment of English. There are many columns in the matrix that are identical, yet the segments represented by those columns are not. For example, the vowels all have the same set of features:

$$\begin{bmatrix} +\text{ vocalic} \\ -\text{ consonantal} \\ +\text{ continuant} \\ -\text{ nasal} \\ -\text{ abrupt release} \\ -\text{ lateral} \\ +\text{ voice} \\ -\text{ strident} \end{bmatrix}$$

In order to distinguish such sound segments from one another, additional features are necessary.

POSITIONS OF ARTICULATION

The position of articulation is an important factor in distinguishing the sound segments of a language. In the articulation of sounds, the shape of the oral cavity is often substantially different from the configuration it assumes just prior to speech (i.e., the configuration illustrated by Figure 7.2). The oral cavity is the primary resonating chamber for the air stream, and a change in the shape of the chamber results in a change in the sound. The principle is the same as that utilized in the different wind instruments in music. The various shapes that the oral cavity can assume are described by phonetic features referring to the position of articulation of sounds. This position is defined as the point (or points) in the oral cavity that is radically different from the prespeech position. Changes from the prespeech position are perhaps most obvious in the case of [+ consonantal] sound segments, when an **articulator** (some movable part of the vocal tract) presents an obstacle to the passage of the air stream. However, [− consonantal] sounds also involve changes in the shape of the oral cavity. It is necessary, then, to describe the position of articulation of all sound segments, vowels as well as consonants.

Traditionally, linguists concerned with articulatory phonetics have described the positions of articulation of consonants with features that are not relevant for vowels. These features indicate the point of maximum interference with the air stream, and each point in the oral cavity is provided with a different label. According to this view, the positions of articulation of English consonants are described by the features given in Figure 8.3. The articulation positions of vowels, in traditional articulatory phonetics, are described by a totally different set of features. These concern the height of the tongue and the position of the highest part of the tongue (whether the highest part is toward the front of the oral cavity, in the center, or at the back). Figure 8.4 illustrates the vowel features of articulatory phonetics. A comparison of Figures 8.3 and 8.4 will show that, in traditional articulatory phonetics, the consonants each have only one relevant feature of articulation

Figure 8.3

Traditional Feature of Position of Articulation	Articulator	Consonants
Labial	one or both lips	[p, b, m, f, v]
Dental	tongue tip at teeth	[θ, ð]
Alveolar	tongue in contact with alveolar ridge	[t, d, n, s, z, l, r]
Palatal	tongue in contact with palate	[š, ž, č, ǰ]
Velar	back of tongue in contact with velum	[k, g, ŋ]

Figure 8.4

		Traditional Features of Tongue Position in Articulation of Vowels		
		Front	Central	Back
Traditional Features of Tongue Height in Articulation of Vowels	High	[i, ɪ]		[u, ʊ]
	Mid	[e, ɛ]	[ə]	[o, ɔ]
	Low	[æ]		[a]

position (for example, [p] is [labial]), while the vowels each involve two features of articulation position ([i] is both [high] and [front]).

More recently, linguists working on systematic phonetics have abandoned the articulation position features of traditional articulatory phonetics in favor of a different set of phonetic features. One reason for the change in the set of features was the recognition that there are similarities among consonants and vowels in terms of their positions of articulation. These similarities were ignored by the traditional approach, in which totally different features were used to describe the articulation of consonants and vowels. The new set of features, on the other hand, captures this similarity by making use of the same features for both types of sounds. A further, and more important, inadequacy of the traditional features was their failure to describe the classes of sound segments that play important roles in the sound systems of human languages. We return to this point when we consider the sound system of English in Chapter 9.

For consonants, the primary point of articulation is the location of the obstruction to the air stream. This is described by the feature **[anterior]**. Since [anterior] refers to the location of an obstruction in the oral cavity, it is relevant only to [+ consonantal] sounds; [− consonantal] sounds are necessarily [− anterior] since they do not involve any obstruction. Sounds that are made by obstructing the air stream in the front half of the oral cavity are [+ anterior]; those involving an obstruction in the back half are [− anterior]. The dividing line is the palate; thus, the labials [p, b, m, f, v], the dentals [ð, θ], and the alveolars [t, d, n, s, z, l, r] are [+ anterior]; the palatals [š, ž, č, ǰ] and the velars [k, g, ŋ] are [− anterior].

In systematic phonetics, the other features describing positions of articulation all involve the fact that the **blade** and the **body** of the tongue, as illustrated in Figure 8.5, may be moved away from their position just prior to speech. The blade is the front part of the tongue, the portion not attached to the floor of the mouth; the body of the tongue is the thicker part in the center region that is connected to the floor of the mouth. The feature [**coronal**] refers to the raising of the blade of the tongue above its prespeech position. When the blade is raised, it naturally approaches the area of the roof of the mouth that lies directly above it, that is, the region from the back of the upper teeth, along the alveolar ridge (the bumpy area directly behind the upper teeth), to the front part of the palate (the smoother, hard, dome-shaped part of the roof of the mouth). Thus, the segments called [dental], [alveolar], and [palatal] in the traditional articulatory phonetic description of English are considered [+ coronal] in systematic phonetics. On the other hand, the segments that are [labial] or [velar] in Figure 8.3 are articulated at the periphery of the vocal tract. In the production of labials, the tongue is not involved at all (and hence is not raised). For velars, the body of the tongue, but not the blade, is raised, and the raising occurs in the vicinity of the velum, not the dental-alveolar-front palatal region. Therefore, the English consonant segments [p, b, m, f, v, k, g, ŋ] are [− coronal]. Observe that the feature [coronal] characterizes two locations of the vocal tract: center [+ coronal] and the periphery [− coronal]; sounds are [− coronal] if they are articulated at the very front or the very back of the oral cavity.

The vowel segments of English all share the feature [− coronal]: for [i, ɪ, u, ʊ], the body of the tongue is raised, but the blade remains in prespeech position; for [e, ɛ, ə, o,

Figure 8.5 _____

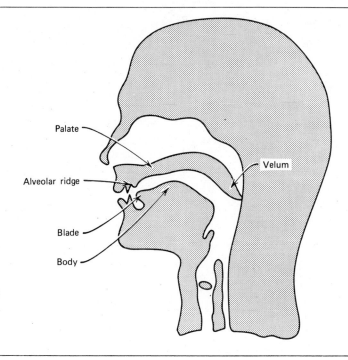

[ɔ], the blade also remains in prespeech position; and for [æ, a] the blade is lowered, not raised. But it should be remembered that the features of systematic phonetics are not designed just to describe the sound segments of English. As was pointed out earlier, the phonetic features should be a universal set that accounts for all of the possible independent activities people can control in their vocal tracts. Since it is possible to raise the blade of the tongue while placing the vocal cords in vibrating position and permitting air to pass freely through the oral cavity, [+ coronal] vowel segments may actually occur in some languages. In fact, they do in some dialects of English. Compare the vowels that you produce in the words *bud* and *bird* and see if, in your speech, the vowel of *bird* is articulated with the blade of the tongue in a higher position than for the vowel of *bud*.

The two features [anterior] and [coronal] divide the vocal tract into four parts, each of which corresponds to an area described by a single feature in the traditional labels for the positions of articulation of consonants. This is summarized in Figure 8.6.

The feature [coronal] refers to the blade of the tongue; three other features involve movements of the body of the tongue. In the articulation of both consonants and vowels, we may keep the body of the tongue in prespeech position, raise it, lower it, or pull it back from prespeech position. The options human beings have regarding the position of the

PHONETIC FEATURES

Figure 8.6 ————————————————————————————————————

Traditional Label	Phonetic Features	Sound Segments
Labial	$\begin{bmatrix} + \text{ anterior} \\ - \text{ coronal} \end{bmatrix}$	[p, b, m, f, v]
Dental and alveolar	$\begin{bmatrix} + \text{ anterior} \\ + \text{ coronal} \end{bmatrix}$	[θ, ð, t, d, n, s, z, l, r]
Palatal	$\begin{bmatrix} - \text{ anterior} \\ + \text{ coronal} \end{bmatrix}$	[š, ž, č, ǰ]
Velar	$\begin{bmatrix} - \text{ anterior} \\ - \text{ coronal} \end{bmatrix}$	[k, g, ŋ]

Figure 8.7 ————————————————————————————————————

Movement of Body of Tongue	Sound Segments of English	Systematic Phonetic Feature Description
Raised above prespeech position	[i, ɪ, u, ʊ, y, w, š, ž, č, ǰ, k, g, ŋ]	[+ high]
Not raised above prespeech position	[e, ɛ, æ, ə, o, ɔ, a, h, p, b, m, f, v, θ, ð, t, d, n, s, z, l, r]	[− high]
Lowered from prespeech position	[æ, a, h]	[+ low]
Not lowered from prespeech position	[i, ɪ, e, ɛ, ə, u, ʊ, o, ɔ, y, w, p, b, m, f, v, θ, ð, t, d, n, s, z, š, ž, č, ǰ, k, g, ŋ, l, r]	[− low]
Pulled back from prespeech position	[ə, u, ʊ, o, ɔ, a, w, k, g, ŋ]	[+ back]
Not pulled back from prespeech position	[i, ɪ, e, ɛ, æ, y, h, p, b, m, f, v, θ, ð, t, d, n, s, z, š, ž, č, ǰ, l, r]	[− back]

body of the tongue are represented by the phonetic features [**high**], [**low**], and [**back**]. The sound segments of English are described in terms of these features in Figure 8.7.

Notice that a sound segment may have the features [− high, −low, − back], as do the English vowels [e] and [ɛ]; in such a case, the body of the tongue has remained in prespeech position. For a segment to be [−high, − low, − back], it is only necessary that the body of the tongue not move; the blade of the tongue may be raised without affecting the body. This, of course, is what happens when you feel the blade move in the production of segments like [θ, ð, t, d, n, s, z]. In any language, there cannot be a [+ high, + low] sound because it is physically impossible to simultaneously raise and lower the body of the tongue.

The five features of articulation position in systematic phonetics are: [anterior], [coronal], [high], [low], and [back]. In English, [anterior] and [coronal] are most important for the description of consonants, while [high], [low], and [back] play a major role in characterizing vowels. Since all vowels are [− anterior] in every language (because a vowel never involves an obstruction to the air stream) and since English vowels are also almost always [− coronal], these two features are usually omitted in descriptions of English vowels. Similarly, the features [high], [low], and [back] generally are omitted from descriptions of English [+ consonantal] sounds (consonants and liquids). [− anterior] consonants in English ([š, ž,č, ǰ, k, g, ŋ]) are predictably, or automatically, [+ high], while the [+ anterior] consonants are [− high]. All of the consonants of English are [− low], and only the consonants [k, g, ŋ] are [+ back] (all other consonants are [− back]). In effect, then, [coronal] and [anterior] are used primarily to describe the position of articulation for consonants, and [high], [low], and [back] are the primary descriptive features for vowel articulation. With the exception of [anterior], however, each of these features is available for use in characterizing both consonants and vowels in other languages. Figure 8.8 provides a summary of the five features of articulation position as they are used for English.

OTHER PHONETIC FEATURES

At this point, the sound segments of English have been described in terms of thirteen phonetic features: [vocalic], [consonantal], [continuant], [nasal], [abrupt release], [strident], [lateral], [anterior], [coronal], [high], [low], [back], and [voice]. In addition to these thirteen, there are at least fifteen other independently controllable activities of the vocal tract represented in the universal set of phonetic features. A complete and explicit account of the sound segments of English would include all of these features for every sound segment. Some of the additional features, however, describe vocal tract activities that do not occur in English. For such features, the sound segments of English would all be marked [−] ("minus"). For example, the feature [**covered**] has been suggested to account for vowel sounds found in some West African languages, where the articulation of these vowels apparently includes a tightening of the walls of the throat. This vocal tract activity never occurs in English, so all English sound segments are [− covered]. We will discuss here only three additional features that are [+] ("plus") for some sound segments

Figure 8.8

PHONETIC FEATURES	SOUND SEGMENTS

Consonants and Liquids

PHONETIC FEATURES	SOUND SEGMENTS
$\begin{bmatrix} + \text{ anterior} \\ - \text{ coronal} \end{bmatrix}$	[p, b, m, f, v]
$\begin{bmatrix} + \text{ anterior} \\ + \text{ coronal} \end{bmatrix}$	[θ, ð, t, d, n, s, z, l, r]
$\begin{bmatrix} - \text{ anterior} \\ + \text{ coronal} \end{bmatrix}$	[š, ž, č, ǰ]
$\begin{bmatrix} - \text{ anterior} \\ - \text{ coronal} \end{bmatrix}$	[k, g, ŋ]

Vowels and Glides

PHONETIC FEATURES	SOUND SEGMENTS
$\begin{bmatrix} + \text{ high} \\ - \text{ low} \\ - \text{ back} \end{bmatrix}$	[i, ɪ, y]
$\begin{bmatrix} - \text{ high} \\ - \text{ low} \\ - \text{ back} \end{bmatrix}$	[e, ɛ]
$\begin{bmatrix} - \text{ high} \\ + \text{ low} \\ - \text{ back} \end{bmatrix}$	[æ, h]
$\begin{bmatrix} + \text{ high} \\ - \text{ low} \\ + \text{ back} \end{bmatrix}$	[u, ʊ, w]
$\begin{bmatrix} - \text{ high} \\ - \text{ low} \\ + \text{ back} \end{bmatrix}$	[ə, o, ɔ]
$\begin{bmatrix} - \text{ high} \\ + \text{ low} \\ + \text{ back} \end{bmatrix}$	[a]

of English. Readers who wish to investigate other possible vocal tract activities may consult "Further Exploration" at the end of this chapter.

In the earlier section on the feature [voice], it was implied that pairs of words such as *pat/bat, to/do, call/gall, few/view,* and *sue/zoo* are phonetically the same except for the fact that the initial sound of the first word in each pair is [− voice], while the initial sound of the second word in each pair is [+ voice]. While the statements regarding [voice] are true, it is a substantial simplification to say that these pairs of words are otherwise the same phonetically. Some people are more aware than others of the phonetic features combined in the articulation of sounds and, in examining their speech production for the feature [voice], may have noticed other features in addition to the vibrating vocal cords. For example, in the production of the [−voice] consonants of English, the muscles in the vocal tract are usually more tense than for the [+voice] consonants. This can be accounted for by the feature [**tense**]. In English, consonants that are [− voice] are [+ tense], while [+ voice] consonants are [− tense]. Nevertheless, the act of tensing the muscles of the vocal tract is independent from the vibrations of the vocal cords. This is demonstrated by the existence of [− voice, − tense] consonants in some languages, such as Korean, and [+ voice, + tense] consonants in other languages, such as Bengali. In all languages [+ tense] sound segments, in addition to involving greater muscular effort, are also slightly longer in duration than [− tense] sound segments. These facts can be observed in the articulation of the pairs of English words given above.

Further careful observation of the vocal tract during the production of the [− voice, − continuant] segments [p, t, k, č] will reveal that, when these sounds occur at the beginning of an English word, there is a buildup of air pressure in the vocal tract, prior to the actual release of the air stream at the position of articulation. When the sounds are produced, this increased pressure results in **aspiration**, a slight puff of breath accompanying the sound. By holding your fingers directly in front of your lips, you will probably be able to feel the aspiration of the first sound in each of the words *pie, toe, kill,* and *chore;* at the beginning of a word, [p, t, k, č] have the feature [+ aspiration]. When these sound segments occur at the end of a word they are sometimes aspirated, sometimes not. Furthermore, when they occur after [s], they are always [− aspiration]. This absence of aspiration can be detected by comparing the pronunciation of pairs of words like *pie/spy, toe/stow,* and *kill/skill.* Notice that there is never any puff of breath accompanying the articulation of the English segments which share the features [+ voice, − continuant], as in the first segment of the words *buy, dough, gill,* and *George.* Such segments are always [− aspiration] in English, as are all segments for which the air stream is not fully blocked. Thus, fricatives, nasals, liquids, glides, and vowels are also [− aspiration].

A complete phonetic description of English must include a discussion of aspiration, in spite of the fact that native speakers rarely notice this phonetic feature unless it is called to their attention. Furthermore, the presence or absence of aspiration can always be predicted in English according to other features of the sound segment or the position of the segment in a word. The predictability of some phonetic features is discussed in Chapter 9.

The feature [tense] plays a more significant role for English vowels than it does for consonants. All vowels in English are [+ voice], but not necessarily [− tense]. In fact, [tense] serves as the chief distinguishing feature for the classes of vowels in Figure 8.8.

Figure 8.9

Vowel Class	[+ *tense*]	[− *tense*]
$\begin{bmatrix} +\text{ high} \\ -\text{ low} \\ -\text{ back} \end{bmatrix}$	[i]	[ɪ]
$\begin{bmatrix} -\text{ high} \\ -\text{ low} \\ -\text{ back} \end{bmatrix}$	[e]	[ɛ]
$\begin{bmatrix} +\text{ high} \\ -\text{ low} \\ +\text{ back} \end{bmatrix}$	[u]	[ʊ]
$\begin{bmatrix} -\text{ high} \\ -\text{ low} \\ +\text{ back} \end{bmatrix}$	[o]	[ɔ, ə]

This distinction is illustrated by Figure 8.9. As with the consonants, a [+ tense] vowel differs from its [− tense] counterpart by involving greater muscular effort and being longer in duration. Furthermore, the [+ tense] vowel usually has a position of articulation slightly higher than the vowel that is identical except for being [− tense]. You can observe these differences by producing a pair of words like *beat/bit* [bit]/[bɪt]. It is clear that the feature [tense] is an independently controllable factor in the production of vowels since the articulatory gesture accompanied by tenseness produces the sound segment [i], while the same gesture without tenseness results in [ɪ].

Another phonetic feature, of particular relevance to vowels in English, may be less obviously independent. **Lip rounding,** also described as lip protrusion, is always present in the English sound segments [u, ʊ, o, ɔ]. These segments are thus [+ round], while all other English vowel segments are [− round]. Notice that the vowels [ə] and [ɔ] are distinguished from one another by the feature [round]; [ə] is [− round] and [ɔ] is [+ round]; [ə] and [ɔ] are the same for all other features. Similar to aspiration, rounding is almost always predictable in English: the [− back] vowels, as well as all of the consonants, are [− round]; the [+ high, + back] vowels are [+ round]; and the [− high, − low, + back, + tense] vowel is [+ round]. The only combination of features for which rounding is not predictable is [− high, − low, + back, − tense]. Although lip rounding is generally predictable in English and, therefore, is normally not noticed by speakers of the language, it is a movement separate from all other features of which a sound is composed. Many languages, including French and German, have vowels which are [− back, + round]. This could not occur if lip rounding were not an articulatory gesture independent from the gesture described by the feature [back].

DIPHTHONGS

Throughout this chapter we have discussed eleven English vowel segments. What about the vowels in the words *bite* and *bout?* For most speakers of English, these words would be represented as [bayt] and [bawt], that is, a sequence of the vowel [a] followed by the glide [y] or [w]. In producing these words, the tongue starts out in the [+low, + back] position of [a] and rapidly moves up to a [+ high] position that is [+ back] for [bawt], [− back] for [bayt]. Vowel sounds in which the tongue starts in one position and rapidly moves to another are called **diphthongs**. A third diphthong in English occurs in words like *boy, toy, annoy, Roy,* and *ploy;* this diphthong is represented as [ɔy]. In addition, the vowels represented here as [i], [e], [u], and [o] are often diphthongs in English. [i] and [e] can be followed immediately by a [y] glide, [u] and [o] by a [w] glide. Diphthongs, as the existence of this special term indicates, are actually halfway between a single sound segment and a sequence of two sound segments.

SYLLABLES AND SUPRASEGMENTALS

The sound segments discussed above, and the various phonetic features of which they are composed, are the basic units of the sound system of a language, but they are not the only units of sound that play a role in speech. Sound segments combine in various patterns to produce syllables, words, phrases, and sentences. The **syllable**, like the sound segment, is a unit of the phonological system, with an arbitrary relationship to meaning and no meaning of its own (unlike the morpheme, which is a unit of meaning represented by sound). Syllables are real, not merely descriptive devices. Speakers of a language can determine the number of syllables in a word, and, in fact, children usually are able to identify syllables before they can identify individual sound segments. Even adults, and especially native speakers of languages such as Japanese and Chinese, frequently report that, for them, syllable identification is easier than segment identification. (This last fact may be due, at least in part, to the nature of the Japanese and Chinese writing systems, discussed in Chapter 11.)

Despite the abilities of speakers to identify syllables, no adequate, formal definition of the syllable is available (recall the similar problem in defining the concept "word" discussed in Chapter 3). One frequently cited definition characterizes the syllable as a sequence of sounds produced with the air from a single **chest pulse** (the muscle contraction in the chest that sends a burst of air from the lungs up through the vocal tract). Records from physical phonetics, however, show that this definition is not always accurate; for example, a one-syllable word such as *blocks* generally involves more than one chest pulse. Furthermore, if each syllable corresponded to a chest pulse, we would expect a clear separation point between the syllables of an utterance, yet in many cases it is difficult to determine the point at which one syllable ends and the next begins. Consider the word *reality;* speakers of English would agree that this word contains four syllables, but where are the dividing points? We could analyze the word as [ri-æl-ə-ti] or as [ri-æ-lə-ti], or maybe even in some other manner (here the hyphens are used to indicate the possible dividing points between syllables). Notice that the conventions of our writing system for syllabification are not always based on phonological units, but instead are sometimes dependent on the morpheme structure of words. In writing, if we needed to divide *reality* into two parts, we would use the division *real-ity,* since we know that the morpheme *real* is part of this word. (*Real,* of course, is a one-syllable word.)

In addition to phonetic features that describe the articulation of individual sounds, there are features characterizing properties of syllables. Such features describing properties of units longer than a single sound segment often are referred to as **suprasegmental features.** The two suprasegmental features pertaining to syllables are [stress] and [tone].

The feature [**stress**] describes the prominence of a syllable. Stressed syllables are sometimes referred to as accented syllables, and usually the prominence is achieved through a relative increase in loudness. However, a syllable that is stressed may also be somewhat longer in duration than an unstressed syllable and be produced at a higher than normal pitch.

Stress is an important phonetic feature of English, for differences in stress may result in different meanings. Compare the prominence of the initial and final syllables of the English nouns *pérmit* and *tránsfer* with the verbs *permít* and *transfér* (the acute accent mark ´ indicates strong stress). The location of stress is important in many languages, including Spanish; compare *háblo* 'I speak' and *habló* 'he spoke'. In some languages, however, although different syllables may be subject to different degrees, or amounts, of stress, there exist no pairs of words differing solely by stress placement. In languages such as Czech, for example, all words have stress on the initial syllable. In cases like this, we say that the location of stress is predictable.

The suprasegmental feature [**tone**] describes the relative pitch at which a syllable is produced. In English, the pitch of a particular syllable is generally unimportant (although a sequence of pitch changes over a phrase or sentence is significant, as discussed below). However, in some languages, such as the African language Hausa, a change in the pitch of a syllable can produce a change in meaning (just as in English the change from [− nasal] to [+ nasal] produces a meaning change from *bean* to *mean*). For example, the Hausa word *jíbí* means 'day after tomorrow' while *jíbì* means 'a meal' (here, the acute accent mark ´ indicates a high pitch while the grave accent mark ` indicates a low pitch). Since the use of tone is significant in reflecting differences in meaning and since the tone remains level throughout a syllable, a language such as Hausa is called a **level** (or **register**) **tone language**. A somewhat different use of tone occurs in Mandarin Chinese. Here we can find four words having identical sound segments but different tones. There is the possibility of a high level pitch, but in addition, the pitch can change during the production of the syllable.

shi	high level tone	(no mark)	'line'
shí	rising tone	´	'stone'
shì	falling tone	`	'to be'
shǐ	falling-rising tone	ˇ	'ambassador'

Languages such as Chinese, where pitch changes can occur during a syllable, are referred to as **contour tone languages**.

When a pattern of pitch changes occurs during a phrase or sentence, we have the phenomenon of **intonation**. In English, as in most languages, different intonations reflect different meanings. Frequently, statements end with a fall in pitch, as in *You are leaving,* while questions end with a rise in pitch, *Are you leaving?* In these examples, the differences in intonation are accompanied by differences in the order of words, but the same distinction in meaning can be obtained solely through intonation: *You are leaving* (statement, with falling intonation) as opposed to *You are leaving?* (question, perhaps indicating astonishment, with rising intonation).

Another suprasegmental feature, **[length]**, refers to the duration, or quantity, of a sound. Notice that unlike [stress] and [tone], which refer to entire syllables, [length] describes the duration of a particular sound segment. In English, a vowel is longer when it occurs before a [+ voice] sound (as in [bi:d] *bead*) than when it occurs before a [− voice] sound (as in [bit] *beat*). The colon is one transcription device used to represent lengthened sounds; it is also possible to double the symbol for the sound segment, so that the transcription [biid] is equivalent to [bi:d]. Length differences do not result in meaning differences in English. In other languages, however, the feature [length] plays an important role. The primary difference between the German words *satt* 'satiated' and *Saat* 'seed' is the length of the vowel: *satt* is [zat] while *Saat* is [za:t]. In Italian, consonants may differ in length; *nonno* 'grandfather' is [non:ɔ] while *nono* 'ninth' is [nonɔ].

SUMMARY

Figure 8.10 is a matrix summarizing the features of systematic phonetics as they apply to a description of the sound segments of English. Note that [p, t, k, č] have been identified in Figure 8.10 as [− aspiration] although these segments are sometimes [+ aspiration]. We return to this point in Chapter 9. In addition to the features listed in the figure, languages also make use of intonation and the suprasegmental features [stress], [tone], and [length].

FURTHER EXPLORATION

For discussion of the features of traditional articulatory phonetics, the references cited at the end of the last chapter are useful (Ladefoged and Sloat, Taylor and Hoard). The features used here for systematic phonetics are based on those presented by Noam Chomsky and Morris Halle in Chapter 7, "The Phonetic Framework," of *The Sound Pattern of English,* a detailed, technical discussion of some difficulty for readers who are new to this subject. More introductory accounts are offered by Sanford A. Schane in *Generative Phonology,* Chapters 2 and 3, and, from a historical perspective that outlines the development of different sets of features, by Larry M. Hyman in Chapter 2 of *Phonology: Theory and Analysis.* Syllables and suprasegmentals are discussed clearly and with examples from several languages in *Introduction to Phonology* by Sloat, Taylor and Hoard.

1. In traditional articulatory phonetics, the descriptions of sounds are organized according to certain conventions (or common practices). Consonants are usually charac-

Figure 8.10

Segments / Features	p	b	t	d	k	g	m	n	ŋ	f	v	θ	ð	s	z	š	ž
Vocalic	−	−	−	−	−	−	−	−	−	−	−	−	−	−	−	−	−
Consonantal	+	+	+	+	+	+	+	+	+	+	+	+	+	+	+	+	+
Continuant	−	−	−	−	−	−	−	−	−	+	+	+	+	+	+	+	+
Nasal	−	−	−	−	−	−	+	+	+	−	−	−	−	−	−	−	−
Abrupt release	+	+	+	+	+	+	+	+	+	−	−	−	−	−	−	−	−
Lateral	−	−	−	−	−	−	−	−	−	−	−	−	−	−	−	−	−
Voice	−	+	−	+	−	+	+	+	+	−	+	−	+	−	+	−	+
Tense	+	−	+	−	+	−	−	−	−	+	−	+	−	+	−	+	−
Aspiration	−	−	−	−	−	−	−	−	−	−	−	−	−	−	−	−	−
Strident	−	−	−	−	−	−	−	−	−	+	+	−	−	+	+	+	+
Anterior	+	+	+	+	−	−	+	+	−	+	+	+	+	+	+	−	−
Coronal	−	−	+	+	−	−	−	+	−	−	−	+	+	+	+	+	+
High	−	−	−	−	+	+	−	−	+	−	−	−	−	−	−	+	+
Low	−	−	−	−	−	−	−	−	−	−	−	−	−	−	−	−	−
Back	−	−	−	−	+	+	−	−	+	−	−	−	−	−	−	−	−
Round	−	−	−	−	−	−	−	−	−	−	−	−	−	−	−	−	−

terized by listing the relevant features in the following order: (1) voicing (voiced, voiceless), (2) position of articulation (labial, dental, alveolar, palatal, velar), (3) degree of obstruction to the air stream (stop, fricative, affricate) or action of the velum (nasal). Thus, [p] is described as a voiceless labial stop, while [z] is a voiced alveolar fricative and [ŋ] is a voiced velar nasal. Vowels are described by citing (1) tenseness [tense, nontense (also referred to as lax)], (2) the tongue height (high, mid, low), (3) the tongue position (front, central, back), (4) rounding (rounded, unrounded), and (5) the fact that the sound

č	ǰ	l	r	h	w	y	i	ɪ	e	ɛ	æ	ə	u	ʊ	o	ɔ	a	Segments / Features
−	−	+	+	−	−	−	+	+	+	+	+	+	+	+	+	+	+	Vocalic
+	+	+	+	−	−	−	−	−	−	−	−	−	−	−	−	−	−	Consonantal
−	−	+	+	+	+	+	+	+	+	+	+	+	+	+	+	+	+	Continuant
−	−	−	−	−	−	−	−	−	−	−	−	−	−	−	−	−	−	Nasal
−	−	−	−	−	−	−	−	−	−	−	−	−	−	−	−	−	−	Abrupt release
−	−	+	−	−	−	−	−	−	−	−	−	−	−	−	−	−	−	Lateral
−	+	+	+	−	+	+	+	+	+	+	+	+	+	+	+	+	+	Voice
+	−	−	−	+	−	−	+	−	+	−	−	−	+	−	+	−	+	Tense
−	−	−	−	−	−	−	−	−	−	−	−	−	−	−	−	−	−	Aspiration
+	+	−	−	−	−	−	−	−	−	−	−	−	−	−	−	−	−	Strident
−	−	+	+	−	−	−	−	−	−	−	−	−	−	−	−	−	−	Anterior
+	+	+	+	−	−	−	−	−	−	−	−	−	−	−	−	−	−	Coronal
+	+	−	−	−	+	+	+	+	−	−	−	−	+	+	−	−	−	High
−	−	−	−	+	−	−	−	−	−	−	+	−	−	−	−	−	+	Low
−	−	−	−	−	+	−	−	−	−	−	−	+	+	+	+	+	+	Back
−	−	−	−	−	+	−	−	−	−	−	−	−	+	+	+	+	−	Round

is a vowel. Therefore, [i] is a tense high front unrounded vowel, whereas [ə] is a lax (or nontense) mid central unrounded vowel. Other features can be added to these descriptions when additional detail is required.

(a) Identify the sounds characterized by the following traditional articulatory descriptions. Write the appropriate phonetic alphabet symbol. (Consult Figures 8.3 and 8.4; features listed below that do not appear in these figures or in the text discussion are the same as those in the systematic feature matrix of Figure 8.10.)

(1) voiceless palatal affricate
(2) voiced alveolar nasal
(3) voiced dental fricative
(4) voiceless velar stop
(5) voiced labial stop
(6) voiceless alveolar fricative
(7) voiced palatal affricate
(8) voiceless alveolar stop
(9) lax mid front unrounded vowel
(10) tense high back rounded vowel
(11) lax high front unrounded vowel
(12) tense mid back rounded vowel

(b) Write traditional articulatory descriptions for the following sound segments.

(1)	[m]	(5)	[g]	(9)	[ɪ]
(2)	[š]	(6)	[d]	(10)	[ɔ]
(3)	[v]	(7)	[ž]	(11)	[e]
(4)	[θ]	(8)	[f]	(12)	[ʊ]

2. Write the phonetic symbol, or symbols, representing the English sound, or class of sounds, characterized by each set of features from systematic phonetics. Check your responses by consulting the matrix in Figure 8.10. (Note that not all sixteen features are necessary to uniquely identify a sound.)

(a) [+ vocalic, + consonantal, − lateral]   r̩
(b) [− vocalic, − consonantal, − voice]
(c) [+ abrupt release, + anterior, + coronal]
(d) [+ strident, + coronal]
(e) [− consonantal, + high]
(f) [+ vocalic, + low]
(g) [+ vocalic, + tense, − high, − low]
(h) [+ nasal, + coronal]
(i) [+ round]
(j) [− nasal, + abrupt release]
(k) [+ nasal, − coronal]
(l) [+ anterior, − coronal]
(m) [− vocalic, + consonantal, + continuant]
(n) [+ vocalic, + back]

distinctive

3. List the feature, or features, from systematic phonetics that the following classes of sounds have in common. (For example, the class of sounds [h, w, y] is [− vocalic, − consonantal, + continuant, − nasal, − abrupt release, − lateral, − aspiration, − strident, − anterior, − coronal].)

(a) [l, r]
(b) [č, ǰ]
(c) [m, n, ŋ]
(d) [b, d, g]
(e) [b, g]
(f) [ɪ, ɛ, ʊ, ɔ́]
(g) [i, e, u, o]
(h) [y, i, ɪ]
(i) [š, ž]
(j) [t, d, s, z, n]

4. Determine the number of syllables in each of the following words as you pronounce them in normal, casual speech. (Pay attention to speech; do not use information about syllable division for writing.) Circle the syllable that has the most prominent stress.

(a) question
(b) dangerous
(c) artificial
(d) sophomore
(e) scorched
(f) examined
(g) presented
(h) books
(i) houses
(j) knives
(k) confide
(l) confidence

5. Refer to the words in (4) above. Provide a broad transcription for items (e), (f), and (g). What do you observe about the pronunciation of the past tense morpheme? Provide a broad transcription for (h), (i), and (j). What do you observe about the pronunciation of the plural morpheme? Notice the different position of the strong stress in (k) and (l). What is the second vowel when it has strong stress? When it does not? Cite two other pairs of words that exhibit similar shifts in stress and vowel changes.

CHAPTER 99999999999999999999999999

PHONEMICS

A systematic phonetic description of sounds covers only a part of the knowledge native speakers have regarding the sound system of their language. Phonetics studies the most concrete, directly observable aspect of language—sounds. But the sounds of a language are organized into a system. The study of this system is known as **phonemics,** and it includes the investigation of the relations among sounds and the rules according to which morphemes are pronounced. Speakers know not only the sounds of their language but also the sound system, and much of this knowledge is described by linguists in the form of generalizations in a grammar. **Phonology** is the study of all aspects of the sounds and sound system of a language, and it includes both phonetics, the topic of the last chapter, and phonemics, which is discussed in this chapter.

Two aspects of phonemics will be treated here. The first concerns the fact that not all phonetic features are of equal importance in a particular language. Some features are **distinctive**; they serve to distinguish one word or morpheme from another. For example, the distinctive difference in sound between the words *bean* and *mean* is that the former begins with a [− nasal] sound while the latter word begins with a [+ nasal] sound. The feature [nasal] is a distinctive feature in English. Two words that are otherwise phonetically identical (share all other phonetic features in common) are differentiated from one another by this feature. Pairs of words such as *bean* and *mean,* distinguished by a single phonetic feature, are called **minimal pairs.** One task of a phonemic study is to determine the set of distinctive features of a language, and this is frequently accomplished by establishing lists of minimal pairs.

Not all phonetic features result in minimal pairs in a particular language. This is because some features are **predictable,** or **redundant**; they occur only when certain other features occur or only in certain environments (in a sequence of sounds). For example, in English, the feature [voice] is predictable (and therefore not distinctive) for vowels. Every English vowel is always [+voice]. In other words, once we know that a sound segment has the features [+vocalic, − consonantal], we can predict that it will be [+ voice] in English. There are no minimal pairs in our language that are phonetically identical except that one has a [+ voice] vowel and the other a [− voice] vowel. Similarly, [aspiration] is predictable in English. All English sound segments that are either [+ voice] or [+ continuant] are always [− aspiration]. We find [+ aspiration] only for sounds that are [− continuant, − voice] (i.e., only for [p, t, k, č]). These four sounds are not always [+ aspiration], however. The aspiration is predictable in a specific environment: when the [− continuant, − voice] sound occurs at the beginning of a word, it will be [+ aspiration]; when such a sound occurs in other positions in a word, it is [− aspiration]. Since the occurrence of [+ aspiration] is limited in this way, there are no minimal pairs in English where one word contains a [+ aspiration] sound and the other a [− aspiration] sound.

The determination of the distinctive phonetic features of a language, along with the set of statements that describe the occurrence of nondistinctive, or redundant, features, is a central goal of phonemics in both traditional structural linguistics and in modern transformational linguistics. A second goal of phonemics, however, was traditionally considered to belong to a different area of linguistics. This second concern involves the fact that morphemes are not always pronounced in the same way. Phonetically, for example, the plural morpheme is sometimes pronounced [s], sometimes [z], and sometimes [əz]. Yet, a morpheme is a single unit of meaning, and, as you may recall from the discussion in Chapter 4, each morpheme is considered to have a single lexical entry. In addition to providing an account of distinctive and redundant features, therefore, it is necessary in phonemics to determine the single set of phonetic features to use in representing a morpheme in the lexicon. The part of phonemics that deals with providing a single lexical entry for each morpheme was known traditionally as **morphophonemics**—a combination of traditional morphology (the study of morphemes) and phonemics.

DISTINCTIVE AND REDUNDANT FEATURES

Consider the words *pea, tea,* and *key.* A full phonetic description of these words would involve a statement about each phonetic feature, as illustrated in Figure 9.1. This phonetic representation is highly specific, but, while it does describe the sound segments of these particular words, it fails to show explicitly that there are certain regularities for the features of the sound segments. Certain features are distinctive, while others are redundant, but the phonetic feature matrix of Figure 9.1 does not reveal this. To demonstrate this point, we can ask the following question: When a speaker of English learns the word

Figure 9.1

Phonetic Features	Sound Segments					
	[p	i]	[t	i]	[k	i]
Vocalic	−	+	−	+	−	+
Consonantal	+	−	+	−	+	−
Continuant	−	+	−	+	−	+
Nasal	−	−	−	−	−	−
Abrupt release	+	−	+	−	+	−
Lateral	−	−	−	−	−	−
Voice	−	+	−	+	−	+
Tense	+	+	+	+	+	+
Aspiration	+	−	+	−	+	−
Strident	−	−	−	−	−	−
Anterior	+	−	+	−	−	−
Coronal	−	−	+	−	−	−
High	−	+	−	+	+	+
Low	−	−	−	−	−	−
Back	−	−	−	−	+	−
Round	−	−	−	−	−	−

pea, is it necessary for the speaker to memorize every one of the sixteen features for [p] and every one of them for [i]? To learn a word is, in effect, to enter it in the lexicon in such a way that the new lexical entry contains enough information so that it is distinct from other entries and can eventually be pronounced. In this particular case, then, what we are asking is whether there is a simpler way of storing information about the pronunciation of *pea*—simpler than storing sixteen features for each sound segment of the word.

Can a speaker limit the number of features that must be memorized and provide other features by means of generalizations, similar to the way in which he or she apparently learns new morphemes and rules of word formation? If it is possible to formulate general rules about the sound system of English, rules predicting the occurrence of particular features, then it might not be necessary to include those features in the lexical entry of morphemes. A lexical entry could consist of the distinctive features only; other features could be omitted from the entry and supplied by statements that predict redundant information. Figures 8.10 and 9.1 provide some basic data that can be analyzed to determine some of the distinctive and the redundant features of English.

In the lexical entry for the word *pea,* the first sound segment must be identified as [p] and not some other segment in the language, such as [t], [m], or [s]; that is, the word *pea* must be distinguished from phonologically similar words like *tea, me,* and *see.* It is necessary, therefore, that the first segment of *pea* be entered in the lexicon with this phonological information:

$$\begin{bmatrix} - \text{ vocalic} \\ + \text{ consonantal} \\ + \text{ abrupt release} \\ - \text{ voice} \\ + \text{ anterior} \\ - \text{ coronal} \end{bmatrix}$$

These six features distinguish [p] from every other segment in English; they are distinctive. No other segment in Figure 8.10 is composed of this combination of features. For example, if you know that the first segment of *pea* is [− vocalic, + consonantal], you know it is not a vowel, liquid, or glide; if you know it is [+ abrupt release], then it cannot be a fricative or an affricate either; [− voice] shows that the segment is neither a nasal nor a voiced stop; [+ anterior] means that it is not [k]; and [− coronal] eliminates [t] as the segment. In other words, just six distinctive features are required to identify the segment in question as [p].

The remaining ten features listed in the phonetic representation of [p] in Figures 9.1 and 8.10 are all predictable. In all human languages, [+ abrupt release] segments always are [− continuant, − strident]. This is a universal fact about human language, and no speaker of any language needs to store these two features for any [+ abrupt release] segment. In English, although not universally, sounds that are [− vocalic, + consonantal] are also [− low, − round, − lateral]. In addition, in English, all [+ anterior] consonants are [− high] and all [− high] consonants are [− back]. As we observed in the last chapter, given information about the feature [voice] for a consonant in English, we can predict the feature [tense]: a consonant that is [+ voice] will be [− tense], and one that is [− voice] will be [+ tense]. Since English has no voiceless nasals, any [− voice] segment is predictably [− nasal], as well. It is also possible to predict whether an English sound segment is phonetically [+ aspiration] or [− aspiration]: any [+ continuant] segment (liquids, glides, vowels, and fricatives) is [− aspiration], as is any [+ voice] segment, including voiced stops and nasals. A segment that is [− continuant, − voice] in English generally will be [+ aspiration] if it occurs word-initially, and [− aspiration] if it occurs elsewhere, as discussed above.

Thus, by carefully describing all of the sound segments in a language in terms of phonetic features, it is possible to study these complete, detailed descriptions and determine which features are distinctive and which can be predicted from the presence of other features. Such predictions are generalizations about the sound system of a language. Each generalization determined by the linguist eliminates the need for including redundant features in the lexical entries of morphemes. Since the grammar of a language, including the lexicon, is intended to reflect the knowledge of its speakers, we may also say that the speaker, in storing entries in his mental lexicon, eliminates any predictable information about phonetic features. In other words, the lexical entry for *pea* may contain only the six distinctive features mentioned above for the sound segment [p]. All other features of [p] can be predicted.

Speakers of English have at least three kinds of knowledge about the sound system of their language:

1. Detailed information about the actual pronunciation of sounds; this information is reflected in a grammar by means of the full set of phonetic features that provide a phonetic representation of the pronunciation of morphemes, as illustrated in Figure 9.1.

2. A set of generalizations about predictable features; this information is reflected in a grammar by means of a set of statements, or rules, that predict redundant phonetic features from information about other phonetic features occurring in the same sound segment or in segments nearby.

3. For each morpheme in their mental lexicon, speakers possess the knowledge of which features are necessary to distinguish that morpheme from all others; this information can be reflected in a grammar in terms of a **phonemic representation** for each morpheme, a list of those distinctive features not predicted by the generalizations in (2).

Figure 9.1 provides examples of phonetic representations for three English words. The generalizations discussed above enable us to eliminate predictable phonetic information not only for [p] but also for other segments in English, such as [t] and [k]. Other generalizations can be formulated for vowels. Thus, a first approximation to the phonemic representation of the words *pea, tea,* and *key* could be that given in Figure 9.2. Speakers who have stored these words in their lexicon with the features listed in Figure 9.2 have only to apply the generalizations to fill in the predictable information; the result would be a full phonetic representation, as in Figure 9.1.

In a linguistic description of English, each morpheme entered in the lexicon contains a phonemic representation—an abstract description containing only essential, unpredictable information—and, for each morpheme, the grammar also provides a concrete phonetic representation containing all information necessary to describe actual pronunciation. Linking these two types of representation is a set of generalizations that convert phonemic representations to phonetic representations. We return to this matter in greater detail below.

TRADITIONAL PHONEMICS AND SYSTEMATIC PHONEMICS

As the field of linguistics developed in the United States during the first half of this century, structural linguists established working procedures and basic assumptions for the

Figure 9.2

Phonetic Features	Sound Segments					
	[p	i]	[t	i]	[k	i]
Vocalic	−	+	−	+	−	+
Consonantal	+	−	+	−	+	−
Abrupt release	+		+		+	
Voice	−		−		−	
Tense		+		+		+
Anterior	+		+		−	
Coronal	−		+		−	
High		+		+		+
Back		−		−		−

Note: Features not listed and blank spaces for those that are listed indicate that the feature in question is predictable for the sound segment involved.

phonological analysis of a language. Although some of the procedures, assumptions, and terminology of structural linguistics are no longer used by modern transformational linguists, it is necessary that at least the basic outlines of this older approach be presented so that readers will be prepared if they encounter structural terms in the material mentioned in "Further Exploration."

In the traditional, structural approach to the analysis of sounds in languages, it became common practice to utilize the shorthand symbols of the phonetic alphabet rather than list all of the phonetic features of a sound segment. When linguists provided a phonetic representation, they enclosed it in square brackets and added extra symbols to indicate particularly noticeable redundant features. For example, a small raised [h] indicated that a sound was aspirated; absence of the [h] indicated absence of aspiration. The word *pea* would be phonetically represented as [phi]. When a phonemic representation was given, it was enclosed in slant lines, and any extra symbol representing a predictable feature was omitted. Thus, a phonemic representation of the word *pea* would be /pi/.

While traditional structural linguists utilized this convention (and some still do), a number of linguists recognized that the use of abbreviated symbols tended to obscure the differences between the phonetic and phonemic representations, differences that are made explicit if both are represented in terms of features. The traditional representations [phi] and /pi/ imply that [aspiration] is the only predictable phonetic feature in the word *pea,* but the systematic representations with features in Figures 9.1 and 9.2 show quite clearly that this is not true. Today, when writing a formal description of the phonological system of a language, linguists who work with systematic phonetics and systematic phonemics consistently use features to represent sound segments at both the phonetic and phonemic levels. Of course, the abbreviated symbols are convenient to use in an informal presentation of phonological facts, but such abbreviations have no place in any full, explicit account of the competence of speakers of a language. Thus, one difference between traditional phonemics and systematic phonemics is the way in which phonetic and phonemic representations are given.

There are differences other than notational ones. An important consequence of using abbreviation devices is that significant facts are not only obscured, but may even go completely unobserved. Consider the words *sea* and *ski.* In the traditional approach, these would be represented as /si/ and /ski/ phonemically. Since the symbol /s/ appears in both phonemic representations, traditional linguistics implies that the /s/ is phonemically the same in *sea* and *ski.* But in the systematic approach, it is clear that the /s/ is different in these two words at the phonemic level, even though the same phonetic sound does occur. The systematic phonemic representations of the first sound segment in *sea* and *ski* appear in Figure 9.3. Notice that for *sea* the initial segment must be specified for six features in order to distinguish the word from all other similar possible words in English, such as *we, Lee, she, tea,* and *knee.* For *ski,* however, the first sound segment need only be represented by one feature, [− vocalic]. This is due to the fact that in English, whenever a word begins with a sequence of two consonants and the second is [− continuant], as [k] is, the first can only be [s]. There are no English words that begin with consonant clusters like [mp], [bd], or [fč]. In fact, if you encountered a word spelled *mpee, bdee,* or *fchee,* you would immediately recognize it as odd, in some way "un-English," and perhaps

Figure 9.3

Phonetic Features	Sound Segments	
	[s i]	[s k i]
Vocalic	−	−
Consonantal	+	
Voice	−	
Strident	+	
Anterior	+	
Coronal	+	

even feel that it was ''unpronounceable.'' Your reaction would be due to the fact that you know a rule predicting all of the phonetic features of [s], except [− vocalic], when [s] appears at the beginning of a word before a [− continuant] sound segment; in other words, in English, the only [− vocalic] sound that can appear in such an environment is [s]. This rule, or generalization, must appear in any description of English phonology that accounts for the linguistic competence of native speakers. And, given such a rule, the [s] in *ski* is different at the phonemic level from the [s] in *sea,* in precisely the manner illustrated in Figure 9.3. If abbreviation symbols, rather than features, are used, this difference, and the generalization that accounts for it, could be overlooked and, in any case, would not be stated explicitly.

The use of shorthand symbols, rather than features, for phonemic representations, involves the **phoneme** concept of traditional American linguistics. The symbols placed between slant lines in a phonemic representation are viewed as abstract units, each of which represents a group of phonetically similar, concrete sounds. These abstract units are said to be phonemes. In determining the phonemes of a language, the traditional linguist would investigate all of the concrete sounds and assign each sound to a phoneme. No two sounds could be members of the same phoneme if they ever constituted the only phonetic difference between two words. [p^h] and [b] must belong to different phonemes since they distinguish many pairs of English words from one another, such as [p^hæt]/[bæt], [p^hɪl]/[bɪl]. On the other hand, [p^h] and [p] do belong to the same phoneme since they are phonetically similar and never serve to distinguish one word from another; that is, in English, there are no pairs of words such as [pɪl]/[p^hɪl]. Each sound is called an **allophone** of the phoneme to which it is assigned. In a particular environment, there is normally only one allophone of a phoneme. The description of when each allophone occurs in speech is accomplished in traditional phonemics by statements somewhat similar to the generalizations of modern phonemics. A traditional phonemic description of English would include a list of the phonemes of the language (roughly equivalent to those segments for which phonetic alphabet symbols were given in Figure 7.1). Accompanying each phoneme would be a list of its allophones, and for each allophone, a statement of when it occurs. For example:

The phoneme	/p/	
has the	{ [p^h]	occurs word-initially
allophones	{ [p]	occurs elsewhere

The term *phoneme* does not normally occur in systematic phonemics, for it is incompatible with the assumption that a phonemic representation is one from which all predictable information has been eliminated. As we have seen, the traditional phoneme /s/, when represented in systematic phonemics, is sometimes [− vocalic] and sometimes as follows:

$$
\begin{bmatrix}
- \text{ vocalic} \\
+ \text{ consonantal} \\
- \text{ voice} \\
+ \text{ strident} \\
+ \text{ anterior} \\
+ \text{ coronal}
\end{bmatrix}
$$

It may have other representations, as well, depending on the environment in which it occurs.

There are a number of differences between systematic phonemics and traditional phonemics, and the reader who is interested in learning more about this issue, which linguists consider of great theoretical importance, may consult "Further Exploration" at the end of this chapter. We have taken the time to discuss the major differences in order to demonstrate that the use of abbreviated symbols obscures important facts about sound systems. The use of phonetic features for both phonetic and phonemic representations is necessary if such facts are to be described in the complete grammar of a language.

REDUNDANCY RULES

In a full description of a language and its sound system, each morpheme has both an abstract, underlying phonemic representation, containing only those features that cannot be predicted by general rules, and a concrete, surface phonetic representation, containing information about all of the phonetic features controlled by the human vocal tract. The relationship between these two levels of representation is provided by the set of phonological generalizations that convert the phonemic representations into phonetic representations. In a formal linguistic description, such generalizations are stated as rules operating in a consistent and explicit manner to insure that, when the rules apply, they do so correctly, producing precisely the correct phonetic forms. The most adequate format for such rules is currently under investigation, and, therefore, suggestions made here regarding format must be regarded as tentative.

The phonological generalizations we have discussed are often referred to as **redundancy rules,** since they add redundant, or predictable, information about features to the phonemic representation. Redundancy rules can be presented as "if . . . then" statements. For example, we have mentioned that if, at the beginning of an English word, there is a [− continuant, − voice] sound segment, then it will predictably be [+ aspiration]. Using the symbol # to represent the boundary (beginning or end) of a word, this generalization may be expressed as the redundancy rule:

(1) If: # $\begin{bmatrix} - \text{ continuant} \\ - \text{ voice} \end{bmatrix}$ ⚹

  Then: [+ aspiration]

In rule (1), the boundary symbol # indicates that the sound segment in question occurs at the beginning of the word, since # precedes the features of the sound segment. Rule (1) is a generalization: it provides [+ aspiration] for a whole class of sound segments ([p, t, k, č]), not just for some particular segment.

Rules (2) and (3) represent the fact that in English, if a consonant is [+ voice], then it is also [− tense], and if it is [− voice], then it is also [+ tense].

(2) If: $\begin{bmatrix} + \text{ consonantal} \\ + \text{ voice} \end{bmatrix}$

Then: [− tense]

(3) If: $\begin{bmatrix} + \text{ consonantal} \\ − \text{ voice} \end{bmatrix}$

Then: [+ tense]

In fact, the two rules really describe a single phenomenon in the sound system of English: tenseness is predictable given information about voicing. This should be made explicit. The best way to reflect the fact that a single phenomenon is involved is to describe it by a single rule. After all, rules are hypotheses about the speakers' knowledge and the way in which that knowledge is organized. If we use two rules to describe some aspect of the language, we imply that the speaker must have learned two separate pieces of information; if we use one rule, then we are hypothesizing that the speaker knows one general fact.

In order to capture generalizations, such as that involved in the relationship between the features [voice] and [tense] for English consonants, **variables** are used in rules. Variables are Greek letters, such as α, β, and γ, and in a given rule the variable replaces both [+] and [−] for a particular feature. Thus, the specification [α voice] means both [+ voice] and [− voice]. Variables always occur with at least two features in a rule, and they indicate a relationship between the features. As a concrete example, recall that, in English, [+ high] vowels and glides have the same specification for [round] as they do for [back]; [i], [ɪ], and [y] are [− back, − round]; [u], [ʊ], and [w] are [+ back, + round]. Without variables, we would need two rules to state this fact:

(4) If: $\begin{bmatrix} − \text{ consonantal} \\ + \text{ high} \\ − \text{ back} \end{bmatrix}$

Then: [− round]

(5) If: $\begin{bmatrix} − \text{ consonantal} \\ + \text{ high} \\ + \text{ back} \end{bmatrix}$

Then: [+ round]

Using variables, however, we can capture what is very clearly a general relationship between the features [back] and [round]:

(6) If: $\begin{bmatrix} − \text{ consonantal} \\ + \text{ high} \\ \alpha \text{ back} \end{bmatrix}$

Then: [α round]

Rule (6) states that any segment that is [− consonantal, + high] will have the same value for [round] as it has for [back]. Thus, if the segment is [+ back], as are [u], [ʊ], and [w], the rule adds to it the feature [+ round]; if the segment is [− back], as are [i], [ɪ], and [y], [− round] is added.

Variables may also occur as opposites, in that [α] may appear with one phonetic feature in a rule and [$-\alpha$] with another. In such a case, when [α] represents [+], [$-\alpha$] will be the opposite, that is, [$-$]. On the other hand, when [α] represents [$-$], [$-\alpha$] represents [+]. This is precisely what is needed to express the relationship between [tense] and [voice] for English consonants.

(7) If: $\begin{bmatrix} + \text{ consonantal} \\ \alpha \text{ voice} \end{bmatrix}$

   Then: $[-\alpha \text{ tense}]$

Rule (7) generalizes rules (2) and (3); it combines them into a single rule, thereby clearly indicating that a single phenomenon is involved.

Rules (1), (6), and (7) represent only three of a large number of redundancy rules that express general facts about the sound system of English. Many others are necessary in order to convert phonemic representations into phonetic representations. Readers who are interested in the explicit formulation of generalizations in terms of redundancy rules may wish to return to the informal discussion of such generalizations earlier in this chapter and attempt to formalize them as "if . . . then" statements.

Note that some linguists specializing in phonology maintain that a list of redundancy statements, when included as part of the description of a language, is sufficient to account for the differences between distinctive and predictable features. Such linguists would not eliminate predictable information from a phonemic representation; instead, they reserve the term *phonemic representation* to refer to the single set of features used to represent each morpheme in the lexicon, as discussed immediately below.

PHONEMIC REPRESENTATIONS AND MORPHEMES: MORPHOPHONEMICS

The purpose of sounds in a language is to provide a way of expressing meaning. The units of meaning are the morphemes, as we have seen. Each morpheme entered in the lexicon is a combination of properties of meaning, syntax, and pronunciation. Linguists, hypothesizing that speakers of a language store information in the most efficient way possible, assume that the lexicon includes a single phonemic representation for each morpheme. By means of phonological generalizations, the phonemic representation can be converted into a phonetic representation appropriate for actual pronunciation.

In the simplest instances, a morpheme will always occur in the same phonetic form, and the difference between its phonemic and phonetic representations will be primarily one of detail. Only redundancy rules will be needed to convert the phonemic representation of a morpheme to its phonetic representation. This is the case for the morphemes described in Figures 9.1 and 9.2. However, human languages are not always so straightforward, and English is no exception. The morpheme meaning 'cat' is always pronounced [kæt], but the morpheme 'plural' can be [əz], [s], or (most often) [z], as demonstrated in Figure 9.4. There is only one lexical entry for 'plural', with one meaning, and, we assume, one phonemic representation from which the various phonetic forms can be derived by means of general rules. These are aspects of English that must be learned by anyone who will speak the language, and the problem for the linguist is to determine both the generalizations and the phonemic representation of this morpheme.

Any description of English must include an account of when 'plural' is pronounced [z], [əz], or [s]. (These three phonetic forms for 'plural' are, of course, the most frequent and the most productive representations of this morpheme; 'plural' may also occur in other phonetic forms, as in *oxen, children,* or even *deer* where there is no actual sound that indicates the word may be plural. Such less common, and essentially irregular, unproductive phonetic representations of a morpheme cannot be described by means of the general rules described below and, like irregularities in morphology, must simply be listed in a complete description of English.)

All speakers of English have mastered rules that enable them to correctly produce the plural forms of the morphemes in their lexicon and also of any new words they may learn. The occurrence of [z], [əz], and [s] is not random in English; it follows a very general pattern, a fact easily proven by nonsense words, such as [bad], [das], and [lap]. Assuming that these are nouns, what is the plural of each? All speakers of English would agree that the correct answer is [badz], [dasəz], and [laps], which demonstrates that there are rules governing the pronunciation of the morpheme 'plural'. The rules can be determined by examining the data given in Figure 9.4. Note that the plural morpheme is most often pronounced with a [z] sound segment (column I). When the sound segment preceding the plural morpheme is [s, z, š, ž, č, ǰ], the vowel [ə] appears between the [z] of 'plural' and the preceding segment (column II). 'Plural' is pronounced [s] after any other voiceless consonant (column III). Remember that the symbols of the phonetic alphabet used above are only abbreviations for the true descriptions of sounds; in a full and explicit description of English, it is necessary to use the phonetic features of the sound segments.

Let us begin with the assumption that the phonemic representation for 'plural' is simply the set of features [− voice, + strident, + anterior, + coronal], that is, a segment which would become phonetic [s] if only redundancy rules applied.* Given this single, underlying phonemic representation, followed by the set of redundancy rules of English, we could produce the correct phonetic representations of words like those in column III of Figure 9.4. In order to produce the correct phonetic forms for the words in columns I and II, we need some way of predicting when [s] changes to [z], or, more accurately, when [− voice] becomes [+ voice] in the plural morpheme. In addition, for the words in column II we must predict when [ə] will occur.

Such predictions are called **phonological rules.** Unlike redundancy rules, which simply fill in information about predictable features in sound segments, phonological rules may add or delete sound segments or even change the features within a sound segment. Redundancy rules are generalizations about the feature makeup of morphemes in the lexicon. Phonological rules account for the fact that the single phonemic representation of a morpheme may appear in a variety of phonetic representations in actual speech, depend-

---

*In a formal description of English, linguists cannot merely make assumptions about phonemic representations. For each morpheme, they must find evidence supporting the representation selected. ''Further Exploration'' at the end of this chapter includes references on determining valid phonemic representations. Our assumption about 'plural' is designed to illustrate the nature and function of phonologial rules and should not be considered the definitive form underlying this morpheme.

Figure 9.4

Column I		Column II*		Column III	
girls	[gərlz]	glasses	[glæsəz]	lamps	[læmps]
bees	[biz]	phrases	[frezəz]	pots	[pats]
bows	[boz]	wishes	[wɪšəz]	cakes	[keks]
pens	[pɛnz]	garages	[gəražəz]†	safes	[sefs]
stoves	[stovz]	churches	[čərčəz]		
fads	[fædz]	judges	[ǰəǰəz]		
cabs	[kæbz]				
bags	[bægz]				

*In many dialects of American English, 'plural' is pronounced [ɪz], rather than [əz].

†In some dialects of American English, *garage* ends in [ǰ], rather than [ž]; for such dialects there are usually no nouns ending in [ž].

ing on the environment of the morpheme—the surrounding sound segments and the grammatical structure of the sentence in which the morpheme occurs. The form of phonological rules is more complicated than the "if . . . then" format of redundancy rules, since redundancy rules only supply predictable features for a sound segment, while phonological rules carry out a number of different, more involved processes. The form of phonological rules is most easily described by means of concrete examples.

We are assuming that the phonemic representation of the 'plural' morpheme is roughly as follows:

$$\begin{bmatrix} - \text{ voice} \\ + \text{ strident} \\ + \text{ anterior} \\ + \text{ coronal} \end{bmatrix}$$

Redundancy rules, when applied to this phonemic representation, would yield the full phonetic representation of the sound segment [s]. There are, however, two phonological rules that apply to this phonemic representation in certain environments, and these rules yield either [əz] or [z]. 'Plural' is always phonetically [əz] when preceded by one of the sound segments [s, z, š, ž, č, ǰ]. This class of sounds can be identified by the phonetic features [+ strident, + coronal]; all these, and only these, segments of English have these two features. It is now possible to write a phonological rule that adds [ə] to the representation of the plural morpheme (in other words, that predicts the occurrence of [ə]).

$$(8) \quad \emptyset \rightarrow [\text{ə}] \ / \ \begin{bmatrix} + \text{ strident} \\ + \text{ coronal} \end{bmatrix} \underline{\quad\quad} \begin{bmatrix} - \text{ voice} \\ + \text{ strident} \\ + \text{ anterior} \\ + \text{ coronal} \end{bmatrix}$$

The rule states: "Given the sequence of segments

$$
\begin{bmatrix} + \text{ strident} \\ + \text{ coronal} \end{bmatrix}
\begin{bmatrix} - \text{ voice} \\ + \text{ strident} \\ + \text{ anterior} \\ + \text{ coronal} \end{bmatrix}
$$

insert the segment [ə] between these two segments." The symbol Ø in the rule indicates that a sound segment not present in the phonemic representation is being introduced into the phonetic representation; the arrow points to the change made by the rule; the slash separates the change from information about the sound segments that must be present for the rule to apply; and the dash shows the place where the change is to be made. Rule (8) is a simplified version of the rule that would actually appear in an explicit description of English; for example, in a complete description, a set of phonetic features would appear rather than the symbol [ə].

Rule (8) provides the [ə] in words like those in column II of Figure 9.4. We must next account for the fact that the plural morpheme is [z] in column I and that it contains [z] (rather than [s], for example) in column II. This is done by a simple phonological rule that changes the value of [voice] in the plural morpheme from [−] to [+] when the sound segment immediately before it is [+ voice].

$$
(9) \ [- \text{ voice}] \rightarrow [+ \text{ voice}] \ / \ [+ \text{ voice}]
\begin{bmatrix} \underline{\hspace{2cm}} \\ + \text{ strident} \\ + \text{ anterior} \\ + \text{ coronal} \end{bmatrix}
$$

The rule states: "Given a sequence of segments

$$
[+ \text{ voice}]
\begin{bmatrix} - \text{ voice} \\ + \text{ strident} \\ + \text{ anterior} \\ + \text{ coronal} \end{bmatrix}
$$

change the [− voice] of the second segment to [+ voice]." Rule (9) describes a phenomenon known as **assimilation,** in which a feature in one sound segment assimilates to, or becomes the same as, a feature in a nearby sound segment. In the case described by rule (9), the feature [voice] in the plural morpheme assimilates to the feature [voice] in the preceding sound segment. After rule (9) applies, both sound segments in question will have the value [+] for the feature [voice]. Additional examples of assimilation and other common phonological processes are presented in Chapter 10.

Given the underlying phonemic representation of the plural morpheme, the redundancy rules of English, and two phonological rules, (8) and (9), we can now produce three phonetic representations from the phonemic representation of this morpheme. Beginning with the phonemic representation, redundancy rules produce the segment [s] for the plural of all English words, except irregular words like *sheep*. Next, rule (8) inserts [ə] immediately before [s] in those words which end in one of the following segments: [s, z, š, ž, č, ǰ]. Finally, rule (9) changes the feature [voice] in [s], thereby producing [z], whenever the segment preceding [s] is [+ voice]. Rule (9), of course, applies to all forms in which a [ə] was inserted by rule (8), since [ə], like all English vowels, is [+ voice]. In

Figure 9.4, the forms in column III are produced by applying only redundancy rules to the phonemic representation. The forms in column I result from the application of redundancy rules and the phonological rule (9). Those forms in column II are derived by redundancy rules and phonological rules (8) and (9). Figure 9.5 illustrates the steps required to produce the three phonetic representations from the single phonemic representation of the plural morpheme. The figure is a simplified illustration since several abbreviated phonetic symbols are used rather than phonetic features in order to save space.

Observe that the phonological rules must apply in a particular order if the correct phonetic output is to be produced. Rule (8) must apply before rule (9), as illustrated by the words in column II of Figure 9.4. If we attempted to apply (9) first, it would produce forms such as [frezz], [gəražž], and [ǰəǰz], which would then undergo [ə]-insertion by rule (8), yielding the correct forms [frezəz], [gəražəz], and [ǰəǰəz]. But rule (9), if applied before rule (8), would not change [s] to [z] in [glæss], [wɪšs], or [čərčs] because the segment preceding [s] at this point is [− voice]. Rule (8) would then insert [ə], but the resulting phonetic forms [glæsəs], [wɪšəs], and [čərčəs] would be incorrect. Therefore, rule (8) must apply before rule (9) in order to yield all of the correct, productive phonetic representations of the plural morpheme.

Note that rules (8) and (9) are very general phonological rules in English. In addition to supplying phonetic representations for the plural morpheme, they also produce the phonetic representations of the possessive morpheme and the third person singular present tense morpheme, both of which have the same underlying phonemic representation and the same three phonetic representations as the plural morpheme, a fact that can be seen by examining the data in Figure 9.6. In Chapter 10, we shall see that rules (8) and (9) are also relevant for still another English morpheme.

Figure 9.5

Phonemic Representation		After Application of Redundancy Rules	After Application of Phonological Rule (8)	After Application of Phonological Rule (9)	Phonetic Representation
gərl	− voice + strident + anterior + coronal	gərls	gərls [Rule (8) does not apply]	gərlz	gərlz
wɪš	− voice + strident + anterior + coronal	wɪšs	wɪšəs	wɪšəz	wɪšəz
læmp	− voice + strident + anterior + coronal	læmps	læmps [Rule (8) does not apply]	læmps [Rule (9) does not apply]	læmps

Figure 9.6

Phonetic Form	Morphemes	
	Possessive	*Third Person Singular Present Tense*
[z]	girl's man's	grabs loves
[əz]	judge's witch's	wishes kisses
[s]	cat's Pat's	bakes tastes

Just as the allophone is a concrete representation of a phoneme in structural linguistics, so the **allomorph** is the concrete representation of a morpheme. For example, a traditional description of the 'plural' morpheme might be:

The morpheme	{Z}	'plural'
has the allomorphs	/əz/ /s/ /z/	occurs after /s, z, š, ž, č, ǰ/ occurs after other voiceless consonants occurs after other voiced sound segments

Note that the traditional statement uses abbreviated symbols and that the morpheme is represented by an ad hoc symbol Z enclosed in braces, { }. The allomorphs correspond roughly to the phonetic representations provided in the systematic approach presented here. For those readers who wish to pursue the matter, "Further Exploration" includes material on morphemes and allomorphs.

DIGRESSION: THE POSITION OF ARTICULATION FEATURES

In the last chapter, we saw that the set of phonetic features must be universal; that is, it must include all of the independent activities that the human vocal tract can carry out in the production of sound segments used in human languages. However, the speakers of a language know certain generalizations about the sound segments in their language. The segments are organized into a system in which various groups of segments play a role. These are natural classes of sounds in that each member of a particular class will share one or more phonetic features with every other member of the class. Rule (8) applies only in the environment of those sounds that are [+strident, +coronal], and we can say that [s, z, š, ž, č, ǰ] constitute a natural class of sounds. It would be highly "unnatural" if a language had a rule like (8) that inserted [ə] after a group of sound segments consisting of

SOUNDS AND SOUND SYSTEMS

[l, p, h, a]. This is not a natural class; there are no phonetic features shared by these four sound segments exclusively.

The universal set of phonetic features, in addition to accounting for man's physical vocal tract capabilities, should also provide a means for describing the natural classes of sounds that play a role in phonological rules. The traditional position of articulation features fail to provide a description of all of the natural classes of sounds in human languages and, for this reason, have been rejected by many linguists in favor of the features of systematic phonetics.

Consider the natural class of sounds [s, z, š, ž, č, ǰ]. In traditional articulatory phonetics, there is no simple, general way of describing this class such that each segment shares a set of features shared by no segment that is not a member of the class. To describe the class, we must talk about the "alveolar fricatives and palatal fricatives and affricates" of English. Even if we used the feature [strident], which does not appear in most sets of traditional articulatory features, we would still have to identify this class of segments as those which are "[+ strident] and either [alveolar] or [palatal]." In other words, the articulatory phonetic features [alveolar] and [palatal] fail to show explicitly that these two positions of articulation are similar and that sounds articulated at either point may operate as a single class in the sound system of a language. In systematic phonetics, on the other hand, the articulation position [coronal] does make this fact explicit. Using the features of systematic phonetics, the natural class of sound segments [s, z, š, ž, č, ǰ] can be identified as all, and only, those sound segments of English that are [+ strident, + coronal].

SUMMARY

A complete description of the sound system of a language must include two types of representation for each morpheme: a single phonemic representation, which identifies only those phonetic features not predictable from generalizations, and one or more phonetic representations, which specify in detail the phonetic features that occur when the morpheme is pronounced. The phonemic representation corresponds to the phonological information entered in the speaker's lexicon about a morpheme. The phonetic representation corresponds to the instructions the speaker issues to his vocal tract in order to actually produce the morpheme in speech.

The levels of representation are linked by a set of phonological generalizations of two types. Redundancy rules describe the speaker's knowledge about sound segments by adding predictable features to the single phonemic representation of each morpheme. Phonological rules account for the fact that a morpheme may have more than one phonetic representation, according to the phonological and grammatical nature of a particular sentence. Unlike redundancy rules, which merely add features to a phonemic representation, phonological rules may add segments, delete them, or change features in the process of converting the single underlying representation of a morpheme into its concrete phonetic representations.

Phonology involves the directly observable aspects of speech and the knowledge that speakers of a language must have in order to produce and understand speech. The former is concrete, the surface of a phonological system; the latter is abstract, the underlying phenomena of a phonological system. Since speakers unconsciously know both the surface and the underlying properties of their sound system, any complete description must include both types of information. The task of the linguist attempting such descriptions is enormous, and, for many of the languages of the world, the task is not even begun. Fortunately, however, several common types of phonological rules seem to be fairly clear at this time, and in the next chapter we shall discuss some additional characteristics of sound systems.

FURTHER EXPLORATION

The most concise introduction to systematic phonemics presently available is the book *Generative Phonology* by Sanford A. Schane. Schane devotes separate chapters to several topics treated here, including Chapter 4 "Redundancy," Chapter 6 "Phonological Rules," Chapter 7 "Underlying Representations" (concerned with morphophonemics), and Chapter 8 "Ordered Rules." The concepts of the phoneme and phonemic representation are discussed by Larry M. Hyman in Chapter 3 of *Phonology: Theory and Analysis;* particularly valuable is Section 3.4, "General Considerations in Setting Up Underlying Forms." In "Phonological Analysis," Chapter 4 of *Fundamentals of Linguistic Analysis,* Ronald W. Langacker provides discussion, data from a variety of languages, and problem exercises.

From the traditional, structural perspective, phonemics, phonemes, and morphemes are discussed in detail by H. A. Gleason in *An Introduction to Descriptive Linguistics;* in the early 1960s, this work served as one of the main introductory linguistics textbooks. Inadequacies of structural phonemics are discussed in a number of articles, almost all of which require substantial background in both traditional and contemporary phonemics. Readers concerned about this topic will find the following of interest: Noam Chomsky's "Current Issues in Linguistic Theory," Sections 4.3, 4.4, and 4.5 (Fodor and Katz 1964) and "Some Controversial Questions in Phonological Theory" by Noam Chomsky and Morris Halle. The latter was written in response to some early questions about systematic phonemics raised by F. W. Householder in "On Some Recent Claims in Phonological Theory." The Chomsky-Halle reply, in addition to contrasting the basic assumptions of traditional and systematic phonemics, provides clear, but extensive, explanations of the principles of the modern approach.

1. Minimal pairs are defined in this chapter as two words, having different meanings, that are distinguished by a single phonetic feature. Actually, this definition is overly rigid, due in part to the interaction of redundant features. Minimal pairs may also be characterized as pairs of words differing by one sound segment. For example, *beet* and *boot* can be considered as a minimal pair since the only difference is in the vowel, [i] for *beet,* [u] for *boot.* Yet, these vowels differ by two features, [i] being [− back, − round] while [u] is [+ back, + round]. In the section on redundancy rules, however, we observed that in English for [+ high] vowels, the value (+ or −) of [round] is predictable given the value of [back]. The following words represent minimal pairs that differ by a single sound segment.

(a) For each pair, identify the sound segments that differ and provide the phonetic symbols for those sounds.

(1)	pit	—	bit
(2)	scream	—	screen
(3)	joke	—	choke
(4)	fun	—	son
(5)	light	—	write
(6)	look	—	luck
(7)	shoe	—	chew
(8)	thy	—	thigh
(9)	tile	—	dial
(10)	weed	—	heed
(11)	feel	—	veal
(12)	hope	—	hop
(13)	cape	—	cap
(14)	mate	—	mat

(b) For each of the distinctions in (a), characterize the distinction in terms of the feature, or features, by which the pair differs. (Consult Figure 8.10 for the feature composition of the sound segments involved.)

(c) Nonlinguistic descriptions of English sounds sometimes identify the difference between the pairs in (12), (13), and (14) as primarily a difference in vowel length. To what extent is such a characterization accurate? Can you explain such a description? What phonetic features are involved in the distinction? *+ vocalic + consonantal*

2. In Chapter 8, the English [1] was described as [− high, − back]. In most dialects of English, however, speakers also use a [+ high, + back] lateral liquid, symbolized as [ɫ]. This sound involves a raising of the body of the tongue ([+ high]) and a retraction of the tongue ([+ back]). The difference between [1] and [ɫ] in English is not distinctive. Whether the lateral liquid will be [+ high, + back] or [− high, − back] is predictable, and, therefore, these features are redundant for this type of sound. Examine the data below and determine the environments in which [ɫ] occurs.

(a) State the environment in terms of the position of the sound in the word (e.g., initially (at the beginning) or finally (at the end)) and in terms of the phonetic features of adjacent sounds when that is relevant. (You may find it helpful to reorganize the data so that all occurrences of [1] are arranged together and similarly for [ɫ].) *lack*

[faɫ]	fall	[lin]	lean
[ɫak]	lock	[feɫ]	fail
[lɪp]	lip	[ɫuk]	Luke
[ɫʊk]	look	[fɛɫ]	fell
[foɫ]	foal	[læk]	lack
[lek]	lake	[fʊɫ]	full
[fiɫ]	feel	[ɫop]	lope
[lɛt]	let	[fɪɫ]	fill

(b) Since the use of [1] and [ɫ] varies from one dialect to another, these data may not reflect your own speech. Test this by comparing forms such as *leap* and *loop*. Do you observe a difference in the tongue position for the initial sound? Also compare *feel* and *fool*. Some dialects use [1] in the former and [ɫ] in the latter, while other dialects (such as the one represented in the data above) use [ɫ] in both of these words.

3. The following are statements of some predictable aspects of the phonetic features of English. Convert each statement into a formal redundancy rule with the *If:/Then:* format presented in this chapter. In the *If:* portion of the rule, use the fewest number of features necessary to identify the sounds to which the rule applies.

(a) All nasals are voiced.
(b) Low vowels are unrounded.
(c) Liquids are lax and voiced.
(d) Vowels are nasalized when they occur immediately before a nasal consonant. (A nasalized vowel is identical to a regular vowel except that it has the feature [+ nasal] rather than [− nasal].)
(e) Of the nasal consonants, only [m] and [n] occur at the beginning of a word; [ŋ] does not occur word-initially. (To write this rule, you must determine the features that distinguish [m] and [n] from [ŋ]; those features are predictable for nasals in word-initial position.)

Note. The two exercises below deal with the methodology of linguistic analysis. They are somewhat more difficult than earlier problems and are most suitable for use as a group project conducted with the guidance of an instructor. Readers who wish to attempt this material on their own are advised to proceed slowly, comparing each point of their analysis with the corresponding points of analysis of the plural morpheme presented in the text of the chapter.

4. In the discussion of morphophonemics and phonological rules in this chapter, it is assumed that the phonemic representation for the plural morpheme is the nonredundant set of features representing [s]; phonological rules (8) and (9) provide for the other regular phonetic forms of this morpheme, namely [z] and [əz].

(a) Now, assume that the phonemic representation for the plural morpheme is the nonredundant set of features representing [z]. List the features that would be needed. What phonological rules are necessary to provide [s] and [əz] for words such as those in Figure 9.4? Is it necessary to apply these rules in a particular order? Why or why not?

(b) We now have two possible analyses for the plural morpheme, the one presented in the text and the other developed in (a) above. This situation is unsatisfactory for several reasons. First, in writing a linguistic description, we are attempting to formulate the unconscious linguistic knowledge of native speakers of the language. Two analyses imply that speakers differ in their knowledge of regular plural formation. Yet, as children, all speakers were exposed to similar samples of the language, and it seems most reasonable to hypothesize that all would arrive at the same conclusion. Second, languages are essentially regular and systematic; it would be highly unusual to find a language in which a phenomenon as basic as plural formation in English was fundamentally irregular or inconsistent. Perhaps additional data will help to resolve this dilemma.

Since a language is a system, the rules and units that comprise the language are interrelated. Consider the consonant clusters (sequences) in the following words.

spy	[sp−]	wasp	[−sp]	lapse	[−ps]
stick	[st−]	test	[− st]	pats	[−ts]
school	[sk−]	ask	[−sk]	axe	[−ks]

What do you observe about the feature [voice] in these clusters? Would you consider the following as normal English words? Try to pronounce them as they are transcribed.

[sbay]	[wasb]	[læpz]
[sdɪk]	[tɛsd]	[pætz]
[sgul]	[æsg]	[ækz]

There is a general principle, or rule, at work here, serving to restrict combinations of consonants. Notice that the rule applies within single morphemes and at both the beginning and the end of words. State the principle.

(c) This general principle applies to both word-initial and word-final consonant clusters in English. If the first consonant of the cluster is [−voice], the next consonant must also be [−voice]. This fact must be stated in any description of English phonology. Now, reconsider the two solutions to plural formation. If we analyze the phonemic representation as [s], we must add to our description of English the special voicing rule (9), and, of course, we must also include the consonant cluster rule that we have just explored. However, if we analyze the plural morpheme with a phonemic representation as [z], no special extra rule is required to handle [voice]. [z] will become [s] according to the general consonant cluster rule that is already part of our description. The [z] solution is preferred. It makes use of a rule already in the grammar for other, related phonological phenomena, thereby increasing the applicability of that rule and achieving a generalization. In this way, the grammar also implies that speakers of English, in learning plural formation, apply to that special task knowledge that they have about other aspects of the sound system of their language.

5. Provide, in phonetic transcription, the past tense of the following words.

Column I	Column II	Column III
examine	present	scorch
lag	land	jump
mire	paint	pick
call	raid	sniff
pay	taste	wash
try	hunt	kiss
buzz	end	fix
seem	wait	
save		
dab		
judge		

(a) What are the three phonetic forms of the past tense? Describe, in terms of phonetic features, the conditions under which each form occurs.

(b) Compare the forms of the past tense with those of the plural. What similarities do you note? Following the same procedures and principles of analysis used in

(c) above, determine the single phonemic representation for the past tense morpheme. What rules are required to produce the remaining two phonetic forms of past tense? Is it necessary to add entirely new rules to the description of English, or can we use (perhaps with minor modification) rules that were formulated to account for consonant clusters and plural formation?

CHAPTER 10

10101010101010101010101010

COMMON PHONOLOGICAL PROCESSES

The relationship between the phonemic representations of morphemes and their phonetic representations is described by the phonological rules of a language. Every language has phonological rules, and all human beings must acquire the rules of their language. Since neither phonemic representations nor phonological rules are directly observable, it may seem amazing that all normal children apparently know the basic phonological rules of their native language by the age of eight. How children acquire language is discussed in some detail later, but here we will begin to explain their accomplishment through an examination of a variety of phonological rules in several different languages.

No two languages have identical sound systems, but there are limits to the diversity that occurs. These limits help to define the concept "human language," and they include the universal set of phonetic features discussed in Chapter 8. In addition, there are limitations on the kinds of phonological rules that actually occur. Phonological rules tend to preserve a natural relationship between the phonemic and phonetic representations of a morpheme. For example, when rule (9) in Chapter 9 changed the

135

phonemic segment [s] to phonetic [z], only one feature, [voice], was changed, and the change was natural in that an adjacent sound was also [+ voice]. But in no language is there a phonological rule that changes a phonemic segment [s] to phonetic [a]. Such a change would be totally unnatural, altering most of the features of the phonemic representation. On the other hand, an examination of the phonological rules of various languages reveals that certain types of changes from phonemic to phonetic representations occur quite frequently.

Thus, the task of learning a language may not be as complex for the child as it seems at first glance. Certain types of rules never occur, and other types occur in many languages. As we shall see, a reasonable hypothesis is that human beings are born with an innate capacity to acquire the kinds of rules that do occur in human languages; the child may be predisposed to learn how the language in the environment makes specific use of the general properties of language. Whether or not this hypothesis is valid, there is no doubt that languages exhibit many similarities in their phonological rules. In this chapter, we examine several of the most common types of phonological processes.

ASSIMILATION

The most common phenomenon expressed by phonological rules is **assimilation,** in which some feature of a sound segment changes to become identical to a feature in a neighboring segment. There are various types of assimilation, depending on the feature affected. The phonological rule (9) in Chapter 9 is an example of voicing assimilation. It should be noted that although rule (9) represented an attempt to describe voicing assimilation only for the 'plural', 'possessive', and 'third person singular present tense' morphemes, the phenomenon is more general in English. Consider the following examples of words with the 'past tense' morpheme: [bekt], [jəmpt], [kɪst], [wɪšt], [læft]. In each case, the phonetic form of the 'past tense' morpheme is [t], which is [− voice] just like the last consonant of the root to which it is suffixed. On the other hand, 'past tense' may also be phonetically [d], as in [tægd], [fezd], [sevd], [kɔld], [bawd], and [tayd], when the last sound segment of the root is [+ voice]. Thus, voicing assimilation occurs in this case, as well as in the others.

Phonological rules involving voicing assimilation occur in many languages. In German, rule (1) applies to [+ voice] consonants when they occur before suffixes beginning with [− voice] stops.

$$(1) \quad [+ \text{voice}] \quad \rightarrow \quad [- \text{voice}] \quad / \quad \begin{bmatrix} - \text{vocalic} \\ + \text{consonantal} \end{bmatrix} \begin{bmatrix} - \text{voice} \\ + \text{abrupt release} \end{bmatrix}$$

Thus, the root morpheme *sag* 'say' is pronounced [zag] in the word *sagen* 'to say', but [zak] in the word *sagte* 'said'.

In a special kind of voicing assimilation, German [+ voice] stops become [− voice] when they occur as the final sound segment in a word. Since the end of a word may be followed by a brief pause, or period of inactivity in the vocal tract, and since the vocal cords do not vibrate during such pauses, a change of [+ voice] to [− voice] may be viewed as assimilation. Examples are given in Figure 10.1. As in all figures in this chapter, the normal spelling of examples in other languages is given in parentheses. In each case, the phonemic representation of the root morpheme ends in a [+ voice] consonant. When a suffix beginning with a [+ voice] sound is attached to the root, the consonant remains [+ voice], but, in those cases where the root occurs without a suffix, the [+ voice] stop is in word-final position and becomes [− voice]. Even though such root morphemes have two different phonetic representations, they have only one phonemic representation.

Nasal assimilation, or **nasalization,** is an assimilation process in French. Consider, the words in Figure 10.2. For each root morpheme, the phonemic representation includes a [− nasal] vowel followed by a [+ nasal] consonant. In the case of the adjectives modifying feminine nouns, this phonemic representation is essentially what occurs phonetically. However, for the adjectives modifying masculine nouns, the [− nasal] vowel becomes [+ nasal], thereby assimilating to the following [+ nasal] consonant; then the [+ nasal] consonant is deleted, or dropped. (In the phonetic alphabet, the symbol [˜] over a vowel indicates that the vowel is [+ nasal]; absence of [˜] means that the vowel is [− nasal].) The precise conditions under which nasalization occurs in French are somewhat complicated and need not concern us here. Readers who are interested in this and other phonological characteristics of French may consult "Further Exploration" at the end of this chapter.

Assimilation can also involve the position of articulation features. For example, in Spanish the morpheme meaning 'a/an' is written *un,* and, in fact, the nasal [n] appears in the phonemic representation of this morpheme. Phonetically, however, the morpheme occurs as [un], [um], [uŋ], or [uñ]—where [ñ] is a [− anterior, + coronal] (i.e., a palatal)

Figure 10.1 _____

Morpheme Meaning	Phonemic Representation	Phonetic Representations	
		Word-finally	*Word-medially*
'dust'	[štawb]	[štawp] 'dust' (*Staub*)	[štawbən] 'to give off dust' (*stauben*)
'child'	[kɪnd]	[kɪnt] 'child' (*Kind*)	[kɪndər] 'children' (*Kinder*)
'day'	[tag]	[tak] 'day' (*Tag*)	[tagə] 'days' (*Tage*)

Figure 10.2

Morpheme Meaning	Phonetic Representations	
	Adjective with Feminine Noun	*Adjective with Masculine Noun*
'full'	[plɛn] (*pleine*)	[plɛ̃] (*plein*)
'level'	[plan] (*plane*)	[plã] (*plan*)
'good'	[bɔn] (*bonne*)	[bɔ̃] (*bon*)

nasal. Figure 10.3 provides examples of the phonetic forms of the Spanish morpheme *un*. Phonetically, the nasal consonant of this morpheme has assimilated to the position of articulation of the first consonant in the following word. For example, if the word begins with a [+ anterior, − coronal] consonant, like [p] or [b], the nasal of *un* is pronounced [m], which is [+ anterior, − coronal]. If the word begins with a [− anterior, + coronal] consonant, [č], the nasal is also [− anterior, + coronal], that is [ñ]. These facts are expressed by a Spanish phonological rule like rule (2).

$$(2) \quad \begin{bmatrix} + \text{ anterior} \\ + \text{ coronal} \end{bmatrix} \rightarrow \begin{bmatrix} \alpha \text{ anterior} \\ \beta \text{ coronal} \end{bmatrix} \Big/ \underline{} \begin{bmatrix} + \text{ nasal} \end{bmatrix} \begin{bmatrix} + \text{ consonantal} \\ \alpha \text{ anterior} \\ \beta \text{ coronal} \end{bmatrix}$$

The use of variables here permits the rule to state several instances of assimilation as a single, general phenomenon. That is, rather than writing several different rules—one to describe the change of phonemic [n] to phonetic [m], another to change phonemic [n] to phonetic [ñ], and still another to provide phonetic [ŋ]—variables show that phonemic [n], the [+ anterior, + coronal] nasal, assumes the same value for [anterior] and the same value for [coronal] as the following consonant.

It might be noted that English has a similar nasal assimilation rule. The prefix *in* 'not' generally is [ɪn] phonetically, but before [+ anterior, − coronal] consonants it is [ɪm], as in the words *impossible, impolite, imbalance*. In some dialects of English, the nasal of *in* also assimilates to [− anterior, − coronal] consonants, so that in such dialects it is pronounced [ɪŋ] in words like *incomplete* and *inglorious*. The English rule is more restricted than the Spanish rule, however, since the nasal does not completely assimilate to the position of articulation of all following consonants; for example, *injustice* is pronounced [ɪnǰəstəs], not [ɪñǰəstəs].

When assimilation involves vowels which are not contiguous, the special terms **umlaut** and **vowel harmony** are generally used to describe the phonological phenomena. In

Figure 10.3 ——————————————————————————————

The Morpheme *un*

Phonetic Representation	Occurs in the Spanish Phrase	Meaning
[um]	[um perro] (*un perro*)	'a dog'
	[um boleto] (*un boleto*)	'a ticket'
[un]	[un sastre] (*un sastre*)	'a tailor'
	[un tako] (*un taco*)	'a taco'
[uñ]	[uñ čeke] (*un cheque*)	'a check'
	[uñ čiste] (*un chiste*)	'a joke'
[uŋ]	[uŋ koče] (*un coche*)	'a car'
	[uŋ golpe] (*un golpe*)	'a blow'

umlauting, the vowel of a root assimilates to the vowel of a suffix. Umlauting has involved the feature [back] in several Germanic languages; if the vowel in the suffix is [− back], then so is the vowel in the root. In Modern German, umlauting occurs in certain morphemes in which the vowel of the root is normally [+ back], but when the suffix *e*, or *er*, meaning 'plural', is added the root vowel becomes [− back], in agreement with the [− back] vowel of the suffix. Note that although the plural suffix is pronounced with [ə], phonetically a [+ back] vowel, the suffix vowel is assumed to be [− back] at the more abstract phonemic level, as indicated by the normal spelling with *e*. Figure 10.4 illustrates German umlaut. A vowel symbol with superscript [¨] indicates that the vowel has all of the features normally associated with the vowel symbol except that the value for [back] is different; thus, [o] is a [− high, − low, + round, + back] vowel, while [ö] is a [− high, − low, + round, − back] vowel.

In the umlauting process, it is a feature of the suffix vowel that leads to a change in the root vowel, but in vowel harmony certain features of the root vowel determine features in the suffix. This occurs in Finnish, Hungarian, and Turkish, as well as in other, less

Figure 10.4 _____

	Without Suffix	*With Suffix*
	[dɛr zon] 'the son' (*der Sohn*)	[di zönə] 'the sons' (*die Söhne*)
	[das dɔrf] 'the village' (*das Dorf*)	[di dörfər] 'the villages' (*die Dörfer*)
	[dɛr tsuk] 'the train' (*der Zug*)	[di tsügə] 'the trains' (*die Züge*)
	[dɛr flʊs] 'the river' (*der Fluß*)	[di flüsə] 'the rivers' (*die Flüße*)

familiar languages. In Turkish, the suffix meaning 'possessive/genitive case' may occur as [in], [ïn], [un], or [ün], depending on the vowels in the root to which it is attached. This is illustrated in Figure 10.5. In a simplified form, the vowel harmony rule of Turkish can be stated as rule (3).

$$(3) \quad \begin{bmatrix} + \text{ vocalic} \\ - \text{ consonantal} \end{bmatrix} \rightarrow \begin{bmatrix} \alpha \text{ round} \\ \beta \text{ back} \end{bmatrix} \quad / \quad \begin{bmatrix} \alpha \text{ round} \\ \beta \text{ back} \end{bmatrix} \cdots \mathbin{/\!\!/} \cdots \underline{\qquad\qquad}$$

In other words, a vowel in a suffix ($/\!\!/$ indicates the boundary at the end of the root and the start of the suffix) will have the same value for the features [round] and [back] as do any vowels in the root (the . . . indicates that the vowels do not have to be contiguous; there may be intervening consonants as there are in all of the examples in Figure 10.5). Thus, in *yol*, the root vowel is [+ round, + back], and so is the suffix vowel [u]; similarly, in *para*, the root vowels are [− round, + back], and so is [ï].

In addition to rules that provide for the assimilation of one vowel to another vowel or of one consonant to another consonant, languages also contain rules by which vowels assimilate to consonants and consonants assimilate to vowels. The French example of nasalization illustrates a [− nasal] vowel that becomes [+ nasal] before a [+ nasal] consonant. Another example of vowels becoming more like a following consonant occurs in Japanese, where vowels, which are normally [+ voice], are phonetically [− voice] when they precede a [− voice] consonant. More common among the world's languages, however, are cases of consonants assimilating to vowels. In many languages, for exam-

Figure 10.5

Noun without Suffix	Noun with Suffix for 'Possessive/Genitive Case'
yol 'road'	*yolun* 'of the road'
gün 'day'	*günün* 'of the day'
kedi 'cat'	*kedinin** 'of the cat'
para 'money'	*paranïn** 'of the money'

*[n] is added between two contiguous vowels in these words by a general rule of Turkish phonology.

ple, [+ back] consonants, such as [k] and [g], become [− back] when they occur before [− back] vowels. This occurs in English, although most speakers are unaware of the change, since it is entirely predictable. Compare the position of articulation of the first sound in [kip] with that of the first sound in [kup]. You will notice that [k] is produced with a position of articulation that is closer to the palate ([− back]) in [kip], which has a [− back] vowel, while in [kup] the [k] is articulated at the velum with the tongue pulled back, before the [+ back] vowel [u]. Consonants also assimilate to vowels in terms of features other than position of articulation. In Spanish, the words *dado* 'gave' and *bebo* 'I drink' have the phonemic representation [dado] and [bebo], but phonetically they are [daðo] and [beβo], respectively (where [β] is the symbol for a voiced bilabial fricative, that is, a fricative formed by both lips). What is happening here is a change of the feature [continuant] from [−] in the phonemic representation to [+] in the phonetic representation. Vowels are all [+ continuant], and in Spanish when a [− continuant] voiced nonnasal consonant occurs between two [+ continuant] vowels, that consonant assimilates to the [+ continuant] feature of the vowels that surround it.

DISSIMILATION AND SEGMENT INSERTION

Dissimilation, in which some feature of a sound segment changes to become different from a feature in a neighboring segment, is less common than assimilation. The most commonly cited example of dissimilation occurred in Sanskrit, a language spoken in India before the time of Christ. In Sanskrit, one means of word formation was reduplication, a process in which a prefix is created by repeating the first consonant and vowel of a root. Thus, from the root [da:] 'give' (where [:] indicates that the preceding vowel has the phonetic feature [+ length]), one forms the word [dada:ti] 'he gives' by adding a suffix and the reduplicated prefix [da] (in Sanskrit, a [+ length] vowel in a root is systematically reduplicated as [− length] in the prefix). Given the root [dʰa:] 'put', one would expect a reduplicated prefix [dʰa]. Instead, we find words such as [dadʰa:ti] 'he puts'. The process at work here is dissimilation. The general rule for reduplication is to copy the first consonant and vowel of the root, but, when this rule would produce a word with two [+ aspiration] consonants, such as *[dʰadʰa:ti], a dissimilation rule changes [+ aspiration] to [− aspiration] in the first consonant. (In linguistic works, * precedes an unacceptable form.)

Dissimilation makes some sound segment clearly distinct from a similar or identical neighboring segment. Another means to accomplish the same end is the insertion of a segment between two segments that are similar, and in Chapter 9, the [ə]-insertion rule (8) did precisely that. It separated two similar sound segments, so that instead of having English words like [wɪšs] or [čərčs], we have [wɪšəz] and [čərčəz] (the result of both rule (8) and a voicing assimilation rule). It should be noted that, like the voicing assimilation rule, rule (8) should also be revised to apply to 'past tense' forms where [ə]-insertion also occurs whenever two similar or identical sound segments would otherwise occur next to one another. Consider the verbs *land* and *hunt*. Without rule (8), their past tense forms would be [lændd] and [hʌntt]; with [ə]-insertion (and, possibly, voicing assimilation to [ə]), we have the actual phonetic forms [lændəd] and [hʌntəd].

Phonological rules introduce segments even when dissimilation is not involved. For example, in English the [+ tense, − low] vowels [i, e, u, o] are predictably diphthongs, that is, phonetically they are followed by a glide. The glide is added by a phonological rule of segment insertion.

$$(4) \quad \emptyset \rightarrow \begin{bmatrix} - \text{ vocalic} \\ - \text{ consonantal} \\ + \text{ high} \\ \alpha \text{ back} \\ \alpha \text{ round} \end{bmatrix} \bigg/ \begin{bmatrix} + \text{ vocalic} \\ - \text{ consonantal} \\ + \text{ tense} \\ - \text{ low} \\ \alpha \text{ back} \\ \alpha \text{ round} \end{bmatrix} \underline{\hspace{2cm}}$$

Rule (4) states that the tense vowels [i] and [e], which are [− back, − round], are followed by the glide [y], which is also [− back, − round]; the tense vowels [u] and [o], [+ back, + round], have the glide [w], which is [+ back, + round].

Spanish has a segment insertion rule that supplies the vowel [e] whenever a word would otherwise begin with [s] followed by another [+ consonantal] segment. For example, consider the morpheme meaning 'write'. In the words *transcibir* 'to transcribe' and *subscribir* 'to endorse', the morpheme is phonetically [skriβ].* However, when this morpheme occurs without a prefix, as in the word *escribir* 'to write', the segment [e] has been added. Many Spanish words show the effect of this rule: *escuela* 'school', *especie* 'species', *estampa* 'stamp', *estuco* 'stucco'.

---

*The assimilation of a [− continuant] segment [b] to the surrounding [+ continuant] vowels has occurred, resulting in [β].

PHONOLOGICAL PROCESSES AND LANGUAGE CHANGE

Assimilation and segment insertion are common phonological processes. Dissimilation, while rarer, does occur, and, as we have seen, is sometimes achieved indirectly by means of segment insertion. In Chapter 9, it was noted that the simplest type of phonological system would be one in which the phonemic representations of morphemes were merely subsets of the phonetic representations; only redundancy rules would be needed to convert the former representations to the latter. A language with such a phonological system would have no phonological rules; however, no such language has ever been discovered. All languages have phonological rules, and many of those rules involve assimilation or segment insertion. Why is this so? The answers lie in the nature of human beings and their languages and are under investigation by linguists. Some possible explanations, however, may be offered even though our knowledge of the nature of language is still far from complete.

The most immediate explanation of why a language contains a particular phonological rule can often be found in the history of that language. At some earlier point in time, the rule was added to the language and may still be operating today. For example, in Latin, the language from which Spanish developed, there was a rule converting [b] to [β] between vowels. After the Latin language was brought to Spain, the rule was gradually extended to include all [+ voice, − continuant, − nasal] segments, and, by the fifteenth century, the assimilation rule that changes [− continuant] to [+ continuant] for phonemic voiced stops between vowels was a part of the Spanish phonological system. Nasalization in French, umlauting in German, and the Spanish [e]-insertion rule have similar, historical sources.

When a rule is added to the phonological system of a language, it may remain in effect for many centuries thereafter. But just because a rule once existed it is not necessarily part of the contemporary language. Sometimes the rule passes out of use, leaving only a few words in the modern language to reveal that it was part of the phonological system at an earlier time. Umlauting, for example, was an active phonological process in Germanic, the language that preceded the development of Old English, as well as Old German. As we have seen, an umlaut rule still exists in Modern German, but in Modern English there is no such rule. However, a few irregular English plurals such as *goose/geese, tooth/teeth,* and *foot/feet,* are the result of an old umlaut rule. In all three pairs, the singular has a [+ high, + back, + round] vowel, while the plural forms have [+ high, − back, − round] vowels. Recall that umlauting is a process in which a root vowel becomes [− back] before a [− back] suffix. In West Germanic, the plural of certain words, including *goose, tooth,* and *foot,* was formed by the addition of a suffix [i], a [− back] vowel. When this suffix was attached to a root with a [+ back] vowel, the vowel of that root became [− back]. An automatic consequence of this umlaut change has been that, eventually, the root vowel also became [− round] since, as we noted in Chapter 9, vowels in English are all [− round] if they are [− back]. Why has the umlaut rule disappeared from English? Such questions are difficult to answer with absolute certainty. We can not go back in time to ask the speakers. Even if we could, it is doubtful whether they could tell us, for the appearance or disappearance of phonological rules in a language usually does not occur suddenly. It is a gradual process, requiring at least a generation and often longer. In this particular case, however, we know that the suffix [i] eventually disappeared, and later, around the fourteenth century, unstressed word-final vowels were no longer pronounced. Thus, there were no forms left to which an umlaut rule could apply. The rule itself disappeared from the sound system, leaving behind in English just a few words that show it once occurred. An umlaut rule has remained in Modern German, however, since the suffixes that are part of the environment in which the rule applies have remained in the language.

The fact that a rule in the contemporary phonological system of a language may have originated at an earlier time does not explain why that rule came into being in the first place. All languages undergo change—change is part of the nature of language. A number of different factors can be correlated with changes in the phonological systems of languages, but, at the present state of our knowledge, it would be false to present these factors as a complete explanation. Among the factors that linguists believe relevant to a discussion of phonological change are: (1) physiological characteristics of the speech and hearing systems of man, (2) language contact, (3) the social nature of language, and (4) the acquisition of language by children.

From the physiological point of view, it is important to recall that a phonological system leads to a systematic phonetic representation that is converted into a set of instructions to the vocal tract. The result, of course, is speech, which must be heard and understood if communication is to be achieved. It is to the speaker's advantage that the instructions that must be transmitted to the vocal tract be as few in number and as simple as possible. This fact may account for the existence of assimilation rules in all human languages. Consider the Spanish rule of [continuant] assimilation. If the speaker wishes to produce the word *bebo* 'I drink', he or she must transmit a large number of instructions to the vocal tract, including information about whether or not the air stream is to be completely blocked for each sound segment. Considering only the latter information, let us look at the series of instructions the speaker transmits. If the phonetic representation of this word were similar to its phonemic representation (i.e., [bebo]), the instructions for the feature [continuant] would be "[− continuant] [+ continuant] [− continuant] [+ continuant]." However, an assimilation rule simplifies the speaker's task; once he or she has completed the instructions to produce [b] at the beginning of the word, he or she has only to send a single instruction "[+ continuant]" to remain in effect throughout the rest of the word—for the vowel [e], the fricative [β], and the vowel [o]. The English voicing assimilation rule is similar, for the speaker has only to leave in effect the instruction [+ voice] or [− voice] (which is issued for the last sound segment of the root) and the suffix will then be [+ voice] or [− voice], respectively. French nasal assimilation and German umlaut also involve anticipation of a later instruction.

Assimilation is a natural phonological process, perhaps related to an innate tendency in all people to minimize the complexity of their basic actions. Complexity of vocal tract movements may also be involved in the existence of segment insertion rules. As mentioned earlier, without the [ə]-insertion rule, the phonetic forms of the English words *wishes* and *churches* would be [wɪšs] and [čərčs]. Sequences of consonants such as [šs] or [čs] apparently require rather complicated vocal tract movements, and such sequences occur only rarely in human languages. In fact, some languages, such as Japanese, have very few consonant sequences. In Japanese, almost every consonant is followed by a vowel, a fact that is apparent when one considers English words that have been borrowed into Japanese: *strike* is [sutoraiku], *baseball* is [beisubooru]. The insertion of [ə] between segments like [č] (or [š]) and [s] simplifies the English speaker's articulatory task. Notice that it also makes it easier for listeners to identify the words they hear; [wɪšs] would sound very much like the singular form [wɪš], but [wɪšəz] is clearly different; an even more obvious example is the word *glasses,* which, without [ə]-insertion, would be [glæss]. Possible physiological explanations for dissimilation are less convincing. They may be similar to those for segment insertion, but examples of dissimilation are fewer and it is difficult to generalize about this phonological process.

In Chapter 5 we saw that language contact, or intercommunication among speakers of two languages, could result in changes in both the lexicon and the rules of word formation in a language. These changes were found to be the result of extensive lexical borrowing by one language from another. The same situation produces changes in the phonological system of a language, that is, changes in phonemic representations, in redundancy and phonological rules, and, consequently, in phonetic representations. For example, in Old English there was a single phonemic representation for the phonetic segments [f] and [v], a single phonemic representation for [θ] and [ð], and a single phonemic representation for [s] and [z]. The feature [voice] was not distinctive for such fricatives. Instead, a redundancy rule supplied [− voice], and a phonological rule of voicing assimilation then converted [− voice] to [+ voice] when the fricative occurred between two vowels or between a vowel and a voiced consonant. During the early Old English period, words borrowed from other languages were adapted to the sound system of Old English. Thus, the Latin word *versus* was written as *fers* in Old English, since [f] occurred word-initially but [v] only between vowels or between a vowel and a voiced consonant. As time passed, Old English, and then Middle English, borrowed an increasing number of words from languages in which [v], [ð] and [z] appeared word-initially. As the number of borrowed words increased, so did the possibility that their original pronunciation would be copied. In Old English, a pair of words like *feel/veal* was impossible; both would have been pronounced with initial [f]. But in Middle English times, when *veal* was borrowed from French, a number of other words beginning with [v] were also borrowed, and the phonological system of English changed. No longer could the feature [voice] be predicted for fricatives; now it was necessary to identify a fricative as [+ voice] or [− voice] in phonemic representations. The information could not be predicted, for the only feature distinguishing *feel* from *veal* was the feature [voice]. The redundancy rule and the phonological rule that had worked in Old English were incorrect for Middle English. The phonological system of the language changed under the influence of extensive contact with another language.

Some linguists believe that another possible explanation for language change in general, as well as for phonological change in particular, may lie in a basic tendency in people to change things periodically. After all, styles of dress, architecture, art, and music change over time in all societies, sometimes slowly, sometimes more rapidly. Why should language be an exception? Language, clothing, housing, and media for aesthetic expression are necessities, but they are also social institutions and therefore subject to change. A basic tendency to change is not unique to language.

At this point, it should be noted that the three factors related to language change —physiological properties of people, language contact, and the social nature of language—are not causes of language change in a strict sense. Thus, assimilation and segment insertion may be explained on a physiological basis, but such phonological processes do not always occur. Many languages do not change voiced stops to fricatives between vowels the way Spanish does (English has words like *baby, ladder,* and *saga*). If there were absolute physiological causes behind phonological processes, all languages should share a largely identical set of phonological rules. Physiological factors are apparently a sufficient basis for phonological change, but they do not necessarily result in such change. The same is true of language contact, which may lead to change but does not always do so. The discussion of the social nature of language may lead us to expect change, but it is only a general expectation. We know that all languages have undergone change and will continue to do so, but there is no way of predicting specifically what changes will take place. Of course, in this respect, linguists are in the same position as others who study phenomena related to people. Political scientists, historians, anthropologists, and sociologists, for example, are also unable to predict future events.

When some aspect of a language system changes, the change is usually a gradual one, in that it takes at least a generation for a large number of people to acquire a new rule, lose an old one, and to make any necessary alterations in the phonemic representations of morphemes. Because of the time span involved, a number of linguists have suggested that children who are in the process of learning their language may play a role in language change. At one time, it was widely believed that children made mistakes in learning a language, and that it was uncorrected mistakes that led to changes in the language. Careful investigation has revealed no cases in which this was actually true. However, children may acquire rules that are different from those of their parents. Children acquiring a language have available two kinds of information: (1) their innate capacity to acquire a human language and (2) spoken examples of the particular language in their environment. They have no immediate access to the underlying representations and the actual rules of the adults who surround them. They must use the general knowledge and particular examples that they do have in order to determine for themselves a set of underlying, phonemic representations and a set of phonological rules. Sometimes the phonemic representations and the rules constructed by children will differ from those of their parents. Consider a plausible example: an adult has different phonemic representations for the words *witch/which* and *wet/whet*. In each pair, the first word begins with [w], the second with [hw]. Should the adult move to an area where everyone uses [w] in all of these words, he or she may add a new rule to his or her phonological system:

(5) [h] → Ø / # —— [w]

The rule eliminates [h] when it occurs at the beginning of a word before [w]. Phonetically *wet* and *whet* become identical in this person's speech. In this case, the adult retains the original phonemic representation and simply adds a phonological rule. That the phonemic representation remains the same is supported by the fact that adult speakers who add such rules often, in rapid conversation or under conditions of stress, fail to use them, thus revealing that the phonemic representation has remained unchanged. The children of this adult hear only the phonetic form of words, not their phonemic representation. If they hear [wɛt] as the pronunciation of both *wet* and *whet,* they construct the same underlying representation for both words, a phonemic representation containing only [w], and never [hw]. Consequently, the children have no reason to develop the adult's rule (5). Thus, the children's linguistic system differs in two ways from that of the parent: (1) the phonemic representations differ for certain words, and (2) the adult's system includes a rule not present in the children's system. The children have not made a "mistake" in learning their language, but the knowledge that is acquired does differ from that of the adult.

The child's linguistic system may differ from the adult's by the addition of rules, as well as by the elimination of rules. Modern English contains the [ə]-insertion rule, which has been discussed previously. This rule was not added by adults to the phonological system of English. During the Middle English period, many words had the plural suffix [əs]. During the fourteenth and fifteenth centuries, unstressed [ə] in the last syllable of a word ceased to be pronounced, except in those cases where it remains today, that is, between [t] or [d] and the 'past tense' morpheme and between [s], [z], [š], [ž], [č], or [ǰ] and the 'plural', 'possessive', and 'third person singular present tense' morphemes. During this period of change, it is reasonable to assume that those adults who, as children, had learned a phonemic representation with [ə] simply acquired a new rule that removed the [ə] in all cases except those just described. Children, however, hearing adults pronounce most instances of these morphemes without [ə] had no reason to develop phonemic representations that included it. Instead, the children developed phonemic representations without [ə], and rather than a phonological rule to remove the vowel in many environments, they learned one that inserted it in a few environments.

It appears that change in the phonological system of a language is usually a two-step process. Adults add new rules, perhaps because of the factors discussed earlier. These rules affect the speech performance of the adults. Children then analyze subconsciously the speech they hear and construct new phonemic representations and different rules when necessary. At this point, the change introduced by the adult becomes a stabilized phenomenon, and the language has changed.

SUMMARY

Phonological rules of assimilation, segment insertion, and, to a lesser extent, dissimilation occur in most, if not all, human languages. It is often possible to find a historical source for such rules. Their widespread occurrence can be explained at least partially through the study of facts related to, but not part of, language itself; such facts include human physiological and psychological characteristics, as well as the environment in which a language is used. Language change usually consists of two steps: the addition of a rule by adults and the child's analysis of the effects of that rule. The consequence is a changed linguistic system.

Phonological processes (or common types of phonological rules) are discussed in all of the introductory studies of phonology mentioned in the "Further Exploration" section at the end of Chapter 8. A brief and straightforward presentation is offered by Sanford A. Schane in a chapter devoted to this subject in *Generative Phonology*. Phonological processes and language change are discussed clearly, with examples from a variety of languages, in Chapter 3, "Primary Change," and Chapter 4, "Grammar Simplification," of the book *Historical Linguistics and Generative Grammar* by Robert D. King; also of interest is Chapter 8, "Causality of Change." Other basic material on this topic appears in the sections on phonological change in *Introduction to Historical Linguistics* by Anthony Arlotto.

The major study of the phonological system of English, technical and demanding, is *The Sound Pattern of English* by Noam Chomsky and Morris Halle. Descriptions of the phonological systems of other languages are also available. For French, a clearly written, minimally technical account is provided by Sanford A. Schane in *French Phonology and Morphology*. Somewhat more demanding but highly valuable is *Spanish Phonology* by James W. Harris. An excellent, but challenging, discussion of the sound system of a less familiar language is presented in *The Phonological Component of a Grammar of Japanese* by James D. McCawley. Numerous, more traditional descriptions of the sound systems of other languages have been published by structural linguists. See, for example, *The Sounds of English and German* by William G. Moulton, one of a series of reference works designed primarily for foreign language teachers, in the *Contrastive Structure Series*, edited by Charles A. Ferguson.

1. Using phonetic features to characterize the sounds involved, explain why the following phonological phenomena are cases of assimilation.

(a) [b, d, g] occur as [p, t, k] respectively before a voiceless stop (as in Spanish, where for some speakers *obtener* is [optener], *vodka* is [botka]).
(b) [t] becomes [d] when preceded by a vowel and followed by a liquid (as in English, where *little* is sometimes [lɪdl] and *butter* is sometimes [bədr]).
(c) [l] becomes [ł] before the vowels [u, ʊ, o, ɔ, a] (see (2) in "Further Exploration," Chapter 9).
(d) [k] is articulated with lip rounding before the vowels [u, ʊ, o, ɔ] (compare the position of the lips for *cool* as opposed to *keel*).
(e) Under certain specific conditions, [k] becomes [s] before [ɪ] (as in English *opaque* [opek] but *opacity* [opæsɪti]).

2. The following are examples of segment insertion and segment deletion. Describe how each may be physiologically based (explained as an instance of the reduction of complexity in vocal tract movements).

(a) Many speakers of English pronounce *warmth* as [wɔrmpθ].
(b) In casual speech, for some dialects of Spanish, the past participle suffix *-ado* is pronounced *-ao*, as in *cantado* 'sung' [kantao].

(c) In French, the definite article 'the' usually has two forms, *le* before masculine nouns, *la* before feminine nouns. However, when the noun following the article begins with a vowel, the vowel of the article is deleted. Compare *le tigre* 'the tiger' and *la tigresse* 'the tigress' with *l'acteur* 'the actor' and *l'actrice* 'the actress'.

(d) Historically, the Modern English words *similar* and *semblance* come from the same Latin source word, *similis* 'like'. Following the deletion of the second vowel, a [b] was inserted between the [m] and the [l] in *semblance*.

(e) In casual, rapid speech, [t] and [d] frequently are deleted in English when both preceded and followed by a consonant, liquid, or glide, as in *wastepaper* [wespepər], *cold-blooded* [kolblədəd], *Second World War* [sɛkən wɔrl wɔr].

3. Not all phonological processes can be characterized as assimilation, dissimilation, insertion, or deletion. In fact, one of the major phonological processes in English involves none of these common types of change. Primarily during the Middle English period in the fifteenth century, the vowel system of English underwent a series of dramatic changes involving the position of articulation of certain tense, long, stressed vowels. Referred to by linguists as the Great Vowel Shift, the changes in the features of tongue height ([high] and [low]) can be summarized, in simplified form, as follows:

$$
\begin{bmatrix} + \text{ high} \\ - \text{ low} \end{bmatrix} \quad \text{lowered to} \quad \begin{bmatrix} - \text{ high} \\ + \text{ low} \end{bmatrix}
$$
[i] [u]   lowered to   [æ] [a]

$$
\begin{bmatrix} - \text{ high} \\ - \text{ low} \end{bmatrix} \quad \text{raised to} \quad \begin{bmatrix} + \text{ high} \\ - \text{ low} \end{bmatrix}
$$
[e] [o]   raised to   [i] [u]

$$
\begin{bmatrix} - \text{ high} \\ + \text{ low} \end{bmatrix} \quad \text{raised to} \quad \begin{bmatrix} - \text{ high} \\ - \text{ low} \end{bmatrix}
$$
[æ] [a]   raised to   [e] [o]

Such tense, stressed vowels occurred primarily in the last syllable of a word when followed by a single consonant or in the next to last syllable of a word. Thus, in Modern English we find such tense, stressed vowels in words like *seréne* and *méter,* where the stressed vowel of the root is [i] (although it should be noted that the spelling reflects the older, Middle English pronunciation with the letter *e* representing the earlier sound [e]). When more than one syllable followed, as would occur with the addition of derivational suffixes, the vowel produced was the nontense counterpart of the original tense vowel. Thus, where we had Middle English *serene* with [e], the related word, *serenity,* had [ɛ]. Originally, then, roots of this type displayed two phonetic forms in Middle English, one with a tense vowel, the other with the nontense counterpart of that vowel, depending largely on the number of syllables following the vowel in question. In Modern English, such roots still display two phonetic forms, but the relationship between the forms is phonetically less close. The Modern English forms differ not only in tenseness, but also, as a result of the Great Vowel Shift (which applied only to tense vowels), in tongue height.

149

(a) In Modern English, the relationship between [i] and [ɛ] is revealed by pairs of words such as *meter-metrical, appeal-appellative, clean-cleanliness.* What two vowel sounds share a similar relationship in the following words: *opaque-opacity, table-tabular, profane-profanity, fable-fabulous?* Following the same pattern discussed for [i] and [ɛ], describe how this relationship developed by means of the Great Vowel Shift.

(b) The high tense vowels of Middle English, [i] and [u], were affected by the Great Vowel Shift and eventually became low vowels, [æ] and [a]. Prior to the change in vowel height, these sounds acquired glides, making them diphthongs. Furthermore, [æ] moved back to become [a], while the nontense counterpart of [u], namely [ʊ], became [ə]. Linguists sometimes disagree on the order in which this complex of changes occurred, but we can summarize them as follows for the purpose of illustration.

	Middle English			*Modern English*
Tense Vowels }	i	iy	æy	ay
	u	uw		aw
Nontense Vowels }	ɪ			ɪ
	ʊ			ə

As a result, in Modern English we find a relationship between [ay] and [ɪ], as in *divine-divinity,* and between [aw] and [ə], as in *pronounce-pronunciation.* Cite two additional Modern English examples of the [ay]-[ɪ] relationship and of the [aw]-[ə] relationship. To what extent does the present spelling reflect the historical vowels in such words? (*Note.* The spelling does not always reflect the phonetic difference between a tense vowel and its nontense counterpart.)

PART 4 WRITING

Speech is the universal manifestation of language; every human language has a sound system. But there are certain limitations inherent in speech. Speech is a momentary phenomenon; when you talk, the sound waves move through the air in fractions of a second, strike the ear of a listener, and are gone forever. Speech has limitations of distance as well as time. Until the recent development of electronic devices that record sound and transmit it over long distances, communication through speech was possible over distances no greater than a few hundred yards at most. Of course, this is still true for the majority of people in the world today who live in societies less technologically endowed than ours. Speech is also inadequate for communication in exceptionally noisy places, such as airports and construction areas. The sounds produced by a human being simply cannot be heard if, nearby, four jet engines are warming up.

The development of an alternative way of manifesting language has provided man with a means to overcome the limitations of speech. When language is represented in written form, noise, time, and distance no longer present problems for communication. Writing has the additional advantage of permitting our performance to more closely reflect our linguistic competence. Written sentences may be longer and more complex than spoken sentences; if readers get lost in a complicated sentence, they can always go back to the beginning and try to find their way. Under ordinary circumstances, listeners cannot return to listen again. The following sentences, for example, might be almost incomprehensible if spoken. In written form, although they are somewhat complicated, the meaning can be determined quite clearly.

I met John's father's stepbrother's mother-in-law's sister at the national conference on ecology sponsored jointly by the Department of Health, Education and Welfare, six major universities, and the Ford Foundation.

151

That the woman the man the actor knew married produced movies astonished Harry.

(It should be noted that these two sentences are complex for different reasons. In the first, it is the length of the sentence that may force listeners to lose their way or readers to return to the beginning. In the second sentence, length is not the major problem; rather, the sentence is grammatically complex. While the written representation of the second sentence offers the reader an opportunity to "study" it, a spoken production would offer a different kind of advantage—stresses, pitches, and pauses could occur in such a way as to facilitate understanding.)

Writing plays such an important role in our society that many educated people believe it to be the primary representation of language. This is wrong, but it is also understandable. After all, a large part of education involves written material. Furthermore, almost no one can recall learning the sound system of his or her language, but many people do remember learning to read and write. Our schools may inadvertently perpetuate this misconception since "language" classes usually turn out to be devoted to composition rather than speech.

The view that language is primarily speech is also questionable, but it has been strongly maintained and defended by many American linguists, especially during the first half of this century. This view, in part, represents an attempt to counteract the incorrect popular notion about writing, but another factor is that many American linguists have carried out extensive studies of languages that have no writing system. Several facts appear to support the view that the chief representation of language is speech. All normal human beings speak; a majority, however, cannot write. All children learn to speak first; writing comes, if at all, later. Speech clearly predates writing in the history of mankind. The earliest evidence of writing comes from less than 5000 years ago; speech undoubtedly has existed for thousands of years longer. Numerically, chronologically, and historically, speech precedes writing. From an objective, contemporary point of view, however, speech and writing can be viewed as simply two different ways of representing language. Some languages make use of both systems of representation; others utilize only speech. Sometimes, writing and speech are related in that the written symbols correspond to units of the phonological system of a language, as is the case in English. This is not always so, for, as we shall see, some writing systems do not correspond to phonological segments at all but represent morphemes instead.

CHAPTER

WRITING SYSTEMS

Not every attempt to communicate through visual material can be called writing. A painting expresses the concepts in an artist's mind, and yet we would not say that it was writing. For written signs to constitute a writing system, they must have some systematic connection with the linguistically significant units of a language.

Man's earliest attempts to communicate via visual symbols were simple drawings. Most of those surviving from ancient times were drawn or carved on rock surfaces, often in caves where they have been protected for thousands of years from wind, sun, rain, and snow. Such pictures are neither art nor writing. Art is generally considered to be an aesthetic experience, without any underlying practical purpose, and yet the pictures produced in the second period of the Stone Age were apparently intended to record events. Pictures of a man with a club and a dead animal at his feet clearly convey a meaning, but they do not correspond to the linguistic units of any particular language. We know nothing about the artist's language, yet we can "read" his drawing with the same level of comprehension as could one of his friends. Furthermore, we can "read" it in any number of ways: "The man took a club and killed the animal" or "The animal on the ground

153

died as the result of receiving a blow from the club held by the man." Drawings represent things and events; writing represents language. In drawings, the symbols bear a physical resemblance to the objects pictured; in writing there is no physical similarity between symbols and objects. Communication through pictures is generally limited to rather concrete things and events; with writing, you can communicate anything which can be expressed in speech.

The linguistic units represented by a writing system may be morphemes, syllables, or sound segments. The oldest writing systems known are all **logographic** systems in which each symbol represents a morpheme, but most modern languages utilize **alphabetic** writing systems in which the symbols correspond to phonological units. **Syllabic** writing systems also exist; in these systems each symbol represents a syllable.

LOGOGRAPHIC WRITING SYSTEMS

Our earliest examples of writing systems come from the eastern Mediterranean region and date back to about 3000 B.C. Seven different logographic writing systems are known to have existed between 3000 and 1000 B.C. in the area extending from Egypt to China. Of these systems, only Chinese remains in use today. Other languages that once had logographic writing systems either are no longer spoken, such as Hittite and Sumerian, or have gradually developed alphabetic systems, such as Hindi.

Authorities on writing systems believe that logographic writing developed from pictures. This is difficult to prove conclusively since the evidence is more than 5000 years old, and the surviving examples of pictures and writing are very few. Nevertheless, the hypothesis is not unreasonable. The process of change from pictures to writing might have gone like this: as pictures representing objects were used more and more for communication, they became stylized and were no longer accurate visual representations of objects but, instead, conventional written symbols representing morphemes.

It should be apparent that a purely logographic writing system would contain an enormous number of symbols. Each morpheme would be represented by a different symbol, and every language contains tens, perhaps hundreds, of thousands of morphemes. The K'ang-hsi dictionary of 1716 (still used today) contains 40,545 symbols for the Chinese writing system, which is essentially logographic. Many are combination signs, consisting of two other symbols, as in 重 力 'to move', composed of the individual symbols 重 'heavy' and 力 'strength'. Nevertheless, children learning to read and write Chinese apparently have a far more difficult task than their English-speaking counterparts, who must deal with only twenty-six letters.

It is not surprising that, among the world's languages today, logographic writing systems are so rare. How did they change? A logographic symbol represents a morpheme, but that morpheme has a phonological representation. It can be pronounced, and the pronunciation is sometimes the same as that of another morpheme, or part of other morphemes. If the logographic symbol is extended to represent not only its original morpheme but also parts of other morphemes that sound the same, the writing system then represents sounds, as well as morphemes. It is no longer purely logographic. Let us take a hypothetical example. Assume that, in prehistoric times, people drew a picture 👁 to represent the eye. Gradually, the picture became stylized to the symbol ⬭ , and this became associated with the morpheme *eye* (if this happened with many other symbols and morphemes, there would be a logographic writing system). Next, because *eye* was pronounced [ay], the symbol ⬭ came to be used for the morpheme *I*, and it was also used as part of the written representation of other morphemes that included the sounds [ay], such as *cry, buy,* and *crisis*. Since a phonological value had been assigned to a written symbol, the writing system was no longer logographic. Of course, the change to a writing system in which symbols represent sounds, rather than morphemes, allows a drastic decrease in the number of symbols needed. In our hypothetical example, the original logographic symbols for *I, cry, buy,* and *crisis* would be eliminated once ⬭ was used in writing these morphemes. I. J. Gelb, an authority on writing systems, reports that Sumerian (spoken in Mesopotamia some 3000 years before Christ) had an essentially logographic writing system of some 2000 symbols; the number was reduced to 600 within a 1000 year period, as many logographic symbols were replaced by symbols representing sounds instead of morphemes.

Apparently because of the enormous number of symbols required, there are no purely logographic writing systems. Even Chinese, which comes closest, utilizes a set of phonetic symbols, representing sound segments, as a supplement to the logographic system. One of the chief uses of these phonetic symbols is in the teaching of reading to children. For example, the morpheme [kwó] 'country' would normally be written with the logographic symbol 國 . However, when children begin to read Chinese, the logographic symbol is accompanied by a set of phonetic symbols representing pronunciation, as in 國 , where ≪ represents [k], × represents [w], ƺ represents [o], and the rising tone is indicated by the acute accent mark (´).

In spite of the disadvantages implicit in the number of symbols required, a logographic writing system does have one very distinct advantage over syllabic and alphabetic systems. Since a logographic system represents morphemes, and not their phonological representation, logographic writing can be readily understood by people who might be unable to understand one another's speech. For example, $3 + 5 = 8$ consists of logographic symbols. The written representation would be understood equally well by speakers of English, German, Spanish, and Russian, although, if it were produced orally by a speaker of any of these languages, it would be unintelligible to speakers of the others: [θri pləs fayv ɪz et], [dray ʊnt fümf ɪst axt], [tres i siŋko son očo], and [trʸi plʸus pʸætʸ vosʸɪmʸ], respectively. A more striking example exists in Chinese. We talk about the Chinese language because of political conditions and the existence of a single writing system throughout the nation. Actually, there are a variety of forms of Chinese, such as Mandarin, Cantonese, Min, and Wu, and people who speak one variety often cannot understand the speech of those who speak another. The differences in the pronunciation of a morpheme are sometimes greater among the so-called dialects of Chinese than they are between English and German. For example, the morpheme 'woods' is pronounced [lin] in Mandarin, [liŋ] in Shanghai (a variety of Wu), and [ləm] in Cantonese (the tones, or pitch and glide of the voice, also differ). Because the writing system is essentially logographic, however, the symbol 林 is used in all of these dialects to represent the meaning 'woods'. Apparently, in most cases this advantage is outweighed by the disadvantages of a logographic writing system, for most such systems in other languages have been replaced by syllabic, and sometimes eventually by alphabetic, writing systems.

SYLLABIC WRITING SYSTEMS

Most of the logographic systems known from ancient times have included a **syllabary,** or set of symbols, each representing a syllable, which usually had the form CV (a consonant followed by a vowel). At the start of the second millenium (2000 B.C.), the 2,000 symbols of the Sumerian logographic system were reduced to 600 logographic symbols, supplemented by some 100 syllabic signs. Gradually, in Akkadian (the language that replaced Sumerian in Mesopotamia but still used the Sumerian writing system), the logographic symbols fell into disuse, and most writing was done with the syllabic symbols. The Akkadian language disappeared in time, and only old inscriptions of this syllabic writing system remain. But a similar development took place in the Far East, beginning about 450 A.D., when contacts between China and Japan had become quite extensive. At that time, the Japanese borrowed a number of logographic symbols from Chinese and actually read them with Chinese pronunciation—a method known in Japan as *on*-reading, which is still in use today. (The Japanese also developed a way of using the sound system of their own language in reading the logographic symbols; this is called *kun*-reading.) The logographic system used in Chinese, however, was not fully appropriate for Japanese. The structure of words in the two languages was, and is, quite different. In Chinese, most morphemes are free forms, and many words consist of either a single morpheme or a combination of free morphemes. In Japanese, on the other hand, words are formed by compounding and also by inflectional processes whereby suffixes are attached to root morphemes. Thus, Japanese had morphemes for which there were no immediate counterparts in Chinese and, therefore, no Chinese logographic symbols. Some way had to be found to write such morphemes in Japanese. This was accomplished by borrowing certain logographic symbols from Chinese and using them to represent sounds rather than meanings in Japanese. In the ninth century, the Japanese converted such original Chinese logographic symbols into syllabic symbols. Once these symbols represented pronunciation, rather than morphemes, they could be used to write all of the morphemes of Japanese. In this way, the Japanese developed a syllabic writing system.

Actually, two Japanese syllabic writing systems were developed: *katakana,* adapted from normal Chinese writing and used today only to represent borrowed words, onomatopoeic words, and in sending telegrams; and *hiragana,* the most common Japanese writing, adapted from cursive Chinese writing. Figure 11.1 illustrates the basic symbols of the hiragana syllabic writing system.

It should be noted that both the katakana and the hiragana syllabic scripts of Japanese contain symbols for every syllable in the language, and, therefore, Japanese could be written entirely in syllabic script. But, because of the logographic origin of their writing system, the Japanese continue to use approximately 1850 logographic symbols for certain root morphemes. Thus, Japanese does not use a purely syllabic writing system, nor, as we have seen, does Chinese use a purely logographic one.

In all languages, the number of syllables is always smaller than the number of different morphemes, and, therefore, a syllabic writing system will always contain fewer symbols than a logographic system. But syllabic systems are not equally practical for all languages. Recall from Chapter 10 that Japanese morphemes do not contain sequences of consonants. Consonant clusters arise only when two morphemes combine. Even then, such clusters are limited to a nasal followed by a consonant (as in [kamban] 'signboard' and [siňča] 'new tea') or to two identical stops, fricatives, or affricates (as in [tappitu] 'skillful penmanship' and [kassai] 'applause'). The result is that, with these exceptions, Japanese words are normally composed of sequences of syllables having the shape CV (that is, a consonant followed by a vowel). But consider the problems of using a syllabic

Figure 11.1

Hiragana Symbol	Syllable Represented	Hiragana Symbol	Syllable Represented	Hiragana Symbol	Syllable Represented
あ	a	た	ta	ま	ma
い	i	ち	ti†	み	mi
う	u	つ	tu‡	む	mu
え	e	て	te	め	me
お	o	と	to	も	mo
か	ka	な	na	や	ya
き	ki	に	ni	ゆ	yu
く	ku	ぬ	nu	よ	yo
け	ke	ね	ne	ら	ra
こ	ko	の	no	り	ri
さ	sa	は	ha	る	ru
し	si*	ひ	hi	れ	re
す	su	ふ	hu	ろ	ro
せ	se	へ	he	わ	wa
そ	so	ほ	ho	を	o§
				ん	n

*Phonetically, [ši].
†Phonetically, [či].
‡Phonetically, [cu].
§Used for [o] only when this sound segment developed historically from the older sequence [wo].

writing system for English. There would be little difficulty for words like *mama* or *tuna* in which each syllable has the shape CV. But English contains many other types of syllables. Each of the following words consists of only one syllable, and, therefore, in a syllabic writing system, each would require a separate symbol: *splash, texts, warped, warmth, strength*. The list could easily be extended. If English were to use a syllabic writing system, several hundred symbols might be necessary. Syllabic writing systems are most appropriate, and manageable, for languages like Japanese, which have very few consonant clusters, but for those languages like English with a large number of such clusters, syllabic writing would require a great many symbols.

The Japanese were not unique in obtaining a writing system by borrowing and adapting a neighboring system. The ancient Greeks modified the syllabic system used by the Semitic peoples with whom they had come into contact. The Semitic system contained symbols representing consonants, but vowels were indicated only occasionally and sporadically. When the Greeks borrowed the Semitic symbols, they used some of the symbols to represent vowels systematically and consistently. The result was an alphabetic writing system that has since been extended and modified throughout the Western world.

ALPHABETIC WRITING SYSTEMS

Alphabetic writing systems are those in which the symbols represent phonological segments. English, Russian, Greek, Italian, and most other languages have an alphabetic writing system. The word *pot,* for example, consists of three sound segments [p], [a], and [t], and it is written with three letters. As we saw in Part 3, however, there are two levels in a phonological system: the level of phonemic representation and the level of phonetic representation. To which does an alphabetic writing system correspond? Consider the words *pod, pot,* and *spot.* If we were to use the detailed symbols of the phonetic alphabet, these would be written phonetically as [pʰaːd], [pʰat], and [spat], respectively. In phonetic writing, such predictable features of English sounds as aspiration and vowel length would be indicated, for phonetic representations, by definition, include full information about concrete sounds. The amount of detail and special symbols necessary in a phonetic writing system would be unwieldy, certainly far more than the twenty-six letters of the English alphabet. Clearly, then, the writing system of English does not correspond to the phonetic representation of morphemes. For the same reason, neither does the alphabetic writing system of any other language. There simply are no phonetic writing systems (except, of course, for those special, technical systems used professionally by linguists and scholars in related disciplines).

From the spellings *pod, pot,* and *spot,* it seems that the English writing system corresponds to phonemic representations. Many of the predictable details about the sounds in these words are not indicated by their written form. The case for phonemic representation is even stronger when we consider words like *cats, dogs,* and *houses.* In each instance, the plural morpheme is written the same way, *s,* and, as we saw in Chapter 9, this morpheme has a single phonemic representation, even though phonetically it may occur as [s], [z], or [əz]. This morphophonemic aspect of alphabetic writing systems, in which a morpheme is written in one way even when it is pronounced in several ways, can be demonstrated for many languages in addition to English. The examples from German, French, and Spanish in Figures 10.1, 10.2, and 10.3 indicate that, even when a morpheme occurs in two or more phonetic forms, the writing systems of these languages correspond to a phonemic representation. For example, the German morpheme meaning 'day' is always spelled *Tag* although it is pronounced as either [tag] or [tak]. Spanish is sometimes said to have a "phonetic writing system," but this is clearly false. We have some evidence in Figure 10.3, and many other examples can be cited to show that the spelling of most Spanish words reflects their phonemic representation, not their phonetic representation. Spanish writing does correspond more closely to actual pronunciation (phonetics) than does English, but this is because Spanish apparently has fewer phonological rules than does English. In other words, phonemic representations are more similar to phonetic representations in Spanish than they are in English.

One might assume that an alphabet that was closer to a phonetic representation than to the abstract phonemic level might in some ways be preferable, and there is some evidence that Spanish-speaking children learn to read Spanish somewhat more easily than English-speaking children master the reading of English. But just because a writing system is difficult to master at the beginning does not mean that it should be revised or replaced by some other system. In the long run, what really matters is how well suited it is to the normal reading of someone who has learned it. In this respect, our writing system works very well indeed. Since any particular morpheme is normally written the same way no matter how it may actually be pronounced, we can immediately identify it when we see it in writing. Consider the additional, and unnecessary, complications which would occur if the plural of *cat* were spelled *cats* but the plural of *dog* were spelled *dogz*. And what about more complicated cases? The words *photograph* and *photography* share a morpheme sequence, *photograph*, which is spelled the same in both words since English writing corresponds to phonemic representation. If English spelling reflected phonetic representations, however, the two words would be written quite differently, for *photograph* is normally pronounced [fótəgræf], while *photography* is [fətágrəfi].

Another argument sometimes advanced against the writing system of English is that foreigners learning to read English have a more difficult time than English speakers do when they learn the alphabetic writing systems of many other languages. While possibly true, this is irrelevant. Writing systems exist for the benefit of the speakers of a language, not for those who are trying to learn it as a second language. Fluent speakers of English know the phonemic representation of every morpheme in their lexicon; if they did not, they would not be able to speak or understand English. When reading some material set down in a writing system that reflects phonemic representations, their task is the simple one of identifying what is on the page with some item in their mental dictionary. If asked to read aloud, native speakers of a language have merely to apply to the written words the phonological rules they use when they speak—the rules that convert phonemic to phonetic representations. While a writing system that corresponded directly to phonetic representations might be convenient for those who do not know the language, it would be a nuisance to native speakers of the language. Reading aloud would not be too bad, since one could proceed immediately from symbol to sound. But, except for reading lessons in primary school, how often do people actually read out loud? Usually when you read you are attempting to understand the meaning of what is written. A phonetic writing system would force readers to mentally convert the phonetic representations on the paper into a phonemic representation, and then they would still have to identify the phonemic representation with some entry in their lexicon. In other words, an extra mental step is required to read phonetic writing; rather than proceeding directly from written symbols to meaning, readers must convert the written, phonetic representation to a phonemic representation, and only then can they determine the meaning of the written passage. We will again consider the question of reading in Part 9, "Language, Linguistics, and Teachers."

The phonemic alphabetic systems so widely used do not look like the linguists' phonemic representations that utilize features. A writing system that did use features like those presented in Chapter 8 would be totally impractical. Think of the amount of space it would take simply to write the word *linguistics* in features! The symbols of our normal alphabet provide an excellent compromise between practicality and accuracy in presenting a written form of phonemic representation for the morphemes of English.

ENGLISH SPELLING

No one would deny that in spite of its advantages, the writing system of modern English contains a number of deviations from phonemic representation. Many of these can be explained historically. The phonological system of every language changes, but writing systems do so very slowly. Many of the so-called silent letters in modern English spelling originated at a time when they actually did represent sound segments. For example, the letters *gh* in *fight, light,* and *night* date back to the Old English sound segment [x] (a voiceless fricative produced at the position of articulation of either [k] or [č]). The sound no longer exists in English (except in Scottish dialects), but it still occurs in German, which came from the same source (as in German *Buch,* [bux] 'book'). There is no need for *gh* in the spelling of such English words. The letters do not correspond to segments in either phonemic or phonetic representations in modern speech, but all attempts to change our spelling in recent years have met not only with failure but sometimes with actual hostility. The great British author and critic George Bernard Shaw was a strong advocate of English spelling reform. In fact, when he died in 1950, he willed part of his estate for the development of a corporation that would promote changes in English spelling. Nothing of consequence has ever resulted. In the United States, President Theodore Roosevelt had plans to use the Government Printing Office as the impetus for changes in the spelling of certain English words (for example, *light* was to become *lite*). Congress reacted so violently to this attempt "to tamper with our language" that the president abandoned his efforts.

Borrowing has also created cases in which English spelling fails to reflect phonemic representations. Just as English has borrowed words, morphemes, and phonological features, so it has borrowed spellings from other languages. In the Middle English period, for example, many literate people knew French as well as English. We saw in Chapter 5 that French was considered more prestigious than English for a time, and it is not surprising that some characteristics of French writing were extended to English. For example, in Old English, the words *choose, chew,* and *cheese* were spelled *cēosan, cēowan,* and *cēse,* respectively. The spelling change from *c* to *ch* was due to the fact that words like *chase,* in which the initial sound was the same as that of *choose, chew,* and *cheese,* were borrowed from French. Since the first sound of *chase* was spelled *ch* in French and since the spelling was borrowed along with the word, it was not surprising that the prestigious *ch* spelling should have been extended to native English words, too.

English spelling has also been affected by well-meaning scholars, who were, perhaps, too enthusiastic about reform. The Latin origin of many English words borrowed long ago became obscured by normal changes in pronunciation (recall the discussion of *cēse* in Chapter 5). During the Renaissance, between 1400 and 1600, there was a revival of interest in the Latin language, and some learned individuals attempted to change the spelling of Latin-based English words in order to clearly show their origin. In many cases, the spelling changes had no relation to Middle English pronunciation. For example, the word *doubt* was borrowed into English from French as *doute.* The Latin source of this word was *dubitum,* and, since the Latin word contained the letter *b,* some people believed that the English word should too, in spite of the fact that no English speaker has ever pronounced *doubt* with a [b] sound. (Notice, however, that the insertion of *b* into the spelling of *doubt* does serve to point out the relation between this root and the words *dubious* and *indubitable.*) Similar interference with spelling also led to the insertion of an *s,* which is never pronounced, in *island* and *aisle.* There are occasions, however, when the spelling of a word has influenced pronunciation; the term **spelling pronunciation** describes this phenomenon. Our Modern English word *perfect* was borrowed into Middle English from French as *parfit.* But the original Latin form was *perfectus,* and, because of this, the spelling *parfit* was changed to *perfect* in English. Unlike *doubt,* in which the inserted letter *b* was never pronounced, people began to use a spelling pronunciation for *perfect,* and in Modern English the word contains a [k] sound where the letter *c* was added. Other, more recent, examples of spelling pronunciations include the *t* in *often* and the *l* in *soldier.* Not too long ago, the most common pronunciations of these words were [ɔfən] and [soǰər], but today [ɔftən] occurs quite frequently and almost everyone says [solǰər].

It is clear, then, that there is mutual influence between an alphabetic writing system and the phonological system of a language. Pronunciation is occasionally affected by the way in which a word is spelled, and spelling may gradually be modified in accordance with changes in the phonological system. Perhaps because writing is visible and permanent and because it is formally taught in schools, many people object to changes or variations in spelling, although they may fail to even notice parallel changes in pronunciation. Interestingly, however, it was not until the appearance of English dictionaries in the seventeenth century that people became so concerned about spelling. Prior to the proclamations on "correct" spelling by self-appointed authorities, everyone spelled words more or less as he wished. Since all used the same alphabetic writing system and the symbols of that system generally corresponded to the phonemic representations that all speakers of the language knew, there was far less variation in spelling than one might expect. In fact, there is no evidence that the spelling differences caused our linguistic ancestors any great problems in understanding written material, although they may well have read more slowly because of both the spelling variations and the extensive use of abbreviations common in medieval manuscripts.

A somewhat similar situation exists today in the differences between British and American spellings for some words; Figure 11.2 provides some examples. For the most part, Americans have little trouble reading British books or newspapers, and the British are also able to read American material without difficulty. Such differences in spelling have essentially the same origin as British and American differences in pronunciation and vocabulary. The natural and inevitable changes of every human institution occurred in the writing system of English. Because Americans and Englishmen were not in everyday contact with one another, spelling changes on one side of the Atlantic were not always adopted on the other. In 1828, for example, Noah Webster recommended that the *u* be dropped from spellings such as *colour* and *honour*. The prestige of his *American Dictionary of the English Language* was so great that his suggestion was generally accepted in the United States. In Britain, however, the American spellings *color* and *honor* were (and for many people still are) regarded as barbaric. Such irrational and emotional responses to spelling are not restricted to the British; many Americans consider the British spellings *colour, cheque,* and *centre* to be pretentious. It might be noted that not all spelling differences are due to changes made by Americans. The use of *re* rather than *er* in the British spelling of words like *center* and *theater* is relatively recent; formerly, the British also used *er*.

From an objective point of view, arguments over the "correct" spelling of a word are often rather silly. It really does not make any difference whether *defense* is spelled with *c* or *s*; both letters are used in our alphabet to represent the sound segment [s] (*fence, tense*). Nevertheless, it is fortunate that people are conservative about accepting changes in their writing system. Sometimes the proposed changes introduce unnecessary complexity, as in the introduction of the *s* in *island*. More significantly, if writing systems did undergo frequent and widespread changes, it would soon be impossible for a contemporary reader to decipher documents and literature of an earlier time. It is precisely the permanence of writing—the possibility of storing knowledge for decades, even

Figure 11.2

American	British
tire	tyre
pajamas	pyjamas
check	cheque
color	colour
honor	honour
center	centre
theater	theatre
defense	defence
offense	offence
traveled	travelled
labeled	labelled

centuries—that makes it such a valuable tool for any society. If writing systems underwent substantial change, that stored knowledge would become inaccessible to all but a few individuals specially trained in the old manner of writing.

DEVISING A WRITING SYSTEM

The great practical value of a writing system is obvious. Even the modern electronic equipment that records, stores, and transmits speech has not replaced writing. It is almost impossible for most Americans to imagine life without writing—no books, magazines, or newspapers, no mail, no signs, no labels with instructions for using, cleaning, or cooking the things we buy. Even when speech is possible, it is often accompanied by writing; in television commercials, for example, the announcer often says no more than what appears in writing on the screen. It is to be expected, then, that efforts are underway to devise writing systems for those languages lacking them. In the past, much of this work has been carried out by missionaries, and they still constitute the major force in this area. More recently, however, the governments of many newly independent nations have also begun work on the creation of writing systems, sometimes with the help of linguists from American service organizations like the Peace Corps. Since those who carry out such projects are generally speakers of languages using alphabetic writing systems, the writing systems they devise are almost always alphabetic. There are practical considerations leading to the use of alphabetic writing systems: logographic systems require thousands of symbols, and the task of teaching people to read and write is enormous; also, languages in which words contain complex consonant clusters are not suitable for syllabic writing. But an alphabetic writing system can be devised for any language, and usually the number of symbols required will not exceed fifty.

New writing systems are rarely new in every respect. Almost all rely on the symbols of existing systems as a base, just as the Greeks originally took the symbols of the Semitic syllabic writing system and adapted them to an alphabetic system by using some of the Semitic consonant symbols to represent Greek vowels. A more recent example of the borrowing of written symbols occurred in the early nineteenth century. Sequoia, a Cherokee Indian, invented a syllabic writing system, which was used for many years in Cherokee books and newspapers, as well as in personal correspondence. Sequoia used many of the symbols of our alphabet, but he arbitrarily assigned to each symbol a syllable (consisting of a consonant and the vowel that followed it) of his own language. The Cherokee syllabary consists of eighty-five symbols. Forms borrowed from the English writing system include J (representing the syllable [gu]), M ([lu]), and S ([du]). Some symbols are apparently modifications of English letters, such as $\sim\!\!\mathsf{Y}$ ([mu]) and G ([yu]); others, for example $\mathfrak{D}$ ([nu]), seem to have originated with Sequoia. Today, Western Europeans and Americans who provide languages with writing systems generally devise alphabets based on our own, often supplementing the symbols with some of those found in the phonetic alphabets used by linguists (see Chapter 7).

The task of devising an alphabetic writing system for a language involves more than merely the choice of symbols. One must also determine the phonological system of the language, for, as we have seen, an alphabetic writing system is never phonetic—it

163

represents the phonemic level of a sound system. When native speakers of a language create their own alphabet, the symbols generally correlate well with phonemic representations since the speakers know these, even if unconsciously. On the other hand, if missionaries or other outsiders who are not fluent in the language attempt to devise an alphabetic writing system, they must first carry out a linguistic analysis of the phonological system to determine the phonemic representations in the language.

Linguistic considerations alone, however, are often not sufficient for the development of a writing system. For example, if some other language with a writing system is also present in an area, it is usually necessary to make the new writing system as similar as possible to the existing one. Many people who are bilingual, speaking both languages, may already be literate in the one, and they might reject a totally different system of writing for their other language. Such factors have played a role in developing writing systems for some American Indian languages in South America, where Spanish is also known, spoken, and written.

Many recently devised writing systems are relatively unknown beyond the small geographical regions in which the languages they represent are used. This is not unexpected since societies without writing systems in the past generally have had little influence on the technological or scientific developments in the rest of the world. In fact, such development is extremely difficult to achieve in a society lacking the means for recording progress and disseminating knowledge in permanent form. Once a writing system is devised and learned, however, formal study and education become possible, and the opportunity for progress is enhanced.

SUMMARY

Speech and writing are the two different representations of language. Although speech takes precedence over writing historically, chronologically, and in extent of occurrence, writing has the advantage of permanence. Most writing systems in use today are alphabetic, like English. The only well-known contemporary syllabic system is Japanese, and Chinese is the main example of a modern logographic writing system. Writing systems change more slowly than phonological systems, and this partially accounts for the fact that English spelling is not always an accurate representation of the phonemic level. Many of the world's languages still lack writing systems.

FURTHER EXPLORATION

A Study of Writing by I. J. Gelb is a comprehensive investigation of the possible origin and evolution of writing systems. Chapters 3, 4, and 5 are devoted to logographic, syllabic, and alphabetic writing, respectively, and include numerous examples and illustrations from a wide variety of languages. Readers should exercise some caution in accepting the author's description of some languages and cultures as ''primitive,'' a designation that modern linguists and anthropologists reject as inappropriate.

Chapter 3, ''Letters and Sounds: A Brief History of Writing,'' in Thomas Pyles' *The

Origins and Development of the English Language outlines the origin of English writing and traces the changes in the system throughout the history of our language. An important article on the relation of modern English spelling to phonology is "Reading, Writing, and Phonology" by Carol Chomsky (Lester 1973).

Kenneth L. Pike, in Chapter 16, "The Formation of Practical Alphabets," of his book *Phonemics,* presents a discussion and some examples of several linguistic and nonlinguistic considerations important in the creation of an alphabetic writing system. Another perspective is offered in Chapter 3, "Language Reform," in the book *Language and Linguistics in the People's Republic of China,* edited by Winfred P. Lehmann. This chapter provides an account of the current movements in the People's Republic of China to simplify the symbols of the Chinese logographic writing system and to develop and implement an alphabetic writing system, known as *pinyin,* for representing the Chinese dialect Putonghua (a dialect that the government is promoting for nationwide usage). The report refers to pinyin as a "phonetic alphabet," although it is more reasonably described in our terms as a phonemic writing system since it does not represent all of the predictable aspects of the sound system of Chinese.

1. (a)　List ten English words that could be represented by the syllabic symbols of the Japanese hiragana writing system given in Figure 11.1. (Base your list on the pronunciation, not the spelling, of the English words.)

　(b)　Use the hiragana symbols to write the words listed in (a).

　(c)　List twenty English words, other than those mentioned in the text, that cannot be represented in the hiragana system.

　(d)　Which list was easier to make? What do you conclude about the practicality of establishing a syllabic writing system for English?

2.　Provide a broad phonetic transcription of your normal pronunciation of the following words; include the acute accent (´) to mark the syllable with the strongest stress in each word.

bomb	—	bombard
malign	—	malignant
medicine	—	medicate
reciprocal	—	reciprocity
sign	—	signature

　(a)　Compare your transcriptions with the normal spellings. List the instances for each pair where the spelling of vowels and consonants remains the same but the pronunciation varies.

　(b)　You have learned the linguistic terms *phoneme* and *morpheme,* pronounced [fónim] and [mɔ́rfim], respectively. Some linguists refer to a sound as a [fon] and use the term [mɔrf] for a morpheme that actually occurs in some speech utterance. Given the existing spellings for *phoneme* and *morpheme,* which spellings would be preferable for [fon] and [mɔrf]: *fone* and *morf* or *phone* and *morph*? Explain.

(c) Based on the words in (a) and (b) above, what advantages for normal (silent) reading are offered by the phonemic nature of our writing system? What disadvantages might there be for (1) spelling, (2) reading aloud, and (3) speakers of other languages learning English?

3. When an alphabetic writing system remains unchanged over time, while the phonological system of the language does change, a common result is the development of **homographs,** words with different meanings but having the same spelling and, sometimes, different pronunciations. Examples:

bow	[bo]	[baw]
lead	[lid]	[lɛd]
read	[rid]	[rɛd]
use	[yus]	[yuz]

Do these homographs cause any major difficulties for comprehension in the following sentences? Explain.

(a) Dr. Johnson made a deep *bow* and his clip-on *bow* tie fell off.

(b) Harry Ellis wanted to *lead* the demonstration by the *lead* metal workers.

(c) The teacher's aid *read* the book to Johnny because he doesn't know how to *read* yet.

(d) Do not *use* this appliance until you have studied the instructions for its *use*.

PART 5555555555555555

SPEAKERS, SENTENCES, AND SYNTAX

When most people hear the word "grammar," they recall the prescriptive rules their teachers insisted must be followed if speech or writing were to be "correct" or "grammatical." This is a very limited use of the term "grammatical" since it refers primarily to artificially imposed, regulative rules and not to the constitutive rules that actually form the basis of speakers' knowledge of their language. When linguists describe a sentence as grammatical, they are basing their judgment on the objective, descriptive system of the constitutive rules of a language.

Normally, we speak or write without paying any attention to how something should be expressed, and yet every time we produce an utterance we are following a set of implicit rules according to which words are combined into sentences. We can say sentence (1), for example, but no speaker of English would ever produce sentence (2).

(1) In a small town, it is difficult to organize a successful boycott of nonunion products.

(2) * Town a small in, to organize it difficult is products nonunion of boycott a successful.

Sentence (1) is **grammatical;** it follows the rules of sentence formation in English. Sentence (2), on the other hand, is **ungrammatical;** it does not follow the rules of sentence formation in English (ungrammatical sentences are preceded by an asterisk).

The set of principles, or constitutive rules, according to which words are combined into sentences in a language is called the **syntax** of the language. Every speaker knows the syntax of his or her language. This knowledge enables the speaker to produce and understand sentences, as well as to recognize certain properties of sentences, and even to make objective observations, such as that regarding the deviant nature of sentence (2) above. The syntactic knowledge underlying speakers' abilities to cope with sentences is not conscious, but syntax is nevertheless quite real. One major task for the linguist is to determine the knowledge of syntax possessed by speakers and to describe this knowledge. Such a description, when presented along with the description of other facets of linguistic knowledge (such as the knowledge of phonology, morphemes, and rules of word formation), is said to comprise a grammar of the language. Actually, of course, the grammar of a language resides in the minds of its speakers. The descriptive grammar produced by the linguist is best referred to as a theory, or hypothesis, of what the grammar of the language really is. (It should be noted, however, that this distinction is rarely made explicit in the texts of linguistic books and articles.)

In some ways, the syntax of a language can be viewed as the core of the language, for it is syntax that links meaning with a concrete means of expression such as sounds or written symbols. This function of syntax will be explored throughout the following chapters, but here we must observe that the term "grammar" is sometimes used in a very limited sense as the equivalent of syntax. Thus, we find that **grammar** may be considered in several different, and sometimes overlapping, ways: (1) as a synonym for syntax, (2) to refer to the entire body of elements and units that constitute a language (including not only syntax, but also phonology and word formation), (3) to label the description of a language prepared by the linguist, (4) to describe the body of linguistic knowledge that resides in the minds of the speakers of a language. In addition, of course, we must also recognize the existence of prescriptive grammar, mentioned above and discussed in Chapter 2. Generally, readers will find that the context in which the word occurs makes it clear which meaning (or combination of meanings) is intended. In this part, we will explore various aspects of the speakers' knowledge of syntax and the linguist's attempt to describe that knowledge.

CHAPTER 12121212121212121212121212

THE SPEAKERS' KNOWLEDGE OF SYNTAX

An attempt to describe the knowledge of syntax possessed by native speakers of a language is an ambitious undertaking. Since not even the speakers themselves are aware of this knowledge, it cannot be observed and then described. Instead, investigators must rely on indirect evidence. They observe how syntactic knowledge is reflected in the sentences people produce and understand and in the judgments they are able to make about sentences they encounter. From this observable information, investigators then formulate a reasonable hypothesis about the kind of knowledge people must possess in order to deal with language as they do.

In this chapter, we discuss several aspects of syntax that are reflected in the linguistic performance of speakers of English. In the following chapters, we attempt to account for the kind of knowledge about syntax underlying such performance.

PRODUCTIVITY

The number of grammatical sentences in any given language is infinite; there is no limit to the number of sentences that might be produced in a language. Even if we had a list of every sentence produced throughout the existence of English, we could immediately add to that list by combining any two (or more) sentences by using *and*. Other ways of producing indefinitely long sentences include the use of multiple relative clauses (see the example in sentence (8) of Chapter 2) and the addition of phrases such as *I know that John knows that Mary is aware that I know* . . . to other sentences.

No individual speaker of English will ever produce or hear all of the sentences of his language. But, on the basis of his knowledge, he is potentially capable of producing any one of them or of comprehending any grammatical sentence he encounters. His knowledge of English encompasses the infinite number of grammatical sentences of the language, although, in terms of actual language usage, no speaker will ever have the opportunity to use all of his knowledge. In other words, productivity in language results from the speaker's underlying linguistic competence, which is never reflected completely by his performance.

A theory of syntax is a theory of what speakers know, not of what they may have the opportunity to do. Thus, a theory of syntax for a language must account for productivity. However the speaker's knowledge of syntax is described, that description must cover all of the possible sentences of the language. Thus, it is clearly impossible to describe syntax adequately by merely listing sentences. The list would be endless. No one could ever learn a language simply by memorizing a list of sentences. Whatever the storage capacity of the human brain may be, it is not infinite, and, therefore, it would be impossible for anyone to store an infinite list. The only way that the human mind can cope with an infinite number of objects (sentences, in the case of language) is if that infinite set is produced by means of a finite (limited) set of principles, or rules. In mathematics, for example, we know that the set of numbers is infinite. For any number, one can always name the next one—the number after 2,397,435,684,162 is 2,397,435,684,163. It is only because we know the principle involved in counting that we can produce the next number, but we may be unable to verbalize the principle itself. The same is true of human language. Since speakers are capable of producing an infinite number of grammatical sentences, they must know the principles that **generate,** or produce, those sentences. These principles constitute the syntactic rules of the language; they must be stated in a descriptive grammar of the language. When the principles are stated formally and explicitly as rules that produce sentences (and, as we shall see, sentence structures), the grammar may be referred to as a **generative grammar.**

SYNTACTIC FACTORS AND GRAMMATICALITY

While both the speakers' internalized grammar and the descriptive grammar that the linguist prepares must contain a set of principles that produce the grammatical sentences of the language, it is not enough for rules to generate strings of words in the appropriate order. Certainly, the syntactic rules of English, for example, produce the grammatical sentence (a) and do not produce the ungrammatical (b) in (1).

170

> (1) a. The boy who sits next to me participated in a sensitivity session last week.
>
> b. *Participated a in sensitivity the session boy next who me to sits week last.

In addition to word order, however, sequences of words may be ungrammatical because of violations of syntactic rules involving proper use of word categories. Thus, in (2), sentence (a) is grammatical, but sentence (b) is not.

> (2) a. The cake is good.
>
> b. *The expire is good.

The problem with (b) is that the rules of English syntax require a particular category, or class, of word to follow *the* and to precede *is*; traditionally, this category has been assigned the label *noun*. In (a), *cake* is a noun, and so the sentence is grammatical, but in (b) *expire* is a verb. All speakers of English can identify the problem with the (b) sentence, whether or not they can cite the appropriate syntactic rule or refer to the word categories by the labels used by linguists. Part of our knowledge of English is that words are grouped into categories (sometimes called parts of speech). The words *cake, men, tree, governor, unicorn, auditorium, happiness, child,* and *peace* all belong together, as opposed to words like *expire, go, imitate, understand, see,* and *interrupt,* which constitute another group of words. Over the years, labels have been provided for such categories, and the first set represents nouns while the second contains verbs. The knowledge of word categories is one of the syntactic factors that enable speakers to produce and comprehend grammatical sentences, and, at the same time, to detect and to avoid producing ungrammatical sentences. Therefore, a description of English syntax must include an account of word categories.

As a brief aside, it may be observed that many schools devote a great deal of time to teaching parts of speech. However, no teacher has ever really taught a native speaker of English the parts of speech of his language. Even children of four know them, although their knowledge is not conscious. Children probably could not respond to the instruction ''list twenty-five English verbs,'' but they certainly have classified the words in their minds. They do not, for example, use a noun where a verb should be. In (3), no native speakers of English, no matter what their ages, would say sentence (b), although (a) might well occur.

> (3) a. The unicorns see the tree.
>
> b. *The unicorns tree the see.

The fact that we all use words correctly indicates that, unconsciously, everyone knows the parts of speech of his language. At most, a teacher or textbook can provide labels for talking about the classes of words we already know.

Another aspect of syntax involves the function that words (and phrases) serve in sentences. A word like *cat* belongs to the category of nouns in English, but that word can be related to other elements in a sentence in more than one way. Thus, in (4), *cat* serves as the subject in (a) but as the object in (b).

> (4) a. The cat chased the dog.
>
> b. The dog chased the cat.

Syntactic functions such as subject and object are actually relations among sentence elements, and a shift in relations will normally result in a shift in meaning. As with word categories, speakers of a language know the syntactic functions of sentence elements, regardless of whether they know the labels used to describe such functions.

Information about syntactic functions provides another basis by which the grammaticality of sentences can be specified. Consider the sentences in (5); (a) is grammatical, but (b) and (c) are not.

(5) a. At the annual banquet for retiring personnel, the company director distributed awards.
   b. *At the annual banquet for retiring personnel, the company director distributed.
   c. *At the annual banquet for retiring personnel, the company director distributed Mary.

Stated formally, we can say that the verb *distributed* requires the presence of a direct object (it is a transitive verb). Notice that this requirement does not refer simply to a word category. It would be insufficient to say that the verb *distributed* must be followed by a noun, for sentence (c) is ungrammatical despite the fact that the verb is followed by the noun *Mary*. Instead, this verb must be followed by a noun that can serve the particular function of direct object for this particular verb. The sentences in (6) show that some verbs are intransitive (occurring only without a direct object), as in (a) compared with (b), while other verbs may occur either with or without a direct object, as in (c) and (d).

(6) a. John complained. ← intransitive
   b. *John complained the policy.
   c. Sarah wrote. } with or w/out a direct object
   d. Sarah wrote a letter.

Thus, the category of verbs in English may be divided into subcategories depending on the possibility of co-occurrence with elements representing the syntactic function of direct object.

To further distinguish word categories from syntactic functions, we may note that within a single sentence, a word will represent only one category but it may represent more than one syntactic function. Thus, in (7), *women* is a noun but it functions as both the object of the verb *force* and the subject of the verb *leave*.

(7) The athletic director forced the women to leave the gym.

A descriptive grammar of English must include an account of the syntactic principles of word order, word categories, and syntactic functions, for this information constitutes part of the linguistic knowledge of speakers of the language.

JUDGMENTS

In addition to determining whether or not a sentence is grammatical, every speaker of English can make other judgments about sentences. Consider the following sentences:

(8) John was too far away to see.

(9) Careless soldiers and politicians are dangerous.

(10) Smoking cigars can be a nuisance.

Each sentence is an example of the linguistic phenomenon known as **ambiguity**—it can be understood in more than one way. In (8) either John cannot see or someone cannot see John; in (9) either all politicians are dangerous or only those who are careless (but, in either case, careless soldiers are dangerous); and in (10) the speaker could mean either that he finds it a nuisance to smoke cigars or that he is bothered by cigars that emit smoke, no matter who is smoking them. Although the ambiguity in these sentences may not have been apparent to all readers at first glance, once it is pointed out, no speaker of English would deny that it exists in these examples. On the other hand, there is no ambiguity in sentences (11), (12), and (13), and no speaker of English would ever claim that there was.

(11) John is too far away to be seen.

(12) Careless soldiers and dishonest politicians are dangerous.

(13) Cigarette smoking is dangerous to your health.

What is it that speakers of English know that enables them to determine when a sentence is ambiguous and, having decided that it was, to understand the different ways in which the ambiguous sentence can be interpreted? A grammar of English must account for such knowledge.

Paraphrase is the converse of ambiguity. In ambiguity, one sentence has more than one meaning; in paraphrase, two or more sentences have the same meaning. Consider the following examples:

(14) a. The man sitting on the edge of the roof threatened to jump.
    b. The man who was sitting on the edge of the roof threatened to jump.

(15) a. Put the bottle away after you've made the drinks.
    b. Put away the bottle after you've made the drinks.

(16) a. The strict teacher knows that the student did not write down the assignment.
    b. The teacher who is strict knows that the student did not write down the assignment.
    c. The strict teacher knows the student did not write down the assignment.
    d. The teacher who is strict knows the student did not write down the assignment.
    e. The strict teacher knows that the student did not write the assignment down.
    f. The teacher who is strict knows that the student did not write the assignment down.
    g. The strict teacher knows the student did not write the assignment down.
    h. The teacher who is strict knows the student did not write the assignment down.

For each set of sentences, (14), (15), and (16), speakers of English recognize that, despite superficial differences in the number or order of words, each sentence in the set has the same meaning as each other sentence in the set. Yet, there are other pairs of sentences where a difference in word order, for example, results not in paraphrase but in a totally different meaning, as in the sentences in (17):

(17) a. A child at the day care center bit the dietician.
     b. The dietician at the day care center bit a child.

Some differences in word order result in ungrammatical sentences. Compare (18) with (15).

(18) a. Come to the living room after you've made the drinks.
     b. *Come the living room to after you've made the drinks.

When do changes in word order lead to paraphrases? When do they result in a sentence with a different meaning? When is the result ungrammatical? More generally, what do speakers of English know that enables them to determine when sentences are paraphrases of one another? This, too, is knowledge of the grammar of their language, and, as such, it must be reflected in any description of that grammar.

Ambiguity and paraphrase are concepts involving the relationship between the syntactic form of a sentence and its meaning. Speakers of a language are also able to make other judgments about sentences with this same kind of relationship. For example, many English sentences are understood by people to include some element of meaning, even though the sentence itself does not actually contain a word or morpheme representing that meaning. Speakers of English all know that the subject of sentence (19) is 'you' but the word *you* does not appear in the sentence itself.

(19) Take this basket of cookies to Grandmother's house.

Similarly, in sentence (20), it is Sylvia who will probably win the game, but in (21) it is Marvin.

(20) Marvin expects Sylvia to win the game.

(21) Marvin expects to win the game.

The name *Sylvia* appears after the verb *expects* in (20), but the name *Marvin* does not appear in that position in (21). Yet any speaker of English knows who it is that is expected to win in both sentences. A linguistic description of English must account for this ability of speakers to understand concepts that do not actually occur in utterances.

Superficially, sentences (20) and (21) seem to differ somewhat in form, yet both express similar concepts. In fact, we might rephrase (21) into (22), which conveys the same meaning although in a form that is not grammatical in English.

(22) *Marvin expects Marvin to win the game.

Two sentences may differ in form and still be similar in the meanings they express. On the other hand, two sentences that seem similar in form may express very different kinds of meanings; the classic example of this situation in English is the following pair of sentences:

(23) John is eager to please.

(24) John is easy to please.

Both (23) and (24) appear to have the same form, but their meanings are quite distinct. Every native speaker of English knows that in (23) it is John who does the pleasing, while in (24) someone else pleases John. What do we know about the grammar of our language that leads to this judgment?

SUMMARY

All human beings who speak a language are potentially capable of producing or understanding any of the infinite number of grammatical sentences in their language. While the number of possible sentences is infinite, the knowledge that enables a person to cope with these sentences must be finite—a limited set of rules that generate all of the grammatical sentences. A grammar of a language consists of such rules. In addition to generating sentences, however, the grammar must account for the syntactic principles of word order, word categories, and syntactic functions; it must also reflect the knowledge underlying speakers' abilities to determine when a sentence is ungrammatical, ambiguous, a paraphrase of another sentence, or related in form or meaning to another sentence. In attempting to account for all of these aspects of syntactic knowledge, modern linguistics faces a challenging task. No complete and adequate grammar has ever been written for any language, but, in the last two decades, substantial progress has been made. In the following chapters, we will survey some of the results of linguistic research on English syntax. It should be noted, however, that although all of our examples come from English, much of what is said is also relevant to the study of other languages. Our attention in this section is restricted to English for two reasons: examples from other languages would be difficult to follow for those readers who do not know the languages, and the most extensive recent work in syntax has been devoted to English.

FURTHER EXPLORATION

The first three chapters in D. Terence Langendoen's book *The Study of Syntax* provide an excellent introduction to aspects of syntax that must be accounted for in a descriptive grammar. More technical discussion, concerned with the goals of linguistics, can be found in two sections of Noam Chomsky's work *Aspects of the Theory of Syntax:* "Generative Grammars as Theories of Linguistic Competence" and "Justification of Grammars" (both reprinted in Reibel and Schane 1969). Of particular interest for its discussion of grammaticality is Chomsky's article "Some Methodological Remarks on Generative Grammar" (Wilson 1967).

1. By using the procedures outlined in the first paragraph on productivity at the start of this chapter, expand the following sentence to a longer sentence at least 25 words in length:

His uncle designs lightbulbs for General Electric.

Could you continue to expand your sentence by repeated use of normal devices of sentence construction for English? If so, the sentence will continue to be grammatical. Does the sentence become stylistically awkward or cumbersome to produce or understand? What does this reveal about the difference between linguistic competence and linguistic performance with respect to syntax?

2. The following sentences are ambiguous; each has at least two distinct meanings. Identify the different meanings by rephrasing the sentences, as in this example:

Ambiguous sentence: That company's hiring policy discriminates against old men and women.

Meaning (1): That company's hiring policy discriminates against old men and old women.

Meaning (2): That company's hiring policy discriminates against women and old men.

(a) Jumping horses can be frightening.
(b) That duck is too hot to eat.
(c) The safety patrol members were ordered to stop jaywalking.
(d) Joan was surprised at Geraldine's appointment.
(e) The pilot decided on an airplane.
(f) Barbara fed her lion meat.

3. The following sentences are syntactically similar to those given above, yet they are not ambiguous. Explain why.

(a) Growling lions can be frightening.
(b) That vegetable is too hot to eat.
(c) The safety patrol members were ordered to wear hats.
(d) Joan was surprised at Geraldine's condescension.
(e) The pilot decided on a procedure.
(f) Barbara fed him lion meat.

4. Consider the following sentences. In each set, which sentences are paraphrases of one another? Which, if any, differ in meaning?

(a) 1. The flowers on the table are pretty.
   2. The flowers are pretty on the table.
   3. The flowers that are on the table are pretty.
(b) 1. That teacher is easy to please.
   2. To please that teacher is easy.
   3. It is easy to please that teacher.
(c) 1. That John disappeared surprised everyone.
   2. Everyone was surprised that John disappeared.
   3. What surprised everyone was that John disappeared.
   4. It surprised everyone that John disappeared.
   5. John's disappearance surprised everyone.
   6. What surprised everyone was John's disappearance.
   7. Everyone was surprised at John's disappearance.

CHAPTER 13131313131313131313131313131:

THE SURFACE
OF SYNTAX

In attempting to describe the speaker's knowledge of syntax, the simplest place to begin is with sentences and the observable aspects of their structure. Given any sentence in a language, we can note the kinds of units it contains and the basic principles of order and organization it reflects. **Surface structure,** which can be roughly described as those aspects of the syntax of a sentence that can be determined by investigating its written or spoken form, has constituted the basis for much of the traditional linguistic and nonlinguistic study of grammar. Labels for parts of speech describe some of the units that sentences contain, while sentence diagramming, or parsing as it is sometimes called, attempts to reflect the organization of the units that make up the sentence.

CONSTITUENT STRUCTURES

Every sentence in English, or in any other language, is a **construction.** Sentences are not merely random strings of words; rather, sentences are constructed of smaller units, known in linguistics as **constituents.** Sentence (1) is a construction consisting of the two constituents (2) and (3).

(1) Rosemary understood.

(2) Rosemary

(3) understood

In the case of sentence (1), the constituents of the construction are only two words. Usually, sentences are more complex than (1), and the construction can then be analyzed as consisting of constituents that are phrases, rather than words. The phrases themselves have constituents, which, depending on the complexity of the sentence, may be either smaller phrases or words. Native speakers of English know the **constituent structure** of the sentences in their language. They demonstrate this knowledge through their ability to diagram, or parse, sentences and to recognize correct parsings when these are presented. Consider, as an example, sentence (4):

(4) The father took the young children to the zoo.

If asked to divide this construction into two phrases, most people would agree that the constituents should be (5) and (6), traditionally called the subject and the predicate of the sentence.

(5) the father

(6) took the young children to the zoo

The constituents of the phrase (5) are the two words *the* and *father*. For (6) the situation is more complex, but, nevertheless, it is usually agreed that the constituents of the phrase (6) are (7), (8), and (9):

(7) took

(8) the young children

(9) to the zoo

(7) has only one constituent, and for (8) the constituents are the words of which the phrase is constructed. (9), however, can be divided into the constituent *to* and the phrase (10):

(10) the zoo

(10), in turn, consists of two constituents, *the* and *zoo*. Figure 13.1 represents the constituent structure of sentence (4) as we have just described it. Such diagrams are called **tree diagrams** (notice the resemblance to an inverted tree). They are also known as **phrase structure markers** (or simply as **phrase markers**) because they explicitly show the constituent, or phrase, structure of a sentence.

Figure 13.1 _____

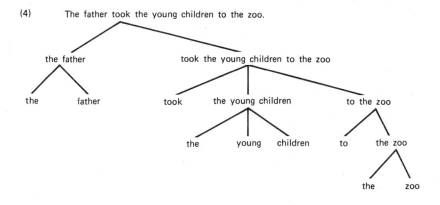

Every phrase marker consists of branches and nodes. A **branch** is a line; if you look down the line you find one of the constituents; if you look up the line you find the construction of which that constituent is a member. In Figure 13.1, *the young children* is a constituent of the construction *took the young children to the zoo*. A **node** is the point at which two or more branches meet; the branches leading down from the node show the constituents of the construction above. Nodes and branches, constructions and constituents, represent the natural dividing points in a sentence or phrase. In sentence (4), *father took* is not a construction, nor is it a constituent of any construction. In Figure 13.1, this is illustrated by the fact that there are no branches leading upward from these two words directly to the same node. This reflects the understanding of speakers of English that *father took* is not a natural grouping of words; no one asked to parse sentence (4) would divide it into the three constituents *the, father took,* and *the young children to the zoo*.

The particular pattern of constituent structure found in sentence (4) and illustrated by Figure 13.1 is not unique to this one sentence. Speakers of English can create any number of other sentences with the same constituent structure, for example:

(11) A strange man offered a green lion to the minister.

(12) The general sent the new recruits on a hike.

(13) The tornado broke our biggest windows in one minute.

(14) The piggle reflicked a tovish gunker at the barble.

Notice that sentence (14) is nonsense, but, nevertheless, it is grammatical in that it appears to follow the same organization of constituent structure as do the grammatical and more meaningful sentences (11), (12), and (13). On the other hand, sentence (15) is ungrammatical because the words, although familiar, are not arranged according to the principles of constituent structure in English.

(15) *Took the young children the father to the zoo.

Knowledge of the constituent structure of the sentences of their language enables speakers to distinguish sentences as ungrammatical or grammatical, depending on whether the sentences violate constituent structure patterns. This same knowledge accounts for the speakers' ability to judge some sentences as ambiguous. Consider again the example from Chapter 12:

(16) Careless soldiers and politicians are dangerous.

This sentence has two different meanings and, in this case, the two meanings are related to two possible constituent structure analyses. Figure 13.2 illustrates the two constituent structures of sentence (16). In the first tree diagram, *careless* is a constituent of a construction that includes both *soldiers* and *politicians;* thus, the meaning of the sentence with this structure is that both careless soldiers and careless politicians are dangerous. In the second tree diagram, however, *careless* is a constituent of a construction that includes only *soldiers,* and, therefore, the meaning of the sentence with this structure is that all politicians are dangerous (along with careless soldiers). The ambiguity of some sentences

Figure 13.2 _____

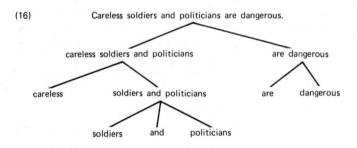

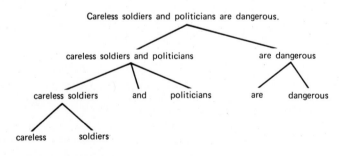

can be accounted for by the fact that each such sentence has two different surface structures. This is true not only for (16) but for many other sentences as well, for example:

(17) Tall boys and girls are needed to participate in the activities of the Square Dance Club.

(18) I want a new car and a boat or a sable coat.

It is not the case, however, that all ambiguous sentences have two different surface constituent structures. Recall the sentence from Chapter 12:

(19) Smoking cigars can be a nuisance.

The only possible tree structure for the phrase *smoking cigars* in this sentence is that given in Figure 13.3. There is more to the syntax of a language than surface structure constituents and constructions, a matter to which we will return in Chapter 14.

Another aspect of speakers' knowledge of syntax can be explained in part by constituent structure. Consider the following sentences:

(20) The bomb blew up the police station.

(21) The wind blew up the busy street.

Normally, we interpret (20) to mean that there was an explosion, whereas in (21) there was merely a strong breeze on a busy street. The two sentences look quite similar, but they have different constituent structures, as illustrated in Figure 13.4. Some readers might argue that these sentences are ambiguous (that the bomb was carried up past the police station by a wind or that the wind was so strong that it caused the street to explode). Although these interpretations are unusual, they are possible, and that, in itself, demonstrates that constituent structure plays an important role in how we interpret the meaning of the sentences of our language. As with ambiguity, not every pair of sentences that seem to have a similar structure but different meanings can be accounted for by differences in constituent structure. There is, for example, no way to explain the difference between the following sentences on the basis of constituent structure; their surface structure is the same.

(22) John is eager to please.

(23) John is easy to please.

Figure 13.3

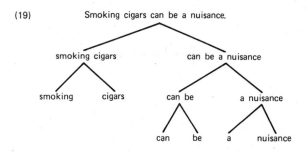

Figure 13.4

(20)

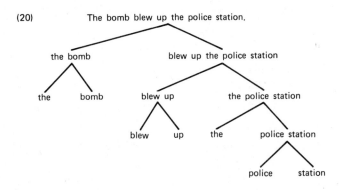

(21)

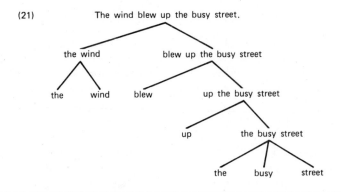

CONSTITUENT TYPES

Just as speakers of a language can recognize the constituent structure of a sentence, they can also identify various constituents as being of the same type. The very basic constituents—words—have well-known labels, for words are classified into the categories referred to as the various parts of speech. Thus, in Figure 13.4, the different constituents *bomb, police, station, wind,* and *street* are all of the same type—they are nouns.

The larger constituents can be labeled in much the same way as words. Using Figure 13.4 again, note the following constituents:

(24) the bomb

(25) the police station

(26) the wind

(27) the busy street

Each of these phrases contains a noun, and so phrases of this kind are called **noun phrases.** Other examples of noun phrases include the following:

(28) careless soldiers and politicians

(29) the father

(30) the young children

(31) the zoo

In spite of differences in the number of words in these phrases, speakers of English will recognize them all as basically similar. That they are alike is demonstrated by the fact that often one noun phrase can be substituted for another. Although the meaning of the sentence changes, the new sentence created by the substitution remains grammatically similar to the sentence that existed prior to the substitution. For example, we can substitute (27) for (25) in the following sentence:

(32) The police station was very noisy.

The result is the grammatically similar sentence:

(33) The busy street was very noisy.

Similarly, (28) can be substituted for (29) in the following sentence:

(34) The father shouted at the children.

The result is as follows:

(35) Careless soldiers and politicians shouted at the children.

It is almost always the case that when one constituent can be substituted for another, the two constituents are of the same type. Of course, there are instances when the meaning of one constituent prevents its substitution for another in a particular sentence. Consider, for example, *smoking cigars*. That this is a noun phrase is shown by the fact that *the father* is a noun phrase and *the father* can be substituted for *smoking cigars* in the sentence:

(36) Smoking cigars can be dangerous.

That is, one can say the following:

(37) The father can be dangerous.

The fact that *smoking cigars* cannot be substituted for *the father* in sentences like (34) is due to meaning and does not negate the fact that *smoking cigars* is a noun phrase.

In addition to noun phrases, several other constituent types occur frequently in English sentences. These include **verb phrases,** which are constructions that contain a verb, and **prepositional phrases,** constructions containing a preposition. Examples of verb phrases are as follows:

(38) took the young children to the zoo

(39) blew up the police station

(40) broke our biggest windows

(41) understood

Note that the verb phrase (41) consists solely of a verb. The reason that (41) must be considered a verb phrase, as well as a verb, is that it can be substituted for other verb phrases. Compare the following:

(42) Rosemary understood.

(43) The father took the young children to the zoo.

(44) The father understood.

(45) Rosemary took the young children to the zoo.

Sentences (42)-(45) also illustrate the fact that a noun phrase can consist of just a single noun, in this case, *Rosemary*.

By providing all instances of a particular constituent type with the same label, a description of surface structure reflects the fact that speakers of the language recognize categories of constituents, just as they recognize categories of words. A further advantage of labeling constituent types is that, by using labels at the nodes of tree diagrams rather than the particular words involved, tree diagrams can show explicitly when two sentences have identical constituent structures. Figure 13.5 shows the surface structure of sentence (4), using labels for constituent types in place of the words that appear in the constituents. The labels used in such trees have the following meanings:

S	Sentence
NP	Noun Phrase
VP	Verb Phrase
PP	Prepositional Phrase
ART	Article
ADJ	Adjective
N	Noun
V	Verb
PART	Particle
P	Preposition

Compare Figure 13.5 with Figure 13.1. Both show the same constituent structure for the sentence, but Figure 13.5 also reflects certain generalizations. One generalization is that, except for the words at the bottom of each lowest branch, the surface structure depicted in Figure 13.5 is the same for sentence (4) and sentences like (11), (12), and (13). Through the use of labels for constituent types, tree diagrams can show why it is that speakers of English recognize (4), (11), (12), and (13) as grammatically similar sentences; except for the words, all have the same structure. Labeled tree diagrams can also make explicit the differences in the surface structure of sentences. Figure 13.6 (p. 186) is a revised version of Figure 13.4. The differences in the structure of the two sentences is made quite clear.

Although we can hear sentences or see them in writing, the constituent structure itself is not directly observable. There are, for example, no detectable pauses in speech that coincide perfectly with the boundaries between each constituent of a sentence. Constituent

Figure 13.5

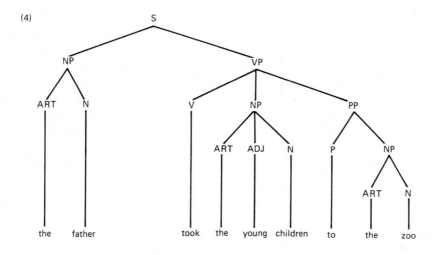

structure, therefore, must be determined by investigating the judgments of native speakers, attempting substitutions, and using other research methods. It is not surprising that speakers will occasionally disagree about the analysis of some particular sentence or will prefer different labels for some constituents. For example, in Figure 13.6, we have analyzed *police station* as a construction, labeled N, consisting of two constituents, both of which are also Ns. On the other hand, the string of words *busy street* in sentence (21) is not itself a construction, although it forms part of the NP *the busy street; busy* and *street* are simply two of the constituents of this construction, the former an adjective, the latter a noun. This analysis seems to be in accord with the judgments of most speakers of English, but it could also be argued that both *police station* and *busy street* should be analyzed in the same way. Such matters cannot be decided quickly and are still unresolved for many structures and constituent types. Nevertheless, tree diagrams do provide some insight into the knowledge speakers of English have about the syntax of their language.

CONSTITUENT STRUCTURE RULES

The tree diagrams represent the constituent structure and the constituent types in the surface structure of sentences. Up to this point, we have presented several diagrams, and discussed some of the judgments native speakers can make about the surface structures of English sentences. What remains to be done, however, is the most important aspect of the study of syntax—to describe the knowledge that enables speakers to make such judgments.

Figure 13.6

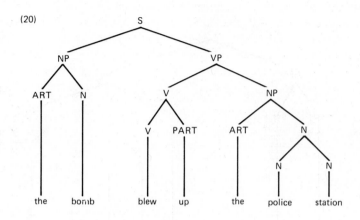

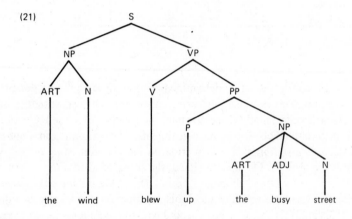

NOTE: In the tree diagram for sentence (20), the construction *blew up* is represented as a V; that is, it is a complex verb consisting of the simple verb *blew* and the particle *up*. This analysis is supported by the fact that verb-particle constructions function much like simple verbs. Note, for example, that if we attempt to substitute a single word for *blew up*, the only type of word we can substitute is a verb, as in *The bomb destroyed the police station.*

Native speakers of English can not only determine the constituent structure of a sentence; they also know when certain strings of words do not follow the permitted structures, that is, they know when a sentence is ungrammatical. Speakers also construct sentences with acceptable constituent structures whenever they speak or write. Similarly, they analyze sentences they hear or read, for, as we have seen, the meaning of a sentence depends in part on its constituent structure. Underlying all of these abilities is the speakers' unconscious knowledge of a set of rules specifying the kinds of constituent structures that are permitted in English. Like constituent structure itself, these rules cannot be observed, nor can one ask native speakers what they are since they are almost always unaware that they even exist. Nevertheless, if we carefully examine the tree diagrams for a large number of English sentences, certain generalizations about constituent structure become apparent. For example, a large number of sentences in our language are composed of two major constituents, a noun phrase and a verb phrase; these two constituents must be arranged in a particular order if a sentence is to be grammatical. This generalization about the surface structure of many English sentences can be expressed in the form of a **constituent structure rule** (also called a **phrase structure rule**):

    (46) S → NP VP

The rule states that the constituents of a sentence (S) are a noun phrase (NP) followed by a verb phrase (VP).

Further examination of tree diagrams reveals other rules that reflect generalizations about the word order and constituent structure organization of the surface structures of English sentences. A noun phrase, for example, may consist of an article and a noun, and it is possible that an adjective may occur between these two constituents. Furthermore, as we have seen, a noun phrase may contain only a noun.

    (47) NP → (ART) (ADJ) N

The parentheses in rule (47) indicate that the enclosed elements are optional; that is, a noun phrase must contain a noun but not necessarily an article, an adjective, or both of these constituents. Thus, a single noun can be a noun phrase, but a noun phrase can also consist of a noun preceded by an article [as in (48)] or of a noun preceded by both an article and an adjective [as in (49)].

    (48) the river
    (49) the polluted river

In fact, a noun phrase can consist of an adjective and a noun without an article, as in phrases such as *silly Mary, tall boys,* and *polluted rivers*.

Verb phrases can also be described by a constituent structure rule.

    (50) VP → V (NP) (PP)

The different possible structures of a verb phrase, as described by rule (50), occur in sentences such as the following:

    (51) The new baby *cried.* (V)
    (52) Don *bought the old car.* (V NP)
    (53) The students from Professor Meyer's German class *flew to Europe.* (V PP)
    (54) Sandy *poured the cereal on her head.* (V NP PP)

The constituent structure of prepositional phrases is described by rule (55):

    (55) PP → P NP

Examples of prepositional phrases occur in (53) and (54).

Although these four rules do not account for all possible surface structures in English, they are very definitely generalizations that describe a large number of sentences. If we hypothesize that underlying the speaker's ability to produce, understand, and judge sentences is knowledge of the kind described by rules like (46), (47), (50), and (55), then we can account for some of the speaker's linguistic abilities. Of course, it would be much too strong to claim that speakers of English actually possess any of the rules that a linguist can write. We know nothing about what actually goes on in the brain with regard to language. What can be said, however, is that the kind of knowledge that speakers have is reflected in such rules.

Constituent structure rules describe part of the syntax of English; therefore, we will say that they are part of the grammar of this language. They provide a description of the structure of many sentences, and they do so by generating, or producing, sentences. Any sentence produced by a grammar is said to be grammatical insofar as that grammar is concerned. The definitive grammar of a language would generate all of those sentences that native speakers agree are grammatical; it would not generate any sentences speakers consider ungrammatical. Of course, rules (46), (47), (50), and (55) do not constitute the complete grammar of English. Figure 13.7 illustrates the way in which this segment of a grammar generates sentences. For convenience, the constituent structure rules are summarized under (56):

(56)

a.	S	→	NP VP
b.	NP	→	(ART) (ADJ) N
c.	VP	→	V (NP) (PP)
d.	PP	→	P NP

not all optional

In Figure 13.7, we begin with S, the construction to be generated. Rule (56a) applies producing the second line of the structure. Now both rule (56b) and rule (56c) apply. It makes no difference which is applied first, for constituents must be provided for both NP and VP. In the application of both of these rules there is some choice. Our grammar can generate the constituents of NP as either ART ADJ N, or as ART N, or as ADJ N, or simply as N. In Figure 13.7, the first has been selected, but any of the latter could have been, in which case the subject of the sentence would have had a different structure. Similarly, there are options in rule (56c); in Figure 13.7, all of the possible constituents of VP were selected. At this point, the constituent structure of the subject NP and the VP has been generated. The VP itself contains NP so rule (56b) is again applicable. It provides constituents for the direct object. VP also contains PP. Rule (56d) produces the constituents of PP, and since one of these is NP, rule (56b) applies again. Constituent structure rules apply until all of the constructions to the left of the arrows have been provided with constituents. In our example, we have now reached that point. We do not yet have a sentence, only the constituent structure for a number of sentences. To produce an actual sentence, lexical items must be drawn from the lexicon, subjected to the rules of word formation, and then the resulting words must be inserted at the bottom of each lowest branch on the tree.

The constituent structure rules (56) do more than produce sentences; at the same time

Figure 13.7 _____

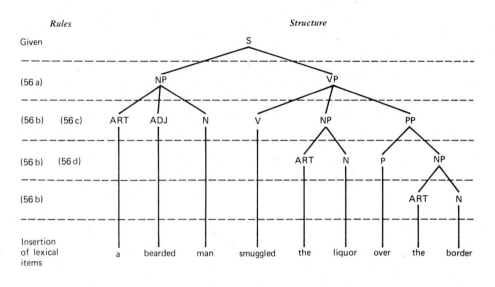

that they generate a sentence, they also provide it with a **structural description**—the constituent structure and the constituent types of which the sentence is composed. In Figure 13.7, we generated a sentence and automatically created the labeled tree diagram for that sentence. Just as speakers of English can produce sentences and recognize the constituent structure and constituent types in sentences, so the rules also produce sentences with this information about their structure. Since the speakers and the rules have the same ability, we can say that the rules and the speakers' knowledge are equivalent. Thus, the rules explain, in part, the speakers' knowledge of the grammar of their language.

Syntactic functions, such as subject and direct object, are not expressed directly by constituent structure rules. However, since these functions are, in essence, relationships among various constituent categories of a sentence, the relationships can be identified in terms of the position of a category in the tree structures produced by the constituent structure rules. Thus, the subject of a sentence can be defined as the NP with a single branch leading upward directly to the node S (with no other node or branch intervening). In Figure 13.7, for example, the subject of the sentence is the NP *a bearded man*. In parallel fashion, a direct object can be defined as the NP with a single branch leading upward directly to the node VP. Therefore, in Figure 13.7, the direct object is the NP *the liquor*. Notice in that figure that the NP *the border* is not a direct object; the upward branch from this NP does not lead directly to VP but rather to the node PP; thus, the NP *the border* has the syntactic function of object of a preposition. Such definitions appear to work well for syntactic functions in simple sentences; we will return to this topic later with reference to more complex sentences.

SUMMARY

The surface structure of a sentence can be represented in the form of a labeled tree diagram, which shows the constituent structure of the sentence along with the constituent types which make up that structure. Speakers of a language know the constituent structure and the constituent types in the sentences of their language. They use this knowledge in determining whether some sentences are grammatical, ambiguous, or similar to one another, as well as in producing and understanding sentences. In part, the speakers' knowledge of syntax can be accounted for by a set of constituent structure rules, which generate sentences and provide those sentences with structural descriptions. The constituent structure rules discussed in this chapter reflect only a small part of the English speakers' knowledge of syntax. Other aspects of that knowledge are discussed in the following chapters, but even that discussion is incomplete for three reasons: (1) no complete description of the syntax of any language has ever been compiled; (2) even the limited descriptions that do exist for English are tentative hypotheses, not positive, definitive statements of fact; (3) a detailed treatment of English syntax is beyond the scope of this textbook.

FURTHER EXPLORATION

Constituent structure is discussed in most introductory syntax texts; see, for example: Chapter 4 in *An Introduction to Linguistics* by Bruce L. Liles or Chapters 2 and 3 in *The New English Grammar: A Descriptive Introduction* by N. R. Cattell. In the following references, discussion of constituent structure follows certain material that is introduced here in the next two chapters. Readers, therefore, may wish to wait until the end of Chapter 15 before consulting the following references; alternatively, they should read the opening chapters of these works, as well as the material devoted specifically to constituent structure: Chapters 6, 7, 8, and 10 of *English Transformational Grammar* by Roderick A. Jacobs and Peter S. Rosenbaum; Chapter 2 of *An Introduction to the Principles of Transformational Syntax* by Adrian Akmajian and Frank Heny.

Of historical interest, but highly formal and difficult, are Chapters 4 and 5 of *Syntactic Structures* by Noam Chomsky. Also relevant, but technical, is Paul Postal's book *Constituent Structure: A Study of Contemporary Models of Syntactic Description*.

1. Consider again sentences (20) and (21) and Figure 13.6. In sentence (20), *up* has been labeled a particle and analyzed as a constituent of the node V, while in (21), *up* is considered a preposition and a constituent of the construction PP. The decisions are based on several types of evidence: the meanings involved, the substitution possibilities (mentioned in the note to Figure 13.6), and, most importantly, the syntactic behavior of the elements in question. For example, with a particle, it is usually possible to move the particle from between the verb and the following noun phrase to a position after the noun phrase and still retain the same meaning as well as the grammaticality of the sentence:

    (a) The bomb blew up the police station.
    (b) The bomb blew the police station up.

This is not possible with a preposition; either the new sentence is ungrammatical or else the meaning changes (with the latter, this indicates that the word operates as both a particle and a preposition).

    (c) The wind blew up the busy street.
    (d) The wind blew the busy street up.

Note that sentence (c), while normally understood as referring to the direction of the wind, is ambiguous; it can also be interpreted as referring to an explosion. Thus, in (c), *up* can be taken as either a preposition or a particle. Sentence (d) can mean only that there was an explosion; in (d), *up* is a particle. Now consider an unambiguous case:

    (e) The boy walked up the stairs.

Here, we must analyze *up* as a preposition (and only a preposition, not as a particle) since the movement of *up* results in the ungrammatical sentence (f).

    (f) *The boy walked the stairs up.

Use this movement test to determine whether the italicized word in each of the following sentences is a particle or a preposition. Note that some sentences may be ambiguous, with the italicized word behaving both as a particle and a preposition. In conducting this analysis, consider the normal, usual meanings of the sentences and avoid bizarre meanings such as the exploding wind example above.

    (i)   The man ran *up* a large bill.
    (ii)   The dog ran *up* a large hill.
    (iii) The mechanic stared *down* the pipe.
    (iv) The speaker stared *down* his opponent.
    (v)   The buyer looked *over* the horses.
    (vi) The horses looked *over* the fence.
    (vii) Susan tore *up* her report card.
    (viii) Jonah looked *around* the room.

2. Use the constituent structure rules given in (56), as well as your knowledge of the lexicon and rules of word formation of English, to generate the following sentences. Produce diagrams like the one given in Figure 13.7.

    (a) The counselor referred the best students to Harvard.
    (b) Little Jack Horner sat in a corner. [*consider the name* Jack Horner *as a single noun*]

(c) An enormous collie chased a tiny kitten through the fields.

(d) The pharmacist prepared the prescription.

(e) Nixon resigned.

3. The following are grammatical sentences of English, but they cannot be generated by the set of constituent structure rules in (56). For each sentence, identify the portion, or portions, that cannot be produced by these rules. For example, the sentence

John can read.

cannot be produced because the rules make no provision for producing a word like *can* (sometimes called a modal auxiliary) between the NP and the V.

(a) Take this basket to Grandmother's house.

(b) The man who came to dinner married Susan yesterday.

(c) Is Muriel at the library?

(d) Rick likes beer and pretzels.

(e) I think Marvin wants an apple.

(f) The reporter brought his article on substance abuse in to the editor's conference room.

CHAPTER 141414141414141414141414141<

DEEP STRUCTURE AND TRANSFOR- MATIONS

The surface structure of a sentence consists of its concrete syntactic form—the form in which constituents occur in actual utterances. But there is more to the syntax of a language than surface structure. The surface organization and arrangement of constituents are the result of complex processes that convert meanings into expressions, and all of these processes must be investigated in the study of syntax.

When people speak, they start out with a set of concepts they wish to express; they then convert these abstract concepts into a form suitable for expression in speech. When people listen, they hear the sounds produced by another; they then attempt to convert those sounds into the meanings the speaker has tried to convey. The same linking of expression and meaning takes place in writing or reading, except that the concrete form of expression is writing rather than sound. The syntactic system of a language is the set of principles that link the meaning of sentences with the form in which they are expressed.

Meaning originates in the mind, and syntax is the study of the relationships between meaning and form. The mind is not directly observable, so there is no reason to assume that every aspect of syntax will be directly observable. The surface structure of a sentence is only the form in which that sentence is expressed. By examining surface structure, one investigates only a single side of syntax. The other side, pertaining to meaning rather than to surface form, is not available for direct examination. Yet, it does exist, for, unless the study of syntax involves meaning as well as form, there is no way to explain how speakers of a language understand the meanings of sentences.

SYNTACTIC RELATIONSHIPS

A description of the syntax of a language must account for relationships among sentences and for the general principles of sentence formation in a language. Consider the following pairs:

(1) a. He will go home.
b. He will go home, won't he?
(2) a. She can read.
b. She can read, can't she?
(3) a. They should leave.
b. They should leave, shouldn't they?

There is a general principle of English syntax that allows speakers to form the (b) sentences, ending with what is called a tag question, given the (a) sentences, which are simple statements. (Reference to a full description of this principle is provided in "Further Exploration.") Informally, the principle says: form a tag question by placing the following elements, in the order described, at the end of the statement: the modal auxiliary of the statement (here, *will, can,* or *should*), the negative suffix *n't,* and the pronoun that is the subject of the statement (here, *he, she,* or *they*).*

Now consider

(4) a. Read the book!
b. Read the book, won't you?

Here, there is a tag question in (b), but by what principle was it formed? The (a) sentence does not contain a modal auxiliary nor does it have a subject, yet the tag portion in (4b) looks just like the tags in the (b) sentences of (1), (2), and (3). If analysis of tag questions is restricted to the surface structure of sentences, then there must be two distinct principles of tag formation in English—one for sentences such as (1)–(3) and another for sentences such as (4).

If there were no other way to describe the formation of tag questions, the linguist would have to be content with presenting such an inefficient grammar and with the lack of a single, general explanation of the form of tag questions. It is possible, however, to retain the one general explanation presented for tag formation in (1)–(3) if we hypothesize that (4a) is really a reduced version of a sentence like (5a).

(5) a. You will read the book!

*Note: *won't* is merely a slightly irregular negative form of *will*.

Both (4a) and (5a) are imperatives, or commands, although (5a) is more forceful and common primarily in contexts such as military training. Furthermore, (4a) and (5a) have the same meaning. Notice that a tag question can be formed from (5a) in exactly the same way as the tag was formed above for (1a). (5b) is simply the result of placing, after the original imperative, the modal auxiliary and the negative suffix (which combine to yield *won't*) and the pronoun that is the subject of (5a).

(5) b. You will read the book, won't you?

Notice also that the tag in (5b) is identical to the tag in (4b). Indeed, any positive imperative like (4a) can have the tag *won't you,* and any positive imperative like (4a) can be rephrased as a longer imperative like (5a) beginning with the subject pronoun *you* and the modal auxiliary *will*. Thus, two imperative sentences, different at the level of surface structure, are related to one another, and the tag questions that appear on both types of imperatives are related to the tag questions that appear with declarative sentences (statements). It would be difficult to explain these relationships through general principles about English syntax if those principles referred solely to surface structures. However, if we consider sentences like (4a) to be derived from (or based on) imperatives like (5a), we not only explain the relationship between (4a) and (5a), but we can also retain the single general principle that describes the formation of tag questions for both statements and imperatives. This is illustrated in Figure 14.1.

Figure 14.1 _____

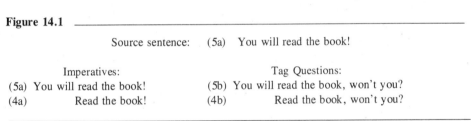

Source sentence: (5a)   You will read the book!

Imperatives:		Tag Questions:	
(5a)	You will read the book!	(5b)	You will read the book, won't you?
(4a)	Read the book!	(4b)	Read the book, won't you?

_____

The hypothesis that some surface structures are derived, or created from, other structures is the basis of the approach to linguistic description known as transformational grammar. The original, or source, structures are referred to variously as **deep structures, underlying structures,** or **remote structures.** (Here, we will use the term *deep structure.*) Some deep structures appear to be similar (or even identical) to surface structures, as in the simple case here where (5a) is posited as the deep structure of (5a), (4a), (5b), and (4b); see Figure 14.1. As will be shown later, however, it is usually necessary to hypothesize rather abstract deep structures that are further removed from actually occurring sentences.

The syntactic rules, or principles, that convert the source, deep structures into actual, surface structures are known as **transformations** (or **transformational rules**). These rules also serve to identify relationships among sentences. Thus, there is apparently a transformation in English that can operate to reduce the sentence structure of (5a) to that of (4a) by deleting (or, in essence, erasing) the subject and modal auxiliary, *you will*. Another transformation relates simple statements and imperatives, such as those in the (a)

195

sentences of (1)–(5), to the corresponding tag question structures, such as the (b) sentences of (1)–(5). This transformation is simply a reflection of the general principle for tag formation cited earlier.

Once it has been established that surface structures are created from deep structures, the role of the constituent structure rules (discussed in the last chapter) is altered. As we will see here and in Chapter 15, constituent structure rules are most effectively used in a grammatical description to produce deep (not surface) structures. These deep structures then may be affected by various transformations and the final result is the surface structures of sentences.

As noted in Chapter 13, most of the work of twentieth-century structural linguists was concentrated on surface structure. The analysis of surface structure, including parts of speech, other constituent types, and constituent structure, has been carried on since at least the fifth century B.C. when Greek philosophers were engaged in the study of language. But deep structure also has been investigated in traditional linguistics. The Modistae and the rationalist philosophers recognized the importance of deep structure, and many of their theories and analyses of language closely resemble those of contemporary transformational linguistics. The insights of these early philosophers were ignored during the first half of the twentieth century by American philosophers, psychologists, and linguists. It has been only in the last two decades that students of language have returned to the study of deep structure and the rules that relate it to surface structure. This is a relatively short period of modern investigation, particularly for a subject as complex and abstract as deep structure. It is not surprising, therefore, that little can be said with certainty about the deep structure of any sentence. Yet, by investigating the relationships among sentences, as well as their meanings and surface forms, it is possible to arrive at some tentative conclusions about the nature of deep structures and the kinds of transformations that link them to surface forms.

In the following material, we begin with a consideration of how the notions of deep structure and transformations may be used to explain the relationship between the form and the meaning of sentences. Later in the chapter, we return to a discussion of imperatives in order to provide additional evidence that surface structure alone does not permit the explanation of the syntactic relationships among sentences or the most general statements of syntactic principles. It should be observed that imperatives are discussed here only as a representative example of the types of evidence linguists use in determining the deep structures and transformations of a language; other sentence structures would also provide similar conclusions, and readers interested in such additional evidence will find references in "Further Exploration" at the end of this chapter.

PARAPHRASE

Most transformational linguists maintain that the essential properties of the meaning of a sentence are represented in the deep structure of that sentence. From this hypothesis, it follows that any set of sentences having the same meaning must have the same deep structure, despite any differences in their surface structure. By attributing to the speakers of a language the knowledge of the deep structures of sentences, we can explain how it is that speakers recognize when two or more sentences are paraphrases of one another. As an example, consider again the sentences of (6) which were given as examples of paraphrase in Chapter 12:

(6) a. Put the bottle away after you've made the drinks.
b. Put away the bottle after you've made the drinks.

The constituent structure of the surface form of these sentences is different. In (a) a noun phrase appears between the verb *put* and the particle *away;* in (b) the particle immediately follows the verb. In spite of this difference in form, every speaker of English knows that the meaning of (a) is identical to the meaning of (b). Therefore, the deep structure must be the same for the two sentences. Although we do not know exactly what this structure is, certain features of it are reasonably clear. It seems that, in the deep structure, *put away* forms a constituent, as it does in sentence (b). This phrase is a complex verb, consisting of a verb and a particle. We know that *put away* is a verb because, if we were to substitute just one word for the expression, the word we substituted would have to be a verb, for example, *smash* or *discard.*

Given that the deep structure underlying both sentence (a) and sentence (b) contains a phrase *put away the bottle,* how does this phrase become changed to the surface form of sentence (a)? The answer lies in the transformational rules that convert deep structures to surface structures. There is, in English, a syntactic transformation that converts deep structures of the form (I) to surface structures of the form (II); see Figure 14.2. The structure underlying sentence (6a), that is, (I), undergoes this transformation, and the result is sentence (6a). However, the rule is generally optional.* The structure (I), underlying both (6a) and (6b), need not undergo the transformation; if it does not, then the surface expression of this meaning will have the form of sentence (6b). The combination of a single deep structure and an optional transformation results in two different surface forms, both with the same meaning. Thus, a grammar in which the sentences of a

---

*It is obligatory (must be applied) when the object NP is a pronoun, as illustrated by the nongramaticality of sentence (a) and the grammaticality of (b):
(a) *Call up her when you arrive.
(b) Call her up when you arrive.

Figure 14.2

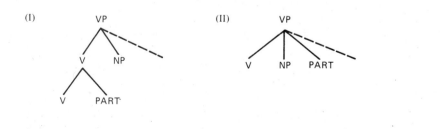

language are described in terms of deep structures and transformations, as well as surface structures, can account for the speaker's knowledge of paraphrases. Any sentences sharing the same deep structure will be paraphrases of one another. The differences in their surface structures are produced by transformations.

Transformations do not convert one sentence to another; rather, they convert one structure to another. The distinction is important, for transformations are generalizations about the syntax of a language. The transformation discussed for the phrase *put away* applies not only to this specific phrase but to any phrase with structure (I). Many sets of paraphrases in English can be accounted for by this one rule, for example:

(7) a. That monopolist took over our family business.
    b. That monopolist took our family business over.

(8) a. The ROTC cadets shouted down the radical speaker.
    b. The ROTC cadets shouted the radical speaker down.

Notice that the transformation that moves particles, or the Particle Movement Transformation as we shall call it, applies only to structures like (I). In other words, transformations apply only in the case of particular structural descriptions provided by the tree diagrams. If a structural description is like that of (I), containing a complex verb made up of a verb and a particle with a following noun phrase, the Particle Movement Transformation can be applied. On the other hand, if we return to the sentence

(9) The wind blew up the busy street.

and the associated structural description provided for this sentence in Figure 13.6, we can see that (9) does not have the same structural description as that required by the Particle Movement Transformation. (9) contains a preposition, not a particle; therefore, the Particle Movement Transformation does not apply to (9) or to other sentences like it. Thus, the grammar does not generate a sentence like (10) with the meaning 'the wind traveled along the busy street':

(10) *The wind blew the busy street up.

The only way in which (10) could be considered grammatical is if it did mean 'exploded', in which case its deep structure would be similar to that illustrated for sentence (20) in Figure 13.6. Any sentence not generated by the grammar is, by definition, ungrammatical. The Particle Movement Transformation does not apply to the structures underlying the sentence in (11a), and, therefore, the sentence in (11b) is ungrammatical.

(11) a. When Charlie looked out the window, there was a dilapidated ambulance parked across the street.
     b. *When Charlie looked the window out, there was a dilapidated ambulance parked the street across.

Thus, a grammar containing the Particle Movement Transformation accounts not only for the ability of speakers to recognize paraphrases but also for their ability to recognize certain ungrammatical sentences.

"MISSING" MEANINGS

Earlier, we presented some syntactic evidence about the need for deep structures and transformations to account for syntactic properties of imperatives and tag questions. It was determined that all imperatives contain *you will* in their deep structures. The *you,* of course, is produced by the constituent structure rules that serve to generate the subject noun phrases of all sentences [see (56) in Chapter 13]. However, our original constituent structure rules did not produce modal auxiliaries and now must be modified to do so. (Words normally classified as modal auxiliaries are *will, would, shall, should, can, could, may, might,* and *must.*) Sentences containing a modal auxiliary always contain a main verb as well, as in the sentences of (12) where the modal auxiliary appears in italic print.

(12) a. You *may* leave the room.
  b. The buyer *must* pay cash at that store.
  c. The state *should* prosecute every official who accepts a bribe.

Therefore, a new constituent, AUX (for auxiliary), should be added to the constituent structure rules of (56) in Chapter 13 so that our descriptive grammar of English will generate sentences containing modal auxiliaries. Most such grammars accomplish this by changing rule (56a), S → NP VP, to S → NP (AUX) VP. The AUX is an optional constituent in this analysis since there are many sentences that lack an auxiliary in their surface form.

(13) a. John understood the question.
  b. The Mets won their final game.
  c. The mailman lost my letter.
  d. A loud noise disrupted the meeting.

We have demonstrated the syntactic need for positing *you* and *will* in the deep structures of imperatives, and we have also indicated how these elements can be generated by the constituent structure rules. Now observe that the *you* of imperatives also accounts for an important aspect of meaning.

In Chapter 12, we raised the question of how speakers understand that some sentences include certain elements of meaning not actually present in the surface structures of the sentences. Now that we are aware of the existence of deep structures and transformations, we can offer an answer to this question. Consider one of the examples cited earlier:

(14) a. Take this basket of cookies to Grandmother's house!

The subject of the sentence is not expressed in its surface form, but every speaker of English knows that the subject is *you* (and not *I, they, the cat,* or *Harry*). This knowledge can be explained by the hypothesis that (14a) has a deep structure which actually contains *you* as its subject. An optional transformation may operate on this underlying structure to delete *you* (along with the modal auxiliary *will* discussed above). The rule is optional, a fact that explains why sentence (14b) is a possible paraphrase of (14a).

(14) b. You will take this basket of cookies to Grandmother's house!

Called the Imperative Transformation, this rule applies only to underlying structures with the form (III) in Figure 14.3. Thus, the (a) sentences of (15), which do not have structures

Figure 14.3

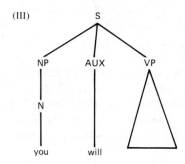

(III)

Note: The triangle under the node VP is used to show that although the verb phrase does have constituents, they are not relevant to the discussion.

like (III), cannot be the deep structures for the surface imperatives of the (b) sentences. Indeed, the corresponding (a) and (b) sentences have different meanings, and some of the (b) sentences are not even grammatical.

(15) a. 1. Harry will study.
      2. That criminal should go to jail.
      3. You might want to carry the books.
      4. I can understand that.
   b. 1. Study!
      2. Go to jail!
      3. *Want to carry the books!
      4. *Understand that!

Knowledge of the deep structure of sentences along with knowledge of the Imperative Transformation accounts for the fact that speakers of English realize that the subject of all imperative sentences is always *you,* even though this particular word may not appear in the surface structure of the imperatives.

    Another transformation that deletes constituents present in the deep structure of sentences is known as the Equi NP Deletion Transformation (or, in its full form, Equivalent Noun Phrase Deletion Transformation). Let us see why this rule is necessary. Recall the sentences from Chapter 12, repeated here as (16) and (17):

(16) Marvin expects Sylvia to win the game.

(17) Marvin expects to win the game.

In both of these sentences, *expects* is the main verb, but *win* is also a verb. In sentence (16) the subject of the verb *win* is *Sylvia;* in (17) the subject of *win* is *Marvin*. This fact would not be disputed by any native speaker of English, although, in the surface structure of (17), *Marvin* appears only as the subject of *expects,* just as it does in sentence (16). How, then, do we know that, in (17), *Marvin* is also the subject of *win?* The explanation again lies in the deep structure rather than at the surface. Underlying (17) is a structure in which *Marvin* appears as the subject of *win*. Were it not for the Equi NP Deletion Transformation, this underlying structure would occur with the surface form (18):

(18) *Marvin expects Marvin to win the game.

This form is ungrammatical as a surface structure in English. *Marvin* must be present as the subject of *win* in the deep structure of (17) in order to account for the fact that speakers of English know that (17) has the meaning reflected in (18). Yet, (18) is ungrammatical; *Marvin* cannot appear as the subject of *win* in the surface structure. Therefore, an obligatory transformation must be applied to convert the deep structure to a grammatical surface structure. This is the Equi NP Deletion Transformation, which, under certain conditions that need not concern us here, deletes the second occurrence of a noun phrase in a sentence containing two verbs, the subject of the first verb being the same as the subject of the second verb. Underlying (17) is a structure with two verbs, *expects* and *win*. The subjects of these two verbs are identical, and, therefore, the second subject noun phrase, *Marvin,* is deleted. It is the obligatory Equi NP Deletion Transformation that accounts for the fact that sentence (a) in each of the following sets is ungrammatical, even though it represents the meaning in the grammatical sentence (b).

(19) a. *I want I to go to New York tomorrow.
    b. I want to go to New York tomorrow.

(20) a. *The Emperor of France preferred the Emperor of France to drink wine instead of water.
    b. The Emperor of France preferred to drink wine instead of water.

(21) a. *Aunt Sally hopes Aunt Sally to win the state lottery so that she can afford to take parachuting lessons.
    b. Aunt Sally hopes to win the state lottery so that she can afford to take parachuting lessons.

Not all "missing" meanings involve the deletion by a transformation of some element present in the deep structure of a sentence. Consider the following sentences:

(22) When he returned home, Mr. Johnson discovered that someone had written dirty words on the front door.

(23) My secretary isn't here yet, and I don't understand why she can't be on time just once.

In (22), who returned home? In (23), who can't be on time? In both cases, the answer is obvious, but note that it is not actually present in the surface form of the sentences. That is, sentence (22) does not have the surface form (24), nor does sentence (23) have the surface form (25). In fact, (24) is ungrammatical, and most speakers agree that (25) is, also.

(24) *When Mr. Johnson returned home, Mr. Johnson discovered that someone had written dirty words on the front door.

(25) *My secretary isn't here yet, and I don't understand why my secretary can't be on time just once.

Yet, (24) and (25) explicitly convey who returned and who can't be on time. The pronouns *he* in (22) and *she* in (23) are apparently surface substitutes for the underlying noun phrases *Mr. Johnson* and *my secretary*. These noun phrases actually occur twice in the deep structures of (22) and (23), but, for each sentence, a Pronominalization Transformation has applied to substitute the appropriate pronoun for one of the specific noun phrases. *He* and *she*, like all pronouns, are quite vague in meaning. The only way we can know which particular person is meant when these words occur is by knowing that the pronouns have been substituted for specific noun phrases that are present in the deep structure.

All elements that constitute part of the meaning of a sentence are present in the deep structure of the sentence, whether or not they actually appear in the surface structure. Elements ''missing'' from the surface structure have been deleted by a transformation or have undergone a substitution transformation that replaces the underlying element by another form, usually a pronoun.

AMBIGUOUS SENTENCES

Ambiguity is the converse of paraphrase. In paraphrase, two or more surface structures that convey the same meaning must have the same deep structure. In ambiguity, a single surface form with several meanings must have several different deep structures. Just as transformations operate to produce several surface structures from a single underlying structure for paraphrase, so transformations apply to create a single surface structure from several different deep structures for ambiguity.

Consider the following sentences:

(26) John is too far away to see.

(27) John is too far away for anyone to see him.

(28) John is too far away to see anything.

(26) is ambiguous, and it has the two meanings expressed by (27) and (28). We could say that (27) is a paraphrase of one of the interpretations of (26), and, similarly, (28) is a paraphrase of the other interpretation of (26). Since paraphrases must have the same deep structure, we know that underlying (26) and (27) is a single deep structure, and underlying (26) and (28) is another deep structure. We have already noted that pronouns often occur in surface structure as the result of a Pronominalization Transformation that replaces a specific noun phrase with a pronominal form. Thus, underlying *him* in (27) is a deep structure constituent *John*. A first approximation to the deep structure of (26)/(27) is (29):

(29) John is too far away for anyone to see John.

We have also seen that the Equi NP Deletion Transformation deletes a noun phrase that is identical to another noun phrase in a sentence. Underlying (26)/(28), then, is a structure similar to (30):

(30) John is too far away for John to see anything.

The words *for* and *to* are simply grammatical morphemes; they do not really contribute to the meaning of the sentence but are present only in order to create a grammatical surface form. Since deep structure is the level of meaning, any element that does not contribute to meaning need not be present in the deep structure but instead can be added transformationally. Thus, a closer approximation to the deep structures under discussion is (31), rather than (29), and (32), rather than (30):

(31) John is too far away—anyone see John

(32) John is too far away—John see anything

(31) and (32) are, of course, not grammatical surface structures but rather structures underlying grammatical surface structures. Let us now see how (27) and (26) are generated from (31).

To obtain (27) from the underlying structure (31), at least two transformations must apply. One inserts the grammatical morphemes *for* and *to*; the other substitutes the pronoun *him* for the noun phrase *John*. These steps are illustrated by (33) and (34):

(33) John is too far away for anyone to see John. (by the *for to* Insertion Transformation)

(34) John is too far away for anyone to see him. (by the Pronominalization Transformation)

To obtain (26), in one of its two meanings, from (31), the following occurs. The *for to* Insertion Transformation applies to (31), yielding (35):

(35) John is too far away for anyone to see John.

Another rule, similar to Equi NP Deletion, applies to delete the second occurrence of *John,* and the result is (36), which is yet another paraphrase of (27) and (26).

(36) John is too far away for anyone to see.

At this point, an optional deletion transformation can remove the pro-form *anyone.* (Like the pronouns *he, she, it,* etc., *someone, something, anyone,* and *anything* are forms with very general meaning related to the meanings of a large number of noun phrases; therefore, they are called pro-forms.) The result is (37):

(37) John is too far away for to see.

In a few dialects of English, (37) is a grammatical sentence. In such dialects, no other transformations need to be applied. This confirms the correctness of an analysis that produces (37) in a grammar of English. For most dialects, however, an additional transformation is needed to delete *for* whenever it is immediately following by *to*. The result of this rule is (38), which is equivalent to (26).

(38) John is too far away to see.

Thus, starting from a single deep structure, a grammar containing the following transformations can generate several surface structures: *for to* Insertion, a transformation like Equi NP Deletion, Pronominalization, the Pro-Form Deletion Transformation, and the *for* Deletion Transformation. For the most part, the same rules are involved in producing the surface forms (26) and (28) from the underlying structure (32).

The surface sentences (26) and (28) are produced from the underlying structure (32) in the following way. The *for to* Insertion Transformation applies to (32) to produce the intermediate structure (39):

(39) John is too far away for John to see anything.

Equi NP Deletion applies to remove the second occurrence of *John,* yielding (40):

(40) John is too far away for to see anything.

For most dialects, (40) is an intermediate structure, that is, not yet grammatical. If no other rule applies to (40), the *for* Deletion Transformation will apply to produce (41), which is one of the sentences we wish to produce, namely (28).

(41) John is too far away to see anything.

But, in addition to the *for* Deletion rule, the optional Pro-Form Deletion Transformation could apply. In this case, the result would be the other sentence we want to generate, (26) which is repeated here as (42):

(42) John is too far away to see.

Again the transformations have produced several surface structures from the same deep structure. But note that, from the two different deep structures (31) and (32), the rules have produced a single surface structure, the ambiguous sentence (26), which was generated as (38) and again as (42).

PROPERTIES OF DEEP STRUCTURES AND TRANSFORMATIONS

The example of ambiguity we have just discussed, although complex and perhaps somewhat difficult to follow, is important for several reasons. First, it illustrates how deep structures and transformations account for the existence of ambiguous sentences in a language. Almost all ambiguous sentences result from similar situations, with several deep structures and a number of transformations that may lead to a single, ambiguous surface structure. Second, the example illustrates a point made throughout this book, namely, that many aspects of language are abstract and not immediately apparent from the surface. Note that the deep structures represented by (31) and (32) are quite different from the actual surface sentences, such as (26) and (27) on the one hand, (26) and (28) on the other. It is in this sense that deep structures are abstract; they may be substantially different from the surface structures that occur in speech or writing. A third point exemplified by our rather lengthy discussion of sentence (26) is that transformations are indeed generalizations—they apply in the production of a variety of sentences with different deep structures. The same rules used in the discussion of (26) also account for the sentences mentioned in Chapters 12 and 13, that is:

(43) John is eager to please.

(44) John is easy to please.

Following the same kind of argument used for (26), we can see that underlying (43) is a deep structure something like (45):

(45) John is eager—John please someone

Underlying (44) is a structure similar to (46):

(46) It is easy—someone please John

The same rules discussed in relation to (26) apply to produce (43) from (45), and, with a few additional rules beyond the scope of this discussion, (44) from (46). The reader might find it interesting to work out the stages for producing (43) from (45), following the pattern used in the discussion of (26). A fourth aspect of the nature of transformations and deep structures illustrated by our account of ambiguity is related to the abstractness of underlying representations. Transformations do not operate directly on a deep structure to immediately produce a surface structure. Deep structures are generally so abstract that it requires a number of transformations to produce a grammatical surface structure. Thus, many transformations apply, not directly to a deep structure, but to intermediate structures produced by other transformations. The general process is illustrated schematically in Figure 14.4. Figure 14.5 refers again to the discussion of sentence (26), in its meaning paraphrased by (27), and summarizes the deep structure, transformations and the intermediate structures they produce, and, finally, the surface structure of the sentence. Note that the deep structure and the intermediate structures 1 and 3 in 14.5 are not grammatical surface forms in most dialects of English.

Since a number of transformations may apply in the generation of a surface structure from a deep structure, it is not surprising that some transformations must be ordered with respect to one another. That is, certain transformations must be applied before others to produce grammatical surface structures. At times, this ordering of rules is self-evident, as with the *for to* Insertion Transformation and the *for* Deletion Transformation. The insertion rule must apply prior to the deletion rule since it is the *for* provided by the insertion

Figure 14.4 _____

DEEP STRUCTURE

Transformation 1 applies to produce

INTERMEDIATE STRUCTURE 1

Transformation 2 applies to produce

INTERMEDIATE STRUCTURE 2

Transformation 3 applies to produce

INTERMEDIATE STRUCTURE 3

Transformation 4 applies to produce

INTERMEDIATE STRUCTURE 4

$\vdots$

Transformation n applies to produce

SURFACE STRUCTURE

Figure 14.5

DEEP STRUCTURE: *John is too far away—anyone see John*

for to Insertion Transformation applies to produce

INTERMEDIATE STRUCTURE 1: *John is too far away for anyone to see John*

NP Deletion Transformation applies to produce

INTERMEDIATE STRUCTURE 2: *John is too far away for anyone to see*

Pro-Form Deletion Transformation applies to produce

INTERMEDIATE STRUCTURE 3: *John is too far away for to see*

for Deletion Transformation applies to produce

SURFACE STRUCTURE: *John is too far away to see.*

---

rule that is in some instances removed by the deletion rule. If the ordering were reversed and one attempted to apply the deletion rule first, there would be no structures to which the rule could apply. If one then applied the *for to* Insertion Transformation, sentences like the following would be generated:

(47) Many linguists like for to read science fiction novels.

(48) John hopes for to be accepted into the Graduate School at the University of California.

(49) We wanted for to see that film but couldn't afford the exorbitant price of admission.

These sentences are ungrammatical in most dialects of English and, therefore, should not be generated by the grammar. The only way to prevent them from appearing as surface forms is to order the *for* Deletion Transformation after the *for to* Insertion Transformation. (In those dialects where sentences (47)–(49) are grammatical, the *for* Deletion rule does not occur, so the question of its order with respect to the *for to* Insertion rule is irrelevant.)

The determination of the proper ordering relations among various transformations is a matter still under investigation. A clear and detailed discussion of the issue is available in one of the works listed in "Further Exploration."

SYNTACTIC EVIDENCE FOR DEEP STRUCTURES AND TRANSFORMATIONS

Up to this point, we have offered deep structures based on evidence from both syntax and meaning. As we will see in Part 6, linguists differ in their conclusions about the relationships among syntax, meaning, and deep structures. Some linguists maintain that deep structures should be determined primarily on the basis of meaning, while other linguists argue that deep structures should be established on evidence from syntax alone. Here in Part 5, both types of evidence are presented, but readers should keep in mind that deep structures may be justified by either the meaning of sentences or by their syntactic form and their syntactic relationships to other sentences.

From the syntactic perspective, deep structures and transformations are necessary because they account for generalizations about the principles of English sentence formation. As in the example above regarding tag questions, the linguist wishes to preserve maximum generalizations in his or her description of the syntax of a language. A single, general rule that applies to a variety of sentences will be preferred to a set of separate rules that account for the same phenomena.

Consider the Imperative Transformation, which applies to underlying structures like (III); see Figure 14.3. (III) contains a subject *you,* and this explains why speakers realize that imperative sentences include 'you' as part of their meaning, despite the fact that the word *you* may not occur at the surface. What syntactic justification can we find for the presence of *you* in the deep structure? To answer this question, we must look at several other aspects of English grammar, for the syntax of a language constitutes a system, and no rule or structure is independent of the other rules and structures in the system. This was demonstrated earlier by the consideration of tag questions in relation to imperatives. Now let us look at yet another aspect of English grammar which provides additional evidence not only for the deep structure occurrence of *you* but also for the systematic interdependence of various aspects of syntax—the set of principles that explain the occurrence of pronouns.

Figure 14.6 illustrates the use of reflexive pronouns in English (such pronouns contain the morpheme *self*). In all of the grammatical sentences, the reflexive pronoun refers to the same person as the subject pronoun, while in the ungrammatical sentences the two pronouns have different referents. A grammar of English could account for this fact by placing a special restriction on the rules that produce sentences—that is, by not

Figure 14.6

Grammatical Sentences	Ungrammatical Sentences
I hurt myself.	*I hurt yourself. *I hurt himself. *I hurt themselves.
You hurt yourself.	*You hurt myself. *You hurt himself. *You hurt themselves.
He hurt himself.	*He hurt myself. *He hurt yourself. *He hurt themselves.
They hurt themselves.	*They hurt myself. *They hurt yourself. *They hurt himself.

allowing the rules to produce any sentence in which the reflexive pronoun has a different referent from the subject pronoun. When we look at other aspects of pronouns, however, we see that this solution is ad hoc (it does not explain the situation). Consider the sentences in Figure 14.7. With a verb like *hurt* any nonreflexive pronoun can occur as object (no matter what pronoun is subject) except a pronoun that refers to the same person as the subject. Again we could state a special restriction on the co-occurrence of nonreflexive subject and object pronouns. But now the grammar contains two statements limiting pronoun occurrence. It would be preferable if these two facts could be accounted for in a single, general way.

The limitations on the occurrence of reflexive pronouns and nonreflexive pronouns are related. Compare Figures 14.6 and 14.7. Only in those cases where an ungrammatical sentence appears with two nonreflexive pronouns do we get a grammatical sentence with a reflexive pronoun as the object; similarly, in those cases where sentences with reflexive pronouns are ungrammatical, there are corresponding grammatical sentences with nonreflexive pronouns. The simplest, most general way to show this relationship in a grammar is to allow the rules to produce deep structures containing all combinations of subject and object in their nonreflexive form. Then a Reflexivization Transformation can be formulated to convert all object pronouns to their reflexive form when a sentence contains a subject pronoun that refers to the same person. (See Figure 14.8.) In this way we do not have to state two different restrictions on the occurrence of pronouns. The restriction is stated once (by means of the Reflexivization Transformation), and the

Figure 14.7

Grammatical Sentences	Ungrammatical Sentences
I hurt you. I hurt him. I hurt them.	*I hurt me.
You hurt me. You hurt him. You hurt them.	*You hurt you.
He hurt me. He hurt you. He hurt them.	*He hurt him.†
They hurt me. They hurt you. They hurt him.	*They hurt them.†

†These sentences are ungrammatical if the two pronouns refer to the same people. They are grammatical if the pronouns refer to different people.

SPEAKERS, SENTENCES, AND SYNTAX

Figure 14.8

DEEP STRUCTURE: *I hurt me.**
Reflexivization Transformation applies to produce
SURFACE STRUCTURE: *I hurt myself.*

DEEP STRUCTURE: *You hurt you.*
Reflexivization Transformation applies to produce
SURFACE STRUCTURE: *You hurt yourself.*

DEEP STRUCTURE: *He hurt him.**
Reflexivization Transformation applies to produce
SURFACE STRUCTURE: *He hurt himself.*

DEEP STRUCTURE: *They hurt them.**
Reflexivization Transformation applies to produce
SURFACE STRUCTURE: *They hurt themselves.*

---

*The difference in form between subject and object pronouns is a relatively minor matter handled elsewhere in the grammar.

---

generalization about the relationship between reflexive and nonreflexive pronouns is described.

We can return now to the syntactic evidence that supports the occurrence of *you* in the deep structure of imperative sentences. Imperatives may contain object reflexive pronouns, as illustrated by the following sentences:

(50) Behave yourself.

(51) Wash yourself.

(52) Don't hurt yourself.

The only reflexive pronoun in imperatives is *yourself;* the following sentences are ungrammatical:

(53) *Behave myself.

(54) *Wash himself.

(55) *Don't hurt themselves.

If no *you* were present as the deep structure subject of imperatives, the fact that only *yourself* can occur as a reflexive object in such sentences would be an unexplained phenomenon in English. Restrictions prohibiting all other reflexive forms would have to be placed on the rules that produce imperatives. However, if we provide imperatives with deep structures containing *you* as the subject, the occurrence of *yourself* is explained: the Reflexivization Transformation can now apply to the object *you* since the imperative contains a subject *you* referring to the same person. Since the reflexivization rule must be included in the grammar to account for the facts in Figures 14.6 and 14.7, we achieve a generalization by also using it for those reflexives appearing in imperatives, and there is no need to add a special restriction to cover this case. We can achieve the generalization

Figure 14.9

Correct Ordering

DEEP STRUCTURE: *You will wash you*
      Reflexivization Transformation applies to produce
INTERMEDIATE STRUCTURE: *You will wash yourself*
      Imperative Transformation applies to produce
SURFACE STRUCTURE: *Wash yourself.*

Incorrect Ordering

DEEP STRUCTURE: *You will wash you*
      Imperative Transformation applies to produce
INTERMEDIATE STRUCTURE: *Wash you*
      Reflexivization Transformation cannot apply
SURFACE STRUCTURE: **Wash you.*

and avoid the restriction only if we hypothesize that there is a deep structure containing a subject *you* for all imperatives. This is syntactic evidence justifying the presence of *you* as the underlying subject.

The ordering of the Reflexivization Transformation with respect to the Imperative Transformation is crucial: the reflexive rule must apply before the imperative rule. If the ordering were reversed, the imperative rule would delete *you,* the reflexive rule could not apply since there would no longer be a subject pronoun, and an ungrammatical sentence would be produced. (See Figure 14.9.)

SUMMARY

Descriptions of syntax restricted to surface structure fail to account both for such syntactic facts as the relationships among sentences with different surface structures and for many of the general principles of sentence formation. In order to provide for such facts in a descriptive grammar, linguists hypothesize that in addition to its surface structure, every sentence has a deep structure. Grammatical relationships between two (or more) sentences can be explained by assuming that such sentences have a common deep structure. Some of the general principles of sentence formation are described by a set of constituent structure rules that produce the deep structures. Other principles are described by transformations that apply to convert deep structures into surface structures.

Deep structures and transformations also provide a means of accounting for relationships between the form and the meaning of sentences, and thus they explain the ability of speakers of a language to understand the meanings of sentences, to make judgments about paraphrase and ambiguity, and to grasp meanings which are not represented in the surface structures of sentences. The deep structure of a sentence contains all of the concepts that speakers understand to be involved in the sentence, but it does not contain those elements of surface structure that contribute nothing to meaning and are present only for reasons of form. Sentences that are paraphrases of one another all have the same deep structure, while an ambiguous sentence has as many deep structures as it does meanings. Deep structures are often highly abstract, quite different in form from the surface structures by which they are expressed.

The transformations that link deep structures to surface structures may carry out at least four kinds of changes: they may rearrange the constituents of a structure (e.g., the Particle Movement Transformation); they may delete certain constituents (such as the Imperative Transformation and the Equi NP Deletion Transformation); they may add certain constituents (as in the *for to* Insertion Transformation); or they may substitute one constituent for another (as does the Pronominalization Transformation). Each transformation is either obligatory (*for to* Insertion, for example) or optional (the Pro-Form Deletion Transformation, for example). Most transformations do not apply directly to a deep structure but rather to an intermediate structure produced by an earlier transformation. Many transformations are ordered with respect to one another.

FURTHER EXPLORATION

The need for establishing deep structures and transformations is discussed informally and concisely by Paul Postal in the article "Underlying and Superficial Linguistic Structure" (Emig et al. 1966; also available in Reibel and Schane 1969), as well as by Adrian Akmajian and Frank Heny in Chapter 3 of their book *An Introduction to the Principles of Transformational Syntax*.

Akmajian and Heny also offer an interesting, yet nontechnical, study of English tag questions in their first chapter; they return to the subject, on a more complex and formal level, in Chapter 6. Reflexive pronouns are a central concern in the first eight chapters of *Beginning English Grammar* by Samuel Jay Keyser and Paul M. Postal; the discussion is quite detailed. Both of these books present data, discussion, and analysis of a wide range of syntactic structures in English, along with the deep structures and transformations that have been proposed to account for the phenomena studied. In each book, emphasis is on the types of data and syntactic evidence and the kinds of argumentation used by linguists in their analyses. *English Transformational Grammar*, by Roderick A. Jacobs and Peter S. Rosenbaum, is a less technical, widely used discussion of the major properties of English syntax.

The ordering of transformations is examined in all three of the books cited above; it is also the central topic of concern in *From Deep to Surface Structure* by Marina K. Burt. In each case, the discussions presuppose familiarity with formalized transformations, so readers might consider consulting this supplementary reading only after they have completed Chapter 16 of this text.

1. The following sentences do not contain an auxiliary in their surface structures. Use your knowledge of English to provide the corresponding tag question for each sentence.

(a) They ride their bicycles to school.
(b) You understand the assignment.
(c) We agree about the menu.
(d) I prepare for my lectures.

What do these tag questions indicate about the deep structure of sentences such as (a)–(d)? (Recall the argument regarding the occurrence of *will* in the deep structure of imperatives.)

2. Describe the principle of English syntax that enables speakers to produce the question forms of (ii) from the statements of (i) in (a)–(d) below. (Such questions are called *yes/no* questions because they can be answered simply by *yes* or *no*.) Restrict your description of the principle to the sentences given (i.e., do not consider other kinds of questions).

(a) (i) You can swim well.
    (ii) Can you swim well?
(b) (i) The patient should follow this diet.
    (ii) Should the patient follow this diet?
(c) (i) A taxi will wait for the doctor until 4 P.M.
    (ii) Will a taxi wait for the doctor until 4 P.M.?
(d) (i) The children who finish their work may read comic books.
    (ii) May the children who finish their work read comic books?

Now examine the following; do not concern yourself with the changes in the tense of the main verb as in *swam* and *swim* in (e).

(e) (i) You swam well in the race.
    (ii) Did you swim well in the race?
(f) (i) The patient followed this diet.
    (ii) Did the patient follow this diet?
(g) (i) A taxi waited for the doctor until 4 P.M.
    (ii) Did a taxi wait for the doctor until 4 P.M.?
(h) (i) The children who finished their work read comic books.
    (ii) Did the children who finished their work read comic books?

Does the principle that you described to account for the *yes/no* questions in (a)–(d) also work as an account of the *yes/no* questions in (e)–(h)? Explain. Is it desirable to have two different descriptions in a grammar for a single syntactic phenomenon (here, *yes/no* question formation)? What hypothesis can you make about the deep structures of the (i) sentences in (e)–(h) that would allow you to retain a single principle of *yes/no* question formation? Is there any relationship between the material considered here and that examined in the first exercise above? Consider the possibility that the constituent AUX occurs in the deep structure of ALL English sentences. If this were the case, how would we have to modify the constituent structure rule $S \rightarrow NP\ (AUX)\ VP$?

3. In this chapter, we have discussed certain aspects of a number of transformations, including the following:

> Particle Movement
> Imperative
> Equi NP Deletion
> *for to* Insertion
> Pro-Form Deletion
> *for* Deletion
> Reflexivization

Consider the following informal representations of deep structure (a formal representation of a deep structure consists of the entire phrase structure tree diagram produced by the constituent structure rules). For each deep structure, (1) provide an actual, surface sentence that could occur, (2) name the transformations that convert the deep structure into the sentence you have provided, and (3) indicate the intermediate structure created by each transformation you name. (Do not be concerned about the ordering of those transformations for which ordering was not discussed in the text.) The first sentence is an example.

(a) The children want something—the children leave.
   Possible surface form:
      The children want to leave.
   Transformations and intermediate structures:
      for to Insertion
         The children want something—for the children to leave.
      Pro-Form Deletion
         The children want—for the children to leave.
      Equi NP Deletion
         The children want—for to leave.
      for Deletion
         The children want to leave.

(b) I may tire out me.
(c) You will behave you!
(d) John is eager—John please someone.
(e) The tenant expects something—the janitor take out the garbage.

handwritten annotations: particle movement / delete imperative & equi / add for to Insertion / subs Pronoun / myself / I may tire out me

4. Keeping in mind the transformations discussed in this chapter, attempt to provide an informal representation of the deep structure that probably underlies each of the following sentences.

(a) Turn the television on!
(b) Bill hoped to marry Charlotte.
(c) He saw himself in the mirror.
(d) The manager, wanted a secretary to type the letter.

CHAPTER 　1515151515151515151515151515

COMPLEXITY AND PRODUCTIVITY

Deep structure, surface structure, and transformations like those illustrated in Chapter 14 account for much of the knowledge speakers of English have about their language. One aspect of this knowledge that has not been investigated in the preceding chapters is the productivity of a linguistic system. Stated briefly, the productivity of all human languages results from the fact that all languages, including English, make use of certain principles for combining simple sentences into more complex sentences. Since there is no limit to the number of simple sentences that can be combined, there is no "longest" sentence for a language and no end to the list of possible sentences. Following a short review of matters involving competence and performance, we will discuss the two basic processes by means of which syntactic productivity occurs in language.

215

COMPETENCE AND PERFORMANCE

Every person who speaks a language possesses the knowledge required to produce an infinitely long sentence, but no human being is actually capable of doing so. Even if people were physically immortal, the need for food and sleep, as well as such factors as mental exhaustion, would cause the end of a sentence produced by even the most loquacious individual. But these are matters of performance; they are nonlinguistic factors. The rules of our language permit an infinitely long sentence, but our bodies and the limitations of our brains do not. Since speakers possess the linguistic competence required for infinitely long sentences, a grammar describing that competence must be capable of producing such sentences.

Other matters of performance affect the sentences that speakers actually use. Certain sentences are grammatical since they are in accord with the rules of the language, but, nevertheless, speakers may tend to avoid them or even to reject them. Here we are concerned with the question of acceptability, which is related to performance, as opposed to grammaticality, which is an aspect of competence. Consider the following sentences:

(1) John is the quarterback and Pete is the halfback.
(2) John is the quarterback and Pete is the halfback and Tom is the safety.
(3) John is the quarterback and Pete is the halfback and Tom is the safety and Bill is a lineman.
(4) John is the quarterback and Pete is the halfback and Tom is the safety and Bill is a lineman and the team is expected to lose every game.
(5) John is the quarterback and Pete is the halfback and Tom is the safety and Bill is a lineman and the team is expected to lose every game but my sister's softball team is very good.
(6) John is the quarterback and Pete is the halfback and Tom is the safety and Bill is a lineman and the team is expected to lose every game but my sister's softball team is very good and
. . .

Any speaker of English, since he knows the processes for combining sentences, can continue sentence (6) and go on to produce longer and longer sentences until he ultimately becomes tired or bored with the task. Sentences (1)–(6), as well as indefinitely many others constructed on the same pattern, are all grammatical; they all are formed according to general principles of English grammar. But it is highly unlikely that anyone would ever say most of them, for, as the sentences become longer, they become monotonous in style and difficult to understand. They vary in acceptability even though they are equally grammatical. Since sentence (1) is clearly grammatical and the other examples are produced by the same rule that produces (1), the others must be grammatical too. There is no point at which we can say that a sentence produced in this way is ungrammatical, and, therefore, they are all grammatical.

A grammar accounts for linguistic competence, and this includes grammaticality. Another theory is needed to account for aspects of performance, including acceptability. As noted in Part 1, a theory of performance has not yet been devised. When developed, it will have to include information about a variety of the characteristics of human beings still under investigation, such as psychological limitations, neurophysiological factors, aesthetic views about language, and a full theory of competence. The description of complex sentences is one aspect of a theory of linguistic competence.

CONJOINING

Conjoining is the process of creating a construction by linking two or more constituents of the same type by a conjunction. The resulting construction is the same type as its major constituents. (Conjunctions are words like *and, but, or;* in the following tree diagrams, CONJ is the label used for a conjunction.) Examples (1)–(6) are all conjoined sentences; each consists of simpler sentences and one or more conjunctions. In their surface structure, conjoined sentences (or compound sentences, as they are also called) have the structure illustrated in Figure 15.1, which probably is also a reasonable approximation of the deep structure underlying conjoined surface structures such as those in sentences (1)–(6).

At the level of surface structure, other kinds of constituents also appear in conjoined phrases. Thus, in addition to conjoined sentences, we have conjoined noun phrases, verb phrases, adjectives, and other examples as well. Some illustrations are presented in Figure 15.2, along with the surface constituent structure of each conjoined construction. Unlike conjoined surface sentences, for which the deep structure also contains conjoined sentences, these other types of conjoined constituents have a deep structure that differs substantially from their surface structure. Consider the full meaning of the sentence (7):

(7) Susan feeds her cat salty peanuts and cold champagne.

Underlying this sentence are two simple sentences:

(8) Susan feeds her cat salty peanuts.

(9) Susan feeds her cat cold champagne.

These sentences, of course, can be conjoined, resulting in the sentence (10), which is a paraphrase of (7).

(10) Susan feeds her cat salty peanuts and Susan feeds her cat cold champagne.

(7) and (10) are paraphrases, and, therefore, they share the same deep structure. Since (10) explicitly provides the information necessary to interpret (7), we assume that the deep structure of (7) is similar in form to (10) itself. Thus, conjoined noun phrases

Figure 15.1

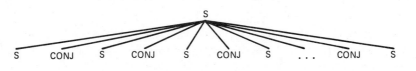

Note: . . . indicates that the sequence of CONJ S may be repeated indefinitely.

Figure 15.2

Conjoined Noun Phrases

a. Susan feeds her cat *salty peanuts and cold champagne.*

b. *My roommate's uncle and the librarian from Big Bluff* became engaged last night.

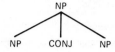

Conjoined Verb Phrases

a. Sam *studied all night but didn't pass the exam.*

b. The University Placement Office *provides reference forms and arranges job interviews.*

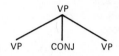

Conjoined Adjectives

a. That *purple and orange* shirt would look terrible on anyone with red hair.

b. Underneath all that dirt, she is an *attractive and interesting* girl.

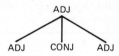

have deep structures containing at least two simple sentences. The same is true of conjoined verb phrases, as indicated by sentence (11):

(11) The University Placement Office provides reference forms and arranges job interviews.

If asked "Who arranges job interviews?" anyone who has heard sentence (11) can respond "the University Placement Office." This indicates that we know the subject of the verb phrase *arranges job interviews* even though the subject does not appear immediately before the phrase in the surface structure. Given this fact, along with sentence (12) as a paraphrase of (11), the underlying structure of both (11) and (12) must consist of conjoined sentences.

(12) The University Placement Office provides reference forms and the University Placement Office arranges job interviews.

Simplified sketches of underlying structures for sentences (7) and (10) and sentences (11) and (12) are provided in Figure 15.3 (the large triangles in the diagrams indicate that irrelevant material has been omitted). The transformations that convert structures like those in Figure 15.3 to surface structures like those in Figure 15.2 involve the deletion of repeated constituents, much as the Equi NP Deletion rule does.

Figure 15.3

(7) and (10)

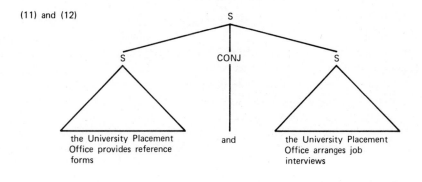

Susan feeds her cat salty peanuts and Susan feeds her cat cold champagne

(11) and (12)

the University Placement Office provides reference forms   and   the University Placement Office arranges job interviews

Conjoining is one of the basic processes by which a language provides for productivity. Underlying all conjoined surface constituents there appear to be structures containing conjoined sentences. These facts can be captured by a constituent structure rule of the form (13):

(13) S → S CONJ S (CONJ S)^n

The raised n indicates that the constituents included in the parentheses may be repeated any number of times. From rule (13), a grammar can generate a single conjoined sentence if the material in parentheses is not selected. Depending on the number of times the parenthesized constituents are repeated, structures of various lengths can be created. (See Figure 15.1.) If we consider rule (13) as a rule that generates deep structures, it accounts for all instances of conjoining discussed above. The surface structures of conjoined constituents such as noun phrases and verb phrases are the result of the transformations that apply to the underlying structures produced by rule (13).

EMBEDDING

The second process that accounts for the productivity of language is **embedding,** whereby one sentence is included within, or forms a constituent of, another sentence. The following examples contain embedded sentences; each embedded sentence is in italic print.

(14) I know *Joe will arrive by midnight.*

(15) *That the elves dug those craters* surprised the scientists.

(16) The hobo *who is sitting on the bench* was once a millionaire.

Each italicized string of words in (14)–(16) has the same fundamental structure as the corresponding independent sentences in (17)–(19).

(17) Joe will arrive by midnight.

(18) The elves dug those craters.

(19) The hobo is sitting on the bench.

(17)–(19) can be generated by a set of constituent structure rules like those proposed for simple sentences in Chapter 13. Now, it would probably be possible to draw up a second set of constituent structure rules to produce the more complex sentences (14)–(16). Such an approach to describing the syntax of English, however, would miss a general fact about this language, that is, that the more complex sentences consist of a combination of two simple sentences, one embedded (or contained) within the other. Rather than complicate our descriptive grammar by including two sets of constituent structure rules (one for simple sentences and the other for complex sentences), it would be preferable to find some means to express the generalization that simple sentences can be combined by the process of embedding. If this can be accomplished, only one set of constituent structure rules will be necessary.

Consider sentence (14). This complex sentence can be analyzed as a combination of two simple sentences, (17) and (20).

(20) I know it.

In terms of the meaning involved, the *it* of (20) clearly refers to (17) when we consider (20) and (17) as a pair of sentences that form a paraphrase for (14). The constituent structures of (20) and (17), as produced by the constituent structure rules for simple sentences, are given in Figure 15.4. Notice that the object of the verb *know* in (20) is a noun phrase (the only type of object our rules will produce); this noun phrase, of course, consists of the simple pronoun *it*. Since the object of a verb must be a noun phrase, and since in the surface structure of (14) the entire sentence (17) appears as the object of *know,* this suggests that the deep structure of (14) is a combination of the two structures presented in Figure 15.4. One way to provide for such a combination is to expand our earlier constituent structure rule for NP. Up to this point, that rule has had the form of (21).

(21) NP → (ART) (ADJ) N

If we now adjust the rule to permit a sentence to form one of the constituents of NP, we will be able to account for the fact that some verbs, such as *know,* have as their object

Figure 15.4

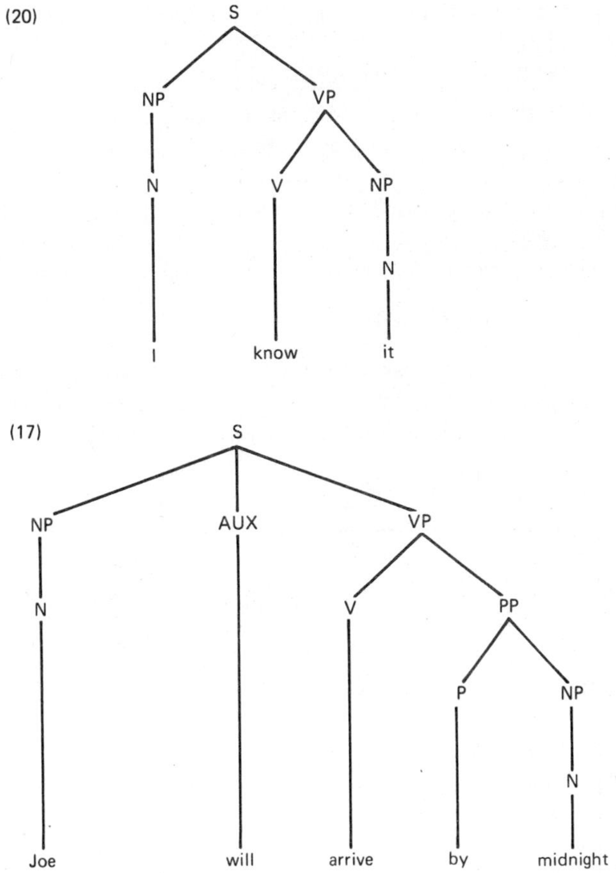

(20)

(17)

a noun phrase that contains a sentence. The adjustment to rule (21) is simple; add S as an optional constituent after N, as in (22).

(22) NP → (ART) (ADJ) N (S)

Rule (22) will generate a noun phrase with the constituents N followed by S (recall that ART and ADJ are both optional constituents and need not be selected). Embedded sentences produced by rule (22) as part of a noun phrase are sometimes referred to as **complement sentences** or, more simply, **complements.** This type of noun phrase is precisely what is needed to describe sentence (14) where, indeed, the object of *know* is a noun phrase containing a sentence. Through rule (22), we can combine the structures in

Figure 15.4 to produce the structure in Figure 15.5; observe that this combination is effected by rule (22). That is, we have taken the S of (17) and made it part of the object NP of (20); in (20), the object NP was simply the N *it;* now, in (14), the object NP is the N *it* followed by the S of (17).

Figure 15.5 represents the deep structure of sentence (14). It is not the surface structure because the tree diagram contains *it* as part of the object of the verb, yet the actual surface sentence itself does not. Therefore, there must be a transformation to convert this deep structure to the surface structure. This transformation will delete *it* whenever *it* occurs between a verb and a sentence, as happens in the structure represented in Figure 15.5. Not surprisingly, the rule is called the *it* Deletion Transformation; this is an obligatory rule since, unless it applies, we have an ungrammatical sentence.

(23) *I know it Joe will arrive by midnight.

At this point, we might ask why *it* appears in the deep structure. Would it not be better to have a deep structure without *it,* that is, a deep structure in which the object of the verb *know* is simply a sentence? Such an analysis has been proposed by some linguists for

Figure 15.5

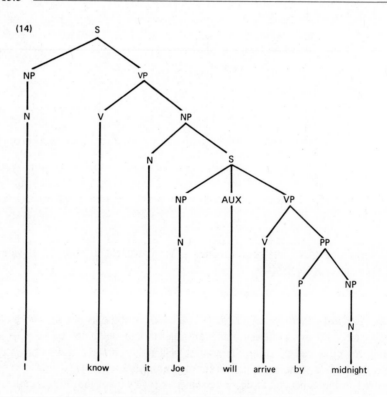

sentences such as (14). However, when other, related aspects of English syntax are investigated, there appears to be some evidence that *it* belongs in the deep structure. First, recall the discussion of noun phrases from Chapter 13. In every case, a noun phrase has contained a noun (and a pronoun such as *it* is simply a special kind of noun). Not only have all noun phrases contained a noun, but in every case, there has been a branch directly downward from the node NP to a node N. This seems to be a general property of noun phrases; in fact, it may be viewed as a defining characteristic of noun phrases. It would be unfortunate if we had to abandon this general statement just so that we could avoid *it* in the deep structure of complex sentences that contain an embedded complement sentence. The second type of evidence in support of the occurrence of *it* in deep structures with embedded complement sentences comes from examples like (15) above, *That the elves dug those craters surprised the scientists*.

Observe that in sentence (15) there is again an embedded sentence functioning as a noun phrase; that is, in (15) the embedded sentence is the subject of the full sentence. The revised noun phrase rule of (22), along with the other constituent structure rules from Chapter 13, can produce the structure in Figure 15.6 as a deep structure for sentence (15). Notice that *it* is present again (as it was in Figure 15.5). Before we consider the evidence in support of this *it,* we must mention that (15) contains the word *that*. Let us hypothesize that in English there is a *that* Insertion transformation that may add the word *that* before an embedded sentence. This rule accounts for the occurrence of *that* in sentence (15), but, in addition, it also accounts for a possible paraphrase of sentence (14). If the *that* Insertion Transformation adds *that* before the embedded sentence in (14), the following paraphrase is produced:

Figure 15.6

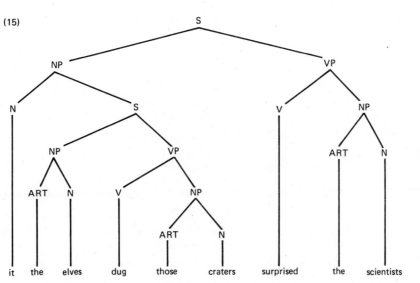

(15)

(24) I know that Joe will arrive by midnight.

Up to this point, we have posited Figure 15.6 as the deep structure of sentence (15). The *that* Insertion Transformation applied to Figure 15.6 will yield the ungrammatical sentence (25).

(25) *It that the elves dug those craters surprised the scientists.

Apparently, once again, an *it* Deletion Transformation is needed to eliminate *it* and thereby produce (15). Yet, there is still evidence that *it* belongs as part of the subject of (15) at the level of deep structure. Consider sentence (26) which is a paraphrase of (15).

(26) It surprised the scientists that the elves dug those craters.

When the embedded sentence is moved to the end of the full sentence, *it* actually occurs in the surface structure. This is evidence that *it* is present in the deep structure. Although the *it* is deleted by an *it* Deletion Transformation in certain cases, there are other cases when the *it* Deletion Transformation does not apply and *it* then appears at the surface.

At this point, it may be helpful to summarize our analysis. Embedded complement sentences can be produced by means of the modified version of the constituent structure rule for noun phrases given in (22). This rule, along with the other constituent structure rules introduced in Chapter 13, generates deep structures for complex sentences that contain complements (see, for example, Figures 15.5 and 15.6). These deep structures are converted into various surface sentences by the application of several transformations. Thus, if *it* Deletion applies to the deep structure in Figure 15.5, the result is sentence (14); if *that* Insertion also applies, sentence (24) is produced. The deep structure in Figure 15.6 can be converted into the surface sentence (15) by the application of both *it* Deletion and *that* Insertion. The same deep structure underlies sentence (26), which is produced through the application of the *that* Insertion Transformation and another rule, called the Extraposition Transformation, which moves (or extraposes) an embedded complement sentence to the end of the full sentence in which it is embedded.

This discussion of embedded complement sentences has become somewhat complicated due to the fact that several types of evidence, sentence structures, and transformations are intertwined. Indeed, this reflects the nature of human languages. Since a language is a system of forms, rules, and structures, no single part of a language can be analyzed in isolation from other, related parts. In fact, it should be noted that, at the present time, no matter how many aspects of a language are described by a particular analysis, it is always possible that consideration of further aspects of the language will lead to a different analysis. Linguists have not compiled a final, complete description of embedded complements in English; many aspects of complements remain to be described and the account here represents only a sketch of one of the possible ways to describe one kind of complement. "Further Exploration" directs the interested reader to more detailed accounts of linguistic research on this topic.

We must now consider the other example of embedding, represented by sentence (16), repeated here for convenience as (27).

(27) The hobo *who is sitting on the bench* was once a millionaire.

In traditional grammatical descriptions of English, the portion (28) is referred to as a **relative clause.**

(28) who is sitting on the bench

Relative clauses are embedded sentencelike structures that follow a noun phrase [*the hobo* in (27)] and that normally begin with a relative pronoun; in English, the chief relative pronouns are *who* (referring to people and, sometimes, animals) and *which* (referring to objects and animals).

Relative clauses differ from complements in several ways. Notice, for example, that unlike embedded complements, the embedded sentence that serves as a relative clause does not have an actual noun as its subject in surface structure. Thus, whereas *Joe* and *the elves* were the subjects of the embedded complement sentences in (14) and (15), the surface subject of the embedded relative clause in (27) is the relative pronoun *who*. Furthermore, several rules that apply to complements do not apply to relative clauses; *that* Insertion would result in the ungrammatical sentence (29).

(29) *The hobo that who is sitting on the bench was once a millionaire.

Extraposition does not apply to relative clauses, nor is there any evidence of *it* in the deep structure of sentences containing relative clauses; (30) is ungrammatical.

(30) *The hobo it was once a millionaire that who is sitting on the bench.

However, despite the above differences between complements and relative clauses, there are also several similarities. Relative clauses, such as (28), do have the basic structure of a sentence; compare (28) with (31).

(31) The hobo is sitting on the bench.

Furthermore, relative clauses are part of a noun phrase. For example, in (27), the subject of the full sentence is (32).

(32) the hobo who is sitting on the bench

As we have seen, the syntactic function of subject is performed by a noun phrase; therefore, (32) must be a noun phrase. As with complements, we must conclude that a phrase like (32) is a noun phrase having a sentence as one of its constituents. In the case of relative clauses, this embedded sentence must follow, not *it* as in complements, but rather a normal noun phrase (such as *the hobo*). Thus, we arrive at Figure 15.7 as a representation of the surface structure of (32), and, in turn, the noun phrase structure of Figure 15.7 can serve as the subject of a full sentence such as (27); see Figure 15.8.

Once again, it has become necessary to modify the constituent structure rule that produces noun phrases; we want to say that, as illustrated by Figure 15.7, a noun phrase may consist of an NP followed by an S.

(33) NP → NP S

Rule (33) should now be combined with rule (22) so that the grammar makes just a single statement about the structure of English noun phrases. This can be accomplished by the use of braces to indicate a choice:

(34) NP → $\begin{Bmatrix} NP\ S \\ (ART)\ (ADJ)\ N\ (S) \end{Bmatrix}$

Figure 15.7 _____

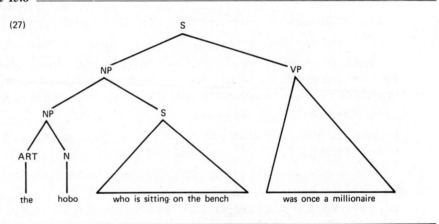

(32)

```
                        NP
                 ┌──────────┴──────────┐
                NP                      S
              ┌──┴──┐              ┌────┴────┐
            ART     N           (triangle)
             │      │
            the    hobo        who is sitting on the bench
```

Figure 15.8 _____

(27)

```
                              S
                 ┌────────────┴────────────┐
                NP                          VP
          ┌──────┴──────┐              (triangle)
         NP              S
       ┌──┴──┐       (triangle)
     ART     N
      │      │
     the    hobo   who is sitting on the bench   was once a millionaire
```

Rule (34) states that a noun phrase in English consists of either NP S (from the top line in the rule) or of a single N optionally preceded by ART, ADJ, or both and optionally followed by a complement S (all of these possibilities are stated by the bottom line in the rule).

Let us return to example sentence (27). Figure 15.8 represents the surface structure of this sentence, but what about its deep structure? If we use meaning and paraphrase as clues to deep structure, we can argue that the subject of the embedded sentence in Figure 15.8 should be *the hobo,* not *who,* in the deep structure. Notice that (27), repeated below as (35a), can be paraphrased by the two simple sentences (35b) and (35c). Thus, we can conclude that (35c) is equivalent to (35d), which is the relative clause embedded in the full sentence (35a).

(35) a. The hobo who is sitting on the bench was once a millionaire.
     b. The hobo was once a millionaire.
     c. The hobo is sitting on the bench.
     d. who is sitting on the bench

In terms of meaning, sentence (27), here (35a), can be represented as (36)—two sentences, one of which, (35c), is embedded within the other, (35b).

(36) The hobo [the hobo is sitting on the bench] was once a millionaire.

Using (36) as evidence for the deep strucutre of (27), it can be argued that the word *who*, although it occurs in the surface structure of (27), is not present in the deep structure. Instead, the actual noun phrase *the hobo* appears in the deep structure as the subject of the embedded sentence; thus, Figure 15.9 provides a plausible deep structure for sentence (27). A comparison of the deep structure in Figure 15.9 with the surface structure in Figure 15.8 reveals that only one transformation is necessary to convert the deep structure embedded sentence into the surface structure relative clause. This rule, commonly called the Relativization Transformation, replaces the subject noun phrase of the embedded sentence (here, *the hobo*) with the appropriate relative pronoun, which, in this case, is *who*. Sentence (37) illustrates that the Relativization Transformation is obligatory; unless it is applied, the resulting sentence is ungrammatical.

(37) *The hobo the hobo is sitting on the bench was once a millionaire.

The Relativization Transformation creates a relative clause from an underlying sentence embedded in a noun phrase. If only the Relativization Transformation applies to the deep structure in Figure 15.9, the result is sentence (27). However, there is a paraphrase of (27), that is, (38).

(38) The hobo sitting on the bench was once a millionaire.

Since (38) is a paraphrase of (27), we can analyze (38) as having the same deep structure as (27), that is, the structure given in Figure 15.9. To create the surface structure of (38),

Figure 15.9

(27) and (38)

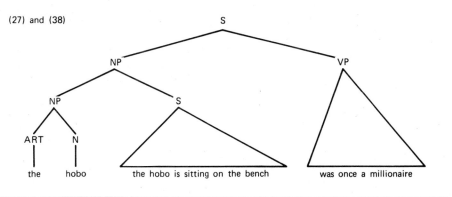

we first apply the Relativization Transformation, which is obligatory, to Figure 15.9. Of course, this yields sentence (27). The only difference in the surface forms of (27) and (38) is that (38) does not contain the relative pronoun *who* and *is* (a form of the verb 'to be'). Therefore, we posit an optional rule, called the Relative Reduction Transformation, which converts the structure of (27) into the surface structure of (38) by deleting the relative pronoun and the following form of the verb 'to be'. In summary, if only the obligatory Relativization rule applies to the structure in Figure 15.9, the result is (27); if the optional Relative Reduction rule applies as well, the result is (38).

A less obvious example of embedding occurs in sentences (39) and (40), which are similar to those we have just discussed:

(39) The hobo who is old was once a millionaire.

(40) The old hobo was once a millionaire.

In (39) there is a relative clause, *who is old,* containing a simple adjective, while (40), which is a paraphrase of (39), contains a noun phrase with an adjective immediately preceding the noun. Most adjectives are implicit propositions. The phrase *the old hobo* contains the proposition 'the hobo is old'. This proposition is part of the meaning of the phrase, and, therefore, must be part of the deep structure from which the surface form is produced in a grammar of English. Likewise, the phrase *who is old* in sentence (39) has as its meaning 'the hobo is old'. Thus, the same deep structure must underlie both (39) and (40), and that deep structure must contain an embedded sentence like (41):

(41) The hobo is old.

Figure 15.10 represents, in simplified form, the deep structure of sentences (39) and (40).

To produce (39) from the structure in Figure 15.10, the Relativization rule applies, substituting *who* for the second occurrence of *the hobo*. But how is (40) produced? Our grammar of English already includes the Relative Reduction rule, for it is needed to

Figure 15.10

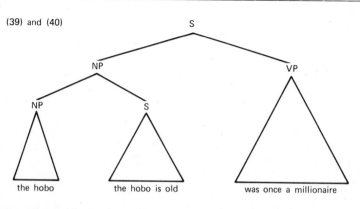

produce sentences like (38). If we apply Relative Reduction to the structure of (39), produced by Relativization from the deep structure in Figure 15.10, the result is (42):

(42) *The hobo old was once a millionaire.

(42) is ungrammatical at the surface level in English, although, in many languages, adjectives do follow the nouns they modify (e.g., in Spanish, 'the old hobo' is *el vagabundo viejo*, literally 'the hobo old'). By using two transformations that must occur in the grammar of English in order to account for relative clauses and reduced relative clauses, the grammar has almost produced noun phrases containing adjectives. All that is needed to convert (42) to a grammatical surface structure is the Adjective Inversion Transformation, which changes the order of a sequence NOUN ADJECTIVE (produced by the Relative Reduction Transformation) to the sequence ADJECTIVE NOUN. The result of applying this additional transformation is the surface structure of (40).

Figure 15.11 summarizes the role of the Relativization, Relative Reduction, and Adjective Inversion transformations in a grammar of English. The particular sentences used in the figure are, of course, only examples. The transformations are relevant to all sentences containing relative clauses and adjectives. With only these three rules, the grammar can produce a variety of grammatical surface structures. Furthermore, although the surface structures of sentences (27), (38), (39), and (40) are different, the Relativization Transformation is used in the production of the surface structures from the appropriate deep structures for all four sentences. The use of one transformation to account for superficially different types of surface structures is an instance of generalization. As discussed in Chapter 2, linguists attempt to describe a language in as general a way as possible, using the fewest number of rules to account for the greatest amount of data.

Traditional grammars defined complex sentences as those that contained clauses consisting of embedded sentences. We can now see that many sentences that appear to be simple at the surface are actually complex, for in their underlying structure an embedded sentence occurs. This is true for all adjectives that precede and modify nouns in English, for example. Underlying them is always a noun phrase that includes an embedded sentence and this is true even in sentences as superficially simple as (43).

(43) Don lost a red book.

GENERATING DEEP STRUCTURES

Once we have accounted for deep structure and have provided the transformations in a grammar, special rules accounting for surface structure are unnecessary. The surface structure of a sentence is the direct result of its deep structure and the transformations that apply during the course of generating the sentence. Thus, all of the constituent structure rules discussed up to this point, if they have any validity and utility, must form deep structures, not surface structures. Any deep structures generated by such constituent structure rules are then subject to the transformations that eventually produce surface structures.

If constituent structure rules produce deep structures, then our noun phrase rule, last formulated in (34), requires yet one more revision. We have just seen that the sequence

Figure 15.11

Deep Structures		**Transformations**		
(See Figures 15.9 and 15.10)				
		Relativization *(obligatory)*	*Relative Reduction* *(optional)*	*Adjective Inversion* *(obligatory)*

cannot apply since structure produced by Relative Reduction does not contain a sequence NOUN ADJECTIVE *

Top row trees:
NP → NP S: the hobo / the hobo is sitting on the bench
NP → NP S: the hobo / who is sitting on the bench
NP → NP S: the hobo / sitting on the bench

Bottom row trees:
NP → NP S: the hobo / the hobo is old
NP → NP S: the hobo / who is old
NP → NP S: the hobo / old
NP: the old hobo

*Some readers may be accustomed to labeling *sitting* as an adjective, but in this type of analysis *sitting* is considered to be a form of the verb *sit;* furthermore, we have simplified our discussion of the Adjective Inversion Transformation. In fact, this rule applies in English only when the noun is followed by a simple adjective; in the example above, the noun *hobo* is followed by a phrase, *sitting on the bench.*

ADJECTIVE NOUN in English always results from an underlying sentence, embedded as a relative clause. In that embedded sentence, the adjective occurs, not in a noun phrase, but rather in the verb phrase. Therefore, we must remove ADJ from the noun phrase rule, as indicated by (44).

$$(44) \quad NP \rightarrow \left\{ \begin{array}{l} NP \ S \\ (ART) \ N \ (S) \end{array} \right\}$$

In addition, the verb phrase rule, last considered in Chapter 13, must be modified so that it can produce both the original type of verb phrase and a verb phrase containing a verb followed by an adjective. The modified verb phrase rule is given in (45).

$$(45) \quad VP \rightarrow \left\{ \begin{array}{l} V \ ADJ \\ \\ V \ (NP) \ (PP) \end{array} \right\}$$

As in the noun phrase rule, the braces indicate a choice. Thus, rule (45) states that in English a verb phrase consists of either a verb followed by an adjective (from the top line of the rule) or of a verb followed optionally by a noun phrase, a prepositional phrase, or both (from the bottom line of the rule).

Figure 15.12 provides a summary of all the constituent structure rules that have been discussed in the last three chapters. These rules produce appropriate deep structures for a wide variety of sentences, but, in addition, they have the important characteristic of **recursion.** That is, they can apply without limit, producing just those types of infinitely long sentences mentioned at the beginning of this chapter as representative of the productivity of human language. We have already observed the way in which the first part of the S rule produces infinitely long conjoined sequences of sentences. Now let us see how the embedded sentences within the noun phrase rule permit recurring application of the rules. Begin with the first rule, which describes the constituents of a sentence. Note that this rule produces a noun phrase. Now note that the noun phrase rule can produce a sentence; this sentence, in turn, must include a noun phrase, and this new noun phrase may contain another sentence, which, in turn, will contain a noun phrase, and so forth. This process of reapplication of the rules is illustrated in Figure 15.13, which represents the deep structure of an indefinitely long sentence such as that of (46).

(46) The old man who is sitting at the table in the corner is a spy who wants to . . .

Both complements and relative clauses, as sentences embedded within noun phrases,

Figure 15.12

Constituent Structure Rules	Discussed in Chapter
$S \rightarrow \left\{ \begin{array}{l} S \ CONJ \ S \ (CONJ \ S)^n \\ \\ NP \ (AUX) \ VP \end{array} \right\}$	15 13 and 14
$NP \rightarrow \left\{ \begin{array}{l} NP \ S \\ \\ (ART) \ N \ (S) \end{array} \right\}$	15 13 and 15
$VP \rightarrow \left\{ \begin{array}{l} V \ ADJ \\ \\ V \ (NP) \ (PP) \end{array} \right\}$	15 13
$PP \rightarrow P \ NP$	13

Figure 15.13 _____

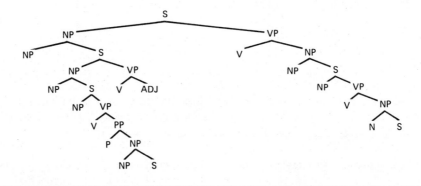

result in the potential production of infinitely long sentences. Conjoining also has this potential.

In Chapter 13, the discussion of constituent structure rules concluded with some comments on syntactic functions such as subject and object. Since syntactic functions are essentially relationships among the constituents of a sentence, we were able to define the relationships in terms of the position of a constituent in the tree structures produced by constituent structure rules. For example, the subject of a sentence was determined to be that NP with a single branch leading upward directly to the node S at the very top of the tree diagram. However, we have now considered sentences much more complex than those discussed in earlier chapters. Reconsider the following sentences:

(47) a. That the elves dug those craters surprised the scientists.
      b. It surprised the scientists that the elves dug those craters.

In their surface structures, (47a) and (47b) have different subjects according to our definition. In the (a) sentence, the subject is the NP *that the elves dug those craters* (an embedded complement sentence), while in the (b) sentence, the complement has been extraposed leaving only the NP *it* as subject. Yet, we understand the sentences to have similar, if not identical, meanings, and it may seem a bit peculiar to conclude that they have such different subjects. We can resolve this problem by considering the deep structure, which is the same for both sentences. Figure 15.6 shows that, in the deep structure of both (47a) and (47b), there is only one NP that meets our definition of subject—the complex NP consisting of the N *it* followed by the embedded S *the elves dug those craters*. We conclude, therefore, that a constituent may undergo changes in its syntactic function through the operation of transformations that convert deep structures to surface structures.

Now, consider sentences (48a) and (48b), which, even in traditional grammars, were considered to be a closely related pair, with (a) referred to as an active sentence and (b) as its passive counterpart.

SPEAKERS, SENTENCES, AND SYNTAX

(48) a. The cat chased the mouse.
      b. The mouse was chased by the cat.

The surface subject of (a) is the NP *the cat,* while the surface subject of (b) is the NP *the mouse*. Similarly, the object at the surface of (a) is the NP *the mouse,* but in (b), *the cat* is the only NP that could possibly be considered the object. Yet the two sentences refer to the same event and appear to have almost identical meanings (only the emphasis changes). As with the sentences of (47), we may appeal to deep structure to resolve this unsatisfactory account of synactic functions. Sentences (48a) and (48b) are grammatically related; given (48a), any native speaker of English can produce its passive counterpart (48b). Furthermore, given almost any active sentence of the syntactic form NP V NP, a speaker of English can produce a passive counterpart. Because of this relationship, linguists generally hypothesize that pairs such as those in (48) both come from a deep structure in which the subject and the object are identical to those found in the surface structure of the active sentence. The changes in syntactic function that we see in the surface structure of the passive sentence are the result of a Passive Transformation that converts the active form into the passive, thereby rearranging the order and relationships of the noun phrases. Thus, in (48b), *the mouse* is the surface structure subject but the deep structure object and, in the same sentence, *the cat* is the only surface structure element that could be object, but it is the deep structure subject. The syntactic function of an element can change as its grammatical relationship to other elements is altered by the operation of transformational rules.

In the last chapter and in this one, it has been noted that the determination of deep structures is a complex and difficult undertaking. The observations that have been made are based on clues to the deep structure level of language, but nothing is known with full certainty. The professional literature of linguistics is filled with other examples of transformations and underlying structures. There is wide debate over whether particular deep structures proposed for even the simplest of sentences are actually valid, and some linguists have suggested that a level even more abstract than deep structure is necessary to account for meaning.

Despite these doubts and qualifications, there can be little doubt that much of what we have said here accounts for many aspects of the linguistic competence of speakers of English. Perhaps the least reliable aspect of our discussion concerns the generation of deep structures by constituent structure rules. It is possible to write a set of constituent structure rules that produce structures with the proper form for the operation of transformations. But whether the structures produced by such rules are actually deep structures or only an intermediate level between deep and surface structure is not fully understood. Furthermore, since many sentence types in English have not yet been examined fully, it is unlikely that any current set of constituent structure rules actually provides the proper underlying structures for all of the sentences of the language. Figure 15.12 provides a summary of the constituent structure rules discussed here, but those readers who go on to examine other books and articles concerning the linguistic description of English should not be surprised to find accounts differing somewhat from this one. The field of linguistics has made striking discoveries about language in the past two decades. Attention is no longer restricted to surface structure, and we are beginning to understand some aspects of the knowledge possessed by speakers of English about their language. The study of syntax, however, is still at the beginning stages. Many years will pass before much is known conclusively or fully agreed on by all linguists.

SUMMARY

The productive nature of syntax is due to two basic processes that combine simple sentences: conjoining and embedding. In conjoining, two or more sentences serve as the constituents of a sentence, these constituents being linked by conjunctions. Although conjoined noun phrases, verb phrases, and adjectives occur at the surface of syntax, underlying such conjoined constructions are conjoined sentences. In embedding, a sentence occurs as one constituent of some construction which itself is a constituent of a sentence. In this chapter, we have examined sentences embedded in noun phrases, but it should be noted that sentences can also be embedded in verb phrases. In surface structure, embedded sentences sometimes have the same structure as corresponding simple sentences, but, more often, one or more constituents of the embedded sentence have been changed or deleted by transformations.

The surface structure of a sentence is the direct result of its deep structure and the transformations that have applied during the course of its generation. Therefore, constituent structure rules, such as those discussed in Chapter 13, are not necessary for the description of surface structure. Instead, such constituent structure rules may be formulated to produce the deep structures of sentences.

FURTHER EXPLORATION

Perhaps because conjoining appears to be a relatively simple aspect of English, few introductory books or articles deal with this productive syntactic process in any greater detail than we have in this chapter. Embedding, however, is widely discussed. Various types of complement structures, along with such transformations as *it* Deletion, *that* Insertion, and Extraposition, are the topic of Chapters 20–24 in *English Transformational Grammar* by Roderick A. Jacobs and Peter S. Rosenbaum. A somewhat more advanced discussion occurs in Chapter 8 of *An Introduction to the Principles of Transformational Syntax* by Adrian Akmajian and Frank Heny. For relative clauses, see Chapter 25 in the Jacobs and Rosenbaum book or Chapter 6 of *An Introduction to Linguistics* by Bruce L. Liles. In Chapter 8, Liles discusses syntactic functions. Recursive, constituent structure rules, their productivity, and their role in generating complements and relative clauses are described by Samuel Jay Keyser and Paul M. Postal in Chapter 14 of *Beginning English Grammar*. In *Foundations of Syntactic Theory,* Robert P. Stockwell includes discussion of most of the topics covered in this and the preceding chapters on syntax; he also includes numerous other relevant topics, as well as data from a variety of languages.

1. Use the constituent structure rules in Figure 15.12 to generate deep structure tree diagrams for each of the following sentences. (Include all of the nodes and branches produced by the rules; do not use the triangles to represent parts of your structures.)

(a) It is obvious that Terry must pass the exam.
(b) The musicians wished the audience would leave.
(c) That Congress squanders money annoys the voters.

For each sentence, provide a paraphrase that results from the same deep structure by application of transformations discussed for complements in this chapter.

2. One of the characteristics of transformations is that they may be ordered with respect to one another, as discussed in Chapter 14. Sometimes ordering is necessary because the change caused by one transformation provides the type of structure to which another transformation applies. The necessary order of application for the transformations involved in embedded relative clauses is (1) Relativization, (2) Relative Reduction, (3) Adjective Inversion. Explain why.

3. In "Further Exploration" at the end of Chapter 13, readers were asked to use the constituent structure rules from Figure 13.7 to generate the sentence:

An enormous collie chased a tiny kitten through the fields.

In this chapter, we have seen that the constituent structure rules actually produce deep structures and that transformations then convert such deep structures into surface structures. Use the revised set of constituent structure rules in Figure 15.12 to generate the deep structure tree diagram of the sentence provided above. (Include all of the nodes and branches; do not use the triangles.) Name, in their order of application, the transformations that must apply in order to convert your deep structure into the appropriate surface structure.

4. In English, the word *that* serves at least four different functions, as illustrated in the following:

Complementizer:	I know *that* dogs have fleas.
Relative pronoun:	I know a dog *that* has fleas.
Demonstrative pronoun:	I know *that*.
Demonstrative article:	I know *that* person.

In this chapter, we have discussed the complementizer *that*. The relative pronoun *that* occurs in the same types of structures as the other relative pronouns *who* and *which*. The demonstrative pronoun *that* occurs wherever a normal pronoun, such as *it*, can occur. Finally, the demonstrative article *that* (related to *this, these,* and *those*) appears in the position of an article (such as *the*); in fact, *those,* a plural form of *that,* occurs as an article in sentence (15).

The descriptions above form the basis for criteria which, in many instances, assist in identifying a particular occurrence of *that*:

(a) *that* is a complementizer when (1) it occurs immediately before a phrase that constitutes a full sentence and (2) when it can be omitted without a change in meaning:

I know that dogs have fleas.
I know dogs have fleas.

(b) *that* is a relative pronoun when *who* or *which* can serve as its substitute:

I know a dog that has fleas.

I know a dog who has fleas.

I know a dog which has fleas.

(c) *that* is a demonstrative pronoun when *it* can serve as its substitute:

I know that.

I know it.

(d) *that* is a demonstrative article when (1) it precedes a noun and (2) *this* can serve as its substitute:

I know that person.

I know this person.

Use these substitution criteria to determine the kind of *that* found in the following sentences.

(i) *That* bothered me.

(ii) *That* conclusion is unacceptable.

(iii) The former president maintained *that* he was innocent.

(iv) The creature *that* dug *that* crater must be very strong.

(v) I suspect *that that* man is the one who did *that*.

5. When the constituent structure rule for verb phrases was revised to include adjectives, it was presented as:

$$VP \rightarrow \left\{ \begin{array}{l} V \ \ ADJ \\ \\ V \ (NP) \ (PP) \end{array} \right\}$$

There are other, equivalent ways to state this rule. Consider the following and explain why it produces the same structures as the rule given above.

$$VP \rightarrow V \left\{ \begin{array}{l} (ADJ) \\ \\ (NP) \ (PP) \end{array} \right\}$$

6. Some linguists maintain that there is insufficient evidence that *it* occurs as an N preceding a complement S in deep structures. In fact, they suggest that a deep structure NP may have a single constituent, S. If this analysis is used, what further modification must be made in the constituent structure rules of Figure 15.12? What generalization about the deep structure of noun phrases would be lost? What new transformation would be needed to account for the complement sentences explored in this chapter? What transformation posited in this chapter would no longer be necessary?

7. In Chapter 14, we observed that linguists hypothesize the existence of deep structures and transformations based on two types of information: syntactic (grammatical) and semantic (aspects of meaning). Linguists differ in the extent to which they depend on each type of evidence, although generally syntactic information is considered primary. It usually happens that syntactic and semantic evidence both point to the same deep structures and transformations. However, there are aspects of English for which this is not the case. Reconsider the data presented in Figure 15.2 and repeated below.

(a) Susan feeds her cat salty peanuts and cold champagne.
(b) My roommate's uncle and the librarian from Big Bluff became engaged last night.
(c) Sam studied all night but didn't pass the exam.
(d) The University Placement Office provides reference forms and arranges job interviews.
(e) That purple and orange shirt would look terrible on anyone with red hair.
(f) Underneath all that dirt, she is an attractive and interesting girl.

In the section on conjoining earlier in this chapter, we argued that sentences such as (a) to (f), each containing a conjoined phrase, had as deep structures full conjoined sentences. For example, underlying (a) we posited a structure with the two simpler sentences (g) and (h), and we supported this analysis by claiming that (g) and (h), taken together, constituted a paraphrase of (a).

(g) Susan feeds her cat salty peanuts.
(h) Susan feeds her cat cold champagne.

However, if we continue this approach, we will find that some conjoined phrases mean more than the individual sentences into which they can be divided. Consider sentence (b) and compare it to sentences (i) and (j).

(i) My roommate's uncle became engaged last night.
(j) The librarian from Big Bluff became engaged last night.

Notice that while sentence (b) implies that the uncle and the librarian became engaged to one another, there is no such implication from the separate sentences (i) and (j); in these sentences the persons involved may have become engaged to two other individuals who are not even mentioned. Syntactically, it is fairly easy to propose transformations to conjoin (i) and (j); essentially, we need rules to delete repeated material and to move constituents—both processes that are found in many other rules that have been proposed for English. In terms of meaning, however, the two separate sentences may not be the same as the single sentence containing a conjoined phrase.

Divide sentences (c) to (f) into two separate sentences and describe any differences in meaning that result for the separate sentences when compared to the single sentence containing a conjoined phrase.

PART 6666666666666666666

SYNTAX, SEMANTICS, AND PRAGMATICS

A language consists of three basic components: meanings, sounds, and syntax. In the preceding parts, we have examined words and lexical items, sounds and sound systems, and deep and surface structure more or less independently of one another. Yet, a language is a single system, and all of these aspects of language are interrelated. In this part, we attempt to provide an overview of the organization of a complete grammar—a framework for the description of all aspects of a human language. In order to accomplish this goal, we must deal more explicitly with meaning.

Throughout the previous chapters, the term *meaning* has appeared without definition, yet most readers probably have encountered few difficulties because of this. Linguists, however, find the study of meaning to be the most challenging aspect of their work. Linguists (and philosophers) engage in more controversy over the analysis of meaning than over any other property of language. Difficulties begin when we try to provide definitions for words, continue as we attempt to account for the meanings of sentences, and expand immeasurably when we consider the effects on meaning of the properties and characteristics of situations, topics, cultures, personalities, beliefs, emotions, and individual experiences.

Resolution of the difficulties is still a goal for the future, but there have been efforts to bring order to the problems through a division into separate areas of research. The study of direct, linguistic meaning —abstracted from such matters as situations, beliefs, and individual experiences—is called **semantics.** This area can be subdivided further into **lexical semantics** (the linguistic meaning of words) and **sentence semantics** (the linguistic meaning of sentences). The properties of the world and of language users, when interacting with lexical and sentence semantics, constitute the domain of **pragmatics.** Chapter 16 includes a brief outline of semantics and its place in a description of linguistic competence; Chapter 17 sketches several current issues in pragmatics.

CHAPTER 16

ORGANIZATION
OF A COMPLETE
GRAMMAR

No complete grammar has ever been written for any language. The reader who has followed carefully the discussion of words, sound systems, and syntax in the preceding sections should have no difficulty in understanding why this is the case. A language is a complex system that constitutes a body of unconscious knowledge in the minds of human beings. As such, this system is neither directly known nor available for direct inspection. Any attempt to describe even a single aspect of language requires intensive study, and, even then, the resulting description must be regarded as a hypothesis subject to expansion and further confirmation or disconfirmation.

We have surveyed some of the hypotheses that have been devised on the basis of linguistic research in phonology and syntax, and we have also mentioned some aspects of meaning. It is necessary now to investigate one way in which these aspects of language might be combined into a single grammar, a complete, overall view of language.

SYNTAX

A complete grammar is a hypothesis about the linguistic competence of speakers of a language. As with any hypothesis, the grammar can be tested for validity only if it is stated as clearly and explicitly as possible. For example, the statement in (1), while possibly correct, is so vague that there is no way to disprove it.

(1) There is a transformation in English that converts underlying structures into imperative surface forms.

In itself, a statement like (1) says very little about the knowledge speakers of English have about imperatives. Even if (1) is true, it is not very informative. If a grammar is to explain English imperatives, it must contain explicit statements regarding the underlying structure of such sentences and the rules that convert such structures to surface forms. We have already seen how phonological rules and constituent structure rules may be formalized, and although we discussed transformations informally, these rules must also appear in a grammar in a fully explicit, formal way. The Imperative Transformation, for example, might be presented in a grammar as follows.

(2) S.D. # *you* *will* VP
       1   2 $\Longrightarrow$ 3   4

  S.C. 1   ∅   ∅   4

Certain details in (2) have been omitted for the sake of clarity, but the formalization exemplifies the way in which transformations frequently appear in formal descriptive grammars of English. The rule is to be interpreted as follows: S.D. represents **structural description;** S.C. represents **structural change.** The first line of the rule, its structural description, shows the type of structure to which the Imperative Transformation applies; the numbers in the second line indicate the order of the constituents before the rule applies. Thus, in (2) we see that the Imperative Transformation can be applied to any structure that begins with a sentence boundary (#) and for which the first three constituents are *you, will,* and some verb phrase (VP). The last line of the rule shows the change this transformation brings about in the structure: the Imperative Transformation deletes the second and third constituents mentioned in the structural description, *you* and *will;* the rule causes no changes in the first and fourth constituents, # and VP.

Figure 16.1 contains simplified formalizations for some of the other transformations discussed in Chapters 14 and 15. The figure also provides an example of the type of structure to which each transformation can apply, the structure produced by applying the transformation, and a phrase illustrating the rule. The results of applying these transformations to a full sentence are shown in Figure 16.4. All transformations can, and must, be formalized in this way. Only by stating them explicitly can we test our grammar to see if it does, in fact, generate all of the grammatical sentences of a language in a way that reflects the knowledge that speakers of the language have. In Parts 3 and 5, we presented several examples of formal rules of phonology and constituent structure. We have now seen that transformations must also be formalized.

Figure 16.1

Particle Movement Transformation

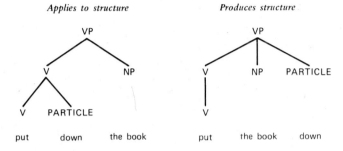

S. D.   V   PARTICLE   NP
         1   2   3
                 ⟹
S. C.   1   3   2

Applies to structure　　　　　*Produces structure*

Note: The lowest V in the structure produced by the transformation is later deleted.

Relativization Transformation

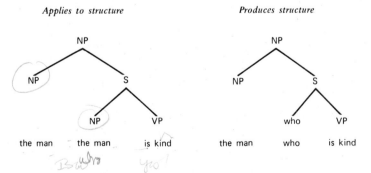

S. D.   NP   NP   (where the NPs are identical)
         1   2
              ⟹
S. C.   1   {who }
             {which}

Applies to structure　　　　　*Produces structure*

Note: The braces in the S.C. indicate a choice: that is, the NP that is numbered 2 is replaced by either *who* or *which,* depending on whether the N in the NP is human or nonhuman, respectively.

Figure 16.1 *(continued)*

Relative Reduction Transformation

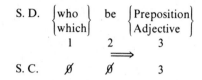

S. D. $\left.\begin{matrix}\text{who} \\ \text{which}\end{matrix}\right\}$ be $\left\{\begin{matrix}\text{Preposition} \\ \text{Adjective}\end{matrix}\right.$
      1   2   3
$\Longrightarrow$
S. C.   ∅   ∅   3

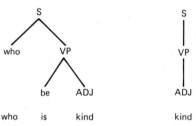

Applies to structure   *Produces structure*

Note: The braces in the S.D. indicate a choice: either *who* or *which* must be the first element; either a Preposition or an Adjective must be the third element; *be* represents any form of the verb 'to be', such as *is* or *are*.

Adjective Inversion Transformation

S. D. N ADJ
       1   2
$\Longrightarrow$
S. C. 2   1

Applies to structure   *Produces structure*

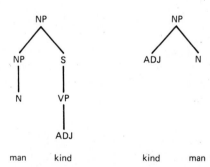

Note: As in the Particle Movement Transformation, this rule ultimately leads to the deletion of certain excess nodes (one NP, the S, and the VP).

Figure 16.2

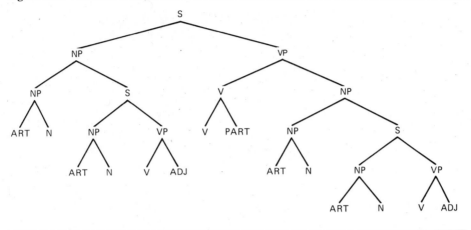

Consider the following sentence:

(3)   The young girl took the artificial flowers away.

A grammar of English will generate (3) in the following way. First, the constituent structure rules apply, producing an underlying structure like that sketched in Figure 16.2. Next, the lexicon and the rules of word formation of the language provide words for each of the constituents of this structure. The result is the deep structure of (3), sketched in Figure 16.3. Now a number of transformations apply, eventually yielding the surface

Figure 16.3

(3)

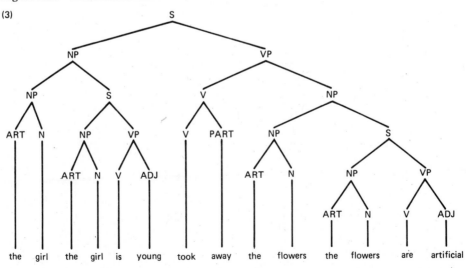

Figure 16.4 ───

The Relativization Transformation applies twice, to the two embedded sentences in the deep structure presented in Figure 16.3, producing the structure

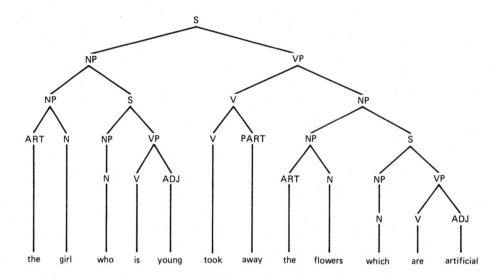

The Relative Reduction Transformation applies twice to the structure above, deleting the relative pronouns *who* and *which* and the form of the verb 'to be' that follows each, producing the structure

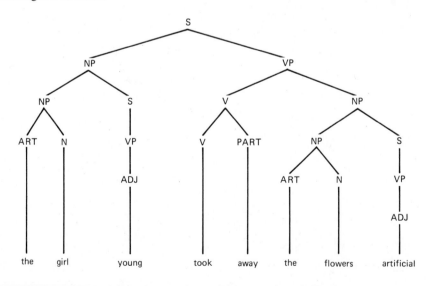

Figure 16.4 *(continued)* _____

The Adjective Inversion Transformation applies twice to the structure above, changing the order of the two sequences of N ADJ, producing the structure

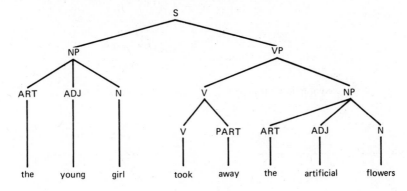

The Particle Movement Transformation applies to the structure above, moving the Particle to a position after the NP, producing the structure below, which is the surface structure of sentence (3)

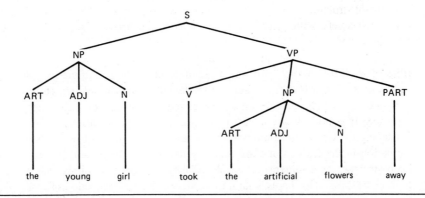

structure of (3). Some of the transformations involved in the generation of (3) from the deep structure in Figure 16.3 are Relativization, Relative Reduction, Adjective Inversion, and Particle Movement. This process, along with the final surface structure of the sentence, is illustrated in Figure 16.4. Note that each transformation applies to the structure produced by the preceding transformation.

Sentence (3) is only one example of the syntactic production of a sentence by a grammar. The process is the same for all other sentences of the language, although, of course, the particular rules that apply will differ. Figure 16.5 provides a schematic

Figure 16.5

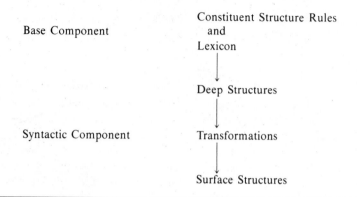

Base Component   Constituent Structure Rules
and
Lexicon

↓

Deep Structures

↓

Syntactic Component   Transformations

↓

Surface Structures

summary of the syntactic portion of a grammar. The constituent structure rules and the lexicon constitute the **base component** by means of which deep structures are generated. The **syntactic component** of the grammar contains the transformations that gradually convert deep structures to surface structures. Do not be confused by the misleading label provided for the component containing the transformations; the base component, with the constituent structure rules, also accounts for syntax. However, the base component is not concerned solely with syntax since it includes the lexicon as well as the constituent structure rules.

In addition to lexical entries, the lexicon may also contain certain kinds of rules. The rules of word formation, for example, seem to be applicable in the lexicon itself. Referring back to Figure 16.5, the reader will note that the constituent structure rules provide a structure into which lexical items are inserted, the result being the deep structure of a sentence. It is not unreasonable to suppose that the deep structure may contain words consisting of two or more morphemes. These words are produced by the rules of word formation in the lexicon and are then inserted into a constituent structure, forming the deep structure of a sentence. The redundancy rules of phonology, since they apply to morphemes, may also apply within the lexicon. The exact location of such rules of word formation and phonological redundancy within a complete grammar is still a matter for investigation, however, and the suggestion here that they occur within the lexicon is speculative at the present time.

PHONOLOGY

The phonemic representations of morphemes are provided in the lexicon of a grammar. After the application of the constituent structure rules, lexical entries are inserted into the structure of a sentence; and, when the transformations all have been applied, the surface structure is produced. But the surface structure of a sentence does not contain all of the information necessary to describe the correct phonetic form of the sentence. If the redundancy rules do apply within the lexicon, as mentioned above, then it still remains for the phonological rules to apply to surface structures in order to produce the correct phonetic forms of words, for, as we observed in Part 3, some morphemes have several pronunciations, depending on the elements with which they are combined. Thus, the phonological rules of a language apply to the surface structures of sentences in order to produce the phonetic forms that represent actual pronunciation. For example, the plural morpheme would be represented at the surface level by a set of features representing [s], whether it was attached to *cat, dog,* or *wish*. To obtain the correct phonetic forms, [s], [z], and [əz], respectively, the phonological rules discussed in Chapter 9 must be applied.

Redundancy rules apply to sound segments on the basis of the features of which a sound is composed or because the sound in question occurs next to, or near, some other sound. Therefore, redundancy rules can operate in the absence of any information about the syntax of a sentence; it was partly for this reason that we proposed above to place the redundancy rules in the base component of a grammar along with the lexicon. However, the situation is different for some phonological rules, particularly for the phonological rules that assign the placement of stress in English. Such rules can predict the placement of stress only after morphemes have been combined into words by the rules of word formation and then those words have been inserted into the constituent structures produced by the constituent structure rules. For example, the pronunciation of the following words differs primarily in terms of the placement of the main stress, that is, in terms of which vowel is produced with the greatest prominence or articulatory force.

(4) *Nouns*   *Verbs*

     cónvict   convíct
     pérmit   permít
     prótest   protést
     tránsfer   transfér

The accent mark indicates the vowel with the strongest stress in each word. The stress placement is predictable if you know the surface structure of the words. For words of this type, stress occurs on the last syllable if the form is a verb, on the next to last syllable if the form is a noun.

It is not only with words that stress is predictable. Given the surface structure of a phrase or a sentence, it is possible to determine the placement of stress. Consider the examples in Figure 16.6. In a noun phrase consisting of an adjective and a noun, the noun receives the primary stress, but, in a complex noun consisting of an adjective and a noun, it is the adjective that receives primary stress. (Note that the spacing conventions of our writing system are irrelevant to stress placement. *Hot dog* is written as two words, but it follows the same rule of stress placement when it is a complex noun as do other complex nouns written as one word, such a *highchair.*)

Notice that the rules for stress placement discussed for the material in Figure 16.6 depend on information that is available only in the surface structures of sentences. While we have not discussed complex nouns of the type illustrated by the second set of words in Figure 16.6, we have attempted to demonstrate in detail that noun phrases composed of an adjective followed by a noun, as in the first set of words, are the result of applying at least

Figure 16.6

Surface Structure	Examples
NP ╱╲ ADJ N	black bírd soft báll sore héad high cháir green hóuse hot dóg
N ╱╲ ADJ N	bláckbird sóftball sórehead híghchair gréenhouse hót dog

three transformations to deep structures: Relativization, Relative Reduction, and Adjective Inversion. Therefore, we must conclude that phonological rules apply only after surface structures have been produced. We can now expand our schematic view of a total grammar to include phonological rules. Such rules constitute the **phonological component** of a grammar and apply after the syntactic component. Figure 16.7 is an

Figure 16.7

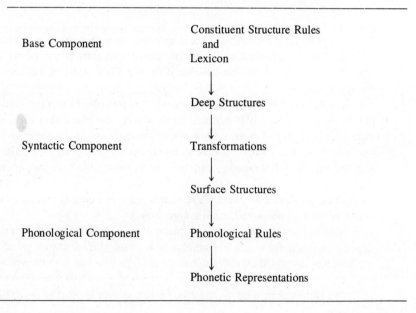

Base Component   Constituent Structure Rules
                                  and
                                Lexicon

Deep Structures

Syntactic Component   Transformations

Surface Structures

Phonological Component   Phonological Rules

Phonetic Representations

expanded version of Figure 16.5. Once the phonological rules have been applied, the result is the phonetic representation of a sentence.

LEXICAL SEMANTICS

Although terminological differences abound in the technical literature, most attempts to describe the linguistic meaning of words (and morphemes) have involved the use of **semantic features.** These features are individual elements of meaning which, when combined, add up to the meaning of a word. (Semantic features, then, are similar to the phonetic features discussed in Part 3 that combine to result in a sound.) As an example, consider the words in (5).

(5) boy   girl
     man   woman

As speakers of English, we know the meaning of these words; even when they occur in isolation from any context or situation, we recognize that the words have, or may have, particular meanings that are different from the meanings of other words. Thus, while *man* in isolation could mean either 'adult male person' or simply 'person', we still know that it does not refer to a kind of plant. Furthermore, we understand certain semantic relationships among the words: all four refer to human beings; *boy* and *girl* are related through the concept of youth (or absence of physical maturity); *man* and *woman* are words for older, more mature individuals; *boy* and *man* are male; *girl* and *woman* are female. These elements of meaning may serve as the basis for definitions; that is, we may use the concepts [human], [young], [old], [male], and [female] as semantic features. These features combine in the four different ways illustrated in Figure 16.8 to represent the meanings of the lexical items *boy, girl, man,* and *woman.*

If we add to the stock of semantic features, other words may be defined. For example, the general feature [animal], along with a more specific feature such as [equine], when combined with [young], [old], [male], and [female], permits the definition of the lexical items in (6).

(6) colt   filly
     stallion   mare

Figure 16.8 _____

boy
human
young
male

girl
human
young
female

man
human
old
male

woman
human
old
female

The examples just cited are quite straightforward, and it should not be difficult to see how the list of semantic features could be extended to provide for other words that refer to animals. A similar procedure has been developed for many other words, including verbs. For instance, the features [motion], [slow], and [fast] could be used for *run* and *walk,* which share the feature [motion] and are distinguished by the features referring to rate of speed.

The determination of the precise set of semantic features necessary to define the lexical items of a language is a monumental undertaking. With phonetic features, as discussed in Chapter 8, linguists are dealing with a relatively limited number of distinct vocal tract activities—a set of activities constrained (or limited) by the observable physical characteristics of a portion of human anatomy. With semantic features, however, we are dealing with concepts that can be formed by the human mind. The mind is not accessible to direct observation, and we do not know what its limits might be. Furthermore, although phonetic features can be defined precisely in terms of physical actions, semantic features must be viewed as **primes**—basic concepts not subject to further division or definition. Given these difficulties, it is not surprising that linguists do not always agree on the specific set of semantic features most appropriate for the definition of a particular word. However, many linguists do seem to agree that some semantic features are a useful descriptive device for the analysis of lexical meaning.

It was observed in Chapter 4 that the lexicon of a grammar contains a list of morphemes; each morpheme is provided with a set of semantic features that serves to describe its meaning. We can now use these semantic features as the explanation for such traditional semantic terms as synonym, antonym, and even homonym.

Specifically, two words are **synonyms** if they have the same set of semantic features; we might refer to synonyms as lexical paraphrases. It is difficult to find a pair of perfect synonyms. It seems that, whenever two words do have the same meaning, they tend to separate, one acquiring an additional semantic feature that distinguishes it from the other. Let us assume, however, that *podiatrist* and *chiropodist* are synonyms. There is certainly some evidence for this assumption. Many people use the words interchangeably. If you look up *podiatrist* in a dictionary, you are often referred to the entry for *chiropodist;* and, in the *Yellow Pages* of the Lansing (Michigan) area telephone book under the heading "Chiropodists," it says "See Podiatrists-Chiropodists." The syntactic and semantic features of *podiatrist* and *chiropodist* are the same. Only their phonological features differ, and since the relationship between semantics and phonology is arbitrary, phonological information is not relevant to the meaning of a word.

It should be noted that common usage of the term synonym is less strict than the more technical definition provided here. Words are described informally as synonyms when they refer to the same thing, as in the case of *child* and *kid* or, for some dialects, *supper* and *dinner*. In such cases, there is generally a stylistic difference involved. *Child* and *dinner,* for example, tend to be more formal than *kid* and *supper*.

Antonyms are two words that share all but one of their semantic features in common. The one exceptional feature must be capable of division into two distinct states along the same dimension. Thus, *big* and *little* are antonyms since both refer to [size] while, at the same time, each involves the opposite dimension of size from the other. Notice that the words *man* and *girl* are not antonyms; they differ by more than one feature.

SYNTAX, SEMANTICS, AND PRAGMATICS

Homonyms are words that share the same phonetic features but have different sets of semantic features; as such, homonyms are the lexical equivalent of ambiguous sentences (which may share a surface syntactic form but have two or more different meanings). Consider the word *bank* in sentence (7).

(7)   We used to meet near the bank on pleasant afternoons.

There are two different interpretations possible for (7). Either the meetings occurred near a financial institution or near an area of land raised above its surroundings. The semantic features are different for the two meanings of *bank*. In one case, *bank* contains semantic features representing the meaning 'financial institution', while in the other case, *bank* contains semantic features specifying the meaning 'land raised above its surroundings'.

Before we conclude this discussion of the lexicon, we must consider one additional aspect of language. We have already observed that the lexical entries of which the lexicon is composed contain semantic features (to account for lexical meaning) and phonetic features (to provide a phonemic representation). In addition, each lexical entry must also specify the syntactic features of a lexical item. Such **syntactic features** are those grammatical properties that are relevant to the production of grammatical sentences. Consider the word *peace*. Sentence (8) is grammatical, but sentence (9) is not.

(8)   No one really expected the participants at the conference to make peace.

(9)   *No one really expected the participants at the conference to peace.

(9) is ungrammatical because *peace* is a noun but has been used in the position of a verb. In order to prevent the insertion of a noun in the verb position, lexical entries must specify whether a word is a noun or a verb. Other syntactically relevant information present in the lexical entry for *peace* includes the fact that it is an abstract, nonhuman noun. Certain verbs can only have human nouns as subjects; thus, no grammar would ever produce a sentence like (10):

(10)   *The peace talked to me for over an hour.

If the lexical entry for *talk* contains the syntactic information that this verb requires a human subject and the lexical entry for *peace* indicates that it is a nonhuman noun, then sentence (10) could never be generated.

It should be noted that the distinction between semantic features and syntactic features, while useful for describing languages, may be arbitrary. That is, certain features may pertain to both semantics and syntax. Thus, it is part of the meaning of *peace* that it has the feature [nonhuman] (recall the use of [human] above as a semantic feature), but, at the same time, we have seen that this feature also plays a syntactic role in the grammar.

In an overview of a complete account of linguistic competence, the description of lexical semantics occurs in the lexicon. The lexicon also contains phonetic features and syntactic features; it forms part of the base component of the grammar (see Figure 16.7).

SENTENCE SEMANTICS

The linguistic meaning of a sentence consists of more than just the sum of lexical meanings involved. In the following examples, the (a) and (b) sentences have different meanings although each pair contains the same words.

253

(11) a. Terry chased the dog.
     b. The dog chased Terry.

(12) a. Janice can swim.
     b. Can Janice swim?

In (11), it is necessary to know which noun phrase, *Terry* or *the dog,* is the subject and which is the object of the sentence, for this information contributes to the meaning of the full sentence. In (12), word order of the subject noun phrase, *Janice,* and the auxiliary, *can,* shows whether the sentence is a statement or a question. These examples indicate that part of the meaning of sentences results from the syntactic structures in which lexical items occur. Consequently, some linguists maintain that sentence semantics should be analyzed and described by rules that operate on the syntactic structures produced by a grammar. Today, this approach is generally referred to as **interpretive semantics,** since semantic rules provide for sentence meaning by interpreting sentences through their structure and the lexical items they contain.

Interpretive semantics first developed in the early 1960s as an attempt to include an account of sentence meaning in descriptive grammars of the form illustrated in Figure 16.7. Over the past fifteen years, linguists have proposed several different hypotheses regarding the type of syntactic structures to which rules of semantic interpretation should be applied. Each proposal succeeds in accounting for certain aspects of sentence semantics but fails to account for other aspects. The arguments and evidence are complex and cannot be described here. We will merely present the basic issues and briefly identify the most well-known hypotheses. "Further Exploration" provides direction to more detailed accounts of sentence semantics.

The fundamental question for interpretive semantics is this: in a descriptive grammar, do semantic interpretation rules apply to deep structures, to surface structures, or to both? The question arises because a descriptive grammar of the form in Figure 16.7 generates several syntactic structures for each sentence: a deep structure (see, for example, Figure 16.3), a variety of intermediate structures (the first three tree diagrams in Figure 16.4), and a surface structure (the final tree diagram in Figure 16.4).

The **standard theory** of interpretive semantics hypothesizes that semantic interpretation should take place at the level of deep structure. In this approach, sentence pairs such as those in (13) and (14) will be assigned the same meaning since they have the same deep structure and it is at the level of deep structure that meaning is assigned.

(13) a. Read the book!
     b. You will read the book!

(14). a. That the elves dug those craters surprised the scientists.
     b. It surprised the scientists that the elves dug those craters.

The deep structure common to (a) and (b) of (13) and the deep structure common to (a) and (b) of (14) are justified by syntactic evidence. (See Chapter 14 regarding the sentences of (13) and Chapter 15 regarding the sentences of (14).) The main advantage to assigning meaning at the deep structure, rather than at the surface structure, is that the deep structure contains elements that may be deleted by transformations, as in (13a), and it provides information about syntactic functions that may be changed by transformations, as in the sentences of (14). In other words, for many types of sentences, the syntactically justified deep structure contains all of the elements necessary for semantic interpretation, whereas the surface structure does not.

Another version of interpretive semantics, the **extended standard theory,** hypothesizes that for limited types of sentences, semantic interpretation depends on both deep structure and surface structure. This hypothesis was developed, in part, because certain syntactically justified transformations appear to cause changes in meaning. If meaning changes between deep and surface structure, then a surface sentence may have a meaning different from the meaning assigned to its deep structure.

Consider the following:

(15) a. The cat chased the mouse.
      b. The mouse was chased by the cat.

As observed in Chapter 15, there is syntactic evidence that these two sentences have a common deep structure and there is a Passive Transformation that operates to change that deep structure into a passive sentence like (15b). In (15), the active and passive sentences have the same semantic interpretation. This is in accord with the standard theory. However, now consider the sentences in (16).

(16) a. Everyone in the room knows two languages.
      b. Two languages are known by everyone in the room.

Syntactically, the sentences of (16) are very similar to those of (15). The (a) sentences consist of the sequence NP$_1$ - V - NP$_2$, while the (b) sentences have the sequence NP$_2$ - be V - by NP$_1$. (*be* stands for *was* and *are,* forms of 'to be'; the subscript numbers show that the subject NP, that is, NP$_1$, in the (a) sentence becomes an object in the (b) sentence, while the (a) sentence object, NP$_2$, is subject of the (b) sentence.) Because of the syntactic similarities of (15) and (16), we would like to say that the sentences of (16) have a common deep structure, as do those of (15), and that, as in (15), the (b) sentence of (16) results from the Passive Transformation. In other words, we wish to retain in our descriptive grammar a generalization about the syntactic rule of Passive. However, we now have a problem for the standard theory. (16a) and (16b) do not have the same meaning. Yet, if semantic interpretation rules apply only to deep structures, (16a) and (16b) will be assigned the same meaning. Apparently, there are certain cases where the Passive Transformation results in a meaning change. (The cases include structures containing words like *two, every, few,* and *many,* which are called quantifiers.) The extended standard theory attempts to account for the data presented here by establishing semantic interpretation rules to apply both to deep structure and to surface structure. In this way, the rules provide the correct meaning both for sentences like (13a), where the subject appears only in deep structure, and for sentences like (16b), where the surface structure has a meaning different from the deep structure.

A third version of interpretive semantics was proposed recently. Called the **revised extended standard theory,** this hypothesis suggests that, in a descriptive grammar, all semantic interpretation occurs at the level of surface structure. This analysis is possible only if we modify our conception of those transformational rules that delete or move constituents in the process of generating surface structures from deep structures. The modification that is necessary requires that such transformations leave a "trace" of the constituent in its original position. This trace would then be available at the surface structure, and, therefore, semantic interpretation could occur. The details of this new proposal remain to be developed. However, we can see some examples of traces in transformations that have been proposed in the past. Consider again the sentences of (14), both of which come from a deep structure in which a complement sentence is embedded in the subject noun phrase. Sentence (14a) results from the application of a deletion transformation, the *it* Deletion rule discussed in Chapter 15. Notice that despite the deletion, the surface structure still contains sufficient information to allow for semantic interpretation. Sentence (14b) results from the application of a movement rule, the Extraposition Transformation, also mentioned in Chapter 15. Again, notice that despite the movement, the surface structure still contains a trace of the subject in its original, deep structure position; that is, *it* remains at the beginning of the surface structure of the sentence. Yet another type of trace that might be left behind following a movement transformation is illustrated in Figure 16.1. The first and last tree diagrams of that figure exemplified the operation of the Particle Movement Transformation and the Adjective Inversion Transformation. In each case, certain constituents were moved but excess nodes remained in the tree structure. These nodes could provide the type of trace necessary to yield semantic interpretations at the surface structure. Therefore, under the revised extended standard theory of semantic interpretation, the excess nodes would not be deleted (as was suggested in the notes to Figure 16.1).

At the conclusion of the discussion of lexical semantics, we observed a problem in attempts to distinguish between semantic features and syntactic features. Notice that the major point of difficulty for sentence semantics also involves the relationship between syntax and semantics. Certain phenomena in the linguistic meaning of sentences are widely recognized: paraphrase, ambiguity, missing meanings, and the contribution of syntactic structure to the meaning of a sentence. What is not clear at the present time is how to organize a formal description of a language to include sentence semantics. Linguists disagree on where the rules of semantic interpretation should be located in the model of a grammar presented in Figure 16.7.

One of the primary reasons for the widespread disagreement about the analysis and description of sentence semantics (in contrast to the more general agreement on phonology, word formation, and syntax) is that semantics is abstract. There are no physical or observable clues to meaning. We can hear sounds, observe the order of morphemes, and detect the sequence of words in the surface structures of sentences; such aspects of the form of language are relatively concrete, and, therefore, they provide fewer problems for analysis. With semantics, however, the linguist is attempting to describe concepts, and relationships among concepts, that reside only in the human mind.

SUMMARY

Figure 16.7 provides a model for a descriptive grammar of a language. The base component contains the constituent structure rules and the lexicon that produce the deep structures of sentences. Transformations then apply to produce surface structures, which are subject to the phonological rules that provide phonetic representations.

The lexicon contains lexical entries, each of which consists of the phonological, semantic, and syntactic features of the morpheme involved. Also included within the lexicon may be the rules of word formation and the redundancy rules that specify predictable phonetic features. While lexical semantics is described by means of the semantic features in the lexicon, it is less clear how sentence semantics should be handled in the model of a grammar offered by Figure 16.7. Three versions of interpretive semantics exist: the standard theory, in which all rules of semantic interpretation apply to deep structures; the extended standard theory, in which semantic interpretation occurs at both deep and surface structure; and the revised extended standard theory, in which deletion and movement transformations leave traces of constituents, thereby permitting all semantic interpretation to occur at the surface structure.

FURTHER EXPLORATION

The formalization and the operation of a number of English transformations are described in several studies mentioned in Part 5: *An Introduction to the Principles of Transformational Syntax* by Adrian Akmajian and Frank Heny, *From Deep to Surface Structure* by Marina K. Burt, and *Beginning English Grammar* by Samuel Jay Keyser and Paul M. Postal. Phonology and its relationship to syntax are discussed in *English Stress: Its Form, Its Growth, and Its Role in Verse* by Morris Halle and Samuel Jay Keyser, an excellent introduction to the prediction of stress from surface structure information about words, phrases, and sentences; particularly relevant are the preface and Chapter 1, "The Stress System of Modern English."

An introductory overview of many aspects of both lexical and sentence semantics is offered by George L. Dillon in *Introduction to Contemporary Linguistic Semantics* and, from a more traditional basis, by Don L. F. Nilsen and Alleen Pace Nilsen in *Semantic Theory: A Linguistic Perspective*. The earliest discussion of the standard theory of interpretive semantics is "The Structure of a Semantic Theory" by Jerrold J. Katz and Jerry A. Fodor (Fodor and Katz 1964); Katz and Paul M. Postal provide a somewhat revised and more detailed discussion in *An Integrated Theory of Linguistic Descriptions*. Noam Chomsky discusses the extended standard theory in the three articles contained in his book *Studies on Semantics in Generative Grammar;* particularly of interest is the article "Deep Structure, Surface Structure, and Semantic Interpretation" (also reprinted in Steinberg and Jakobovits 1971). At this time, relatively little published material is available on the revised extended standard theory, but the hypothesis does appear in the following works, both by Noam Chomsky and valuable for their discussion of many issues in semantics and the goals of linguistics: "Questions of Form and Interpretation" and *Reflections on Language*.

1. Use the constituent structure rules of Figure 15.12 and the formalized transformations of Figure 16.1 to produce the deep structure, intermediate structures, and surface structure of the following sentence. (Follow the pattern provided by Figures 16.3 and 16.4.)

The man who came to dinner turned the radio off.

2. Consider the following phrases, ignoring the spacing between the words. Each is ambiguous when considered in this way, without context, syntactic sentence structure, or stress. Determine two different meanings for each phrase, and, using the phrase, construct a pair of sentences, each representing one of the meanings. Now produce each pair of sentences aloud. Compare the stress placement on the phrase in each sentence pair. What differences, if any, do you observe?

(a) light house keeper
(b) American history teacher
(c) psychotic development expert
(d) black board eraser

3. Metaphors, or metaphorical uses of words, frequently arise through a shift in semantic features. Compare *Willy laughed at the joke* with *Willy cackled at the joke*. The word *laugh* includes the feature [human], but *cackle* usually involves [animal]. Consider the italicized word in each of the following phrases, and describe the semantic feature or features that differ from the normal, non-metaphorical use of the word.

(a) *leg* of a table
(b) *mouth* of a river
(c) *slip* of the tongue
(d) *pulse* of the nation
(e) *head* of a pin

Make up a similar list and description for the metaphorical uses of five additional words.

4. Provide a list of five pairs of antonyms and identify the semantic feature by which the members of each pair differ.

5. Name the semantic or syntactic features that account for the ungrammatical, metaphorical, or otherwise deviant nature of the following sentences.

(a) My sister bought himself a new car.
(b) The coffee pot tried to burn me this morning.
(c) The elephant read the newspaper.
(d) Mary flew up the stairs when she heard the baby cry.

6. Consider the following pair of sentences:

(a) Even Susan could swim the length of this pool.
(b) Susan could swim the length of even this pool.

To what extent do these sentences have the same meaning? Does (a) imply anything different than (b) about Susan's swimming ability or about the length of the pool? If, in a descriptive grammar, (a) and (b) shared a common deep structure and their difference in surface form was the result of some *even* Movement transformation, which theory of interpretive semantics would result in the correct assignment of meaning for both sentences—the standard theory or the extended standard theory? Why?

171717171717171717171717171

MEANING
AND USE

In the last chapter, the study of semantics was introduced within the context of a model for a descriptive grammar in which syntax played the central role. This approach to semantics was the first developed within contemporary transformational linguistics, and it is not surprising that when such linguists turned their attention to meaning, they attempted to relate semantics to those portions of the grammar that had already been explored and to limit the study of meaning to linguistic competence. However, a more traditional approach to semantics, as well as to meaning in a broader sense, begins, not with syntax, but with meaning itself. When approached in this way, the study of meaning includes not only the exact, literal meaning of words and sentences, but also aspects of meaning that derive from linguistic performance, intentions of the speaker, knowledge of the world shared by speaker and listener, expectations of the participants in a conversation, and other matters that relate linguistic utterances to the general context in which they occur. This approach to meaning is sometimes referred to as pragmatics, and, in this chapter, we will sketch some aspects of the study of pragmatics and its relationship to literal, linguistic meaning (i.e., to semantics). We begin, however, with one aspect of semantics that has not been discussed as yet.

SEMANTIC RELATIONS

In Chapters 13 and 15, we described the syntactic functions that are fulfilled by noun phrases as these occur in various relationships to other elements of a syntactic structure. For example, a noun phrase that occurs sentence-initially as a constituent of a sentence can be described as the subject of that sentence, while the same noun phrase, in another sentence, will serve the function of direct object of the verb if it follows the verb and is a constituent of the verb phrase construction. Syntactic functions are, indeed, syntactic: they refer to positions and relationships among elements in a syntactic structure. However, when we emphasize the meaning of a sentence, syntactic functions provide only an incomplete account of the necessary semantic interpretation.

Consider the following sentences:

(1) John opened the door.
(2) The key opened the door.

In (1), *John* is the subject; in (2), the subject is *the key*. If we described these sentences only with such syntactic functions, however, we would miss an important aspect of meaning. In (1), *John* is the agent, the "doer" of the action. In (2), though, *the key* is not the agent at all; it is the instrument by means of which some (unspecified) agent has accomplished the action. Now consider sentence (3).

(3) John opened the door with the key.

Here *John* is the subject and the agent, but *the key* is now object of the preposition; nevertheless, *the key* remains the instrument. Such relationships of meaning among noun phrases, as agent and instrument, are known as **semantic relations,** or **case relations.**

Figure 17.1 provides brief definitions of four case relations commonly used in English, along with examples that demonstrate the distinction between the semantic relations expressed by cases and the syntactic functions performed by noun phrases. Notice that a noun phrase, such as *the key,* may have several syntactic functions (object of a preposition, direct object, subject) and several semantic relations (instrument, patient). However, while there are few restrictions on the variety of syntactic functions a particular noun phrase can perform, there are restrictions, related closely to meaning, on the number of semantic relations expressed by a particular noun phrase. Thus, an inanimate noun such as *door* is rarely, if ever, the agent or experiencer, while an animate noun such as *John* is seldom an instrument. Only under bizarre circumstances, or in metaphorical uses, would a sentence like (4) occur; (5) rarely means that John was the object by means of which Bill opened the door.

(4) The door saw John arrive.
(5) Bill opened the door with John.

In order to understand the linguistic meaning of a sentence, it is necessary to know, not only the syntactic functions of noun phrases, but also their semantic relations. For this reason, it is necessary to include an account of semantic relations in a complete descrip-

Figure 17.1 _____

Case Relations	*Definitions*
agent	that which actually performs an action specified by the verb; usually the agent is an animate noun (animal or human).
patient	that which is directly affected by the action specified by the verb; the patient may be either an animate noun or an inanimate noun (a physical object); this case relation is also referred to as the recipient or the object.
experiencer	that which participates in the nonaction experience specified by the verb; the experiencer is generally an animate noun.
instrument	that which serves as the tool, instrument, or means by which the action of the verb is accomplished; the instrument is almost always an inanimate noun.

Examples

AGENT		PATIENT		INSTRUMENT	
John	opened	the door	with	the key.	
SUBJECT		DIRECT OBJECT		OBJECT OF PREPOSITION	

EXPERIENCER		PATIENT		PATIENT	
John	saw	the door	and	the key.	
SUBJECT		DIRECT OBJECT		DIRECT OBJECT	

PATIENT
The door opened.
SUBJECT

INSTRUMENT		PATIENT
The key	opened	the door.
SUBJECT		DIRECT OBJECT

---

tive grammar of a language. Some linguists have proposed that this can be accomplished by considering combinations of semantic features (such as [animate] and [inanimate]) and syntactic functions. (For example, if an [animate] noun is the subject of a verb with the semantic feature [action], that noun usually will be the agent; if the [animate] noun is the subject of a verb with the semantic feature [nonaction], that noun normally will be the experiencer.) Other linguists maintain that semantic relations are primes and should be part of the deep structure of sentences. One version of the latter position is called **case grammar** and references are provided in "Further Exploration;" another version is discussed later in this chapter under the heading of "Generative Semantics." No matter which alternative is selected, it is clear that semantic relations are an important aspect of meaning.

PRAGMATICS

Semantics is the study of the direct, literal, purely linguistic meaning of a sentence. However, in many cases when people actually use sentences, in natural, normal, real-life situations, they mean more than what they actually say. Further, listeners understand this "additional" meaning despite the fact that there may be little or nothing present in the sentence itself to convey it. Consider (6).

(6)   Can you take out the garbage?

Linguistically, (6) is a question, specifically a *yes/no* question formed by the syntactic rules explored at the conclusion of Chapter 14. If we restricted our analysis of the meaning of (6) to its semantics, we could stop at this point and simply apply the rules of semantic interpretation for questions in English. But this approach would eliminate an important aspect of the broader meaning of (6). In the real world, (6) may be an imperative. That is, despite the fact that (6) is syntactically a question and that it does not have the syntactic form of a command [compare (7)], (6) is frequently used as a (rather polite) request for action.

(7)   Take out the garbage!

Indeed, the appropriate response to (6) is often the same as the appropriate response to (7)—the person addressed, if willing to respond positively to the request, picks up the garbage and takes it out; the person does not respond simply by answering "yes" or "no." When we discuss sentences in this way, referring to actual utterances in particular circumstances, including both semantic and pragmatic factors, we are considering concrete acts of speech (or, **speech acts,** as they are called by linguists).

A concept useful in describing speech acts such as the one just mentioned is **illocutionary force.** The term refers to the speaker's communicative intention in producing an utterance. Types of illocutionary force include assertions, requests for action (imperatives), and requests for information (questions). In (6), the illocutionary force involved may indeed be a request for information, but in many real-life situations, the illocutionary force is a request for action. (7), however, can represent only the intention of a request for action. Since illocutionary force is defined in terms of the speaker's intent, and not the strictly linguistic meaning of a sentence structure, it is an aspect of pragmatics.

Whenever we speak, we have some intention in speaking. Sometimes, the intention is implicit; it is not conveyed directly by the utterance produced, as above in (6). At other times, however, the utterance itself directly signals our intention to a listener. Consider the following sentences:

(8)   I promise to arrive on time.

(9)   I pronounce you man and wife.

(10)   I command you to salute.

In each of these utterances, the act of saying the sentence actually constitutes a performance of the intention. Thus, one makes a promise by virtue of saying (8). A minister performs his intention of marrying a couple by stating (9). And a military officer explicitly commands through an utterance like (10). Verbs such as *promise, pronounce,* and *command* are thus called **performative verbs.**

Compare (8) with (11).

(11) I try to arrive on time.

The verb *try* is not a performative verb; in saying (11) the speaker may be asserting his or her efforts to arrive punctually but to utter (11) is not the same as to actually try.

Now compare (10) with (12).

(12) Salute!

Notice that both have the same illocutionary force—they are both imperatives in that they request an action. In (10), the illocutionary force is actually specified in the utterance, while in (12) it is not. Similar situations hold for other speech acts. Consider the sentence pairs below.

(13) (a) I tell you that John did read the book.
    (b) John did read the book.

(14) (a) I ask you whether you are going to Chicago.
    (b) Are you going to Chicago?

Tell and *ask* function in the (a) sentences as performative verbs, just as *command* does in (10). Because of the clear relationship between sentences such as (10) and (12), and between the (a) and (b) sentences of (13) and (14), some linguists have maintained that, in their deep structures, all sentences contain performative verbs. Under such an analysis, for example, (13a) and (13b) would have the same deep structure, and these sentences will be described as having the same semantic and pragmatic aspects of meaning. A simplified deep structure for the sentences of (13) is offered in Figure 17.2.

Figure 17.2 _____

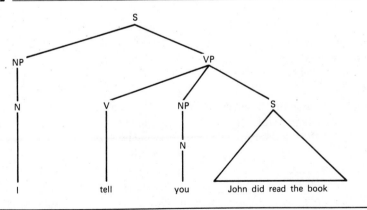

Note: that, which appears in the surface structure of (13a), is added by the transformational rule of *that* Insertion, mentioned in Chapter 15.

Observe that if all sentences are analyzed with deep structure performative verbs, the difference between sentence (8) and sentence (11) becomes clear. Informally, the deep structure of (8) is much like its surface structure—*I promise you* [*I arrive on time*]. The deep structure of (11), however, contains a different performative—*I tell you* [*I try* [*I arrive on time*]]. (The square brackets here are used to show the boundaries of the sentences embedded within the full sentence.)

The examples above, and that in Figure 17.2, illustrate another way in which performative analysis reflects pragmatic as well as semantic aspects of meaning. Notice that in each case, the performative verb is part of a sentence sequence *I VERB you: I tell you, I promise you, I command you*. In a practical sense, for actual communication to occur, someone must produce an utterance (*I*) and someone else must hear or read it (*you*). These participants are part of the speech act and, therefore, part of the pragmatic meaning of an utterance.

The act of communication involves other pragmatic factors beyond the participants and the illocutionary force that concerns the speaker's intent. In normal conversations, the participants share certain expectations about the way in which the dialogue will be conducted. These expectations, or **conversational principles,** include the following: (1) the speaker will be sincere and will tell the truth, (2) what is said must be relevant to the topic, the situation, the relationships between the participants, and so on, and (3) an appropriate amount of direct information will be conveyed, neither more nor less than is necessary for communication. Perfectly grammatical sentences, from the syntactic perspective, may be inappropriate in speech situations if they violate one or more of the conversational principles. Confusion, boredom, or anger may result; communication will be disrupted. Consider, for example, sentence (10), repeated here as (15), produced by a general addressing a private.

(15) I command you to salute.

If the general is not sincere in wanting the private to actually carry out the command, and yet the general produces (15), the private will salute, the general will become angry, and total confusion may result. Similarly, (15) can be produced appropriately only by the general addressing the private (not by the private addressing the general) and only when the private is not saluting or has not saluted the general during this encounter. Furthermore, in producing (15), the general need not offer any detailed explanation for his command; that is, he need not provide his listener with a full account of military rules and regulations regarding a general's authority to issue commands, his right to be saluted, or the physical motions involved in executing a proper salute.

The same principles hold for ordinary conversation. If I ask you what time it is, you will expect that I am sincere in my question and that I don't know the answer; I will expect you to answer and to answer truthfully. Furthermore, you must respond appropriately (you may not say *It rained yesterday*) and at reasonable length (do not embed the time in a long description of your watch or of the internal workings of an electric clock).

Since pragmatics involves human beings, as well as the utterances that they produce, it should not be surprising that conversational principles can be, and often are, violated under certain circumstances. In this society, all but the most naive consumer realizes that at least some of the principles are suspended in a commercial for a soap product. No advertiser provides all of the information a consumer might need in order to evaluate a product fully. Thus, we may hear that the product *cleans 40% better*. Better than what? The principle requiring sufficient information has been ignored.

PRESUPPOSITION

Another aspect of meaning concerns the knowledge of the world and of situations that participants in a conversation have. Certain phenomena of language use are controlled by principles relating to such knowledge. For example, it usually is not appropriate to open a conversation with a stranger by saying (16).

> (16) Hello. It's very nice to meet you. By the way, have you seen the flashlight?

Unless you are sure that the stranger knows about a particular flashlight somewhere in the vicinity of the conversation, (16) does not make much sense. When we use the word *the*, we generally are referring to some object that is known to both speaker and listener. The word *a,* on the other hand, is used when neither speaker nor listener are certain of a particular object. Thus, if we replace *the flashlight* by *a flashlight* in (16), we have an utterance that would be appropriate under conditions where the listener may be unaware of the presence of any flashlight in the vicinity and the speaker may not know of a particular flashlight. Whenever we speak, we make assumptions, perhaps unconscious assumptions, about the knowledge that we share with our listeners. Such assumptions which affect our use of language are called **presuppositions.**

The sentences from exploration (6) of the last chapter concerned presupposition. They are repeated here as (17) and (18).

> (17) Even Susan could swim the length of this pool.

> (18) Susan could swim the length of even this pool.

(17) presupposes, or assumes, that Susan is not a very good swimmer and that the pool is relatively small. (18), on the other hand, presupposes that Susan is an excellent swimmer and that this pool is extraordinarily long. An interesting property of presuppositions is that sentences seem deviant when they violate one of their own presuppositions. For example, consider (19) and (20).

> (19) Even Susan, who won a gold medal in swimming, could swim the length of this pool.

> (20) Susan could swim the length of even this pool, which is exceptionally short.

(19) and (20) seem to involve contradictions, despite the fact that neither sentence contains an explicit statement of the presupposition that is contradicted by the added relative clause.

All sentences involve presuppositions. Sentence (21), for example, is a very simple sentence, yet it includes all of the presuppositions of (22) and probably others as well.

> (21) Alan's wife works for the state of Michigan.

(22) a. A person named Alan exists.
    b. The listener knows Alan.
    c. Alan is an adult male.
    d. Alan is married.
    e. Alan's wife is alive.
    f. There is a state named Michigan.
    g. Michigan has employees.

Some of these presuppositions appear rather clearly in (21), so that the fact that the verb *works* is in the present tense directly implies that Alan's wife is alive. Other presuppositions are not directly stated; here, the speaker simply assumes that the listener knows Alan. The knowledge of the world, semantics, and pragmatics that enables speakers and listeners to communicate the meanings of (22) through the utterance (21) is a part of language use. How information about presuppositions is to be included in a descriptive grammar is a matter on which linguists do not agree, but it is beyond dispute that presupposition plays an important role in the production and comprehension of speech acts.

GENERATIVE SEMANTICS

The aspects of meaning that have been outlined in this chapter are difficult, but not impossible, to incorporate into a descriptive grammar of the form presented in Figure 16.7. Readers will recall that semantics in such a grammar is described by rules of semantic interpretation that operate on syntactic structures (although, as was discussed in Chapter 16, there is some debate over which syntactic structures provide the appropriate location for semantic interpretation). An alternative to interpretive semantics is offered by the theory of **generative semantics.**

Generative semantics accounts for meaning directly, not through syntactic structure. In generative semantics, a descriptive grammar begins with a deep structure that is semantic and, to some extent, pragmatic. This deep structure consists of combinations of semantic features, semantic relations, performatives, and presuppositions. Deep structures are then subject to lexical insertions and transformations to ultimately yield surface structures, which then serve as the structures to which the rules of the phonological component apply.

In a generative semantic account of a language, all meaning is present in this deep structure (sometimes called **logical structure** in order to distinguish it from the syntactic deep structures of interpretive semantics). Syntactic constituent structure rules do not produce the deep logical structures and transformations never result in changes of the meaning of a sentence. Furthermore, since this deep structure is purely semantic, generative semantics appears to be a clever means for describing paraphrase and ambiguity, both for syntax and for lexical items. This is particularly clear when we consider that some paraphrase relations hold between a single lexical item and a phrase with syntactic structure.

Consider the following sentences:

(23) In the old westerns, the hero would always kill his opponent in a gunfight.

(24) In the old westerns, the hero would always cause his opponent to die in a gunfight.

Although they are stylistically distinct, (23) and (24) can be understood as paraphrases of one another. Yet, these two surface structures are very different syntactically. (23) contains the single lexical item *kill,* while the corresponding portion of (24), *cause to die,* is a phrase. In interpretive semantics, the rules of semantic interpretation can be stated in such a way as to provide the same interpretation for *kill* and *cause to die.* In generative semantics, however, the issue can be handled more directly—the corresponding elements simply have the same deep semantic structure, a possible solution since deep structure in generative semantics does not include any syntactic information.

One difficulty with the generative semantics approach is its failure, up to the present time, to provide a detailed account of how the semantic deep structures are converted into syntactic structures. However, interpretive semantics has been criticized for failure to provide a sufficiently formal account of the rules of semantic interpretation and the principles by means of which the theory incorporates information about presupposition, illocutionary force, and semantic relations. Which approach to the description of human languages is more adequate remains an open question of great concern to those linguists who seek to develop a model for descriptive grammars.

LINGUISTICS, PSYCHOLINGUISTICS, AND SOCIOLINGUISTICS

Part 1 of this book provided a distinction between descriptive linguistics and linguistic competence, on the one hand, and other approaches to the study of language and linguistic performance, on the other hand. The distinction has been useful in guiding working, professional linguists in their efforts to cope with the complexities of language, but it has resulted in a somewhat artificial division between language and language use. Psycholinguistics and sociolinguistics attempt to avoid this division by investigating the connections between speakers' linguistic competence and their linguistic performance in natural language use. At the same time, linguistics has begun to incorporate into descriptive grammars data on such matters as illocutionary force and presupposition. Thus, the dividing line between language and language use is beginning to disappear. However, it is still necessary to recognize that much of the linguistic material available in print consists of descriptive grammars of linguistic competence.

A descriptive grammar is a set of rules that reflect the kind of knowledge people have of their language. It is not a reflection of the process they use to produce or to understand sentences. The grammar is neutral with regard to the speaker and the hearer. It represents the knowledge that both require to carry out their language performance, but it is neither a model of the speaker nor a model of the hearer. This point is sometimes misunderstood, possibly because the grammar generates sentences, starting from meaning and ultimately yielding a phonetic representation. It may seem to be a model of the speaker, but it is not. What is centrally important about a grammar is the information it contains about the sentences of a language, and that information must be possessed by speaker and hearer alike.

That people do possess the kind of linguistic knowledge represented in grammars is beyond doubt, but in what form this knowledge is stored and utilized is largely unknown. It may be that people know a set of rules very much like those in a grammar and that they also command certain processes for speaking and listening that are based on those rules. The question of how linguistic knowledge is actually utilized in linguistic performance is a matter for research by psychologists, neurophysiologists, and others who deal with people and their psychological and physiological characteristics. Many aspects of language use are determined, not by linguistic rules, but rather by physiological and psychological properties of human beings. Memory span prevents overly long and complex utterances from occurring or, if they should occur, from being understood; attention span of listeners discourages monotonous repetition of identical syntactic structures in speech or writing; physical properties of the brain, the vocal tract, and the hearing mechanism result in certain productions and perceptions and prohibit others. Some of these factors were mentioned in earlier chapters; others are discussed in Parts 8 and 9, which deal with language acquisition, reading, and writing. For additional information, see the references in "Further Exploration" at the conclusion of this chapter.

The use of linguistic competence is also affected by social factors. The social status of speaker and listener may indicate that only certain styles of speech are appropriate. In societies where individuals speak several dialects, or even several languages, there are conventions that govern the particular dialect or language that is most suitable for particular topics of conversation or for conversation among particular people. Chapter 6 included discussion of certain social aspects of word use; Chapters 20 and 26 deal with social dialects; other information about sociolinguistic topics can be found in the references provided below under "Further Exploration."

LINGUISTIC UNIVERSALS

A descriptive grammar of a particular language, as an account of speakers' linguistic competence, still does not reveal very much about the nature of language. If only a single language is described, it is not possible to tell from that description which aspects of the language are general properties of all human languages and which are particular aspects of the language in question. The general properties of all human languages are known as **language universals.**

In any discipline involving the study of natural phenomena, scholars are concerned not only with describing what they observe but also with determining the general properties of the phenomenon under investigation. So, in the study of language, linguists are interested in determining language universals as well as in writing grammars of particular languages. In fact, the two tasks are interrelated. Once the universal properties of language have been discovered, it is no longer necessary that these universal aspects be mentioned in the grammar of each language. At the same time, the study of particular languages provides evidence for hypotheses about universals. If, after investigating a wide range of different languages, the linguist finds the same characteristics over and over again, he can begin to assume that the recurring property is universal.

There are any number of conceivable ways in which people could communicate with one another. For example, there seems to be no reason why a language could not exist without transformations; that is, deep and surface structure could be identical. But, in fact, no such language exists. The distinction between an abstract, underlying structure and a different, concrete, surface structure for sentences is universal. All languages follow the same general pattern.

Generally, we are more aware of the diversity among languages than of the similarities. Even when we listen to someone who speaks a dialect of our own language, we notice the differences but ignore all of the similarities between his speech and ours. But the diversity among languages and dialects is superficial. It occurs primarily at the level of surface structure and phonetics. Careful investigation of the underlying structure of languages has demonstrated that at this more abstract level, the similarities among languages are very great indeed.

Although we find great diversity in the sounds used in different human languages, there are certain general patterns in all languages. No matter how distinct two sounds may seem to be, all sounds are the result of a very limited number of vocal tract activities. The phonetic features needed to describe all of the sounds in every human language probably do not exceed thirty-five in number. The set of phonetic features is universal; every language must make use of some of the features in this set and no others, although not all languages use all of the features.

In drawing from the universal set of phonetic features, languages are constrained in very definite ways. A language need not use the feature [covered], but it must utilize the feature [continuant]. All languages have stops and at least one fricative. Furthermore, certain sound segments occur in almost all languages. There are few reports of languages that do not have the vowel [a]. Among the consonants, almost every language makes use of [p, t, k, s, n]. In addition to such specific limitations on diversity in sound systems, there are also general patterns to which every language must conform. Although the human vocal tract can produce more than a dozen different affricates, no language makes use of all of them. In fact, the number of affricates in a language is never greater than the number of stops in that language. Similar pattern restrictions occur for vowels. Any vowel can be nasalized, and it is therefore conceivable that a language could have only [+ nasal] vowels. However, no such language exists, and, in fact, no language has more [+ nasal] vowels than [− nasal] vowels. The number of [+ nasal] vowels can never be greater than the number of [− nasal] vowels in any language.

Not only are the actual sounds of language based on a universal set of features and general patterns of organization, the kinds of phonological rules that link phonemic and phonetic representations are also limited. Rules of assimilation, for example, appear to operate under universal constraints that do not allow a rule to change more than a few features of a sound. We find examples of stops becoming voiceless in word-final position (a simple change of [+ voice] to [− voice]), vowels becoming nasalized before nasal consonants ([− nasal] to [+ nasal]), and nasals assimilating to the position of articulation of the following consonant (involving a change in only the position of articulation features). However, in no language is there a rule that changes [č] to [o] in any environment. Such a change would involve almost every feature, and it is part of the nature of language that radical changes of this kind simply do not occur.

There are also universal limitations on the kinds of sound sequences. No language contains words made up of an initial consonant cluster containing six consonants in a row, nor do languages contain words consisting of a long sequence of vowels. Three consecutive vowels seem to be the limit in language, and, even when three vowels are in sequence, one or more of them is usually converted into a glide.

We have presented only a few examples of phonological universals, but these are sufficient to illustrate the fact that, although sound systems differ from one language to another, there are limitations to diversity. It may be said that people are usually unaware of just how limited diversity is because unconsciously they expect to find the similarities. The universals are not striking because they constitute part of every language, and, as human beings, we know what language is. A similar situation exists for syntax, semantics, and pragmatics.

We have already stated that all languages contain deep structures, surface structures, and transformations, but there are even more specific universals of syntax. There is no known language that lacks ambiguity, paraphrases, or processes for forming imperatives, questions, and negatives, as well as declarative, affirmative statements. Furthermore, in all languages words are organized into classes, such as nouns, verbs, and adjectives, and sentences are always subject to constituent structure analysis.

No matter how superficially different from English a language may appear to be, the same kinds of transformations will occur. Transformations that delete, add, and rearrange constituents, as well as those that substitute one form for another, occur in every human language under investigation. Just as there are constraints on the kinds of changes that can be brought about by phonological rules, there are also limitations on the changes made by transformations. Deletion transformations, for example, are highly restricted. They can eliminate material from an underlying structure only when the constituent that is deleted occurs elsewhere in the structure or when it is a pro-form or when it is highly specific. The Equi NP Deletion Transformation in English obeys the first restriction, the Pro-Form Deletion rule follows the second, and the Imperative Transformation, which specifies *you* in its structural description, is an example of the third restriction. On the other hand, there is no transformation in any language that deletes the last word in every sentence or every third word in questions. There is a reason for these limitations. Since the function of language is to convey meaning, transformations must not destroy the meaning of a sentence. Listeners must be able to recapture the basic meaning of a sentence from the surface structure they hear. If transformations could delete any and all constituents without limit, there would be no way for a listener to determine what had been eliminated from a sentence. By limiting deletion to the three situations described above, languages provide listeners with enough information in surface structures to recapture the meaning. It should also be noted that addition transformations are constrained, too. No transformation can add morphemes that change the meaning of a sentence. The *for to* Insertion rule is an example because these morphemes do not contribute to the meaning of sentences to which they are added. Sentence (25) is not grammatical in English, but it contains all elements necessary for the interpretation of its meaning. Sentence (26) is a grammatical surface structure, but the morphemes added transformationally do not add to its meaning. As we observed earlier, a sentence similar to (25) underlies (26).

(25) *John leave early is unusual.

(26) For John to leave early is unusual.

Many of the observable differences in the syntax of languages are matters of surface structure. One common distinction, for example, is whether adjectives precede or follow the nouns they modify. Although English and Spanish differ in this respect at the surface, we have seen that, at an intermediate level, adjectives do follow nouns in English, just as they do in Spanish. They are moved to a position before nouns by the Adjective Inversion Transformation, which occurs in the grammar of English but not in that of Spanish. Although (27) is a grammatical phrase in Spanish, its word-for-word translation into English as (28) would be only an intermediate English structure that is converted into the grammatical surface form (29) by the Adjective Inversion rule.

(27) *una brisa suave*

(28) a breeze soft

(29) a soft breeze

As we move below the surface of language, we find more and more similarities among languages. At the same time, it becomes more difficult to collect evidence in support of the analysis of individual languages at the deeper, more abstract levels. Thus, as we approach the level of deep structure, we expect to find that languages share a great deal in common; perhaps all languages even have the same rules to generate deep structures. It may be that there is a set of constituent structure rules that are correct for every human language—a universal set of rules. Alternatively, within the generative semantics approach, the semantic deep structures posited for English may also be appropriate for other languages. We must admit, however, that at the present time, our knowledge of deep structures, even for English, is still too limited to support either hypothesis.

There is one rather convincing argument in support of a theory of a universal underlying structure, but it is indirect and not drawn from completed descriptions of languages. The argument is based on the fact that all children master their native language perfectly and in a very short period of time, despite great variation in the amount and kind of language samples to which they are exposed. To learn a language means to learn the structures underlying sentences, as well as their surface forms. Yet, deep structures are not observable; they are highly abstract. How, then, do children manage to learn them? The hypothesis shared by many modern linguists and psychologists is that human beings are born with an innate capacity to learn language, and this capacity includes the universal properties of language. Any universal aspect of language does not have to be learned by children. Their only task is to determine the language-specific aspects of the language spoken in their environment. If the underlying structures of sentences are universal, then children do not really have to learn them. In an unconscious sense, they already know these structures and the principles that produce them. Their task in learning their native language is less complex than might be expected at first glance, for they do not have to learn underlying structures. They need only determine the specific rules in their language for converting these structures into their surface forms. A theory of universal underlying structure may explain, in part, how it is that children accomplish the task of learning their native language. We will return to this topic in Part 8, "Language Acquisition."

SUMMARY

The meaningful role of noun phrases with reference to other noun phrases and verbs in sentences is described by semantic relations. Commonly used semantic relations in English include agent, patient, experiencer, and instrument. Such relations are correlated with, but not equivalent to, syntactic functions. For example, an inanimate noun phrase such as *the key* may have the semantic relation of instrument when it is functioning either as a syntactic subject or as the object of a preposition.

In addition to semantic relations and those aspects of semantics surveyed in Chapter 16, a complete investigation of meaning must involve the pragmatic factors that concern illocutionary force, performative verbs, conversational principles, and a variety of psycholinguistic and sociolinguistic principles that affect actual language use. Presupposition also plays an important role in the production and comprehension of speech acts. Generative semantics provides an alternative to the interpretive semantics theories for the inclusion of semantic and pragmatic information in a linguistic description. In generative semantics, the deep (logical) structure includes no information about syntax but rather is a purely semantic combination of semantic features, semantic relations, performatives, and presuppositions.

Although there is widespread diversity among human languages, much of this diversity exists at the surface of language. When deeper, more abstract aspects of language are investigated, it becomes clear that there are many universals, common to all languages. These universals establish limits to the diversity and provide for a core of shared features in all languages. We have presented only a small sample of the universals of phonology and syntax. Other universals, particularly those in semantics, are more difficult to determine, but it is reasonable to hypothesize that the closer one comes to semantics, the more universals one will find.

A strong theory of language universals, one which removes many aspects from particular grammars by explaining them as properties of all languages, may explain how it is that children are able to learn a system as complex and abstract as human language in a relatively short period of time.

The grammar of a particular language, as well as a set of universals, is a description of the knowledge people have of their language. It is not an account of language use, but rather of the knowledge underlying such use. As we come to understand more about language, it becomes more feasible to develop a theory of language performance.

FURTHER EXPLORATION

Many of the topics of this chapter are discussed in three introductory works on semantics: *Introduction to Contemporary Linguistic Semantics* by George L. Dillon, *Semantic Theory: A Linguistic Perspective* by Don L. F. Nilsen and Alleen Pace Nilsen, and *Semantics: A New Outline* by F. R. Palmer. Semantic relations, and case grammar, were brought to the attention of modern American linguists by Charles J. Fillmore in the article "The Case for Case" (Bach and Harms 1968).

A detailed but quite clear presentation of illocutionary force and performative verbs is *Toward a Linguistic Theory of Speech Acts* by Jerrold M. Sadock. A variety of conversational principles are discussed by H. Paul Grice in "Logic and Conversation" and by David Gordon and George Lakoff in "Conversational Postulates;" both of these articles, and others of similar interest, appear in *Syntax and Semantics Volume 3: Speech Acts,* edited by Peter Cole and Jerry L. Morgan.

Informal discussion of generative semantics and interpretive semantics, as well as such matters as presupposition and pragmatic aspects of language, appears in interviews with Noam Chomsky and George Lakoff in *Discussing Language,* edited by Herman Parret. Somewhat more demanding is the chapter entitled "Generative Semantics versus the Extended Standard Theory" in *Guide to Transformational Grammar* by John T. Grinder and Suzette Haden Elgin.

Psycholinguistic aspects of language and language use are described by Dan I. Slobin in *Psycholinguistics* and, in more detail, by Jerry A. Fodor, Thomas G. Bever, and Merrill F. Garrett in *The Psychology of Language.* Two surveys of sociolinguistics are: *Sociolinguistics: An Introduction* by Peter Trudgill and *The Sociology of Language* by Joshua A. Fishman.

The classic work on phonological universals is Roman Jakobson's *Child Language, Aphasia, and Phonological Universals.* A number of articles on linguistic universals appear in *Universals of Language,* edited by Joseph H. Greenberg. More demanding are the articles in *Universals in Linguistic Theory,* edited by Emmon Bach and Robert T. Harms.

1. Identify the case relation of each noun phrase in the following sentences.

(a) Harry trained the dog.
(b) The dog was trained by Harry.
(c) The butcher cut the steak with a knife.
(d) Joan left by train.
(e) The watchman became ill.

2. Identify both the syntactic form (statement, question, imperative) and the illocutionary force (assertion, request for information, request for action) of each of the following utterances. If more than one illocutionary force is possible, describe a context in which each possibility might occur.

(a) I wish that you would finish your dinner.
(b) Why don't you stop hitting your brother?
(c) Have some of this candy!
(d) Shouldn't we leave soon?
(e) I wonder if Gerry knows that.

3. For each of the following sentences, draw a deep structure that includes a performative verb. (See Figure 17.2 for an example.) Provide as much detail as possible based on the discussion in this chapter and on the information about deep structures that was presented in Part 5.

(a) Are you going to Chicago?

(b) Salute!

(c) Explain the problem!

(d) The talented dancer fell.

(e) Bill knows that Mary is ill.

4. If all sentences are analyzed to include a performative verb in their deep structure, then the following pairs of sentences will have different deep structures.

(a) (i) You will salute. (statement)

(ii) You will salute! (imperative)

(b) (i) John has finished his work. (statement)

(ii) John has finished his work? (question)

Explain why.

5. Describe, as fully as possible, a set of conversational principles and presuppositions that would have to exist for the following utterance to be appropriate in a conversation.

I received the latest hospital bill only this morning.

6. Explain the following in terms of presupposition.

When did you stop beating your wife?

PART 7777777777777777777
VARIATION

The flexibility inherent in human language is one of its most important characteristics. On the one hand, every human language must make use of certain universal properties, a fact which limits the amount of diversity possible among different languages. On the other hand, within any particular language, it is difficult to find any two speakers who use their language in exactly the same way. Our speech is somewhat like our signature—it is unique. We all differ to at least a slight extent in the lexical items we use, in our pronunciation, and even in the syntactic structures that occur in our speech. Yet, there are limits to this diversity among individual speakers, for communication is possible only because all speakers of a language share a certain basic, underlying system of knowledge about phonology, semantics, and syntax.

When we investigate language, we are faced with the dual problem of universality and diversity. In the broadest sense, all human languages are the same—all are instances of the general, universal phenomenon **language.** But, since no two people use their language in the same way, there are as many representations of language as there are human beings who use language. The term **idiolect** has been devised to describe the speech of a particular individual.

If we study many samples of idiolects from all over the world, we find that some idiolects are more similar to one another than are other idiolects. In other words, certain idiolects share linguistic features not found in others. By comparing idiolects in this way, we can arrive at a view of the different languages of the world. And, of course, in exactly the same way, we can divide the speakers of a language into groups, where the speech of each group contains certain features not found in the other groups. A procedure such as this would serve to identify the **dialects** of a language.

277

The difference between a language and a dialect is a matter of degree. Both terms refer to a system of communication that is used by one group of people and contains some characteristics not present in the communication system of another group. There is a kind of hierarchy in the organization of idiolects, dialects, languages, and human language in general. If we start with individual speakers and their idiolects, we can see that a dialect is simply a set of similar idiolects, and a language is a set of similar dialects. Human language in general is composed of a number of languages, all of which are similar to one another in that they contain the universal properties that characterize human language.

In this part, we will investigate some of the sources of the linguistic variations that result in separate languages, dialects, and idiolects. We will survey some of the basic characteristics of regional and social dialects of American English and attempt to point out the major dialect divisions and their distribution within our society.

CHAPTER 18 18 18 18 18 18 18 18 18 18 18 18 18 18 18

LINGUISTIC CHANGE: RELATED LANGUAGES AND DIALECTS

The study of language change is referred to as **diachronic** (or **historical**) **linguistics,** in contrast to **synchronic linguistics,** which investigates languages at a particular point in time (usually the present). For the most part, this text has concentrated on a synchronic perspective, although diachronic issues have been mentioned, especially in Chapters 5 and 10.

A major concern in diachronic studies are the types of changes that occur over time in the various subsystems of language. Lexical change includes several phenomena: additions and deletions of morphemes in the lexicon, changes in the meaning of morphemes, and alterations in the rules of word formation. These matters were discussed in Chapter 5. Phonological change, surveyed briefly in Chapter 10, involves the addition and deletion of sounds from the set of sounds used in a language, changes in redundant and distinctive features, along with corresponding changes in redundancy and phonological rules and, therefore, in the phonemic representations of lexical entries. Syntactic change is less common, and so it was not discussed in the chapters on syntax. Frequently, syntactic change is interwoven with lexical change. For example, in Old English, inflectional affixes attached to noun roots were used to indicate grammatical relations among the elements in a sentence. Thus, the indirect object was marked by a suffix; for 'men' the suffix was *um*. To express the meaning 'to/for men', Old English used a single word, *mannum*. As such affixes disappeared from use (and from the grammar of the language), prepositions such as *to* and *for* were required to convey such relations, and so in Modern English we must use a syntactic construction *to men* rather than a single word. "Further Exploration" directs the interested reader to diachronic accounts of English, as well as to several sources on types of language change.

In addition to the kinds of changes that occur in languages, historical linguistics also explores dialects, related languages, the reconstruction of older forms in a language, and the factors that are associated with linguistic change. These topics are discussed in this chapter.

DIALECTS AND RELATED LANGUAGES

Change is part of the nature of language, but particular changes are not predetermined. Any one of a number of changes may or may not take place in the development of a language. If one group of speakers is separated from other speakers, the subsequent changes in the language of the two groups are often quite different. While both groups initially may have spoken the same language and the same dialect, after a period of separation and normal linguistic change, their speech will no longer be the same. New dialects or even new languages may evolve.

The origin of dialects and of languages is the same—linguistic change. The chief difference lies in the degree of change: if it is extensive, we generally say that a new language has developed; if it is moderate, we say that a new dialect has been created.

No language in widespread use today is free of dialect variation. With the possible exception of some languages used by only a few speakers (such as some American Indian languages), all languages have dialects and always have had dialects. In fact, when we look back over a sufficiently long period in the history of any language, we will find a time when the language itself was simply a dialect of some other language. This matter was discussed briefly in Chapter 5, where we observed that Old English is merely a label for a dialect of Germanic. Old English was highly similar to other Germanic dialects, which have since developed into distinct modern languages such as German, Norwegian, and Swedish. The linguistic changes during this period were, for the most part, gradual, and therefore, it is not possible to pinpoint a particular time at which we could say "it was here that English ceased to be a dialect of Germanic and became a separate language."

Distinct languages which can be traced back to a common source are said to be **related languages.** In the case of modern German, Norwegian, Swedish, English, and other languages of this group, historical records reveal that these languages were much more similar to one another in the past than they are today. In fact, the similarities were so great 1500 years ago that it is clear the languages were at one time mutually intelligible (speakers of one could understand and be understood by speakers of the others), just as are the dialects of modern English, for example. When we say that these modern languages are related, we are actually stating a hypothesis. Although accepted by all scholars of language as fact, this old Germanic language existed prior to the time of extensive writing in northern Europe. By the time written records were frequent, Germanic already had developed from a language with several dialects into a set of distinct languages.

An indisputable case of language change resulting in new languages where once there were dialects is found in a study of Latin and the modern Romance languages, such as Spanish, French, Italian, Portuguese, Romanian, Provençal, and Catalan. The Roman Empire, at its height during the first two centuries after Christ, extended from the British Isles to northern Africa and from the Atlantic coast of modern Portugal eastward to the Caspian Sea. Roman administrators, military personnel, and other officials engaged in the business of the empire carried the Latin language with them throughout this region, and the language was adopted by many of the peoples under the rule of Rome. The Latin of this period (the second, third, and fourth centuries) had already changed substantially from the older, Classical Latin that is still taught in some of our schools. Classical Latin remained the language of scholarship and learned conversation, but the people did not speak it. Instead, they used a more modern form of the language, known as Vulgar Latin (from the Latin word *vulgaris* meaning 'of the common people'). Where ties with Rome were strongest, Vulgar Latin replaced the original languages and gradually acquired special, local variations; in other words, there were a number of different dialects of Vulgar Latin in the different Roman colonial areas. With the collapse of the empire, the outlying regions once dominated by Rome lost contact with one another and with Rome itself. The result was that each dialect continued its linguistic development independently of the others. By the end of the fifth century, the dialects of Vulgar Latin were quite distinct; and, by the ninth century, Vulgar Latin texts show so much variation and so many changes that scholars have applied new labels to these dialects, such as Old Spanish, Old French, and so on.

There are many historical records and documents providing positive proof that the modern Romance languages are related because they all derive from a common source, Vulgar Latin. But even if such direct evidence were lacking, it would still be possible to determine this fact. Consider the data presented in Figure 18.1. There are great similarities among the words for 'friend' in each of four Romance languages; the same is true for the three other meanings listed. In fact, there are thousands of examples illustrating such similarities. When several languages all make use of the same linguistic form, with only minor differences, there are three possible explanations:

1. The existence of similar forms is accidental.
2. The languages borrowed the forms from the same source or the form was original in one of the languages and was borrowed from it by the others.
3. The form dates back to a time when the distinct modern languages were all the same language.

Although it is possible for two languages to develop the same form independently of one

Figure 18.1

Meaning	French	Spanish	Italian	Romanian
'female friend'	*amie*	*amiga*	*amica*	*amică*
'flowers'	*fleurs*	*flores*	*fiori*	*flori*
'they are'	*sont*	*son*	*sono*	*sînt*
'Monday'	*lundi*	*lunes*	*lunedì*	*luni*

another, this rarely occurs. In the case of the languages listed in Figure 18.1, accidental similarity cannot be the explanation, for there are far too many similar forms in far too many languages for this to be possible. Explanation (2) is more likely than (1). Readers will recall that modern English and French share many similarities in their vocabulary due to borrowings during the Old and Middle English periods from both Latin and French. For borrowing to occur there must be contact between two languages, and, if the borrowing is extensive, the contact must be longlasting and widespread. This condition for borrowing is not met by the examples in Figure 18.1. Although French, Spanish, and Italian are in close geographical proximity to one another, Romanian is very far removed and therefore unlikely to have borrowed large numbers of lexical items from any source that also could have affected the languages farther west. The similarities in Figure 18.1 can be explained neither by accident nor by borrowing. They must, therefore, result from the fact that all of these languages are modern developments of the same original source language. This is the only possible explanation for the situation illustrated in Figure 18.1. Even without the confirmation of historical documents, the student of language history must reach the conclusion that the Romance languages all developed from a single language. Of course, we have historical evidence to confirm this hypothesis, for we know that the common source was Vulgar Latin. The Latin words from which those in Figure 18.1 developed are as follows: *amica* 'friend', *flores* 'flowers', *sunt* 'they are', and *lunae diem* 'Monday'.

RECONSTRUCTING THE PAST

When we compare forms in a number of modern languages in an attempt to determine whether those languages have developed from the same source, we are making use of a technique of linguistic research known as the **comparative method.** The comparative method was developed by linguists during the nineteenth century, a time when there was great interest in linguistic change. Originally, scholars believed that change in language was random, but, as more and more examples of change were examined, it was discovered that language change is generally ordered and systematic. This fact made it possible for linguists to discover not only whether two languages were derived from the same source, but also the pattern of their development and the nature of the source language. Consider again the words for 'friend' in Figure 18.1. There is evidence that in older forms of French, 'friend' was more like the modern Provençal form *amiga*. If we compare all of these forms, we can see that there is really only one basic difference among them: whether or not the intervocalic stop is [+ voice] ([g]), as in Provençal and Spanish, or [− voice] ([k]), as in Italian and Romanian. The same distinction exists in many other sets of forms; for example, 'to change' is *mudar* in Provençal and Spanish, with a [+ voice] segment intervocalically, but *mutare* in Italian and *a muta* in Romanian, both with a [− voice] intervocalic segment. Clearly, at some point in the historical development of these languages, a systematic change occurred. The comparative method can aid us in determining that change.

If we try to determine the original form by comparing its modern versions, it seems only reasonable to hypothesize that any sound segments occurring in all or almost all of the forms in the modern languages were probably present in the original form. Thus, we assume that the original form of 'friend' was something like *amiKa*, where the asterisk indicates that this is a hypothetical reconstruction of the original based solely on the modern forms. We use the *K* to indicate that the intervocalic segment may have been either [+ voice] or [− voice]. How do we determine which value for voicing was original and which represents a change that several of the languages have undergone during the course of their development? According to the comparative method, our hypotheses concerning sound changes and original forms must take into account the kinds of changes known to be natural and common in human language. Readers may recall from Chapter 10 that assimilation is a common phonological process, whereas dissimilation is less common. In the particular case we are discussing, there are two possibilities. Either the original form was *amiga* or it was *amika*. In the former case, it would be necessary to hypothesize that Italian and Romanian underwent a rule that dissimilated the [+ voice] segment [g] to [− voice] [k] when the segment was surrounded by [+ voice] vowels (the letter *c* in the Italian and Romanian spellings represents a [k]). The dissimilation of a consonant from vowels is an unusual process in language. But if we hypothesize the original form to be *amika*, the situation is far more natural. In this case, we would maintain that Provençal and Spanish made use of the common process of assimilation by converting a [− voice] consonant [k] to its [+ voice] counterpart [g] between two [+ voice] vowels. Thus, the comparative method would lead us to select *amika* as the most likely original form, since assimilation is more common and natural than dissimilation in this case. We know that the Latin form was *amica* (where *c* did represent [k]), so the principles of the comparative method are supported by historical facts.

The comparative method would work in much the same way for our other examples. Consider again 'to change': Pr. *mudar*, Sp. *mudar*, It. *mutare*, and Ro. *a muta*. Our first hypothesis about the original form would be *muTar(e)*; that is, the original contained *m*, *u*, *a*, and *r*, as well as a stop that was either [+ voice] or [− voice], and possibly a final *e*. Following the same line of reasoning as in the discussion of *amika*, we must hypothesize that the original form of 'to change' was *mutar(e)*. But how do we decide about the *e*? Again the answer rests basically on the question of naturalness. Would it be more natural for languages to lose an unstressed vowel in word-final position or for a language to add an unstressed vowel in word-final position? The former is more likely to occur, as illustrated by English, where unstressed word-final vowels have ceased to be pronounced, leaving us with a writing system that represents many "silent *e*'s" at the ends of words. Thus, we establish **mutare* as our reconstruction of the original form from which the various modern forms have developed. This reconstruction is confirmed by historical evidence, for the Latin verb was, indeed, *mutare*.

The comparative method provides a means for reconstructing the past. Even in the absence of older written records to demonstrate (or attest to) the actual occurrence of forms like *amica* and *mutare,* diachronic linguistics can determine, with some assurance, many of the forms and properties of languages from the past. (Such hypothetical, reconstructed forms, produced by application of the comparative method, are called **proto-forms,** and the language in which they are assumed to have occurred is called a **proto-language;** thus, our reconstructions above, based on the modern Romance languages, represent Proto-Romance.) The comparative method not only establishes hypothetical reconstructions for particular words; it also provides insight into the types of changes that have occurred. The differences between a reconstructed proto-form and the known forms on which it is based require an explanation. The explanation is provided by the proposed changes that occurred between the proto-language and the more modern languages.

The past is never totally reconstructable through the comparative method. We can go back only one step prior to the time for which we have records. Yet, it must be assumed that the reconstructed forms themselves had undergone changes from still older forms. Even those reconstructions that are possible may still be incomplete. For example, if a sound present in the original language disappears over time and leaves no trace in any of the more modern languages, there is no way to determine that it was ever there. Consider the *m* in the Vulgar Latin *lunae diem* 'Monday'. None of the modern Romance languages in Figure 18.1 has such a consonant in its word for 'Monday'; we would not be able to reconstruct the *m* here for Proto-Romance unless we found other data in which it occurred.

For the Romance languages, the comparative method is really not necessary. The history of these languages is well documented and can therefore be determined directly. This is not the case for most languages, however. In fact, there is little concrete evidence available regarding the history of the majority of the world's languages. The problem is particularly great, of course, for those languages that lack, or have only recently acquired, a writing system. In such cases, the comparative method can achieve some insight into the history of the languages involved. But, even then, extensive borrowing may complicate the picture to such an extent that it becomes difficult to determine which languages are actually related to one another and which have merely influenced others and served as a source for borrowing. Although linguists are reasonably confident that they have established the relationships among many of the well-known languages of Europe, there is far less certainty when discussion turns to linguistic relationships among the languages of Africa or North and South American Indians, for example. Readers who are interested in a survey of language relationships throughout the world should consult Chapter 1, where this was discussed briefly, as well as the sources in "Further Exploration" at the conclusion of this chapter.

Another means for reconstructing language history is **internal reconstruction.** Unlike the comparative method (which utilizes, and requires, data from two or more related languages), internal reconstruction is based on evidence from within a single language. Here, the diachronic linguist also attempts to establish the older forms of a language, as well as the rules of change that have resulted in the modern form. With internal reconstruction, the data for such analyses come primarily from the variations in the phonetic representations of individual morphemes. The linguist operates under the assumption that, at an earlier point in time, a morpheme had only a single phonetic form and that any modern situation with more than one form is due to language change. In other words, a change during the history of a language will often leave traces of the older forms, thus permitting the analyst to gain insight into an earlier stage of the language. The older stage proposed as a result of internal reconstruction is referred to as the **pre-language** stage. If, for example, we use data from Modern English and the principles of internal reconstruction, we can establish forms of Pre-Modern English. Internal reconstruction posits only that such forms existed before the Modern English period; it cannot locate a precise point in time for the forms (such as Middle English or Old English).

In Chapter 10, we examined several situations in which a contemporary language possesses morphemes having two phonetic representations, along with a synchronic phonological rule that serves to relate the phonetic forms to a phonemic representation. The same data that served as the basis for that analysis can also be used to explore the history of a language. For example, the alternation in Spanish of voiced stops, [b, d, g], with voiced fricatives, [β, ð, ɣ], points to a single phonemic representation and a phonological rule converting voiced stops to fricatives intervocalically. Through internal reconstruction, it is assumed that in an older stage of Spanish (Pre-Spanish), only the voiced stops existed. Then, Pre-Spanish changed by adding the rule altering the value of [continuant] from [− continuant] to [+ continuant] between vowels. A similar argument can be offered for a historical change in the voiced stops of German. As noted in Chapter 10, Modern German has only voiceless stops in word-final position, but many morphemes show an alternation of voiced and voiceless stops, the latter occurring only word-finally; for example, [hʊnt] 'dog' and [hʊndə] 'dogs'. When considered from a historical viewpoint, this data can be used to reconstruct an older variety of German (Pre-Modern German) in which the only phonetic form of 'dog' was [hʊnd], whether in the singular or the plural. Following this stage, we hypothesize that Pre-Modern German added a diachronic phonological rule changing [+ voice] to [− voice] for stops in word-final position. This analysis can be confirmed by comparative data, since the Modern English word [hawnd] *hound* is related historically to the German [hʊnt] 'dog'. The English word has retained the voiced [d] word-finally; English did not undergo the same phonological change that occurred in German.

Alternations in the phonetic representations of a modern morpheme are only one indication of language change. Among others, there is also the situation in which some sound segment is relatively rare in the synchronic system. For example, the sound [ŋ] occurs far less frequently in Modern English than do the other nasals [m] and [n]. Furthermore, there are relatively few minimal pairs distinguished by [ŋ] and another nasal, although many minimal pairs occur for [m] and [n], such as *might/night,* *mine/nine, map/nap.* This indicates that, at an earlier time, [ŋ] was not a distinctive sound segment of English. Synchronically [ŋ] occurs in Modern English primarily before [g] and [k] (both of which have the same position of articulation as [ŋ]) and sometimes at the end of a word. The modern minimal pairs of [ŋ] and either [m] or [n] occur almost solely when the nasal is in word-final position: *seem* [sim], *seen* [sin], *sing* [siŋ]. For internal reconstruction, this limited occurrence of [ŋ] indicates that historically [ŋ] never formed a minimal pair with [m] or [n], but rather [ŋ] appeared only before [k] and [g]. Later, the [g] sound after [ŋ] was dropped word-finally, thereby creating the Modern English minimal pairs. Thus, we would hypothesize a Pre-Modern English form of the root *sing* to be *[siŋg], and, indeed, there are written records of Old English indicating that the [g] was present. This is supported by the spelling used in both Old and Modern English, *sing*.

Many of the limitations of the comparative method also hold for internal reconstruction. Nevertheless, these two approaches to diachronic studies provide substantial insight into the history of languages and the nature of linguistic change.

INTERCOMMUNICATION

The chief factor involved in the creation of dialects or related languages is the degree of intercommunication among the speakers of a language. If all speakers of a language come into contact with all other speakers, then, although linguistic change will occur, it will not result in division of the language into dialects or new languages. Of course, for almost every human language, there are too many speakers for them to be in total contact with one another.

In addition to the number of speakers involved, lack of complete intercommunication may be due to several factors. Geographical features may prevent contact among peoples; a broad river or a mountain range was sometimes a great obstacle to intercommunication in the past. Thus, we often find that dialects or related languages are separated by rivers, mountains, lakes, and so on. For example, the Catalan language is separated from Castilian Spanish by the Iberian Mountains in northeastern Spain, and Andalusian Spanish is set apart from Castilian in the south of Spain by the Sierra Morena mountains. Similarly, the eastern coast of the United States can be divided into three main dialect regions, commonly termed the North, the Midland, and the South. The extent of these regions is indicated by Figure 18.2. If we superimposed a topographical map on Figure 18.2, we would find that, to a great extent, the line separating the Midland from the South coincides with the Blue Ridge Mountains in Virginia and North Carolina.

The obstacles that inhibit intercommunication among the speakers of a language are not always as concrete as a mountain range. When a particular portion of the population is separated from others because of social class, for example, there is little opportunity for intercommunication and thus a strong possibility for the development and maintenance of separate dialects. Dialects resulting from such social class divisions in a society are social in nature, not regional; that is, the dialect is characteristic of people from a particular social class, not of those from a particular region of the country. In recent years, a number

VARIATION

Figure 18.2

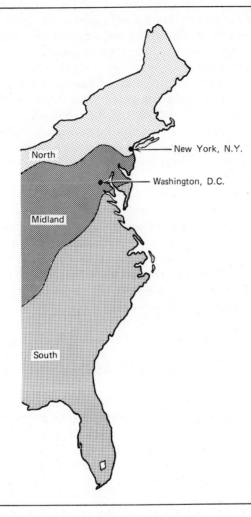

North

New York, N.Y.

Washington, D.C.

Midland

South

of linguists and sociologists have been investigating a form of language commonly referred to as Black English. This is a social dialect, used by many American black people who are (or at one time were) constituents of the lower socioeconomic strata. It exists because of patterns of segregation and cultural and linguistic isolation that were, and in some cases still are, prevalent in our society. We will return to a more detailed study of social dialects in Chapter 20.

Just as lack of intercommunication tends to create dialect distinctions, so the existence of intercommunication may prevent the development of separate dialects. In fact, intercommunication may even bring about **dialect leveling,** the situation in which dialect differences disappear. Population mobility is one of the chief factors involved in dialect leveling. As people move from one region to another, they carry with them their original dialect. Encountering a new dialect, they may then lose some of their old features while at the same time acquiring new ones. In this way, a new dialect is created, one that replaces two formerly distinct dialects.

In more recent times, another possible cause of dialect leveling may be increased exposure to various forms of mass communication. The first communication channel that comes to mind is television, but the effects of television on the speech of the nation have never been fully investigated. It should be noted that television does not provide actual opportunity for true intercommunication. People listen to television, but they do not talk back to it; communication is one-way.

NONLINGUISTIC FACTORS

The distinction between a language and a dialect is not purely a linguistic one. Two systems of communication may be similar enough to be mutually intelligible, and yet they may be labeled as separate languages. For example, we generally recognize Dutch and German to be distinct languages, although speakers of German in the north of the country communicate readily with their neighbors who speak Dutch. The two systems are accepted as separate languages, rather than simply as dialects of a single language, primarily for political or nationalistic reasons. That is, there is a national boundary separating two distinct countries, and it is assumed that a major linguistic boundary exists along the same line. Even though there is no such boundary, the nonlinguistic factor of national identity is so strong that it overcomes linguistic reality, and the popular belief that different countries should use different languages remains in effect.

National boundaries also play a role in the classification of language in China. Reference is made frequently to the Chinese language, yet the dialects of Chinese differ from one another far more than do Dutch and German. In many instances, different dialects of Chinese are mutually unintelligible. Linguistically, one would be justified in speaking of different languages, but the political situation and the fact that all of China shares the same logographic writing system lead to the view that the Chinese language contains a number of unusually distinct dialects.

One interesting illustration of how nonlinguistic factors may play a part in the classification of dialects can be found in the recent history of the study of black Americans. When interest in dialects arose in this country during the second quarter of the century, social dialects were overlooked and efforts were concentrated on the investigation of regional variations. When some attention was paid to black speech, the investigators generally insisted that there was little or no difference between the speech of blacks and whites of the same region and social class. This, of course, reflected society's growing awareness of the question of civil rights and the need for recognition of equality among the races. During the 1960s, as blacks asserted their own cultural and linguistic heritage, linguistic investigators began to talk about a special dialect of English, namely Black English. One may choose to emphasize the similarities and thus say that there is a single dialect, or one may choose to emphasize the differences and distinguish a black dialect. The conclusion depends not so much on the language itself as on personal, psychological, and sociological factors. Scientists are no more immune from such factors in their research and conclusions than are other people although scientists do attempt to filter out their personal views when presenting their results. As indicated by the study of social dialects in American English, however, the identification of dialects has been influenced by the views of society.

ATTITUDES

A dialect is simply one of several different "versions" of a language. Earlier, we defined a dialect as a set of idiolects that shared certain linguistic characteristics not found in the speech of other speakers of the language. Clearly, then, everyone speaks a dialect. Yet, for some reason, many people share the popular misconception that it is bad, wrong, or incorrect to speak a dialect. To say of someone "He speaks a dialect of English" somehow implies that the person does not speak English, or, at least, does not speak "good" English. In other words, the term *dialect* has come to mean 'unacceptable dialect' for many speakers of English. This is an unfortunate change in meaning, for underlying it is a tendency of our society to judge people by the way they talk. And yet, what is it that makes some dialects acceptable while others are not? All dialects of a language, like all languages, are fully adequate vehicles for communication. They are equally systematic, expressive, complete, capable of changing to meet future needs of their users, and so forth.

In most societies, there is some model of language usage that members identify as highly acceptable. Those who use this particular variety of the language are accorded some prestige, and speakers of other varieties may attempt to model their own speech after this variety. In such cases, we may speak of the **standard dialect** of the language. Other dialects, which differ from this standard, are sometimes subject to criticism from those who use the standard dialect. Dialects that differ to some extent from the standard are referred to as **nonstandard.** The bases for classifying a dialect as standard or nonstandard have little or nothing to do with the linguistic facts about the dialect. Rather, such judgments are based on nonlinguistic facts. The selection of a model, standard dialect is determined by such matters as the political, cultural, or social prestige of those who speak the dialect. The speech of those who have such prestige within a society is considered standard; the speech of those who lack the prestige may be considered nonstandard.

The situation of standard and nonstandard dialects exists in many languages. For example, Parisian French is generally accepted as the standard dialect of French. Other regional dialects possess less prestige. Yet, the prestige of Parisian French has nothing to do with the linguistic features of the dialect. Rather, Parisian French is the model others try to attain because of the political, cultural and economic prestige of Paris. To speak Parisian French is to be identified as either a Parisian or an educated, cultured person.

In the United States, there is no one regional dialect that serves as the model. What is considered standard English in New York City would not be considered standard in Fort Worth, Texas. Each region of the country has its own standard. Thus, when we speak of standard English, we are actually oversimplifying a highly complex dialect situation.

Since almost all dialects of American English are mutually intelligible, there is really no linguistic need for a single, standard dialect known and used by people in addition to their native, local dialect. Even without a single standard dialect, all speakers of American English are able to communicate with one another. Although the main function of language is communication, it can serve other purposes as well. Regional dialects can be viewed as a means of expressing pride in one's state, county, or town. In fact, some of our humor reflects this, as with the stories and jokes about people from Texas, for example. Social dialects also provide a way in which one person can set himself or herself apart from others, or, on the other hand, by using a particular social dialect, an individual can express identification with the speakers of that dialect. By using a dialect associated with the middle or upper class, a person can reveal to others that he or she has acquired a certain amount of education and a certain income level. Part of upward social mobility is the acquisition of a new dialect to reflect the new social position. Of course, care must be taken not to overgeneralize. Many people with substantial education, high incomes, and all of the other characteristics of the higher social classes speak dialects that others might call nonstandard. Judging people by the way they speak is almost as unreliable as judging intelligence by eye color or weight.

SUMMARY

Linguistic change is the underlying cause of dialects and related languages. The comparative method and internal reconstruction provide means for exploring language change, establishing types of changes that occur, and reconstructing proto-language and pre-language forms. Such change is most likely to result in new dialects and languages when the speakers of a language are not in full intercommunication with one another. Intercommunication can be prevented by physical obstacles, such as rivers or mountains, or by less concrete barriers, such as social stratification. On the other hand, population mobility and mass communication increase contact among speakers of different dialects and may ultimately result in dialect leveling. In linguistic terms, one dialect is as good as another. All dialects are systematic, expressive, productive varieties of language.

FURTHER EXPLORATION

Several excellent introductory books on historical linguistics are available for the interested reader. All contain sections on the main topics: types of language change, factors that influence change, internal reconstruction, and the comparative method. The most elementary of those mentioned here is *Introduction to Historical Linguistics* by Anthony Arlotto. Also at the introductory level is Winfred P. Lehmann's *Historical Linguistics: An Introduction*. More comprehensive, with numerous examples, is *An Introduction to Historical and Comparative Linguistics* by Raimo Anttila. In *Historical Linguistics and Generative Grammar*, Robert D. King relates the concepts and goals of diachronic studies to synchronic issues in transformational linguistics.

For studies on the history of English, see Thomas Pyles' *The Origins and Development of the English Language*. A more specific study is provided by Elizabeth Close

Traugott in *A History of English Syntax*. Suggestions for readings on regional and social dialects of English are offered in the "Further Exploration" sections of the following two chapters.

1. Some of the principles of the comparative method have been discussed and illustrated in this chapter. The readings suggested above provide additional principles. Along with positing rules that are natural, the diachronic linguist also works under the assumption that language changes in general and phonological changes in particular are regular, operating on all relevant forms without exception. For example, a historical study of Spanish, in comparison with the related Romance languages, demonstrates that Spanish added a phonological rule which inserted [e] word-initially before consonant clusters that began with [s] (see Chapter 10 for synchronic discussion of this). For EVERY Proto-Romance form beginning with a cluster such as [sp-], the Modern Spanish equivalent will have the phonetic shape [esp-]. In using the comparative method, the linguist must check the proposed proto-forms and diachronic rules to be sure that each rule is tested against each proto-form and that the rule produces the correct modern language form in every case, without exception.

For each row in the following data, use the principles of the comparative method to establish a proto-language form that could have been the source of the three words in the artificial "languages" A, B, and C. To do this, it is necessary to propose, for each modern language, a diachronic rule that serves to explain the phonological change that occurred between the proto-language and the modern language. Check each rule with each proto-form. (*Hint*. The most acceptable solution will require only one natural phonological rule for each of the three languages.)

Meaning	Language A	Language B	Language C
'tree'	[bal]	[balo]	[balo]
'wind'	[kantid]	[kantid]	[kantit]
'sky'	[pit]	[pit]	[pit]
'moon'	[upar]	[ubaru]	[uparu]
'thunder'	[tudab]	[tudab]	[tudap]
'grass'	[ebig]	[ebig]	[ebik]
'lake'	[kamp]	[kampe]	[kampe]
'rain'	[amegog]	[amegog]	[amegok]
'sun'	[pitad]	[pidad]	[pitat]
'mountain'	[gonum]	[gonum]	[gonum]
'star'	[tik]	[tigo]	[tiko]
'valley'	[otupid]	[odubid]	[otupit]
'shrub'	[sitep]	[sidep]	[sitep]
'weed'	[dorak]	[dorago]	[dorako]
'hill'	[inogeb]	[inogeb]	[inogep]
'stream'	[idirek]	[idirek]	[idirek]

2. Internal reconstruction is based on the fact that diachronic changes within a language often leave behind traces of the earlier system. The most common type of trace is the presence of two or more phonetic representations for a single morpheme. Reconsider the Great Vowel Shift of Middle English in terms of internal reconstruction (the Great Vowel Shift was discussed in item 3 of "Further Exploration" at the end of Chapter 10).

The Great Vowel Shift left evidence in Modern English of the older, early Middle English vowel system; before the Great Vowel Shift, tense vowels and nontense vowels alternated in the Middle English pronunciation of certain morphemes (e.g., [e] in *serene* alternated with [ɛ] in *serenity*). The alternations that occur in Modern English would provide clues (even without direct written evidence from Middle English) for the internal reconstruction of a Pre-Modern English stage, one that would actually be close to Middle English. Now consider the Middle English situation prior to the Great Vowel Shift. On the basis of internal reconstruction, what hypothesis, if any, might be offered about Pre-Middle English vowels?

CHAPTER 1919191919191919191919191919

REGIONAL DIALECTS

In the last quarter of the nineteenth century, the study of language change led to an interest in dialects, and a number of scholars in Germany, Switzerland, France, and Italy began to investigate regional variation in language. Their work established a basic pattern for **dialect geography,** or **regional dialectology,** a pattern of research still followed by those American linguists who study dialect geography today.

After sampling the speech of people in a particular region, the dialectologist will transcribe his or her data in phonetic symbols to provide a detailed record of even the smallest differences in pronunciation. Variations in syntax and vocabulary are also noted. All of this information is then transferred to maps of the area, one map for each feature of language use. For example, one map may indicate the word used for a particular type of container: *pail* in some regions, *bucket* in others. Another map will show the regions where people say *greasy* with the sound [s] and those where it is said with [z]. On each map, it is usually possible to draw a line separating two areas; for example, the area in which *pail* is used can be separated from the area in which *bucket* occurs. Such a line is called an **isogloss.** A single isogloss is not sufficient to establish a boundary between two dialects, but, when several maps are superimposed upon one another, several isoglosses may coincide. The map in Figure 18.2, which illustrates the three major dialect areas of the East Coast of the United States, is based on a large number of more detailed maps, each showing the distribution of one linguistic feature in the area. The isoglosses on each of these maps bundle together in such a way that the general outlines of the major dialect regions are clear. In other words, a dialect boundary occurs whenever a bundle of isoglosses occurs. People on each side of the dialect boundary use certain forms not used by those on the other side, and, therefore, we say that they speak different dialects.

The study of the regional dialects of American English began over forty years ago when the American Council of Learned Societies initiated a research project known as the Linguistic Atlas of the United States. Early work was concentrated on the New England area, and this was followed by studies of the Midland and South regions of the East Coast. Other studies have been conducted in the central and western sections of the country, but the features and areas investigated have generally remained quite scattered. It is only with difficulty that we can construct a picture of the regional dialect situation beyond the East Coast area.

INVESTIGATIVE PROCEDURES

Most work on American regional dialects has been carried out either as part of the Atlas project or at least in cooperation with it. Therefore, the procedures used for the collection and analysis of data generally have followed the same pattern. First, a number of towns or counties within the area to be studied are selected as sampling points. For each point, at least two persons are interviewed by a trained investigator familiar with phonetic transcription, linguistic analysis, and dialectology. The investigator works from a questionnaire to be filled in with information about pronunciation, vocabulary, and grammar. All investigators in a particular region use the same questionnaire, and, in this way, the results are compatible and can be combined when the research is completed.

Although some dialect research has relied on mailed questionnaires, most has been carried out by means of personal interviews between linguists and natives of the communities under investigation. This is an expensive and time-consuming approach to the problem of gathering information about regional dialects, but it is necessary, especially if valid data are to be obtained for pronunciation. Linguistically untrained people are often totally unaware of their own pronunciation, and they make notoriously unreliable sources of information about their own speech. Mailed questionnaires are sometimes useful in collecting material on vocabulary, but, again, personal interviews are more satisfactory. Since so many people are concerned about ''good'' English, they may deny using a word that others might consider unacceptable, even if the word is common and accepted within their own community. A trained interviewer can usually uncover such little deceptions.

The need for personal interviews has limited the amount of coverage possible for regional dialect studies. An interview may last only an hour or it may take an entire day, depending on how completely the region is to be studied. If at least two people are interviewed in each town or even in each county, the task of gathering data for even a single state becomes substantial. It is not surprising that many states have not yet been investigated in detail, especially if it is kept in mind that the collection of information is only a small part of a regional dialect study. Preparations prior to actual interviewing, such as selecting communities and speakers, training the interviewers, finding some source of financial support for the project, and so on, may require years of work. And, even after the information has been obtained, it must be analyzed, reviewed, transferred onto maps, and studied. Isoglosses must be drawn, and only then may it be possible to determine dialect regions.

The entire process of regional dialect investigation takes many years, even for a small area. In selecting speakers to interview, dialectologists often choose older, less educated people since they are more likely to use local, or regional, vocabulary and pronunciation than are the younger people with more education and more contact with other dialects. The result is that, when a dialect study is finally published, its information about regional features may be substantially out-of-date. For example, a very careful study of vocabulary in the Hudson Valley area of New York and New Jersey reports the words *pot cheese* 'cottage cheese' and *darning needle* 'dragon-fly' as local forms. The author, who lived in the area for many years, is familiar with *darning needle,* but *pot cheese,* even at the time this study was published over twenty years ago, was used almost solely by old people. Young and middle-aged people said *cottage cheese.*

Some of the regional features discussed below may also be out-of-date, already disappearing from the speech of young people. The reader should expect this, for it seems that some dialect distinctions are undergoing a leveling process in the United States, especially among members of the middle and upper classes who have a college education and have traveled beyond their native dialect region.

EAST COAST DIALECTS

The divisions between regional dialects are most sharply defined along the East Coast. As you move westward, it becomes increasingly difficult to find isoglosses, either individually or in bundles. This situation is primarily due to population mobility. The earliest settlements were along the East Coast, and dialect patterns have had a long period of time in which to become stabilized. Many New England residents, for example, can trace their ancestors back in New England for more than two hundred years. The central and western areas of the nation are more recently settled, and the settlers in any given community often came from several different areas in the east. The result of this is that it is difficult to separate one dialect area from another west of the Appalachian Mountains. Nevertheless, in such regions it is generally possible to identify dialect features that originated in one of the three major East Coast areas (see Figure 18.2).

Figure 19.1 illustrates several of the vocabulary features that distinguish the North, Midland, and South dialect regions of the eastern section of the country. Notice that most of the terms refer to common, rural objects. In part, this is due to the fact that the Linguistic Atlas investigations relied heavily on the speech of the more rural, less educated, older population. Rural areas tend to preserve regional dialect features to a greater extent than urban areas. After all, the population of a rural area generally remains quite stable. Once it is settled, very few outsiders come in, and, therefore, a local dialect can

Figure 19.1

North	Midland	South
string beans	green beans	snap beans
darning needle	snake feeder	snake doctor/mosquito hawk
sweet corn/corn-on-the-cob	roasting ears	roasting ears
pail	bucket	bucket

survive with few changes. In a city, however, the population mix changes much more rapidly. People migrate to cities from nearby rural areas, from distant regions, and even from other countries. Thus, the city-dweller is constantly exposed to other dialects, and his own dialect is likely to change accordingly.

Figure 19.1, in addition to providing a small sample of the distinctive linguistic characteristics of these dialect areas, also gives a clear indication that dialect regions are not always sharply defined areas. Whereas all three regions have different words for 'dragonfly', the Midland and the South do have some terms in common, such as *bucket* and *roasting ears*. A similar situation can be found in a study of pronunciation differences in these regions. Consider the word *greasy*, one of the key indicators of dialect regions in the east. In the North, the word is normally pronounced with [s], but in the Midland and the South the most common pronunciation is with [z]. Other aspects of pronunciation show the eastern North and South to have features in common, distinct from the Midland. Perhaps one of the best known characteristics of New England and Southern speech is the absence of [r] in preconsonantal and word-final positions. While someone from the Midland would pronounce the word *barber* as [barbər], those from New England or the South would more likely say [babə], without the preconsonantal [r] (before [b]) and without the word-final [r].

The distribution of this particular dialect feature can be explained by the settlement history of the Atlantic Coast. Early colonists of New England, Virginia, and the Carolinas came from southern Britain where [r] was not pronounced preconsonantally or word-finally in the seventeenth century, so, naturally, they brought with them this "*r*-less" dialect of English. Later colonists, who settled the Midland area, came from northern Britain where [r] still occurred before consonants and at the end of words, so these settlers kept an "*r*-full" dialect.

Although the North and South eastern dialect regions are both characterized by absence of [r] in certain environments, the eastern New England area is distinct from the South in that the former, but not the latter, contains a phonological rule that inserts an [r] whenever a word ending in a vowel is immediately followed by a word that begins with a vowel. Thus, in this eastern New England dialect, one says *Cubar and Africa* or *Africar and Cuba*, but never **Cubar and Africar*.

Although many more examples could be given from the dialect areas of the East Coast, we will consider only one: the pronunciation of words written with *wh*, such as *which, whine,* and *whet*. Throughout the Midland, much of the North and South, and, in fact, throughout most of the nation, these words are pronounced exactly like *witch, wine,* and *wet,* respectively. Only in a few more or less isolated areas in the North and in some regions of the South is a distinction made between words spelled with initial *w* and those spelled with initial *wh*. Where the distinction is made, words spelled with *wh* are pronounced with the initial sequence [hw]. Although [hw] is disappearing from the dialects of American English, it is interesting to note how many teachers try to impose this pronunciation on their students; it is now primarily a spelling pronunciation, with little relationship to what the majority of speakers say. One argument sometimes offered for retaining [hw] in speech is that it eliminates the possibility of misunderstanding due to homonyms, but it is a weak argument. In almost any sentence, the context and the syntactic information, such as part of speech, make it quite clear whether the speaker means *which* or *witch,* for example, and there is no need for these two words to be pronounced differently.

CENTRAL AND WESTERN SPEECH

West of the Appalachian Mountains, dialect boundaries are no longer clear. Nevertheless, we can find some basic patterns that reflect the movements of those who settled these regions. The earliest settlements present the clearest dialect divisions. Thus, in Michigan, Ohio, and Indiana, we do find some bundles of isoglosses indicating dialect distinctions. But, as we move further west, where settlers tended to come from all regions of the east, dialect maps take on the appearance of random distribution.

We find mostly North dialect features in Michigan, while Midland features predominate in southern Illinois, Indiana, and Ohio. Between these two areas is a transition zone with both North and Midland characteristics. For example, *pail* is common in Michigan, *bucket* in southern Illinois, Indiana, and Ohio, and both *pail* and *bucket* occur in the area between these. These areas, of course, adjoin the eastern dialect regions, and there is no sharp line dividing Michigan, for example, from the North dialect region shown in Figure 18.2. Thus, it is not surprising to find features of the North dialect in Michigan but features of the Midland dialect in Ohio. Since dialect lines tend to follow migration patterns, and migration tends to follow reasonably direct routes, we expect adjoining areas to share linguistic characteristics. This expectation is fulfilled in a study of Texas, as well as other states. Eastern Texas shows a number of vocabulary items common in the South dialect region, such as *snap beans*. In western Texas, however, we find *green beans,* as well. The fact that some Midland words also occur is explained by settlement patterns since western Texas was settled by people from the Midland region, as well as from the South.

In the western states, the most common dialect situation resembles that of Washington, Oregon, and Idaho in Figure 19.2. For the northwestern states, we find a blend of many dialect features. North, Midland, and South dialect areas are all represented but not in any neatly patterned arrangement. For example, although *darning needle,* the North term for 'dragonfly', occurs in northwestern Idaho, it is more or less isolated from other occurrences of the same term in the rest of Idaho and in Washington and Oregon. There is no way of drawing an isogloss to separate the *darning needle* regions from those of other terms, such as Midland *snake feeder* or Southern *snake doctor*.

Figure 19.2

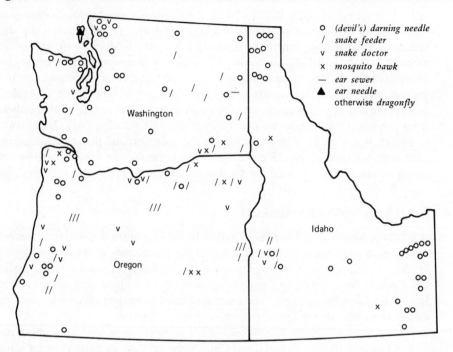

Source: Map No. 19 from *Dialects of American English* (Revised Edition) by Carroll E. Reed. Amherst, Mass.: The University of Massachusetts Press, 1977, page 116. Reprinted by permission of Carroll E. Reed.

It should be remembered that here, as in our earlier discussion of dialect features in the eastern United States, the most striking regional features may be rural. Urban areas tend to display fewer local characteristics because of their greater mixture in population. In fact, when we examine the speech of people in the cities of the West Coast, we often find greater similarities to East Coast speech than to nearby western rural areas. Once again, this is due to patterns of migration. Many of the recent settlers in Los Angeles, for example, have come from New York City.

One interesting tendency in the use of dialect forms appears especially in those regions where dialect features from several areas occur. For some reason, speakers dislike having two words for the same thing, and when two terms are used in an area, people often assign slightly different meanings to them. This occurs in the transitional region of northern Indiana, Ohio, and Illinois, where both *pail* and *bucket* are used. Many speakers will insist that the two words refer to different objects, but few speakers agree on just what the difference is. Similarly, people who have encountered the words *string beans, green beans,* and *snap beans* may maintain that these refer to different vegetables, although the difference is rarely explained. An individual speaker may be consistent in using such terms differently, but there is often substantial variation from speaker to speaker in cases like this.

VARIATION

298

LIMITATIONS OF DIALECT GEOGRAPHY

The investigation of regional dialect characteristics and the mapping of these features provide an interesting survey of the variations in speech throughout a country. But such dialect geography, unlike other areas of linguistics we have discussed in this book, is primarily the study of language performance. Dialect geography asks "What do people say?" but not "What do people know?" It is much easier to observe what is said than to determine the knowledge underlying what is said. We have already noted how complicated a task it is to carry out even a survey of regional dialects. In earlier sections, we observed some of the problems involved in understanding linguistic competence—the knowledge that underlies language use. The future task for dialectologists is to combine these two areas of research. For example, to truly understand language and people, it is not enough to know that some people say words like *whine* with an initial [w] and that others use [hw]. The linguist wants to be able to account for this difference. He or she wants to know if both kinds of speakers have the same underlying, phonemic representation, perhaps with [hw]. If so, speakers who say [w] must also have a phonological rule that deletes [h] before [w] at the beginning of a word, while those who actually say [hw] have no such rule. Underlying our use of language is a grammar consisting of forms and rules. Full understanding of dialect distinctions requires that we investigate dialect differences in terms of differences in underlying forms and the rules that convert them to surface forms. Such investigations have scarcely begun, but this is one area in which dialectology can develop in the future.

SUMMARY

The regional dialects of American English are quite distinct in the eastern section of the country where settlement patterns have long been established. This area has been investigated by dialectologists working on the Linguistic Atlas of the United States, and, for the most part, linguists working on regional dialectology have followed the same procedures for collecting and analyzing data. Once we move beyond the original American colonies, west of the Appalachian Mountains, the dividing lines between regional dialects are less clear. In the central region of the nation we find certain dominating characteristics from the East Coast, depending on the origin of the settlers, and so, for example, Michigan has basically a North dialect. But the further west one goes, the less patterning one finds in the distribution of dialect forms. In addition to further investigation of regional variation, dialectologists in the future must also turn their attention to determining the forms and rules that underlie dialect differences.

FURTHER EXPLORATION

In *Dialects of American English,* Carroll E. Reed surveys the origins and settlement patterns that are the basis of modern American regional dialects; lexical, phonological, and grammatical characteristics of regions throughout the United States are discussed and illustrated in an informal and nontechnical manner. An excellent source for active investigation of dialect variation is *Discovering American Dialects,* by Roger W. Shuy; this booklet provides sample questionnaires that readers can use to explore aspects of their own dialects or that of their communities.

More technical works resulting from the Linguistic Atlas project are valuable resources for those interested in the details of regional variation. Examples: E. Bagby Atwood, *The Regional Vocabulary of Texas;* Hans Kurath, *A Word Geography of the Eastern United States;* Hans Kurath and Raven I. McDavid, Jr., *The Pronunciation of English in the Atlantic States.*

1. American regional differences in pronunciation tend to occur more frequently with vowels than with consonants, and vowels before [r] are particularly subject to dialect variation. In the North section of the East Coast, many speakers have different vowels in the words *merry, Mary,* and *marry: merry* with [ɛ], *Mary* with [e], and *marry* with [æ]. In the Midland region, as well as in the Mid West and West, however, all three words are often homonyms, normally pronounced with [ɛ]. However, there are speakers in these areas who use [ɛ] only in *merry* and *Mary* and have [æ] in *marry.* How do you pronounce these words?

Provide the phonetic transcription symbols that represent the vowel sounds you use in the following words. Then, have a speaker of a different regional dialect pronounce the words and record his or her pronunciation. What differences do you observe?

(a)	orange		(f)	fog
(b)	creek		(g)	dog
(c)	root		(h)	can't
(d)	on		(i)	hawk
(e)	pen		(j)	hoop

2. Consider the words in Figure 19.1, as well as those given below. Which of these terms do you use in your own speech?

Meaning	North	Midland and South
'animal that emits a strong odor'	skunk	polecat
'container made of paper'	bag	sack
'drainage devices on roof'	eavestroughs	gutters
'frying pan'	spider	skillet
'hard core of fruit (e.g., cherry)'	pit	seed
'small woodland animal'	chipmunk	ground squirrel

If you use more than one term in a set (e.g., both *chipmunk* and *ground squirrel*), do the terms have different meanings? Check any such differences in meaning with any distinction made by other speakers of your dialect. Age is sometimes an important factor with regard to the use of vocabulary items. If possible, compare your own usage of these terms with that of an older speaker from your region (your grandparents, for example).

3. The nationwide distribution of canned, and more recently frozen, food products requires labeling that will describe the product to speakers of a variety of regional dialects. Consider the terms *string beans, green beans,* and *snap beans,* originally East Coast North, Midland, and South, respectively. Which term has been selected for the label on nationally distributed canned goods? What reasons can you provide for the selection of this term, as opposed to the others? Can you cite other examples where canned or frozen food products are labeled with a term different from that used by speakers in your community? Compare the labels on canned goods with the signs in the fresh produce department in a grocery store.

CHAPTER 2020202020202020202020202020

SOCIAL DIALECTS

We all possess certain attitudes toward our own speech and that of other people. Consciously or not, we tend to judge ourselves and others according to language, and these judgments affect many aspects of life. If individuals use language in a way that others consider incorrect, or unacceptable, or nonstandard, they may be denied a job, a promotion, or, in the case of children, a passing grade in school. In the last chapter, we discussed regional variations in language; now we will consider variations correlated with social class.

Although there is no single regional dialect of American English that is generally accepted as the ideal standard, the speech of educated upper- and upper-middle-class Americans is commonly considered as "correct" within their own locality. Departures from such regional standard dialects, whether in pronunciation, grammar, or the use of lexical items, are viewed as uneducated and, therefore, nonstandard. Since the standard dialects that members of a community use as models of socially acceptable speech are based on the speech of those who constitute the higher social classes, it is to be expected that the dialect variations that differ most from the standard are to be found in the speech of those at the lower socioeconomic levels of society.

The study of social, nonstandard dialects is a relatively recent concern among scholars of language. In fact, it is only within the last two decades that linguists and sociologists have joined forces to create the interdisciplinary field of **sociolinguistics** within which it has been possible to objectively investigate language and the social factors most closely associated with it.

POPULATION MOBILITY

In our survey of regional dialects, we noted that mass migration from one section of a country to another carries with it dialect features. The state of Michigan, for example, has a number of dialect characteristics found in the northern regions of the eastern part of the country because the early settlers in Michigan came primarily from the northeast, and they brought their native dialect with them when they moved. The same factor of population mobility is often at work in the creation of dialect distinctions associated with social classes.

In general, the speech of people with relatively high incomes and educational backgrounds tends to be quite similar no matter which region of the country they live in. This is due, in large part, to the mobility of the middle and upper classes in our society. Young people go away to college and then often find positions far from their home towns. Even then, they may move several more times, seeking better jobs, climates, or general environments. Each move results in some dialect leveling, for, although people will carry their native dialect with them, it is subject to change in the direction of any new dialect they encounter. Since members of the middle class tend to assimilate quite rapidly to their new environment, many noticeably different features of their speech usually disappear quickly. At this level of society, it is often difficult to distinguish long-time residents of an urban or suburban area from those who have only recently entered the community.

The situation is somewhat different for members of the lower socioeconomic classes, who have far less flexibility regarding migration and settlement possibilities. Whereas middle-class individuals usually have a job awaiting them at their destination, as well as the money to buy a house in the community, lower-class people often move in order to find work. Having little money, they are forced to settle in low-rent, ghettolike areas, close to the public transportation that may enable them to find a job. Of course, the people who have already settled in such areas may be in exactly the same position—relatively recent settlers who came to the city seeking work. In fact, when people move, they often try to settle in neighborhoods where others from the same background and even from the same original neighborhood have settled. The result can be seen in any major American city. It accounts for the "foreign" communities in our urban areas—Irish, Italian, Polish in and around New York; Ukranian and Arab in Detroit; Chinese in San Francisco; and so forth. The settlement patterns of poor people also account in part for the class and racial makeup of some areas in cities, such as the black ghettos, Chicano areas, and poor southern white neighborhoods. Racial or class prejudice in housing is often a factor in determining where new arrivals to a city may live. However, such neighborhoods also develop because of the choice made by migrating people to live in a community where others of the same background have settled.

Unlike middle-class mobility, the population movement of members of the lower class generally does not lead to dialect leveling. The assimilation to the new environment resulting in dialect change does not occur. In fact, the linguistic environment in a new area may be much like the one left behind. Consider, for example, a family that moves from rural Mississippi to Detroit and settles in the same neighborhood as a number of other families from Mississippi. As far as language is concerned, the family might just as well have never left home. All around them, people speak in the same way as they did in the south, and, if the family has limited financial resources, they are unlikely to spend much time outside of their immediate neighborhood. They will not have the opportunity to hear, learn, or use the local Detroit dialect.

The result of such social and linguistic isolation is that some dialect features (which may have been standard in the region from which people move) come to be considered nonstandard in their new environment. If a dialect feature is different from the new regional standard and if those who use that feature are not members of the upper or middle class, any differences in their speech are interpreted as nonstandard. Consider, for example, the pronunciation [grizi]. We have seen that this is standard in the south but that the northern pronunciation is [grisi]. In Chicago, Detroit, and Buffalo, for example, the form [grizi] is considered nonstandard by the local population. Of course, this pronunciation is used there and elsewhere by those who have come from the south. The fact that these speakers often have low incomes and have not assimilated to the regional dialects of the north makes their speech nonstandard as far as the natives of the north are concerned.

The interrelationship between regional and social dialects is often very close. Features considered marks of low social class in one area may be regional features transplanted from another area in which they are standard. Other examples include the use of the word *anymore* and the pronunciation of the words *root* and *roof; merry, marry,* and *Mary;* and *pin* and *pen.* Differences in these forms are regional in origin, but it is not uncommon to find people who attach some social significance to them. In certain areas of the midwestern section of our country, *root* and *roof* are pronounced with the vowel [ʊ], and the pronunciation with [u] is considered nonstandard. But, in the northeast section, [u] is standard, and those who use [ʊ] in these words are viewed as uneducated. Similarly, speakers for whom *merry, marry,* and *Mary* are homonyms may be judged as lower class if they move to a region where the vowels in each of these words are different. *Pin* and *pen* are homonyms for many southern speakers of all social classes because it is a regional feature of the south that [ɪ] and [ɛ] are pronounced the same before a nasal consonant. In the north, however, failure to distinguish [ɪ] and [ɛ] before nasals is often considered representative of low social class. In many northeastern dialect areas, the word *anymore* is used only in sentences containing a negative element. One can say *I don't do that anymore,* but it is ungrammatical to say **I do that anymore.* Instead, one would have to say something like *I do that nowadays.* Other dialect regions, however, make use of all three of these sentences, and there is no restriction on the use of *anymore* without a negative element. From the objective point of view, neither approach to the use of *anymore* is better than the other, but those whose dialect includes the restriction may look down on speakers whose dialect does not.

In summary, some grammatical features, like the use of *anymore,* and many phonological features are socially nonstandard in one part of the country but regionally standard elsewhere. The judgments of individuals about whether someone's speech is "correct" or "standard" are based primarily on familiarity. What is accepted is what is familiar in one's own regional and social dialect; differences in speech incorrectly are considered to be defects. It should be clear that such attitudes reflect a lack of understanding about the nature of language, language change, and dialect variation.

STYLES OF SPEECH

In the section on situations and styles in Chapter 6, it was pointed out that language usage varies as situations vary. Every speaker controls a variety of language styles, and he selects the style appropriate to the context, topic, and people involved in any communication situation. Style in language usage involves more than the selection of lexical items discussed in Chapter 6. There are also phonological characteristics of different speech styles, and some of the same phonological features that distinguish styles may play a role in distinguishing social dialects. For example, it is commonly believed that members of lower social class groups consistently pronounce the suffix *ing* with an alveolar nasal [n] rather than the velar nasal [ŋ]. This view is reflected in literature where some attempt is made to represent pronunciation by altering normal spelling, as in *runnin'* in place of *running*. But this belief is a substantial oversimplification of the facts of English social dialects. Everyone, no matter what his social status, uses [ŋ] in highly formal situations, such as the reading aloud of word lists for a teacher, and, at the same time, everyone uses [n] in highly informal situations. The difference in usage, if any exists at all, is generally only one of style. It may be that people at lower socioeconomic levels do use [n] more than [ŋ] in *ing,* but this may merely reflect fewer occasions in which a formal style of speech is appropriate. Similarly, there are social dialects in which [t] or [f] is frequently heard in place of standard [θ], as in the pronunciations [wɪt] or [wɪf] for *with*. But, in all such dialects, speakers can and do use [θ] when the occasion is sufficiently formal.

Very often the same features of speech people judge as nonstandard in the speech of others occur in their own speech. Few of us, for example, are generally aware of whether we use [n] or [ŋ] in *ing,* but we may notice use of [n] in the speech of someone else, especially if the context in which it occurs is one where we would use a formal style in which [n] would not be appropriate. Given [æst] and [sɪks] for *asked* and *sixths,* respectively, many people would judge these pronunciations as nonstandard, but consider the following sentences and say them aloud as you would if talking casually with a friend.

(1) I asked him to come home.

(2) Take one and five-sixths cups of sugar.

Although the formal pronunciation of *asked* is [æskt] and that of *sixths* is [sɪksθs] in standard English, even the most highly educated, socially prestigious speaker would be very likely to reduce these word-final consonant clusters in rapid, informal speech. The result would be [æst] and [sɪks], pronunciations that would be nonstandard in highly formal situations although standard in informal speech. Basically, many aspects of language usage that are judged to be nonstandard are actually standard, informal usage in a formal situation.

Those speakers who are the most insecure about their own speech tend to be the most critical of the speech of others. A common example is the use of the pronouns *I* and *me*. Most speakers say *it's me* in casual speech. But some teachers feel that this expression is incorrect and instruct their students to say *it is I*. As a result, some speakers become sensitive to the use of *me* and *I*. Upon hearing others use the nonstandard form *John and me went home,* for example, they react strongly. However, they may overreact in their own speech. In an effort to avoid the incorrect use of *me,* they may begin to substitute *I* for *me* in the wrong situations, so that they say *between you and I* rather than the standard, correct *between you and me*. Such **hypercorrections,** which extend a correction beyond its proper domain and result in nonstandard forms, are marks of a linguistically insecure person. Often hypercorrections are indications that an individual originally spoke a nonstandard dialect, but this is not always true. Sometimes people start out with a standard dialect, but, by accepting the artificial standard imposed by some teachers, they hypercorrect and end up with nonstandard features in their speech.

Thus, many of the features found in lower-class social dialects of English are also present in middle- and upper-class dialects, as well. The difference lies in the situations in which the features are utilized.

ASPECTS OF NONSTANDARD ENGLISH

Although many features of nonstandard English can, upon careful investigation, be identified as either mislocated regional features or as informal speech used in a formal context, there are certain characteristics that never occur in any form of standard English. Although most of these characteristics involve aspects of syntax, some are phonetic.

Since all speakers of English can produce [θ] and [ð] in appropriate words under formal conditions, it is clear that words such as *through* and *that* have phonemic representations containing these segments. But in the informal speech of certain social dialects, [θ] and [ð] are replaced by [t] and [d] respectively, so that *through* is pronounced something like [tru], while *that* occurs as [dæt]. This substitution is an identifying characteristic of many nonstandard dialects, for it does not occur in any standard dialect of English; it is never regionally standard or informal, but simply nonstandard.

Although the origin of many nonstandard aspects of English has not been determined, it is widely believed that some of the features involved could be traced back to an earlier time when newcomers to America learned English as a foreign language. As we will discuss later in Part 8, adults often have difficulty in mastering the sounds of a foreign language, and the sounds most difficult to learn are those that do not occur in one's native language. [θ] and [ð] are relatively rare phonological segments among the languages of the world, and few foreigners who came to the United States, whether from Europe, Africa, or elsewhere, were accustomed to these sounds. So, as almost all adults do in learning a foreign language, those who learned English very likely substituted for [θ] and [ð] sounds of their native language that were most similar to these unfamiliar continuants, namely, the noncontinuants [t] and [d], which occur in most languages. Naturally, not everyone whose ancestors learned English as a foreign language uses [t] and [d] for [θ] and [ð]; social dialects are not transmitted genetically. The dialects we speak depend on our environment. When substantial contact with speakers of standard English occurs, a nonstandard feature can readily be replaced by standard usage. But for those who are exposed primarily to a dialect that does not fully utilize [θ] and [ð], these segments play a different role from the one they have in standard English.

Among the grammatical aspects of nonstandard English, the best known is probably the phenomenon commonly referred to as the double negative, illustrated in sentences (3) and (4):

(3) You can't have no more.

(4) John never did know nothing.

Contrary to the purists' view, two negatives do not "make an affirmative." In the dialects that include them, sentences (3) and (4) are as negative as their standard equivalents (5) and (6):

(5) You can't have any more.

(6) John never did know anything.

Although double negatives are always viewed as nonstandard in English, this syntactic pattern is apparently a highly natural one in human language. Many languages make use of more than one negative element in a negative sentence, as shown by the Russian and Spanish sentences (7) and (8):

(7) Вера ничего не знает.
     'Vera nothing not know'
     (Vera doesn't know anything.)

(8) Diego no conoce a nadie aquí.
     'Diego not know nobody here'
     (Diego doesn't know anybody here.)

Double negatives are also very common in the speech of young children who are in the process of acquiring English as their native language. Even children whose linguistic environment consists solely of standard English are likely to produce sentences such as (9):

(9) Don't take no candy!

The naturalness of double negation may well be a factor in the explanation of its occurrence in nonstandard English, since nonstandard dialects are generally those that have not been subjected to alteration by traditional, formal, school instruction.

[θ] and [ð] and double negation are only two examples of features often found in nonstandard dialects of English; others are listed in the books and articles mentioned in "Further Exploration." No matter how many examples of nonstandard features we might list, it should always be kept in mind that, when compared to the full range of phonological and syntactic properties in our language, those that may be nonstandard represent only a very small percentage. It is precisely because of this that all speakers of English, no matter what their social dialect, are able to communicate with one another with relatively little difficulty. Those dialect differences that do occur appear to be essentially phenomena at the surface level of language. Investigations of social dialects, for example, indicate that in almost every case there is strong evidence to set up the same underlying phonemic representations and deep structures for nonstandard and standard dialects. The observable differences apparently are due to phonological rules and transformations that apply very close to phonetic representations and surface structure, respectively.

BLACK ENGLISH

Much of the sociolinguistic research on social dialects has been concentrated on the speech of black people of the lower socioeconomic classes, largely because this group has captured the concern of society at large during the last two decades. Although much more remains to be learned, it has become clear that certain grammatical features are present in the speech of lower-class blacks throughout the country, in both urban and rural areas. This fact has led scholars to suggest that there exists a special variety of English, which has come to be known as Black English. The term is perhaps misleading since not all black people are speakers of Black English. Black English is a social dialect, not a racial one; it is a variety of English used by black people who are at the lower socioeconomic levels of our society (or who have moved from such a level to the middle-income range but retain contact with their earlier social group). Furthermore, not all speakers of Black English are black; in New York City, for example, some Puerto Rican people living in, or near, predominantly black communities use Black English, as well as their native variety of Spanish. In the past, even otherwise reputable scholars sometimes claimed that the speech of blacks differed from whites because of supposed physical and mental differences. Scientists have shown conclusively that there are no mental differences among races, and the physical differences that sometimes exist are unrelated to speech differences. Dialect variations are due to regional and social environment alone, a fact demonstrated by those blacks who speak standard English identical to that of whites of the same regional, social, and educational background.

The similarities in the speech of lower-class black people across the country must be accounted for. We noted in Chapter 18 that when different languages are found to have features in common, this is generally the result of some form of intercommunication or it is due to the fact that the languages were derived from a common source. The same considerations can be used to view the origin and history of Black English (or of any language or dialect).

Most speakers of modern Black English are descendants of the slaves who were brought to the United States from West Africa. These original slaves had a variety of native languages, which prevented full intercommunication among them. Furthermore, slave traders followed a practice of "language mixing," designed to separate those groups who did speak the same language and thereby to prevent whatever intercommunication might have been possible. The tactic was not effective for very long; all people possess an inherent need to communicate, and the result was the development of a lingua franca among the slaves. A **lingua franca** is a common language that can be used by members of a community who do not share a native language in common. Frequently, a lingua franca is just some ordinary language known to all members of the group, as English might serve as the lingua franca at an international meeting of scientists. In the case of the original black slaves, however, no such common language was available, except for English, which the slaves still had to learn. The resulting lingua franca was a special variety of English called Pidgin English. (The term may seem somewhat unusual, but it is a technical term not intended to convey any negative attitude.) A **pidgin language** has no native speakers. Instead, it is a variety learned by adults as a foreign language. The pidgin created in such cases frequently reflects some of the features of the learners' native languages (as is normal when adults learn a foreign language). Furthermore, the more complicated aspects of ordinary language may be omitted from the pidgin, leading to a somewhat simpler linguistic system that can be mastered more readily. Thus, the Pidgin English created by black slaves did not use all of the inflectional morphemes of English to indicate such matters as past tense or subject noun-verb agreement. Today, in modern Black English, therefore, we can find *he go* where standard English requires agreement, *he goes*.

As a pidgin language develops and is acquired and used by more and more members of a community, it increases in complexity and gains all of the characteristics of ordinary languages. If the pidgin eventually replaces the speakers' native languages as the normal means for communication, it will be acquired as a native language by the children of the community, and it is then identified as a **creole language.** It appears that modern Black English developed in large part from the creole English used by black slaves in the South; this creole, in turn, had its origin in the pidgin English of the earliest slaves, and that pidgin contained a number of the linguistic features of its speakers' native West African languages.

One feature of language that is not strongly utilized in standard English but does occur in Black English is the phenomenon of **aspect,** in which verbs indicate the duration, completion, or repetition of an action, sometimes with little or no attention to tense (the time at which the action occurred). For example, when asked where his or her mother is, a child may answer with sentence (10):

(10) She is in the hospital.

This sentence gives no information about the duration of the mother's absence. Sentence (10) is standard English. Consider sentences (11) and (12), which are typical forms of Black English.

(11) She in the hospital.
(12) She be in the hospital.

These two sentences convey different meanings, and the difference is one of aspect. (11), in which no form of the verb *be* occurs, means that the mother is there right now and that her confinement is probably unusual and has been for a relatively short time. (12), on the other hand, in which *be* is present, means that the mother has been hospitalized for a long time or that she is often hospitalized. The presence of *be* in a Black English sentence can indicate a basic, inherent quality, while absence of *be* may indicate a temporary quality. Thus (13) means 'she is a silly person' and (14) means 'she is being silly now'. (Those readers familiar with Spanish will recognize this as similar to the distinction in meaning of *ser* and *estar*.)

(13) She be silly.

(14) She silly.

It is interesting to note that a similar distinction occurs in many West African languages, a fact that may account for its presence in Black English. While such a hypothesis is appealing, it is necessary that some caution be used in accepting as fact the view that all aspects of Black English can be traced back to features in the native languages of slaves from more than a century ago. Research into Black English is a recent interest of students of language, and there may well be aspects of this social dialect that cannot be accounted for by this hypothesis.

OTHER SOCIAL DIALECTS

In addition to lower-class blacks, there are two other major linguistic minority groups in the United States: the Spanish-speaking Americans and the American Indians. One might ask whether these groups utilize special social dialects parallel to Black English. In neither case has there been sufficient investigation to provide an answer to the question, but some tentative discussion is possible.

The nonstandard speech of Spanish-speaking Americans in the lower social classes shows certain basic similarities in all areas of the country where native speakers of Spanish learn English as a second language, from the southwest to New York and the Miami area of Florida on the East Coast. Examples range from phonetic differences, such as the simplification of word-final consonant clusters, to syntactic distinctions, such as the placement of adjectives after nouns rather than before them, to variations in the use of lexical items, as with the preposition in sentence (15).

(15) Peter married with her.

In the cases listed, the features in these nonstandard dialects are also features of Spanish, in which word-final consonant clusters do not occur, adjectives generally follow nouns, and the expression 'to marry' is conveyed by *casarse con,* in which *con* is a preposition usually translated into English as *with*. It seems that, at least in some cases, nonstandard features of the English used by lower-class Spanish-speaking Americans are due to their native language, Spanish. It must be pointed out, however, that children also use these features, in spite of the fact that most young children can learn a foreign language perfectly, given sufficient exposure to that language. The key point here is exposure to the language, for the English learned by children is that which they hear around them. If they grow up in a community where they hear primarily nonstandard English strongly influenced by Spanish, that is the dialect of English they will learn.

Studies of the English used by American Indians are almost nonexistent. It is known that many Indians never acquire standard English, a situation that is not surprising since they are often taught English in reservation schools or boarding schools where they come into contact with only a few teachers who speak standard English and their fellow students are all learning English as a foreign language. Unlike Spanish-speaking Americans, who share a linguistic background of a single language, American Indians do not all share one language. In fact, some American Indian languages differ from one another more than do the languages of Europe or those of West Africa. Thus, it would be surprising if future investigations were to reveal a single, nonstandard dialect of English shared by all lower-class Indians, although certain features common to many nonstandard dialects might occur.

COMMUNICATION AND SYSTEM

It is extremely important to recognize that all dialects, of English as well as of any other language, are equivalent from an objective point of view. No single dialect, regional or social, is superior to others in terms of its capabilities for expressing concepts. Every dialect is an adequate system for communication by the people who use that dialect. Although individuals who are not familiar with a particular regional or social dialect may have some difficulty in understanding that form of speech when they first encounter it, the users of the dialect clearly have no such problems. And, of course, this situation is parallel to that which exists among different languages. It is interesting that few people object to the fact that there are languages they have difficulty understanding, and yet there are often very strong reactions to dialect differences. As we have seen, whether a form of speech is termed a dialect or a language is basically a matter of degree of difference, coupled with such nonlinguistic factors as national boundaries.

It should also be noted that every dialect consists of a full linguistic system. It is totally incorrect to label a social dialect as "sloppy speech" or as "inconsistent." The speakers of every dialect know an extensive and complex set of rules that they utilize when they talk. People who simplify word-final consonant clusters, for example, pronouncing *texts* as [tɛks], are not being careless in pronunciation; they are simply following a phonological rule of their dialect that deletes certain consonants other dialects allow word-finally. Although the presence of *be* in sentences like (11) and (12) may appear to be inconsistent to those who do not know Black English, speakers of this dialect are completely consistent in distinguishing aspect by the use or nonuse of *be*. The systematic nature of all dialects is demonstrated conclusively by the fact that people learn them. Anything as complex as language can be acquired only if it is systematic. The alternative would be that a dialect is a random set of forms and rules, and, if this were so, it would be impossible to learn.

It cannot be denied, of course, that some people find certain dialects to be more aesthetically appealing than others. To some, southern English is "charming;" to others, it is "annoying." Upper-class British English may sound "sophisticated" to one person, "pretentious" to another. People have always made such judgments about speech, and there is no reason to believe that they will ever cease to do so. But it must be kept in mind that personal reactions of this kind are highly subjective, generally dependent on one's past experiences with language, and, as with all subjective judgments, subject to wide differences of opinion.

SUMMARY

Within their own locality, the speech of upper- and upper-middle-class Americans is commonly accepted as standard English. Such regional standard dialects serve as models for language use, and departures from standard usage are often considered to be representative of uneducated, nonstandard speech. Yet, all social dialects are equally systematic, consistent, and adequate for communication among the people who use them.

Population mobility plays a major role in the development of social dialects, just as it does for regional dialects. In fact, there is a strong interrelationship between regional and social dialects since linguistic features considered nonstandard in one area may be standard in another. Other features judged as nonstandard can often be found in informal standard dialects. For those aspects of English that are always nonstandard, a number probably can be explained by considering the history of the users of these features. In some cases, for example, phonological differences apparently can be traced back to a time when people learned English as a foreign language under conditions in which they were not exposed to a sufficient amount of standard English. Certain syntactic nonstandard features may be due to similar situations or to the fact that they are natural linguistic phenomena. The linguistic, as well as social, isolation of many people who use nonstandard dialects is an important factor in the retention of these dialects, for no one will learn standard English unless he or she is exposed to it.

FURTHER EXPLORATION

An excellent introduction to social dialects is *The Study of Social Dialects in American English,* by Walt Wolfram and Ralph W. Fasold. In *The Study of Nonstandard English,* William Labov provides a brief, interesting overview of the nature of nonstandard dialects, as well as some enlightening discussion about the implications of sociolinguistic research for teachers whose students speak nonstandard English. More demanding are two collections of Labov's papers and research reports on social dialects: *Sociolinguistic Patterns* and *Language in the Inner City: Studies in the Black English Vernacular.* A detailed history of Black English, with substantial documentation and numerous examples, is presented by J. L. Dillard in *Black English: Its History and Usage in the United States.* A recent collection of articles on the interactions of Spanish and English in the southwestern United States appears in *El Lenguaje de los Chicanos: Regional and Social Characteristics of Language Use by Mexican-Americans,* edited by Eduardo Hernandez-Chavez, Andrew D. Cohen, and Anthony F. Beltramo. Also of interest is *Spanish and English of United States Hispanos,* edited by Richard V. Teschner, Garland Bills, and Jerry Craddock. *Contemporary English: Change and Variation,* edited by David L. Shores, is a collection of articles devoted primarily to social dialects.

Another issue in the study of social dialects, dependent on sex differences rather than distinctions in general socioeconomic class, involves aspects of language use by and about women (as contrasted with language use by and about men). This topic is pursued from a personal, feminist perspective by linguist Robin Lakoff in her brief study *Language and Woman's Place.*

1. Consider your own social dialect in terms of the concepts discussed in this chapter. Have you ever moved from one region of the country to another and encountered negative reactions to features of your speech that were normal and accepted in the region from which you came? List several systematic differences in your pronunciation in casual as opposed to formal situations. Have you ever made a conscious effort to change some aspect of your native dialect (in pronunciation, vocabulary, or syntax)? Why? Did hyper-correction occur?

2. Reconsider item 1 in "Further Exploration" at the end of Chapter 19, "Regional Dialects." What social class reactions, if any, do you have to pronunciations that differ from your own for the words listed? Have you ever attempted to change your native dialect pronunciation of any of those words? If so, why?

3. In addition to the types of social dialects discussed in this chapter, sociolinguists recently have become interested in differences between the speech of men and women from the same region and social classs. Among the variations that have been reported for certain groups are the following:

(a) Women tend to use more modifiers than men (e.g., more adjectives and words like *very, frequently, some*).
(b) Many women frequently employ a rising intonation, even in statements, so that the resulting utterance gives the impression of a question.
(c) Adolescent men are more likely to reduce word-final consonant clusters in informal speech than are adolescent women.

These and other variations can be investigated in several ways. Simple observation of conversations may reveal some features. For a more systematic approach, cut out a news photograph from a paper or magazine and ask several men and women to describe the picture. Approach each person individually so that his or her response is not influenced by what others say. Tape-record the responses and compare them, noting systematic differences in phonology, lexicon, and syntax.

PART 8 LANGUAGE ACQUISITION

The ultimate goals of children mastering their native language and adults studying a foreign language are often the same—to acquire a knowledge of the language sufficiently rich and correct to result in fluent performance equivalent to that of adult native speakers. It is a well-known fact that all normal children, and many who have mental or physical abnormalities, succeed in achieving this goal without any formal teaching. In this sense, children acquire a language; they do not learn it in the way that they learn geography. On the other hand, adults, even with the guidance of experienced teachers, often fail to achieve fluency in a foreign language. There is apparently a difference between native language acquisition and foreign language learning.

How can this difference be explained? How does a child, apparently too young to carry out many of the reasoning processes used by adults, acquire language perfectly in just a few years time while learning many other activities as well? Are there ways of teaching foreign languages so that adults will learn more quickly and more accurately? In this part we will examine some of the contributions modern linguistics can provide in answering such questions.

These areas of investigation are by no means new. Educators and psychologists have been concerned with them for many years. But it is only recently that linguistic theory has become sufficiently well developed to provide a basic understanding of the nature of language and thereby a basic framework for investigation.

CHAPTER **21212121212121212121212121212**

NATIVE LANGUAGE ACQUISITION: THE DATA

Modern linguists are especially interested in the study of native language acquisition. By examining what children learn, in what order, and what kinds of "mistakes" they make as they attempt to learn a language, the linguist hopes to obtain additional insights into the nature of language itself. By investigating how children acquire their native language, the linguist, as well as the psychologist, expects to find evidence about the nature and properties of the human mind. The "what" of language acquisition serves as the topic for this chapter; the "how" of language acquisition is discussed in the following chapter.

Superficially, it seems that the study of what children learn when they acquire their native language is a relatively straightforward task. One might simply observe and tape-record the speech of a number of children at regular intervals over a sufficiently long period of time and then analyze the recordings to determine which aspects of language have been mastered at different ages. This type of study has indeed been carried out by many investigators, and the results are well-established developmental norms. Such norms are important to teachers, speech therapists, physicians, and psychiatrists, all of whom may wish to determine whether a particular child is making normal progress in language acquisition.

Unfortunately, the matter is not that simple. To begin with, many studies of this type have been conducted by people with relatively little knowledge of linguistics. For example, they confuse sounds with letters, and one finds statements such as "By the age of five, most children have mastered the *th* sound." But what does this mean? As we know, the letters *th* represent two different English sounds, [θ] and [ð]. Further problems arise because of a lack of sophistication about language on the part of many investigators. It is not enough to say that children know the sound [š] just because they use it in words like *shine* and *ship*. If we are to understand children's mastery of English, we must also know whether they have acquired the sound system of their language. For example, do they know that [t] alternates with [š] in certain English words, as illustrated by the pairs *act/action, construct/construction?* Linguistically naïve investigators also tend to analyze children's speech in terms of adult speech. Thus, if children use only four words, and two of them are *go* and *cookie,* the adult may report that the children have acquired nouns and verbs, in spite of the fact that there may be no evidence that these words constitute different parts of speech for the children themselves.

When investigators attempt to determine what children know, they are dealing with a highly complex problem. The knowledge involved is implicit. It is unconscious knowledge, acquired by the child without obvious teaching. Such knowledge may not be fully represented by what children say or by how they respond to the speech of others. Thus, investigating language acquisition merely by collecting samples of speech and then organizing the data is subject to important limitations. Speech itself is only an imperfect reflection of what an individual knows. Adults, for example, can understand very complex sentences if they are written down. However, they may never utter such sentences, and they may be unable to comprehend them if they hear them. Their linguistic competence is the same whether they are speaking, listening, reading, or writing, but their performance differs. The case is similar for children. What they have learned of their language may not be obvious from their speech. For example, all children appear to comprehend utterances before they are able to produce such utterances spontaneously. Few studies of language acquisition have involved investigation of children's comprehension. Most studies currently available concentrate on production. Thus, there are even aspects of linguistic performance that have not been investigated fully.

At the current state of our research all that can be described is what is readily and directly observable—what children say. Recently, a number of linguists and psycholinguists (scholars with a background in both linguistics and psychology) have attempted to improve this situation by new approaches to the study of native language acquisition. Such approaches are designed to provide further information about linguistic comprehension in children and also to obtain other information that will give a better picture of what children at various levels of linguistic development actually know. Research of this kind, however, is still quite limited.

INFANT VOCAL PRODUCTION

Newborn infants are not the charming, cooing little people presented so beautifully in advertisements for baby products. For the first month or two of life, babies cry, and their vocal performance is limited to these crying noises. Fortunately for those around them, children soon replace some of their crying with cooing noises, usually during the third month of life. During this **cooing** period, the sounds a child produces are primarily consonants formed at the back of the mouth, such as [k] and [g], and nonlow vowel sounds, such as [i], [ɛ], and [u]. The cooing period varies in length from one child to another, but by the age of five months, most children have entered into the **babbling** stage, characterized by an ever increasing variety of sounds.

The crying and cooing stages apparently play no significant role in the acquisition of language. No matter what language is spoken in the environment, all children sound the same during these periods. In fact, children who hear no language at all for the first few months of life, whether because of deafness or other unusual conditions, cry and coo just like more fortunate children. Children who are prevented from crying and cooing because of physical problems suffer no ill effects insofar as later vocal development is concerned, provided that the physical problem involved is corrected. There is, then, no concrete evidence that these periods are important for the eventual acquisition of language. A number of people have speculated as to the reasons why children make such vocal noises during the first few months. For example, some maintain that children are exercising and strengthening their vocal tract; others feel that they make noise in order to gain some control over their environment. Regarding the former, it is of interest to recall that the vocal tract is used only secondarily as a sound producing mechanism; its primary functions are eating and breathing. The muscular control and effort required for such a simple procedure as swallowing are as great as those involved in many speech sounds. All infants are able to swallow and, we must assume, physically capable of producing some speech sounds even if they are not yet able to consistently or consciously articulate them. It seems that any exercise provided by crying and cooing is not really necessary. Whether or not crying and cooing are efforts by children to control their environment is something known only to the children themselves. Noises made during these periods very often do have this effect, but whether they are made in order to create the effect is another matter altogether.

The babbling period extends from the age of four or five months until the child is approximately one year old. During this time, the child produces a great variety of sounds. Babbling appears to be an innately determined activity. All children, even those who are deaf, reportedly babble in much the same way. The language spoken in the child's environment has no effect on the sounds in early babbling, so, for example, a child brought up in an English-speaking situation does not show any preference in his babbling for the particular sounds of English. It is not clear, therefore, whether babbling plays any true role in the acquisition of language. There is a very definite distinction between babbling and the initial stage of talking. Children can and do produce many sounds during the babbling period that they do not use in actual speech. For example, [k] occurs as early as the cooing stage and is also used in babbling, but, when children begin to produce their first words, they may not use [k] in any of those words. Where adults do use [k], the child may substitute another sound, as in the word *cookie* (a word many young children pronounce [tuti]). If babbling were directly related to language acquisition, we would expect there to be some kind of continuity between the two stages. It should be noted that children, in the early stages of actual language production, frequently have two separate vocalization systems: babbling occurs on some occasions, with its typical wide diversity of sounds; on other occasions, children will produce their new words, utilizing only the very small number of sounds that comprise their developing linguistic systems.

Late in the babbling period, the effect of children's linguistic environment begins to appear in the sounds they make. It is at this point that children seem to recognize and understand a few of the words they hear, such as their name and commands like ''No!'' In terms of production, children at about the age of ten months have usually acquired the basic intonation patterns of the language they are about to learn. Thus, if you listen to a ten-month-old child babble, it often seems as if he or she is trying to communicate, for some utterances sound like statements, with falling intonation, and others sound like questions, with rising intonation. The babbling of a child in a Chinese-speaking environment, toward the end of the babbling stage, is quite distinct from that of an American child. Since the Chinese language makes use of tone (the pitch of the voice) in distinguishing words from one another, a child raised in this linguistic environment begins to make pitch distinctions in babbling at about the age of ten months. This phonological feature does not play the same role in the sound system of English, and, therefore, children learning English do not utilize such tones in their late babbling.

FIRST WORDS

It is usually said that children have begun to talk when they first begin to consistently use a particular sequence of sounds that corresponds roughly to a sequence of sounds used by adults for approximately the same meaning. This is recognized as the child's first word. However, there is a certain bias in this view. The adult investigator may credit the child with a productive linguistic system only if the child's speech corresponds to the adult's in some obvious manner. Yet, it may be that some children, if not all, begin using sounds consistently and with specific meanings at an earlier point in time. For example, [bababa] may occur when the child apparently is pleased about something; [nana], with rising intonation, may be uttered in seeking an object, such as a cookie that is beyond reach or a toy that has been put away. Such utterances represent the child's first attempt to use sounds to convey meanings. When the correlation of sound and meaning is not related to the adult language of the child's environment, however, it is not recognized as language; instead, it is viewed simply as babbling. This problem of adult recognition of children's early language production is due to a common phenomenon of linguistic perception. As linguistically mature individuals, we perceive the speech of others in terms of our own internal linguistic system. Thus, in listening to a foreign language, we may take note of phonetic differences that are redundant in that language (but distinctive in our own) and, at the same time, we may be unaware of features that are distinctive in the foreign language (but predictable or absent in our own language). The same phenomenon can affect our perception of the linguistic efforts of children. It may well be, therefore, that researchers in the past have underestimated the emerging linguistic abilities of children under the age of one year.

The appearance of the first recognizable word may occur at any time from eight months up to eighteen months of age. There is very wide variation in the age at which normal children begin to talk. In fact, some completely normal children do not produce recognizable words until they are two years old. But, once children do begin to talk, they all follow the same general pattern of development in acquiring phonology, syntax, and semantics. Occasionally, it is reported that some child has skipped a step in the process of language acquisition, but upon investigation it usually turns out that the step was not skipped at all, but rather was completed in a very short time and the observer overlooked it.

The first stage of actual language acquisition is the **holophrastic** stage—"expressing an entire sentence in one word." During the holophrastic stage, which begins with the production of the first word, children use only single words; they do not yet combine two words to produce simple phrases. The length of the holophrastic stage, like all stages of language acquisition, varies from child to child. For some, it may last as long as a year; for others, especially those who enter this stage later than usual, it may occur for only a few days. The normal length appears to be between three and nine months.

Relatively little is known about what children learn during the holophrastic stage. It is clear that they are beginning to acquire the sounds of their language, and since sounds are directly observable, there are a number of studies of the order in which children master sounds. At the same time, a child in this stage is also learning phonological rules, meanings, and probably the rudimentary aspects of syntax. These aspects of language, however, cannot be directly observed, and children under two years of age do not make very good subjects for experiments and research. Investigation of these matters is underway, but thus far results are few.

No matter what language they are learning, children all seem to follow the same order in the acquisition of sounds. Possible explanations for this fact are presented in the next chapter under discussion of how children acquire language. For now, let us simply describe the normal order.

The first words which many children produce are *papa* and *mama,* and these are the **nursery words** for parents in a great many languages. (Nursery words are those words that are not normally used by adults speaking to one another, but adults commonly use them when talking to very young children. **Baby talk** makes use of nursery words as well as intentional deviation from normal pronunciation whereby adults attempt to pronounce words as they believe the child would.) *Mama* and *papa* illustrate a universal fact about native language acquisition. The first vowel most children acquire for use in language is [a]; the first consonant is almost always a bilabial noncontinuant, that is, [p], [b], or [m]. Even when children do not begin with the particular words *mama* and *papa,* they still usually conform to this fact. The author's daughter Tanya, for example, began the holophrastic stage at fourteen months with the words *bad, up,* and *potty,* which she then pronounced as [ba], [ap], and [pa], respectively.

The course of the acquisition of language sounds follows a pattern of differentiation.

It should be noted that the first vowel, [a], is produced with a maximally open vocal tract; the body of the tongue is lowered from prespeech position allowing the air stream as much room as is possible to move freely through the oral cavity. On the other hand, the first consonant, [p] for example, involves a maximally closed vocal tract; the air stream is completely blocked by the lips at the very front of the oral cavity. Thus, the child's first two language sounds are as different from one another as any two sounds can be. This holds true even for those children who do not follow exactly the pattern described here. Thus, a child whose first word is [kiki] 'kitty' is still making use of the maximal distinction between the sounds in the word: [k] is a voiceless stop formed at the back of the oral cavity, while [i] is fully voiced and is the vowel articulated most toward the front of the oral cavity.

From this point on, children master the grossest distinctions among sound segments, then the finer ones, until ultimately they have acquired all of the segments of the language they are learning. Distinctions among vowels proceed side by side with distinctions among consonants, and any given child may learn some vowel distinction before a distinction between consonants, or vice versa. Let us consider the order of acquisition of vowels, then that for consonants.

[a] is a [− high, + low] vowel. Therefore, the vowel most distinct from [a] is one that is [+ high, − low], and these are the phonetic features of the second vowel that most children acquire. Thus, the second vowel will be either [i] or [u]. The third vowel normally learned is also a [+ high] vowel. [i] and [u] are distinguished primarily by the feature [back]; whichever of these segments was not acquired as the second vowel, the child learns as the third vowel. Thus, at a particular stage in the acquisition of phonology, children will have a three-vowel system consisting of [a], [i], and [u]. This system makes use of the opposition between front and back and between high and low. From this point on, the child refines control of such features, learning the mid vowels, such as [e] and [o]. Last to be learned are those vowels that, in addition to the basic position of articulation features, involve features describing supplementary articulatory activities. For example, French-speaking children do not learn the [+ nasal] vowels of their language, such as [ã], until after they have learned the corresponding [− nasal] vowels, in this case [a].

In learning to distinguish consonants from one another, children follow the same pattern of first acquiring the major distinctions, later mastering the finer ones. The first consonant is [− coronal, − continuant]; the second consonant is usually [+ coronal] (normally, it is [t]). Only later do children master another [− coronal] consonant, like [k]. Only after children have acquired several [− continuant] sound segments do they begin to learn [+ continuant] consonants. It is clear that this is a process of moving from gross articulatory gestures to finer ones. To produce a [− continuant] sound, one simply has to block the air stream completely. [+ continuant] consonant sounds require greater control, since one must interfere with the air stream but neither block it nor allow it enough room to pass freely through the oral cavity. Thus, fricatives are learned after stops. Similarly, if the language the child is learning has affricates, these will be learned relatively late, only after the corresponding stops and fricatives have been mastered. As we observed in Chapter 8, an affricate, such as [č], involves total blockage of the air stream followed immediately by gradual release that results in some friction noise. This type of sound requires finer control over the vocal tract than do either stops or fricatives.

In Chapter 8, it was noted that liquids, such as [l] and [r] in English, share features with both consonants and vowels; furthermore, they involve vocal tract activities not associated with other sounds in the language, such as the [+ lateral] feature of [l]. It is not surprising, therefore, that children tend to master liquids quite late compared to all other sound segments in their language.

The acquisition of the phonological system of a language involves more than learning to produce the sound segments of the language. As we observed in Part 3, a phonological system consists of underlying phonemic representations and surface phonetic representations for the morphemes of a language, as well as a series of rules linking these two types of representation. Therefore, we must ask when children determine phonemic representations, to what extent they differ from their actual phonetic forms, and at what points and in which order children master the phonological rules. Very little is known about the answers to such questions, in large part because of the general problems involved in carrying out research with children and because such aspects of phonology cannot be directly observed. We can examine only children's phonetic forms, their actual pronunciation. From this the investigator must attempt to determine the underlying knowledge that children could reasonably be expected to possess in order to produce such forms. Let us consider the problem of word-initial consonant clusters as an example.

In the acquisition of consonants, children almost always master the production of single segments before they are able to produce sequences of consonantal segments. Thus, children may be quite accurate, from the adult point of view, in their pronunciation of words like *see* and *key* but be as yet unable to produce the word *ski* with the normal, adult initial consonant cluster [sk]. By the age of nineteen months, the author's daughter Tanya had mastered the production of all English stops, nasals, and all fricatives except [θ] and [ð], but she did not use any consonant clusters. The word *sky* was pronounced either as [say] or [kay]; *spoon* was sometimes [sun] and sometimes [pun]; *stool* was either [su] or [tu]. From the point of view of her phonological system, one can ask what her underlying phonemic representation was for such words beginning with [s] followed by a consonant. Did she have two phonemic representations for each word of this kind, identical to the phonetic representations, one with just [s], the other with just the other consonant? This is possible, but it is highly unlikely since the child treated all words beginning with *sC* (where *C* stands for any consonant) in exactly the same way (each had two possible pronunciations). Clearly, some kind of system was at work. It seems more likely that she knew that each of these words began just as they do in adult speech, but she had not yet reached the degree of muscular control necessary to produce the proper sequence of sounds. Since in performance she was limited to producing only one consonant before a vowel, she selected one of the two that were present at her level of phonemic representation. Her performance in comprehension supports this hypothesis that her knowledge of English was much more sophisticated than her production performance indicated. If asked whether she wanted her [spun], for example, she would respond appropriately. If an adult used HER pronunciation and asked if she wanted her [sun] or [pun], the child simply rejected the utterance; she acted as if she did not know what the adult was talking about. In other words, at the level of comprehension she demonstrated that she knew the correct forms of the words even though she could not produce them. Similar observations have been made for many other children.

It is difficult to determine when children learn such facts about their language since their knowledge is not directly reflected in their speech. One further example will suffice to illustrate this matter. At sixteen months, Tanya pronounced the words *bad, bath,* and *back* all as [bæ]. Yet, in a completely neutral context, such as her room, one of these words would be produced by an adult. Although Tanya did not distinguish the words in her own speech, she always knew which one had been said. She would walk to the bathroom in response to [bæθ], stop or turn around in response to [bæk], and look very worried if the adult said [bæd]. She knew the pronunciation of these words, even though she could not yet implement such knowledge when speaking herself.

Another problem in many studies of language acquisition involves the fact that people tend to hear in terms of their own phonological system. Investigators report that a particular child has not yet acquired [θ] and that in words where [θ] appears in adult speech, "the child substitutes [t]." But recently, examination of such "substitutions," using the detailed records of physical, acoustic phonetics, has revealed that the child may actually be making a distinction between words such as *thank* and *tank*. The [t] used in *tank* is different from the [t] used in the child's pronunciation of *thank*. Since the particular way in which the child distinguishes these sounds is not used for the same purpose in adult English, the adult fails to notice the distinction.

It should be noted that, although the preceding discussion of phonological acquisition has occurred within the division on the holophrastic stage, children actually learn the phonological system of their language over a long period of time, extending well beyond the holophrastic stage. Since phonological acquisition begins at this point, however, it has been included here.

At the onset of the holophrastic stage, most children acquire words quite slowly, adding as few as one or two new words a week to their lexicon. This may be due in part to the fact that, since the child is still mastering the sound segments of his language, he does not yet have enough different language sounds to use. But homonyms do not seem to bother children, as evidenced from the example [bæ] in Tanya's speech. The initial, gradual development of the lexicon may also be due to the way in which children learn meaning. The same process of differentiation observed in phonological acquisition appears to be at work in the acquisition of lexical semantics.

Many investigators have noted that children in the holophrastic stage extend the meaning of the words they learn. For example, a child may use the word *car* for any motor vehicle, such as a truck or bus. The meaning of the word, for the child, is apparently 'a large object that moves on the street'. This meaning is refined as the child acquires different words, such as *bus* or *truck*, and once such words are learned, *car* comes to have the same, more limited meaning it has for adults. Figure 21.1 illustrates the process of semantic development for Tanya during the holophrastic stage. It is interesting to note that, the first few times a word occurred in her speech, it had a highly specific meaning. This was followed by a period in which the child generalized, or extended, the meaning.

LANGUAGE ACQUISITION

Figure 21.1 ——

Age (in months)	Word*	Meaning
15	[pa]	potty seat
16	[pa]	any small, chairlike object, including potty
18	[tu] or [su]	stool
	[tæ]	chair
	[pa]	only potty seat
17	[dus]	only fruit juice given in highchair
18	[dus]	any liquid
19	[miw]	milk
	[wɔyi]	water
	[dus]	only fruit juice
18	[opi]	open
18.5	[opi]	open or close
19	[kwo]	close
	[opi]	open

*Some phonetic details have been omitted.

Finally, as other semantically similar words were learned, the meaning of the original word was narrowed down to the equivalent of the meaning for adults. This same process of very limited use at first, overgeneralization beyond the adult meaning, and finally narrowing can be observed in the acquisition of syntax during the next stage of development.

During the holophrastic stage there is little direct evidence that the child is learning syntax. Since, by definition, the child does not combine words at this point, we do not observe the phrases or sentences from which information about syntax is available. But, nevertheless, some kind of syntactic knowledge seems to be at work even during the holophrastic period. Children do not use their words merely to name objects, and, contrary to some reports, many, if not all, children are capable of talking about people, objects, and events that are not present (so-called "displaced speech"). For example, children may say *dada* as they hear father's car come up the driveway, in which case *dada* seems to be functioning as the subject of the sentence, 'Dada is coming'. Children may also say *dada* when father is not present, perhaps as a request to be taken to see the father ('I want to see *dada*'); in this case, *dada* is the object. Attributing knowledge of parts of speech or syntactic functions, like subject or object, to the child is somewhat tricky, for, in any investigation of child language acquisition, there is a strong tendency for researchers to interpret the child's knowledge according to their own. But the fact that even at the holophrastic stage children are quite consistent in using their words in appropriate grammatical and situational contexts seems to indicate that children know more about the syntactic properties of words than might be assumed initially from their speech.

EARLY SYNTAX AND SEMANTICS

If you had to send a telegram notifying someone of your arrival at the airport, which of the following messages would you send?

(1) I am arriving at ten tomorrow morning at the John F. Kennedy International Airport on American Airlines flight number 72.

(2) Arrive ten A.M. tomorrow JFK, American flight 72.

The second message, of course, represents normal telegram style. In addition to the abbreviation of certain words, telegraphic messages eliminate many of the morphemes found in the regular sentence, in this case morphemes such as *ing, at, the,* and *on.* The speech of children for roughly two years after the end of the holophrastic stage is similar to the telegraphic style of adults, and, therefore, this period in the acquisition of language is often referred to as the **telegraphic** stage.

Sometime between the ages of one-and-a-half and two years, children generally produce their first two-word sentence, such as *byebye daddy.* Prior to this time, both words occurred holophrastically, but never in combination. Once children have produced a combination they usually follow up by producing several more that contain one of the words in their first combination; for example, a child who begins with *byebye daddy* may then say *byebye mommy, byebye car, byebye TV.* The word that occurs over and over again in such two-word sentences is often referred to as the **pivot** word; the variety of words that co-occur with the pivot are called **open class** words. In the early stages of telegraphic speech, children seem to organize their vocabulary into these two classes. The pivot words consist of a small number of words used very frequently, but rarely alone. The open class consists of a large number of words used both holophrastically and in combination with pivot words and with other open class words. An example from Tanya's speech at eighteen months is given in Figure 21.2. The pivot class is listed in its entirety, but, as noted, only representative examples are given from the open class. In two-word utterances, the pivot word always preceded the open class word for this child, but investigators report that other children sometimes have pivot words following open class words, for example, *it* in *want it, see it, do it.* Not every pivot word actually occurred in Tanya's speech with every open class word, but from the large number of actual combinations, it was clear that many of the gaps were accidental. Perhaps no situation arose in which they would be appropriate, or possibly the combination was not observed when it did occur. It appears, then, that the child had learned two classes of words and a rule for combining the members of the classes:

$$S \rightarrow \left\{ \begin{array}{cc} (P) & O \\ O & O \end{array} \right\}$$

Figure 21.2

	Pivot Class	Open Class	
	byebye	daddy	mommy
	hi	juice	book
	my	TV	cracker
	more	car	kitty
	want	cow	bath
	allgone	cookie	house
		nose	applesauce

as well as approximately fifty lexical items learned during the holophrastic stage and others acquired during this stage

Note: Words are given in normal spelling since phonetic details are irrelevant.

The rule notation is the same as that introduced in Part 5. This rule, therefore, states that a sentence consists of (1) an open class word by itself, (2) an open class word preceded by a pivot word, or (3) two open class words.

Apparently, the speech of all children at this stage can be characterized in terms of the pivot/open class distinction. Although research results are limited, the distinction has been reported for the speech of children learning languages such as Russian and Spanish, as well as English. One interesting characteristic of this stage of linguistic development involves the number of two-word sentences that children produce. In the study on pivot and open class words listed in "Further Exploration," Martin Braine reports the following figures for one child whose speech he investigated. Gregory began the two-word sentence stage with 14 combinations the first month of two-word sentence production; by the second month, he had 24 combinations, 54 for the third month, 89 for the fourth, and then a rapid increase to 350, 1400, and more than 2500 for the fifth, sixth, and seventh months, respectively. The great increase in new word combinations at about the fifth month may indicate that, at the beginning, the two-word combinations produced were simply memorized forms. Later, when Gregory had actually mastered a rule for combining words, he no longer had to rely on memorization, but instead could produce sentences by means of a generalization. It is the generalization that accounts for the child's ability to produce hundreds of two-word utterances. This pattern of development is not unique to Gregory; it has been observed in a number of other children as well.

The pivot/open class analysis provides a useful characterization of the observable syntactic nature of the speech of children at the onset of the telegraphic stage. However, there are serious questions as to whether this type of analysis truly captures all of the child's developing linguistic knowledge. There is an increasing body of evidence that children at this point actually know much more about syntactic and semantic properties in their language than is reflected by a simple rule such as the one cited above. For example, a child may use a two-word utterance at various times to represent a variety of syntactic relations such as subject-verb, verb-direct object, or possessor-possession, and in each case the utterance will be appropriate to the context and situation in which it occurs. Investigators have reported numerous instances of utterances such as *baby candy,* where on one occasion the meaning may be that of possession, 'baby's candy', on other occasions it may reflect the indirect-direct object relation, 'I am giving the baby some candy', and yet another time the relation may be that of subject-direct object, as in 'baby ate the candy'. A simple rule of word combination does not reveal the fact that the child apparently has learned these different relations among words. The study and description of child language acquisition must include information about the context in which utterances occur and the various syntactic functions that may be represented in what at first glance appears to be a simple combination of two words.

It is important to recall that syntactic functions serve a semantic purpose—they are one means for the expression of meaning. For example, in English, the relation of subject-verb can be used to express the meaning of some agent carrying out some action, as in the sentence *David ate.* A child who produces this sentence has learned more than a grammatical fact about word order; the child has also acquired knowledge about meaning, not only of the specific lexical items but also the meaning of the structure itself. The same syntactic structure may be used for the expression of a different semantic relation. Thus, while subject-verb expresses agent-action in most cases where the subject is human, or at least animate, there are other cases where the same syntactic structure has a different meaning. Consider the sentence *The door opened.* In this case, *the door* is the subject, but it is not the agent at all (the agent may be some person who turned the knob and pushed the door); instead, *the door* is the patient, or recipient, of the action.

In English, syntactic functions are commonly expressed by word order. Semantic relations are related to, but independent of, syntactic functions. A child occasionally may express a semantic relation, such as action-patient, without utilizing the normal, adult word order. Thus, a child who says *doll get* when he or she has gotten a doll has mastered the semantic aspects of the language but may not control fully the particular grammatical element of word order. Semantic relations are acquired early; we can observe their expression in the speech of children who are still at the two-word level. The relations acquired earliest appear to include agent-action (*Mommy spank*), action-patient (*get doll*), item-location (*cup sink*), and possessor-possession (*Daddy car*). It also appears to be the case that word order is acquired early. Although examples such as *doll get* for the adult order *get the doll* do occur in some children's speech, they are relatively rare. In a language like English, where word order is an important grammatical device, children seem to master the appropriate word order of their language almost as soon as they begin to combine words.

The transition period between holophrastic speech and the two-word stage frequently shows instances of children producing a series of one-word utterances in close succession. A child may say *Daddy* and then, a few seconds later, *car.* We know that these utterances reflect separate sentences because each is usually produced with the intonation of a complete sentence and there is an observable pause between the two words. The progressive step that results in combining the two separate one-word utterances into a single two-word utterance is reasonably simple and straightforward. The same type of transition appears between the period of two-word sentences and the more advanced stage of longer sentences. The child may say *Mommy get* and then *get doll*. Very soon, the same child will produce a sentence reflecting all three of the semantic relations, agent, action, and patient: *Mommy get doll*. Generally, utterances at this point consist of just such overlapping combinations of the earlier two-word sequences.

With the onset of sentences longer than two words, the "telegraphic" structure of children's speech becomes apparent. These sentences consist primarily of nouns, verbs, and adjectives (sometimes called **lexical morphemes,** or content words, since they represent the types of morphemes and words that express complexes of semantic features of great importance for communication); morphemes such as articles, prepositions, and affixes are generally absent (these are referred to as **grammatical morphemes** and provide small modifications to the meanings of the lexical morphemes; grammatical morphemes are generally short elements, represented phonetically by only one or a few sounds and rarely occurring with strong stress). The following sentences are representative of this period:

(3)   Mommy cook hotdog.

(4)   Mary go home!

(5)   No want supper.

(6)   Where Daddy go?

(7)   Why Grandma can't come?

Such utterances differ from adult speech in several ways. Word order may be different, as in sentence (7). The most characteristic property, however, is the absence of certain grammatical morphemes, a fact that will be readily apparent to the reader who compares (3)–(6) with their equivalents in normal adult production.

As with the acquisition of so many other aspects of language discussed earlier, the acquisition of grammatical morphemes appears to follow a general pattern with all children learning English. In fact, there is some evidence that children acquiring other languages follow similar orders insofar as their languages utilize semantically and syntactically similar morphemes.

A number of studies indicate that the earliest grammatical morphemes acquired in English are the inflectional suffixes. Within this set of morphemes, certain developmental generalizations can be established, at least tentatively. Thus, for many children who have been observed with respect to this aspect of acquisition, the first grammatical morphemes to appear in spontaneous speech are the present progressive (*ing*) and the plural morphemes. Next, we usually find the past tense forms, followed by the possessive. Finally, the verb suffix representing third person singular present tense occurs. What is particularly interesting about this pattern is the fact that although the plural, possessive, and third person singular present tense all have the same general phonetic representations, the morphemes do not all emerge at the same time. Thus, it is not phonetic form that is responsible for order of acquisition of grammatical morphemes. Nor does the frequency with which children hear a morpheme seem to influence directly their order of acquisition. For example, the suffix *s* representing the third person singular present tense occurs far more frequently in the speech of adults than does the suffix *s* representing possessive. Yet, the possessive is almost always produced before (sometimes several months before) the third person singular present tense. Order of acquisition may be dependent, at least partially, on the mental, or cognitive, development of the child. Perhaps children understand the concept of possession earlier than the complex of concepts involved in third person singular present tense and, for that reason, produce possessives before they produce the verb forms.

Following the acquisition of the highly productive and systematic inflectional affixes, the child begins to acquire those grammatical morphemes that are, in a syntactic sense, closest to lexical morphemes. In other words, the next step is the appearance of grammatical morphemes such as articles and prepositions, morphemes that in English are also words. Last to be acquired are the derivational affixes, and these are usually mastered in an order directly reflecting their productivity. For example, children will learn the highly productive suffix *ly* before they learn the less productive prefix *re*. Of course, this sketch of the order of acquisition of grammatical morphemes is somewhat oversimplified. With some children, for instance, articles may be used before the appearance of the present tense verb suffix, and a few derivational affixes may occur prior to the acquisition of some of the pronouns. In fact, it is not unusual to find scattered instances of any one of the affix morphemes as early as the holophrastic stage. However, in such cases, these cannot be considered as actual morphemes for the child, no matter what their status might be for the adult. The child can use words holistically, considering *cats,* for example, as a single, whole unit, with no recognition of the fact that the unit consists of two morphemes. When we describe the acquisition of grammatical morphemes, we cannot consider a morpheme to have been acquired simply because it appears in the child's speech on a few occasions. That could be merely a reflection of the memorization of a whole word. What concerns the linguist and psycholinguist is the point at which children have entered such morphemes into their lexicons and mastered the appropriate rules of word formation necessary for them to use the morpheme in the productive manner that characterizes normal, creative adult speech. The investigator cannot be confident that this point has been reached until the child's speech reveals frequent usage of the morpheme in almost all those situations where the morpheme would be used by the linguistically mature adult. For most children, the basic grammatical morphemes of English have been mastered by about the age of five.

It was observed earlier that certain aspects of word order are acquired very early by children. Other types of word order, however, come about only later, during the more advanced period of telegraphic speech. What the child masters earliest are the most general principles of word order—those reflected in the most frequent types of utterances that he or she encounters, such as the order of adjective and noun within phrases or the order of words in statements. For such syntactic constructions as negatives, questions, and passives, however, acquisition of appropriate order comes later. This is due partly to the relatively infrequent occurrences of such structures when compared to active, affirmative statements (few adults would say to a child *The candy was eaten by Brian*) and partly to the fact that such constructions incorporate morphemes and words that the young child has not acquired (such as *be,* auxiliaries like *can* and *may,* and prepositions such as *by*). Other factors are probably at work here, too.

For childen acquiring English, the first means of expressing a question is typically by retaining the word order of a statement but supplying a question intonation with a rise in pitch at the end of the utterance:

(8)   Mommy cook hotdog?

Next, as the child acquires question words such as *who, where,* and *what,* these forms are placed at the beginning of the question but no other changes in word order occur:

(9)   What you are doing?

And, finally, the special word order used for English questions is mastered, so that sentences such as (10) are produced:

(10)   What are you doing?

Negatives develop in a parallel manner. Initially, the negative element is simply preposed to the statement.

(11)   No Mommy get babysitter.

The negative element is then moved into the appropriate position.

(12)   Mommy no get babysitter.

And, as the child approaches adult competence in negation, the required additional morphemes occur.

(13)   Mommy did not get the babysitter.

In the case of passives, the situation is somewhat different. Observations have revealed that children rarely produce passives until they have reached school age. Prior to that time, they may understand passive sentences such as

(14)   The candy was eaten by Brian.

However, for sentences such as (14), it cannot be determined whether the child has actually understood the passive as a syntactic construction (where the surface subject is actually the object of the verb at the deep structure level). Notice that (14) allows only one possible interpretation, since the alternative meaning, that the candy ate Brian, is inconceivable in our world. When investigators explore children's comprehension of passives such as (15),

(15)   The dog was chased by the cat.

the results indicate that children four and five years of age do not really understand the passive structure. In the case of (15) it is semantically possible for either animal to have chased the other. Yet children of this age are quite consistent in interpreting (15) as equivalent to (16).

(16)   The dog chased the cat.

Apparently, such children are attending to the word order of the lexical morphemes and are using a generalization that is true for many English structures, namely, that the first noun is the agent and the noun after the verb is the recipient of the action expressed by the verb. These children have not learned the passive structure, and so, in cases where the semantic relations are not determined fully by the state of the world, the child interprets the passive as if it were an active. Such difficulties in comprehension, as well as a low incidence of passives in children's spontaneous speech production, frequently continue until the age of nine or ten.

INVESTIGATION OF LATER LANGUAGE ACQUISITION

At one time, it was believed that children had mastered most of the linguistic properties of their language by the age of seven. We have just seen that this is not the case with passive constructions, and, as more investigators turn their attention from the preschool child to the child beyond the age of five, they are discovering a substantial number of different linguistic phenomena that are acquired quite late in childhood.

While early school-aged children do utilize rather complex syntactic structures in their spontaneous speech, there are apparently a number of syntactic facts that children do not control until close to the age of puberty. Many of these facts involve minor deviations from the most general rules of English or semantic properties unique to a small group of words. Similar to the problem of the passive construction is the difficulty that children encounter with sentences involving words such as *ask* and *promise*. Under most circumstances in English grammar, the noun that comes just before the verb is the subject of that verb. Children apparently learn this as a principle of English syntax, and this principle accounts for their misinterpretation of certain passives, as in example (15), where the principle does not apply. More complex sentences that contain embedded sentences generally do follow the principle:

(17) I want you to put the book here.

(18) Mommy told Michael to bake some cookies.

In these cases, there are two verbs in each sentence (*want* and *put* in (17), *told* and *bake* in (18)) and for each verb the subject is the immediately preceding noun or pronoun. Thus, *I* do the *wanting* and *you* do the *putting*; *Mommy* did the *telling* and *Michael* is to *bake*. However, compare this situation with the sentences of (19) and (20).

(19) I asked you where to put the book.

(20) Mommy promised Michael to bake some cookies.

Here, the subject of the second verb in each sentence is not its immediately preceding noun but rather the noun at the start of the full sentence. That is, in (19), *I*, not *you*, will do the *putting*, and in (20), it is *Mommy*, not *Michael*, who will *bake* the cookies. (19) and (20), then, do not follow the general subject-verb order principle, and it is just such sentences that are acquired late. Some children up to nine years have difficulties with sentences like (20) with the verb *promise*; even older children may fail to interpret (19) correctly.

Certain grammatical morphemes used in complex syntactic structures also undergo development during this later period. During the early grades of elementary school, children rarely use such words as *but* and *unless*. In experimental studies where children are asked to interpret sentences containing these words, it is quite common for those up to the age of ten to interpret *but* as 'and' and *unless* as 'if'.

The acquisition of lexical morphemes continues not only throughout childhood but throughout life. Even as adults, we continue to encounter new words, to enter in our lexicons any new morphemes contained in those words, and perhaps we even adjust or add to our set of rules for word formation. Children do so on an even larger scale. This is particularly true for those words that constitute the learned vocabulary of English. Words such as *explanatory, opacity,* and *substantiation* occur primarily in written material and in formal speech. Young children rarely have the opportunity to acquire learned words, or the morphemes of which they are composed, for such words do not occur in the average child's linguistic environment. Only when children become older, cognitively mature, and fluent readers will they acquire this aspect of English. In fact, some people never acquire the elements of a formal, learned vocabulary. The context and conditions of their lives are such that they are never exposed to such words (as discussed in Chapter 6 with respect to situations and styles).

It is also known that the acquisition of phonology is not complete when a child enters school. Certain sound segments, such as [r], [l], and [θ], may not be articulated correctly until the age of seven. Consonant cluster articulation, particularly in word-final position as in *warmth,* is sometimes not achieved with adult perfection until the age of eight. Another aspect concerns children's ability to recognize the sounds that make up a word. Studies of children acquiring languages as diverse as English and Russian have shown that five or six year olds normally are unable to isolate the sounds of a word. For example, if asked to say just the first sound of a word such as *sink,* children at this age will reproduce the entire word, name the letter of the alphabet used to represent the sound, or simply fail to respond. Their responses are equally unsuccessful with sounds in word-medial or word-final position, and, in fact, until the age of eight, many normal children continue to have difficulty isolating sounds in any position except word-initially. The implications of this for some widely used methods of teaching reading are discussed in a later chapter.

The sound system of a language also involves phonological rules. In English, some phonological rules apply primarily to learned words; such rules cannot be acquired until the relevant vocabulary has been encountered. Consider again the alternation of [t] and [š] in words such as *act/action, construct/construction.* For the adult, it seems reasonable to hypothesize that the phonemic representation of the root morphemes in such words ends in [t]. The adult also possesses a phonological rule that converts this [t] to [š] before the derivational suffix *ion.* Children cannot possibly have acquired such a rule until they have been exposed to the English vocabulary affected by the rule, and it cannot be taken for granted that learned words like *explanatory/explanation, delegate/delegation,* and *indicate/indication* are known to all eight-year-old speakers of English. Such phonological rules are apparently learned quite late in childhood.

Only within the past few years have investigations of the linguistic performance of children from kindergarten age on been conducted by linguists and psycholinguists. Prior to this, most studies of school-aged children's language development were conducted by specialists in elementary education. Generally, these studies were aimed at providing representative norms of rather superficial aspects of language; the norms, in turn, could provide the basis for the sequencing and organization of teaching materials. Looking for a method of evaluating children's linguistic maturity, most educators concentrated on the extent of vocabulary and average sentence length. Unfortunately, vocabulary is highly dependent on environment. Many children have been classified as "language-deficient" because the words they know do not happen to correspond to those that middle-class children have learned by a particular age. Such "language-deficient" children are as competent in their own dialect as "normal" children are in theirs. The use of average number of words per sentence is also a misleading, and basically invalid, test of linguistic development for school-aged children. Long sentences are not necessarily syntactically complex, whereas short sentences may be quite sophisticated. A child who uses a great deal of sentence conjoining, for example, will produce longer sentences than one who utilizes embedding, yet embedding is apparently a more complex syntactic process than conjoining. Sentence (21) seems to represent a more mature level of speech than does sentence (22).

(21) At the circus I saw an acrobat who jumped into a net.

(22) I was at the circus and I saw an acrobat and the acrobat jumped into a net.

Yet, tests of linguistic maturity that rely primarily on sentence length as an indication of development will select (22) as more mature than (21) when, in fact, it seems that the opposite is the case. Investigation of language development in school-aged children is still at a relatively unsophisticated level. Much remains to be done in devising methods of studying the more complex aspects of language that every child must learn.

It should also be noted that the common tests of language maturity used in many educational systems involve a basic confusion between linguistic competence and linguistic performance. It is not always clear which of these is being tested. Tests have almost always indicated that knowledge of certain sentence types does not increase beyond a certain point. In other words, children from first through fifth grades (the ages most frequently examined for language maturity) all seem to know the same basic syntactic structures. We must assume, then, that for such structures, their linguistic competence is approximately the same at these different grade levels. Yet, in language performance, there are differences in the frequency with which children of different ages use certain structures. The concept of linguistic maturity, therefore, involves factors of performance, as well as the linguistic knowledge underlying such performance.

SUMMARY

Children's acquisition of language probably begins well before they produce their first recognizable words. As early as the babbling period, children have acquired at least some of the intonational characteristics of the language of their environment, and some children, if not all, begin to use sounds consistently for specific meanings. During the holophrastic period, in which recognizable single word utterances occur, the child begins to acquire aspects of the phonological and semantic systems of a language. Syntactic properties of language emerge most clearly during the two-word period. At that time, the child learns the relations among the elements of a sentence and the semantic properties of structures. As the length of utterances increases, grammatical morphemes are acquired. Certain aspects of phonology, syntax, and semantics are not acquired until the age of ten or twelve.

FURTHER EXPLORATION

An important source about research on child language acquisition is the extensive anthology, *Studies of Child Language Development,* edited by Charles A. Ferguson and Dan Isaac Slobin. Many classic articles are collected in this work, covering the acquisition of phonology, inflectional morphemes, syntax, and semantics and including studies of children acquiring not only English but also languages such as Chinese, French, and Russian. Sources for some of the discussion in this chapter appear in this anthology: on pivot/open class analysis, Martin D. S. Braine, "The Ontogeny of English Phrase Structure: The First Phase," and Lois Bloom, "Why Not Pivot Grammar?;" on the acquisition of questions and negatives, Edward S. Klima and Ursula Bellugi, "Syntactic Regularities in the Speech of Children."

In addition to the material in Ferguson and Slobin's book, the acquisition of phonology is discussed in the classic work *Child Language, Aphasia, and Phonological Universals* by Roman Jakobson. A laboratory study of the acquisition of initial consonants is presented by J. R. Kornfeld in "Theoretical Issues in Child Phonology." "The Child's Learning of English Morphology" by Jean Berko Gleason reports on children's mastery of the various phonetic forms of certain inflectional morphemes in English; the article appears in a collection of some sixty papers edited by Aaron Bar-Adon and Werner F. Leopold, *Child Language: A Book of Readings.*

The most comprehensive study of holophrastic and early telegraphic speech is *A First Language: The Early Stages* by Roger Brown. This book presents detailed reports of the acquisition of grammatical morphemes, relations among grammatical elements, and semantic properties of structures. Also of interest is an article by Eve V. Clark, "What's in a Word? On the Child's Acquisition of Semantics in His First Language" (Moore 1973).

For language acquisition by older children, David S. Palermo and Dennis L. Molfese provide a summary in "Language Acquisition from Age Five Onward." In *The Acquisition of Syntax in Children from 5 to 10,* Carol Chomsky reports on her experiments indicating that children continue to learn certain aspects of language (such as *ask* and *promise*) well beyond the age of five.

At a more introductory level than the articles and books mentioned above is *Language Development: Structure and Function* by Philip S. Dale.

1. Adults' use of nursery words and baby talk may reflect their unstated beliefs about what children's language is like. Make a list of such words and see if you can determine what these beliefs might be. How accurately do your conclusions correspond to what you have learned about children's language? Do you think that the use of either baby talk or nursery words might have a harmful effect on a child's linguistic environment? Explain.

2. To study language acquisition scientifically, it is necessary to observe children as they develop over an extended period of time or to devise sophisticated experimental studies such as those discussed in some of the readings cited above. However, much can also be gained even from brief, informal observations. Volunteer to work for a few hours in a day care center or offer to babysit for a friend's child. Depending on the age of the child or children, you can check on various aspects of language acquisition. Can you detect basic intonation patterns or systematic use of sounds in an eight-month old? Is a two-year old still using holophrastic utterances? How does a three-year old form questions or negations? Does a five-year old understand the passive sentences mentioned in the text? What sounds (of mature English) do not occur in the child's speech? Other questions may occur to you as you look back through the chapter.

3. An analysis of the "errors" children make frequently provides evidence of their linguistic development. Try to obtain copies of the written work of several children in second, fourth, and sixth grades. What errors do you find? Consider each error. Does it reflect lack of knowledge of the language? Could it be an overgeneralization of some kind? Is it merely lack of familiarity with the conventions of written language (spelling, punctuation, capitalization)? Can you detect any systematic differences in the writing of the children in the three different grades?

CHAPTER 2222222222222222222222222222

NATIVE LANGUAGE ACQUISITION: SOME EXPLANATIONS

In just a few years, a crying, newborn infant becomes a linguistically mature individual. Although the linguistic capabilities of a six or seven year old are not entirely equivalent to those of an adult, the aspects of language that must still be acquired are minimal when compared to the acquisition that has already occurred. In the last chapter, we surveyed what the child acquires. Now, we must ask what is known about how he accomplishes this task.

In the strict sense, of course, theories of learning belong to the realm of psychology, but in the particular case of native language acquisition the linguist and the psychologist must each contribute to the subject. In fact, the investigation of how children acquire language constitutes a primary area of research in the interdisciplinary field of psycholinguistics. In this chapter we will survey the main conclusions of modern psycholinguistic research regarding native language acquisition, concentrating our attention on the adequacy of various theories about how children acquire language.

THE NATURE OF THE TASK

In one way, the task of children acquiring their native language is similar to that of the linguist who is attempting to describe a language. Both start out by observing samples of the language, and, for each, the eventual goal is a grammar of that language. The linguist's grammar is, of course, a descriptive device—a theory of what speakers know. The grammar children construct is not a descriptive device, but rather a body of knowledge—the forms and rules that constitute the language they are acquiring. Linguists set about their task with the conscious knowledge of what they are doing; their grammar is fully explicit, carefully describing all aspects of the language. Children, on the other hand, are not aware of what they are doing; they simply and unconsciously acquire internalized knowledge of their language. This knowledge is complete in every detail, certainly more complete than any grammar that linguists have ever been able to write, yet children are totally unaware of it. They cannot tell you what rules they have learned, nor can they tell you how they learned them. Here, then, lies the task of the linguist and the psychologist. Based on what is observable, they must formulate a reasonable hypothesis about what is not observable. Figure 22.1 illustrates the task of language acquisition in a schematized manner. Aspects I and III are known. The investigator can directly observe I, and III, while only indirectly observable, is beyond question. Given these two aspects of language acquisition, we must now attempt to determine the nature of II—the process of language acquisition. Before proceeding to this attempt, however, let us first note some of the general characteristics of the linguistic environment of the child (aspect I in the figure) and the nature of the knowledge he or she attains (aspect III).

DIVERSITY AND UNIFORMITY

In all aspects of language acquisition there is both diversity and uniformity. The linguistic environment differs for every child. Given the productivity of human language, it is obvious that no two children will encounter exactly the same set of utterances. However,

Figure 22.1 _____

Aspect I	Aspect II	Aspect III
Samples of the language that the child encounters in the environment	Process of language acquisition—how the child acquires language	Knowledge of the language that the child eventually attains

since every human language is a system composed of a basic set of sounds, morphemes, semantic properties, syntactic structures, and several types of rules, each child will encounter samples that reflect these general properties. The process of language acquisition is uniform in certain respects, as discussed below, but there is also diversity here. Some children, for example, appear to imitate frequently, while other children rarely do so. The linguistic knowledge ultimately attained by each child acquiring a specific language is largely uniform. It is precisely this uniformity that makes possible communication and understanding among people. Yet, again, there seems to be some diversity, at least with respect to the lexicon. Let us consider these matters in more detail.

The particular language that children acquire depends upon the language to which they are exposed. In some cases, children may be exposed to more than one language, and, if they hear enough samples of each, they will become bilingual, having mastered each language. One fact that should be obvious but is sometimes overlooked is that children will acquire the particular dialect of their environment. Thus, a five year old who pronounces both *pin* and *pen* as [pɪn] is not necessarily in need of speech therapy. If the dialect heard at home is one in which [ɪ] and [ɛ] are not distinguished before a nasal consonant, the child will not make the distinction. If sufficiently exposed to another dialect in which the distinction is made, the child will acquire pronunciations such as [pɪn] and [pɛn] without any formal teaching or speech therapy. Educators and speech therapists must be careful to differentiate between normal language acquisition of particular dialects and actual problems in language acquisition.

Although certain children have language disorders that make it difficult for them to follow the normal pattern of language acquisition, most children have no such problems. A large majority of children acquire their native language perfectly, in spite of great variations in their environments. Any theory of how children learn language must account for the fact that the samples of language heard differ greatly from child to child, both in kind and in quantity. For example, the language development of hearing children born to deaf parents is reported as usually normal even though such children are exposed to less language usage than children born to hearing parents. The difference in quantity is apparently irrelevant for language acquisition. Some children hear little language from their parents other than commands, but, nevertheless, they learn all of the sentence types in their language.

It is sometimes observed that children from backgrounds in which language contact was restricted do not speak as much as those from more normal backgrounds. This does not mean, however, that the child does not know the language. At issue here is the distinction between competence and performance. If children have been discouraged from speaking at home, they will not do so readily when they enter school. But there is no way of discouraging children from acquiring a language (except by totally depriving them of contact with language). Children who do not talk may possess full knowledge, competence, of their language even though they do not make use of that competence in producing language. This can often be noted in children with complex psychological problems, who may comprehend everything they hear but, for a variety of reasons, simply never say anything. It is necessary to distinguish between children's linguistic ability and their nonlinguistic ability or willingness to use language.

Although there is great variation in the quantity and in the structures of the language to which children are exposed, there is little variation in the knowledge of the language they eventually achieve. All normal children acquire their language completely and perfectly. There are no instances of children learning only part of a language, for example, statements but not questions, affirmatives but not negatives. Given the uniformity of output in Figure 22.1 (knowledge of the language) and the diversity of environmental input (samples of the language), it seems that the child himself contributes a great deal to the process of language acquisition.

Certain aspects of II in Figure 22.1 are known. For example, whatever it is that constitutes the ability to learn language, it is definitely species-specific. Only human beings acquire human languages. Furthermore, the ability to acquire language is species-uniform in that all human beings learn language. Even children with severe mental or physical illness generally make some progress in language acquisition. Sometimes this progress is amazingly good when compared to other kinds of learning that such children attempt. Children learn language whether their linguistic environment is very rich or very poor. All that is necessary for language acquisition to take place is some exposure to a language. Children succeed in acquiring their native language even though the examples of speech they hear contain ungrammatical utterances (slips of the tongue, uncompleted sentences, etc.), syntactic structures that may be well beyond their level of comprehension at a particular time, accidental mispronunciations, and so forth. Children do not have to be taught their native language, and, in fact, attempts to instruct children in the holophrastic or telegraphic stages usually end in failure. Children proceed at their own pace in language acquisition, just as they do in developing various motor skills, such as sitting, standing, and walking. All of these factors concerning the process of language acquisition point strongly to one conclusion: that human beings are born with an innate capacity to acquire language.

CAPACITIES AND STRATEGIES

What is it that constitutes the universal human capacity to acquire language? This is, of course, the fundamental question in any attempt to explain child language acquisition. Many responses have been offered by psychologists and linguists over the years, but, unfortunately, no single response is sufficiently sophisticated to account for the complexity, diversity, and uniformity involved. Clearly, the capacities of the human mind are central factors in the acquisition of language. Language is a mental phenomenon and it cannot be acquired or used without the active participation of the mind. All explanations of language acquisition, therefore, refer to properties of the mind. The explanations differ, however, in whether the properties are considered specific to language acquisition or are viewed as more general capacities, necessary for other matters such as perception, cognition, and the learning of nonlinguistic material. The explanations also vary in the quantity and quality of the mental processes suggested as the basis for language acquisition. We cannot hope to survey all of the explanations that have been offered in the psycholinguistic research literature, but we will discuss the most widely known suggestions, along with the evidence and counterevidence related to each hypothesis.

In the first half of the twentieth century, most of the hypotheses on language acquisition were formulated from an **empiricist** viewpoint. At the basis of empiricism lies the assumption that the scientist must rely solely on experimentation and direct observation of phenomena. Explanations of phenomena, such as language acquisition, must be directly linked to observable facts and should include an absolute minimum of hypothesizing about unobservable aspects of the subject. Empiricist views of language acquisition, therefore, tend to be extremely limited since what is observable in the process of language learning constitutes only a small part of the entire process.

Many children, at one or more stages in language acquisition, have been observed to repeat utterances produced by other people in their environment. One possible explanation for how children learn language, therefore, is that they imitate what they hear, and, by means of imitation, they memorize the structures of their language. But, clearly, this is not an adequate explanation, for any human language is far too complex to be mastered through imitation and memorization. In addition, one of the basic characteristics of language is its productivity; speakers of a language are capable of comprehending and producing an infinite number of novel sentences. If language were learned simply by imitation and memorization, no one would ever be able to understand or to say anything he had not heard before.

Furthermore, from the very earliest period of the telegraphic stage, many children produce utterances that could not possibly be the result of imitation. The classic example, which occurs in the speech of many children, is *allgone candy, allgone car, allgone kitty,* etc. If children learned solely by imitation, they would never produce such sentences, for the normal adult equivalent in each case would place *allgone* after the noun, not before, as in the sentence *The candy is all gone.* Given the complexity and the productivity of language, as well as observable instances of children's speech, imitation cannot be the primary process at work in language acquisition.

The rejection of imitation as the chief explanation of language acquisition should not be taken as a denial of imitation as ONE strategy in the child's process of learning his language. Many children do utilize imitation, and they do so in a highly systematic manner. A number of studies have been reported on (1) children's spontaneous imitations in naturalistic (i.e., normal, homelike) settings and (2) children's responses when they were instructed to imitate adult utterances in experimental situations. For spontaneous imitation, there are two important results. First, while some children imitate a great deal, others scarcely imitate at all. From this we can conclude that while imitation may be a useful strategy for the acquisition of language, it is not a necessary one. No substantial differences have been found between the level and rate of acquisition of children who do imitate and those of children who do not. Second, those children who do imitate tend to imitate only utterances that are somewhat more advanced linguistically than their nonimitative speech. Imitation, therefore, is not random. If an utterance is too much beyond a child's normal speech production, it will not be imitated; if the utterance reflects linguistic material that the child can already produce spontaneously, it will not be imitated. Children have the capacity to select for imitation precisely those aspects of language that are appropriate for their next stage of acquisition. The studies of elicited imitation in experimental settings offer similar conclusions.

Somewhat more sophisticated than imitation is the empiricist theory that **contextual generalization** is the basic process involved in language acquisition. The term is meant to describe a proposed innate ability of children to learn syntactic facts on the basis of generalizing from the contexts in which a word appears. For example, it is maintained that a child who hears the expressions *byebye daddy* and *byebye mommy* will generalize from these contexts to the use of *byebye* before all nouns. Again, it may be that something like a process of contextual generalization is at work when children learn simple structures, but this process cannot account for the normal, complex structures of language they eventually master. Furthermore, contextual generalization fails to explain how children acquire the underlying structures of sentences, which are often quite different from the surface structures they hear and on which any process of contextual generalization must be based.

Perhaps the best known of the empiricist theories regarding language is the **stimulus-response** approach in which it is maintained that children learn to talk because adults selectively reinforce (or reward) certain responses that the child makes to particular stimuli. In this view, children themselves make little or no contribution to their own linguistic development. Their language is assumed to be molded in much the same way that psychologists mold the behavior of rats finding their way through mazes or pigeons learning to peck at a certain place in order to receive a grain of corn. It was, in fact, such simple experiments with animals that initially led to the general stimulus-response theory of learning, but the extension of this theory from animals to humans is questionable. One major issue is that the behaviors developed in the animals had to be taught; they were not natural. But children do not have to be taught language; for them, language acquisition is a natural undertaking. A further argument against the stimulus-response/reinforcement theory is that, like other empiricist theories, it fails to account for the productivity of language. If children acquire language solely on the basis of reinforcement of a response they make to a particular stimulus, then how do they ever manage a linguistic response to some situation, or stimulus, they have never encountered in the past?

As with imitation, the importance of reinforcement by adults of the child's early linguistic production cannot be discarded completely. If children received no response to their communication efforts, it is unlikely that they would continue them. However, it should be noted that the type of response, or reinforcement, that children do receive from adults normally emphasizes the success of their speech in communicating meaning. Parents and other adult caretakers correct pronunciation and syntax only rarely. Studies of adult reactions to children's speech have shown that the adult seldom corrects the child unless the meaning of the child's utterance is incorrect. For example, if *Daddy go Chicago* is a true utterance, the adult may respond simply by indicating agreement or by a further comment on the situation, despite the immature grammatical nature of the utterance. However, if the child says something false, the adult is likely to correct the utterance no matter how mature it may be from a grammatical perspective. Thus, it is possible that adult reinforcement assists the child in his or her semantic development and understanding of the world, but it is unlikely that such reinforcement plays any major role in the acquisition of the linguistic properties of phonology and syntax.

By focusing attention almost solely on observable behavior and refusing to accept hypotheses that deal with mental phenomena, empiricists may so restrict their observation of language and language learning that their explanations cover only the most superficial aspects of these topics. There are some psychologists who attempt to adapt empiricist theories in order to account for the complex, abstract, and productive nature of language. The adaptations are generally less than satisfactory, for they often consist of the addition of labels for what cannot be explained by the more traditional empiricist theories. By labeling an unknown, you do not explain it. For example, within the stimulus-response theory, the attempt to account for productivity resulted in the empty concept of "stimulus generalization," which apparently means that somehow the child generalizes information about one stimulus to other stimuli. But the question of how he does this remains unanswered, as does the question of how the child knows which generalizations are linguistically significant.

One very popular explanation for why children learn language requires discussion at this point, in spite of the fact that it does not result from the type of direct observation characteristic of empiricist theories. Some people claim that children learn language because of "need." Infants have all of their needs met, it is believed, and thus have no reason to learn language. As children grow older, their needs become more complex and may no longer be immediately apparent to adults. Thus, children must learn to talk in order to convey their needs to others, and, it is argued, their language becomes more complex as their needs do. For one who knows little about the nature of language or the way in which children actually proceed in acquiring it, this attempted explanation may be appealing. But, in fact, it explains nothing and is contradicted by rather convincing evidence. In the first place, there is no way to determine whether the needs of toddlers are stronger for them than those of an infant. Second, if this theory were correct, then we would certainly expect neglected children to learn to talk more quickly than those who are cared for. But both groups learn at approximately the same speed. For example, the development of linguistic knowledge in children raised in orphanages is apparently the same as that of children from normal home environments. The former perform somewhat less well in tests of speech production at the early stages of language acquisition, but there is no evidence that their comprehension is any less than that of other children. In any case, this early performance inadequacy is rapidly overcome by the time the children reach school age. Yet the institutional setting of most orphanages surely must create greater needs for the children.

All scientists, including linguists and psychologists, seek the simplest explanation possible to account for the phenomena they are investigating. A complicated hypothesis will always be rejected in favor of a simpler one that explains the same thing. There is little doubt that the theories of imitation, contextual generalization, stimulus-response, and need are simple explanations of how and why language is acquired. But simple explanations alone are not enough. The explanation must also account for the facts. And the facts are that language is far too complex, too abstract, and too productive to be acquired solely by these processes.

As contemporary linguists began to understand the complexity of human language, the inadequacies of traditional empiricist explanations of language acquisition became increasingly apparent. Some linguists and psychologists began to explore a **rationalist** approach to the issues of language acquisition. Sometimes referred to as the nativist view, this approach permits emphasis on unobservable properties of the human mind. It is maintained that human beings are, in a sense, "programmed" to acquire the specific type of communication system that constitutes human language. The brain may be structured and may function in such a way as to direct children's acquisition of the language to which they are exposed. Perhaps children are born with a general framework of language; it is not necessary for them to learn that language consists of rules. Instead, their task is to learn which rules are utilized in the language of their environment. Some rationalists even hypothesize that children possess at birth those properties of human language that are universal.

While many aspects of the rationalist hypothesis are supported by relatively little evidence, this approach can account for some of the facts of language acquisition. We have noted several times that children's language acquisition is not random. Instead, children acquire language systematically even at the earliest stages of development. Furthermore, all children appear to pass through similar stages in the acquisition of language, despite variations in the speech samples to which they are exposed. Many of these similarities hold true even for children acquiring different languages, as we observed in the discussion of phonological acquisition in the preceding chapter. The rationalist position hypothesizes that such similarities are due to the fact that all normal children are endowed with similar brains and mental capacities that direct the way and the order in which language is acquired.

No adult has to teach a child that a language is organized according to general principles, or rules. Most adults are not even aware of this fact. Yet every child acquires language as a set of rules. This is apparent when we observe the types of "mistakes" children make. The "mistakes" are organized; they reflect generalizations that the child is making. For example, it is common to all children that in mastering aspects of language such as inflectional morphemes, they begin by producing a variety of forms correctly, including the apparently irregular ones like English *brought*. Then they learn the generalizations reflected in regular forms (English *baked*), and these generalizations are extended to cover the exceptions (so the child would say *bringed* rather than *brought*). Only as the last step does the child learn which forms are exceptions to the generalizations he has acquired. Similar overgeneralizations occur in the acquisition of semantics (see Figure 21.1 for examples) and syntax (recall the overgeneralization discussed above for the acquisition of passives). The generalizations and the overgeneralizations that a child makes reflect the mental structures and capacities that he possesses. Generalizations, in this rationalist sense, are not to be confused with the empiricist hypothesis of contextual generalization. Contextual generalization is a behavioral process, strongly dependent on observable context and relevant, at most, to the acquisition of surface syntactic structure. Generalization in the broader rationalist hypothesis is a mental process and capacity resulting in the formulation of linguistic rules for all aspects of language.

The child's initial formulation of a linguistic rule is not a simple undertaking. Before a general rule can be acquired, the child must encounter data—a number of examples which reflect the operation of the rule. In many cases, such early data may be simply memorized. Examples appear in the child's speech, but the child does not yet know that a general principle of the language can account for these examples and even be utilized to produce other examples. Recall the data for Gregory cited in the last chapter, as well as the examples of the past tense grammatical morpheme discussed above. Only after children have formulated a rule will they be able to produce new examples spontaneously. Even then, the rule may not be entirely accurate. Children may overextend their generalization to forms or structures where it is inappropriate. When this happens, it is normally the case that children have applied their generalizations to forms that are exceptions in adult language or to forms that follow another, very similar rule that the children have not yet mastered. This is illustrated by the types of overgeneralizations discussed above. Overgeneralized rules must be reformulated to conform to the adult linguistic system. This process can be accomplished in several ways. In some cases, the child will learn that certain forms are simply exceptions to the generalization (e.g., *bring* has the past tense form *brought,* not *bringed*). In other cases, the generalization itself will be modified through the addition of other aspects of the language. The word *juice* will be used for any liquid only until the child acquires new lexical items that refer to other specific liquids such as milk and water; the meaning of the word *juice* is then narrowed.

The child's mental capacities are not all linguistic. The study of cognitive development in psychology has important implications for language development. There is substantial evidence that the order of acquisition of linguistic material is partially determined by the process of cognitive development. Generally, children will not acquire the linguistic means to express a concept until they are intellectually capable of understanding that concept. When we find, for example, that children do not comprehend cause and effect relations until the age of six, it is not surprising to also find that the linguistic representations of cause and effect are not used maturely by children in the first grade. First graders may produce utterances containing the word *because,* but, for them, the meaning is merely that of a sequence of events rather than the cause and effect relation. For example, to a six year old, the sentence *You can't go out because it's snowing* is equivalent to two separate sentences *You can't go out* and *It's snowing;* the fact that the latter is the reason for the former is not comprehended. Many of the details of cognitive development in the child are still unknown to investigators. Yet, these may provide explanations for many aspects of linguistic development, such as the late acquisition of *but* and *unless* mentioned in the last chapter or the fact that children acquire the plural morpheme before the past tense. Cognitively, plurality may occur earlier than tense, and this aspect of cognitive development may determine the order of acquisition of these two grammatical morphemes.

Physiological and neurophysiological development also affect linguistic development. The brain, the nervous system, and the muscular control system of the vocal tract are not fully mature at birth. All undergo development throughout childhood. Until children are physically mature enough to control vocal tract activities, they will not be able to produce sound segments. And, since sounds differ in the degree of control required for their articulation, the order in which certain sounds are mastered will be at least partly dependent on the child's physiological development. Thus, children almost always acquire stops before fricatives. The complete blockage of the air stream necessary for stops requires less careful control of the vocal tract than does the partial closure necessary for fricatives.

This section began with a question: What is it that constitutes the universal human capacity to acquire language? The question has not been answered fully, but it should be clear at this point that there are many partial answers. The capacities for language acquisition and the strategies that are used come from a variety of sources within and around the human being. Mental processes, neurophysiological and cognitive development, and the linguistic environment that surrounds the child all have an effect on the acquisition of language.

DEVELOPMENT OF THE BRAIN

Just as the study of child language acquisition was one of the primary factors in bringing together linguists and psychologists in the interdisciplinary field of psycholinguistics, so this same area of study has been partly responsible for cooperative efforts among linguists and neurophysiologists. The interdisciplinary field of **neurolinguistics** has emerged as the study of the relations between language and the brain. While the central concern of this field initially involved the study of **aphasia** (linguistic disorders caused by brain damage), the research findings are also relevant to issues in child language acquisition.

Structurally, the human brain is divided into two sections, the left hemisphere and the right hemisphere, which are connected by a mass of fibers. Each hemisphere is composed of a cover layer of nerve cells called the **gray matter** (or **cortex**) and an inner mass of nerve fibers called the **white matter.** As with other parts of the body, the brain at birth is not fully mature. Maturation occurs throughout childhood, reaching a peak at about the age of two years, when the brain has attained roughly 65 percent of its mature characteristics, and then developing more slowly up to the age of puberty when a fully mature state is achieved. Note that the child's native language development shows its most remarkable progress at about the age of two and that such development is completed by the onset of puberty.

The functioning of the brain is as significant for language acquisition as its structure. Although the two hemispheres of the brain are structurally very similar, they each serve different functions. Early in life, for the first two years, this is not the case, but at about the age of two, evidence emerges to indicate that each side of the brain is assuming specific duties not assumed by the other side. This process is referred to as **lateralization.** One of the earliest observable signs of lateralization is hand preference. Somewhere between the ages of two and three years, children begin to show a preference for either the right or the left hand, the right hand being the preference of the majority of people. Hand preference is the result of lateralization, but contrary to what might be expected, lateralization of the brain is to the opposite side of the observed result. Thus, the right hand, and in fact the right side of the entire body, is controlled by the left hemisphere, while the left side of the body is controlled by the right hemisphere of the brain.

Language also lateralizes. Between the ages of three and five years, the left hemisphere usually takes over the function of language. Initially, this lateralization is not total, and if some injury to the left hemisphere occurs, it is possible for the right hemisphere to assume the language function. By the time the brain is fully mature, however, lateralization is complete and established. At that point, for the adult, an injury to the language-dominant left hemisphere can have very serious consequences, for the right hemisphere is no longer sufficiently flexible to take over. In the case of older stroke victims, for example, loss of speech may be permanent.

Evidence for the lateralization of language comes from a variety of sources. The majority of investigations have resulted from cases of brain damage due to lesions. Such lesions may be caused by accidents, such as a fall or a bullet wound, or by physical malfunctions, as in the case of stroke. When surgery is required, it is possible to observe the lesion. Language is affected when the lesion occurs at certain points in the left hemisphere, but when such lesions appear on the right hemisphere, language is generally not affected. It can be concluded, therefore, that language is located in the left hemisphere. (It should be noted, however, that for a very small number of people, less than 5 percent of those examined, the two hemispheres may function in precisely the reverse manner, with the right hemisphere assuming dominance in language; the brain is still lateralized, but in the opposite direction).

One common type of experimental work on lateralization involves a test of auditory (hearing) perception called **dichotic listening.** When listeners are presented with different sounds or words offered simultaneously through headphones to each ear, the right ear perceives linguistic material better than the left ear. Recall that the right ear is controlled by the left hemisphere. On the other hand, when the sound stimuli are not linguistic but just noises, such as an animal cry, the left ear perceives the material more accurately than the right ear. Thus, the right hemisphere is capable of dealing with sound, but the specific, structured sounds of language are better handled by the left hemisphere.

The development and functioning of the brain constitute a critical area of research for the understanding of language acquisition, not only in the case of the normal child acquiring a native language, but also in the case of individuals who have suffered some type of aphasia, and, as we shall see in the following chapters, in the case of adults who are attempting to learn a foreign language.

ANIMAL COMMUNICATION

All animals appear to possess some type of communication system, but the evidence that has been gathered so far indicates that only man possesses language. There are a number of differences between language and other communication systems. Perhaps the most significant of these differences is the fact that many nonlanguage communication systems are highly limited in terms of what may be expressed, whereas human language is highly creative and productive. Scientists have studied a wide variety of animal communication systems, and in all such studies it is clear that the animals involved are able to communicate only about a limited range of information. For example, bees use a system of various bodily movements to communicate information regarding a source of food. A foraging bee returns to the hive and "dances" on the surface; the pattern and rate of the "dance" are actually determined, at least in part, by the distance the bee has traveled, its state of physical exhaustion, how thirsty it is, and so on, but the effect of the "dance" is to provide information to the other bees about the direction, distance, and location of the food source. This is a remarkable system; the bees respond to the information conveyed and the source of food can be utilized. However, although the system is capable of transmitting information about any distance, direction, or level of quality, it remains limited to communication about this one topic: source of food. Bees cannot alter their "dance" to communicate about other matters such as the location of another hive or the fact that it is raining a short distance away.

Other animals utilize sound to convey various meanings, but here, too, the limitations are very great. For example, rhesus monkeys are reported to communicate alarm, defeat, and threats by means of distinct noises, such as barks, screams, and screeches. In such cases, however, the set of distinct noises is limited and so is the type of information that is systematically conveyed by such noises. All of the natural communication systems of insects and animals are limited in terms of both the form of expression (e.g., types of body movement or limited range of sound production) and the content of expression (e.g., source of food or danger signals).

Since no natural animal communication system exhibits the creativity of human language, some scientists have begun extensive training programs to teach chimpanzees a communication system that approximates human language. Chimpanzees were selected for this research because, of all animals, they are most similar to humans physiologically, mentally, and socially. Several different research programs have emerged in the past decade. In one, a chimpanzee named Washoe was raised from the age of one year in a homelike environment and taught American Sign Language (a manual system of communication used by many deaf people). Since the vocal tract of chimpanzees is not suited to the controlled production of humanlike speech sounds, investigators hoped that some insight into a chimpanzee's possible linguistic capabilities could be achieved if the chimpanzee were offered a communication system that utilized the animal's natural manual abilities. Washoe's achievements are impressive over the four-year period of training for which reports have been issued. At age five, she was able to produce and to understand one hundred and thirty signs, and she also was capable of combining some individual signs into short sentences. This places her at about the communication level of a two-year-old child. However, the number of signs, and even their combination into longer sentences, is not sufficient for us to conclude that Washoe has learned a human language. In human languages, the relation between sounds and meanings is arbitrary. For Washoe, a number of her signs are not arbitrary—rather, they bear a physical resemblance to the meaning, as in the case for 'give' where the sign consists of a gesture moving toward one's body or 'eat' indicated by moving the fingers toward the mouth (as if placing food in the mouth). Not all of Washoe's signs are nonarbitrary, but another cause for caution in evaluating her achievements is her progress in sentence formation. Washoe appears to have paid little attention to word order, yet this aspect of language is one of the earliest mastered by human children who acquire languages like English in which word order is important. Furthermore, although Washoe was raised in a humanlike environment, receiving the type of care and attention that humans receive, her training situation differs from that of children in that much more attention was paid to communication development by her trainers. Washoe was taught American Sign Language; children acquire the language of their environment without being taught.

Another chimpanzee, named Sarah, has been taught a different communication system. In Sarah's case, communication is achieved through the movement and placement of a variety of colored plastic chips on a board. The experiment with Sarah avoids the problem of nonarbitrary relations between the form of the word and its meaning. In the chip that represents 'banana' for Sarah, for example, there is nothing that resembles an actual banana; the chip is neither yellow nor shaped like a banana; instead, it is a red square. Sarah's communication system is a devised, artificial system that Sarah has been taught through a training program employing methods such as reinforcement and the carefully controlled introduction of data. We have discussed both of these for children and have found that while the child probably does need some type of response from the caretakers, it is not necessary to provide a child with a reward (such as a piece of candy) each time he or she produces a correct sentence, nor is it necessary to restrict a child's language exposure to just one type of grammatical structure at a time. Sarah does appear to have mastered syntax to a greater extent than Washoe. Sarah controls word order and is even capable of producing new sentences that she has not previously been taught. However, Sarah differs from children in that all of her new sentences are closely modeled on those she has already learned. We do not observe in Sarah the type of overgeneralization that children display as evidence of their mastery of the rules of language. A major difference between Washoe and Sarah in their reactions to the communication systems is that Washoe has been observed to initiate communication; she apparently enjoys using sign language and makes signs to her caretakers without any noticeable prompting from them. Sarah, however, has not been reported to begin a communication on her own; she uses her system only with prompting and in the presence of rewards. It is not clear what implications this may have for the understanding of the chimpanzees' abilities to learn a communication system.

Another interesting project is being conducted with Lana, a chimpanzee who utilizes a complex computer display board in order to put arbitrary symbols together in sentence form. Lana's communication system is an artificial language, especially designed for her. Each symbol is arbitrary, bearing no physical resemblance to its meaning. The communication system involved uses word order distinctively, so there is a difference in meaning, for example, between the symbols for 'Tim groom Lana' and 'Lana groom Tim' (Tim is one of Lana's caretakers; grooming is a partly social behavior in chimpanzees involving a cleaning of the hair). Lana, like Sarah, appears to have mastered this aspect of syntax. A particularly important aspect of the project with Lana is that through the use of the computer, it is possible to keep detailed records of all of Lana's efforts at communication. Eventually, this will provide researchers with data not only about Lana's successful attempts to utilize her communication system but also about any errors that she makes. Such detailed records are not now readily available for Washoe and Sarah, yet much can be learned from the analysis of errors.

At the present time, there is not enough information available to enable scientists to determine with certainty whether or not animals other than man have the capacity to acquire a communication system with all of the properties and complexities of human language. For the chimpanzees discussed above, it seems that natural acquisition does not occur; rather, a communication system must be taught. Furthermore, none of the chimpanzees studied has achieved the level of sophistication in communication of even a three-year-old child, nor have the chimpanzees demonstrated the quality of creativity found in children's language acquisition. Finally, there is no evidence to indicate that such chimpanzees, trained to communicate with a limited number of human caretakers, have ever attempted to use their communication systems with other chimpanzees. Manual communication systems, whether by signs or the manipulation of objects, are not natural to chimpanzees. Language is natural to human beings.

SUMMARY

On the basis of a scattered sample of utterances in a language, the child must acquire a complex, abstract, productive linguistic system. The fact that all human children accomplish this task in a relatively short period of time, regardless of the quantity and type of language samples to which they are exposed, indicates that they are equipped with an innate capacity for language acquisition. This capacity directs the way in which children observe and analyze the linguistic data they encounter and makes it possible for them to accomplish a task that linguists are only beginning to resolve—to determine the nature and form of the system constituting a particular language. This rationalist hypothesis about how children acquire language attributes to the human mind certain properties that cannot be directly observed. But only by positing such mental capacities is it possible to account for the facts of language acquisition. The various empiricist theories of how language is learned are simpler and based on observable facts, but they are inadequate. Something as complex as human language would never be acquired by a child who relied solely on imitation, stimulus-response, contextual generalization, need, or even a combination of all of these processes. Language acquisition by children may also be influenced by cognitive development, physiological maturation, and lateralization of the brain. Studies of animal communication systems indicate that no animal or insect possesses anything like human language; all such natural systems are highly limited in both their means of expression and the content that can be expressed. Some success has been achieved by rigorous training programs designed to teach artificial communication systems to chimpanzees, but even then, there are numerous differences between the learning and use of such systems by the animals and the acquisition and use of language by children.

FURTHER EXPLORATION

There is a wide range of books and articles offering both speculations and evidence for different hypotheses about how children acquire their native language. A strong nativist view is presented throughout *The Acquisition of Language: The Study of Developmental Psycholinguistics* by David McNeill. An early formulation of the rationalist approach appears in the section "Linguistic Theory and Language Learning" in Noam Chomsky's book *Aspects of the Theory of Syntax*. Chomsky discusses the inadequacies of stimulus-response explanations of language acquisition in "A Review of B. F. Skinner's *Verbal Behavior*" (Fodor and Katz 1964; Jakobovits and Miron 1967). Contextual generalization is the topic of the following series of articles (all in Jakobovits and Miron 1967): Martin D. S. Braine, "On Learning the Grammatical Order of Words;" T. G. Bever, J. A.

Fodor, and W. Weksel, "On the Acquisition of Syntax: A Critique of 'Contextual Generalization';" Martin D. S. Braine, "On the Basis of Phrase Structure: A Reply to Bever, Fodor, and Weksel;" and T. G. Bever, J. A. Fodor, and W. Weksel, "Is Linguistics Empirical?" More recent studies include the articles "Imitation in Language Development: If, When, and Why" by Lois Bloom, Lois Hood, and Patsy Lightbown and "Cognitive Prerequisites for the Development of Grammar" by Dan I. Slobin (in Ferguson and Slobin 1973).

Physical and neurophysiological development and their relation to language acquisition are discussed technically and in depth by Eric H. Lenneberg in *Biological Foundations of Language;* less demanding and less detailed surveys of the same topics by this author appear in the articles "The Capacity for Language Acquisition" and "On Explaining Language" (both in Lester 1973). Language and the brain are discussed informally by David Krech in "Psychoneurobiochemeducation" (informal despite the title, in Lester 1973). More extensive treatment is offered in the standard book on this subject, *Speech and Brain-Mechanisms* by W. Penfield and L. Roberts, as well as in the more recent, technical article, "Neurolinguistics" by Harry A. Whitaker (Dingwall 1971).

Animal communication is the topic of several articles by Allen and Beatrice Gardner, who trained Washoe, and by David Premack, who trained Sarah (detailed reports on Lana are not yet available from the Yerkes Regional Primate Laboratory). The Gardners report in "Two-way Communication with an Infant Chimpanzee" (Schrier and Stollnitz 1971) and "Teaching Sign Language to a Chimpanzee." Premack discusses Sarah in two articles, "The Education of Sarah: A Chimp Learns the Language" and "Language in Chimpanzee?" Communication systems in other animals and insects are surveyed by McNeill in *The Acquisition of Language* and discussed more technically by specialists in *Approaches to Animal Communication,* edited by Thomas A. Sebeok and Alexandra Ramsay.

1. Explore for yourself some of the research findings discussed in this chapter. Spend some time with a child and determine his or her approximate stage of language acquisition. Observe whether the child spontaneously imitates things that you say and examine the imitations, comparing them with both the child's nonimitative speech and with the utterances that he has attempted to imitate. (It is best to have a tape recorder, if possible, and to record your entire session with the child, leaving the analysis until later.) If the child does not imitate spontaneously, try to involve him or her in a game where the child must imitate or repeat something you say to a doll or another person. In this case, you can offer for imitation carefully selected utterances at various levels of complexity (at, below, or beyond the child's production level). Examine any imitations that occur in the same manner as suggested above for spontaneous imitations. Compare your results with those of Bloom, Hood, and Lightbown (mentioned in "Further Exploration"); try to account for any differences.

2. Observe the linguistic interaction between a child and an adult. What types of responses does the adult make to the child's utterances? Does the adult expand on the child's comments (e.g., by responding *Yes, Daddy is in Chicago today* when the child says *Daddy in Chicago*)? Do the adult's responses refer mainly to the meaning of the child's utterances? How often, if at all, does the adult apparently ignore meaning and, instead, explicitly correct the child's pronunciation or grammar? Consider whether your presence has affected the adult's behavior toward the child.

3.   The following is an informal way of exploring the phenomenon of dichotic listening and lateralization. Go to a place where people are talking or turn on the radio or television to a talk show or news broadcast. Try to read something and observe whether the talking distracts you. Cover your left ear. Are you less distracted? Cover your right ear. How annoying is the talking now? Try to hold a conversation or listen to an individual talk when there is another kind of noise nearby (such as traffic or laughter or a vacuum cleaner). What effect is there when you cover your left ear? Your right ear? What conclusions can you draw? Are you left-handed or right-handed? How might that affect your results?

232323232323232323232323232:

FOREIGN LANGUAGE LEARNING: FACTORS AND APPROACHES

In order to understand foreign language learning, it is necessary to examine not only the linguistic properties of the languages involved but also the physical, psychological, and sociological characteristics of the learner. Just as children play an active role in acquiring their native language, so foreign language learners approach their task with established capacities, strategies, physical and cognitive development, goals, attitudes, and motivations, all of which interact to affect their success. With so many different factors involved, there is great variation from one person to another. However, there are also a number of general conclusions and implications that arise from research into these matters, and it is these that will serve as the basis for discussion in this and the following chapter.

Students of a foreign language are faced with an extremely

difficult task. Whether they wish to acquire nativelike mastery of the language in all aspects or merely to learn to read foreign language material in their own professional field, they must cope with the complex and abstract system of rules and forms that constitute every human language. When we consider this along with the variety of nonlinguistic factors mentioned above, it should not be surprising that methods for foreign language teaching frequently fail to assist learners in attaining their goal. The phenomenon of foreign language learning is enormously complex, and until it is understood fully, the development of effective and efficient teaching methods and materials will remain a difficult, if not impossible, goal.

To see how far we are from achieving this goal, we have only to observe that foreign language learning is frequently best accomplished without any teaching at all. That is, the preferable course of action for people who really want to learn a language is to go to an area where that language is spoken and immerse themselves in the new environment, gaining maximum exposure to, and practice in, the language. However, not everyone can afford the time and money required for such an experience. The only practical procedure, then, is to enroll in a foreign language class, where the teacher can facilitate learning by presenting samples and descriptions of the language, along with opportunities for its use, in such a way and to such an extent that the students, consciously or subconsciously, internalize the forms and rules sufficiently well to meet their performance goals.

BRIEF HISTORY OF TEACHING METHODS

Many foreign language teachers are interested in determining new methods and materials that will help their students learn. The relatively poor results of existing pedagogical techniques make this search especially important and, at times, even desperate. But the same situation has existed for decades. As an existing approach was recognized as ineffective, any suggestion for a different method seemed attractive, particularly when the new proposal differed greatly from the method being used. The history of trends in foreign language teaching is essentially a series of reactions, overreactions, and counterreactions. In order to understand some of the current issues in the field of foreign language instruction, it may be helpful to examine the strengths and weaknesses of past and present trends in American language teaching.

Prior to the twentieth century, most language instruction was carried out by a method known today as **grammar-translation.** In this approach the student memorized lists of vocabulary items, sets of words with inflectional affixes, and formal statements of grammatical rules. Use of the foreign language was restricted to translating, either from English or into English. When the goal was similarly restricted, and an acceptable end result was only the ability to translate written material, the grammar-translation method worked reasonably well. In fact, it is still widely used today in teaching Latin and ancient Greek. But in the first quarter of this century, a number of other factors arose that changed the goals and methods of language teaching. Substantial immigration of speakers of other languages led to an increased awareness of language as a vehicle for oral communication. Travel to foreign countries became more accessible and popular with affluent Americans, and it became clear to them that the ability to translate a French novella was of little use in asking a Paris policeman for directions to the Louvre. It is hardly surprising that the grammar-translation method did not help people learn to speak a foreign language; it was not designed to accomplish this task. People began to seek a new method to match the new goal of an oral command of foreign languages.

As a reaction to grammar-translation, the **direct** method soon acquired advocates. This was, in fact, an overreaction, for, with the direct method, the memorization of word lists and rules and the practice of translation were totally abandoned. English was never used in the classroom and there was no discussion about the structure of the language. Instead, an attempt was made to create an artificial linguistic island in the midst of an American school. The teacher used only the foreign language, relying on pictures and props to help students understand what was said. Underlying this approach was the theory that adults could learn a foreign language in the same way that children acquire their native language. Children, it was reasoned, learn a language by being in an environment where all communication takes place in the language they are trying to master. If adults are placed in a similar situation, according to this theory, they too will learn. As is discussed below, it is not entirely true that native and foreign language acquisition are the same, but even if this were the case, the direct method still would not succeed in a foreign language classroom. The student in a direct method class is exposed to the language for, at most, one hour a day, five days a week. For an entire school year, this adds up to no more than 200 hours. The child, on the other hand, receives at least 200 hours of exposure to language per month, and probably more. From the practical point of view, there is no way to recreate this extensive and intensive linguistic experience in the normal high school or college language class. In spite of this limitation, however, the direct method was partially successful. Students at least were able to learn something of the phonological system of the foreign language, and they had both an incentive and an opportunity to use the language for communication. But the same method that encouraged some students led to rejection or inhibitions with others. Unlike children acquiring their native language, adults who study a foreign language already know a language in which they can communicate. Many find it impossible to accept the restriction against the use of the native language that is imposed under the direct method. Furthermore, adults enter a foreign language class with a wide range of experience in studying a variety of subjects; in all of their prior experiences, they have been provided with descriptions and explanations of the subject matter. The direct method prohibits this type of instruction, and the result is that students sometimes come to the conclusion that the method is inadequate. Believing that they cannot learn in this way, they do not. An additional difficulty lies not with the method itself but with the kind of teacher it requires. To successfully conduct classes solely in another language, one must be a fluent speaker of that language. During the 1920s and 1930s, when the direct method was utilized in a number of American schools, relatively few foreign language teachers were fluent in the languages they taught. They themselves had often studied the language in school under the grammar-translation approach. Such practical weaknesses in the direct method soon became apparent. Some former advocates returned to grammar-translation, others devised combinations of the two approaches, and most were seeking a more effective way to teach foreign languages.

It was at this point that linguists entered upon the scene. Prior to World War II, American linguistics had been closely associated with the field of anthropology. Linguists investigated the languages of American Indians, just as anthropologists examined their cultures. Neither linguistics nor anthropology was concerned with the modern languages and cultures of Western Europe. Since it was precisely those languages that were taught in the schools, linguists had little contact with foreign language instruction. But the war changed this situation. In the Pacific, the armed forces came into contact with languages that were unfamiliar to most Americans—Chinese, Japanese, and the languages of the Philippine Islands, for example. Some military personnel had to be taught these languages so that they could communicate with the local people in establishing bases, supervising workers, and obtaining information. Few competent language teachers and almost no teaching materials existed for these languages, and so linguists were called in by the government to develop language courses for the military. Linguists were selected for this task because, even though few of them knew the particular languages involved, they had acquired substantial experience in working with unfamiliar languages. The foreign language teaching method that evolved in the military language training programs supervised by linguists became known as the **mimicry-memorization** approach (or simply as the Army method). A native speaker of the language served as the linguistic model for the students; they mimicked his production of basic sentences in the language. The linguist then provided descriptions of the phonological and/or grammatical points illustrated by these sentences. In addition, the linguist, working with the native speaker, devised lengthy dialogues to be memorized and practiced by the students.

Mimicry-memorization was extremely successful in meeting the particular goals of language training in the armed forces. Students assigned to the classes were highly motivated. Many had been selected for this training precisely because they had already demonstrated an aptitude for foreign language acquisition. The native speakers provided excellent models of speech from which the students learned, and classes were small and intensive (in most programs language training was a full-time activity with formal classes and informal practice sessions scheduled all day, almost every day for up to nine months). Furthermore, attention was generally concentrated on speech since there was little need for most military personnel to read or write these languages (some of which did not even have a writing system). The sentences and dialogues that were memorized were generally designed to reflect actual situations the student might expect to encounter in his later duties in the Pacific area.

News about the success of the mimicry-memorization method gradually spread to teachers outside of the armed forces language program. The American Council of Learned Societies sponsored a series of textbooks based on this method. These texts were largely devoted to the less commonly taught languages, such as Vietnamese and Korean, but they served as models for the preparation of new texts for more familiar languages, such as Spanish and German. In the late 1940s, mimicry-memorization was extended to some college foreign language classrooms, but it was far less effective there than it had been in military training programs. The reason for this is obvious: the environment was completely different. The high motivation was generally lacking; classes were bigger and met much less often; native speakers were not always available; and the students were often dissatisfied with an approach that stressed speaking and listening almost to the exclusion of reading and writing. In fact, it seems that the language programs developed for the armed forces succeeded not so much because of the mimicry and the memorization but rather because of the high motivation of the students, the relatively limited performance goals, and because of the intensive nature of the program. Nevertheless, many linguists and teachers viewed the initial success of this method as an indication that, modified somewhat, it could also be made to work in contexts other than military language programs. The result was a method developed during the 1950s and still widely used in both high school and college foreign language classes—the **audio-lingual** approach.

The essential characteristics of the audio-lingual method of foreign language teaching directly reflect the views about language held by the linguists who were instrumental in developing the approach. Largely under the influence of the empiricist theories that dominated American psychology during the second quarter of this century, linguists at that time considered language use as a set of ''habits'' acquired primarily through imitation and repetition and set into motion by some external stimulus. The structural linguistic theory of this period emphasized the diversity among languages, and research was concentrated on phonology and morphology (the study of morphemes). Little had been done with syntax, and the modern distinction between deep and surface structure was as yet unrecognized. Furthermore, much linguistic investigation of the time involved languages without a writing system, and linguists tended to regard writing as a relatively unimportant aspect of language. Based on these assumptions, the audio-lingual approach to foreign language teaching, as its name indicates, emphasizes speaking and listening; reading and writing usually are considered secondary goals. When the principles of this method are strictly observed, students are never presented with written material until they have mastered it orally.

Also characteristic of the audio-lingual method is the use of **pattern practice** in teaching syntax. An attempt to create in the student the ''habits'' of language use through imitation, repetition, and highly controlled practice, pattern practices are oral exercises in which a particular grammatical structure is presented. For example, in teaching English as a foreign language, one might use the pattern practice in Figure 23.1 to teach the fact that adjectives precede nouns in this language. The teacher provides the stimulus, the students respond. The response to the first stimulus is simple repetition; each additional stimulus

Figure 23.1 _____

TEACHER:	I have a big book.
STUDENTS:	I have a big book.
TEACHER:	blue
STUDENTS:	I have a blue book.
TEACHER:	heavy
STUDENTS:	I have a heavy book.
TEACHER:	funny
STUDENTS:	I have a funny book.

consists of an adjective that students must then substitute for the appropriate word in the sentence.

Despite a number of problems, some of which will become more apparent as discussion proceeds, the audio-lingual approach is usually more successful than either grammar-translation or the direct method in teaching pronunciation and basic control of the simpler syntactic structures of a foreign language. The systematic arrangement and presentation of material, in contrast to the almost random nature of the direct method, appeals to both teachers and students. But the audio-lingual approach is limited to first- and second-year courses. Once the student has mastered the sounds and rudimentary surface structure aspects of syntax, the audio-lingual method has little more to contribute, for it is based on a traditional approach to linguistics that did not go much beyond these areas of investigation. In third-year language courses, and often as early as the second year, emphasis switches from language to literature, in spite of the fact that few students have yet mastered the language.

The audio-lingual approach views the foreign language learner as an essentially passive recipient of stimuli provided by the teacher. The learner is "trained" to "perform" the "habits" of the new language. In fact, one proponent of this approach has characterized language learning as "the acquisition of nonthoughtful responses." This characterization reveals that the audio-lingual approach to foreign language learning is closely related to the empiricist views of child language acquisition, and the two share many basic inadequacies.

Paralleling the rationalist view of child language acquisition is the recent **cognitive** approach to foreign language learning. Here, the learner is viewed as an active participant in the process of acquiring a language. Learners come to their task equipped with the ability to reason and to acquire a new linguistic system. The ultimate goal is not merely the display of certain types of performance but the development of an internalized linguistic competence. Therefore, teachers and teaching materials are expected to offer samples of the language in natural contexts, as well as explanations and descriptions of structures when students request such information. The cognitive view assigns less importance than other approaches to highly structured methods and materials and, instead, places primary emphasis on providing meaningful examples of the language, organized to activate the students' natural language learning strategies and capacities. Although it is by no means a "linguistic teaching method" (no such method exists), the cognitive view gains much support from theoretical aspects of transformational linguistics and cognitive psychology. Many foreign language teachers, however, have been somewhat reluctant to adopt for classroom use an approach that lacks a fully developed set of materials and teaching procedures. At the present time, the cognitive view might be characterized more as a theory of foreign language learning than as a detailed method of foreign language teaching.

Rarely does one find a foreign language class conducted strictly according to the principles and procedures of any one of the methods discussed above. Most teachers choose elements from several approaches, combining them in a manner that they find helpful to their students and in agreement with their own background and views. Since no single method or theory has been proven fully effective, perhaps this eclectic approach is the best possible at the current time.

IMPLICATIONS AND CONTRIBUTIONS FROM LINGUISTICS

We begin this section with the statement of a fundamental principle: there is not now, nor can there ever be, a "linguistic method" of foreign language teaching. Application of the results of contemporary linguistic knowledge alone cannot provide all of the insights and information necessary for successful foreign language instruction. Obviously, if students have no motivation other than the completion of a requirement for graduation, no teacher can force them to master a foreign language, no matter how much time is spent on the task or what methods and materials are used. And, if the teacher does not speak the language fluently, students will never learn it unless they are able to find some additional source from which to learn.

A linguistic description of a language will indicate which forms and features must be learned, but the linguist cannot offer valid professional advice on how such learning is best achieved. This is an area in which language teachers must turn to studies by psychologists on factors such as attention and memory span. Psychology may also be able to provide some insight into the necessity of grammatical explanations for adult students or the most effective ratio between actual language usage and descriptions of usage, grammar, or pronunciation. As with the contributions of linguistics, the suggestions made by psychologists regarding foreign language acquisition will be only as valid and adequate as the assumptions, techniques, and research results on which they are based.

There are also limitations inherent in the present limits of the discipline. Modern linguistics is the study of the nature of language and the linguistic competence of the people who use a particular language. How this linguistic competence is actually put to use in the production or interpretation of speech or writing is a matter that currently lies beyond our understanding. Actual language performance is the goal of most foreign language learners, but linguistics has little to say about performance itself. Of course, performance does presuppose competence, and, in this sense, linguists can make a contribution by describing some of the knowledge that foreign language learners must acquire. Another limitation should be apparent from the section on syntax. Many linguists are only beginning to concern themselves with units of language larger than the sentence, but the kind of normal language performance sought by the language learner involves not just individual sentences but monologues, dialogues, conversations, paragraphs, chapters, and books. Yet, in spite of the limits of most modern linguistic research, some contribution is possible here, for one could neither understand nor produce sequences of sentences unless one also knew how to produce single sentences. A grammatical description of the sentences of a language, therefore, is an account of part of the knowledge that underlies the ability to engage in the normal use of language.

The proper application of linguistics to language teaching lies in an understanding of what language is. The insights linguists have attained about the complex, abstract, and systematic nature of language are helpful to both teachers and students of foreign languages, for such insights provide an understanding of the enormity of the task they are attempting to accomplish. But the proper application of linguistics is not a classroom presentation of a formal grammar, no matter how valid that grammar may be as an account of the competence of native speakers of the language. Modern linguists do not claim that the rules of their grammars actually exist in the same form in the minds of speakers. The grammars merely capture the same kind of knowledge the speakers have. Human beings may store this knowledge in a totally different form; we know too little about the human brain to make any claims of identity between our grammars and the speakers' minds. Consequently, there is no claim by linguists that speakers of a language actually produce sentences by a process of selecting underlying structures, inserting lexical items, applying transformations one at a time, and then passing this surface structure through a set of phonological rules. Just because a grammar is arranged to begin with meaning and end with phonetic representations is no reason for language learners to put off mastering pronunciation until they have learned how to produce all of the meaningful, grammatical sentences in the language they are studying. Although the informal presentation of some transformations and phonological rules may help a student to master some aspects of a foreign language, undue emphasis on formal rules and the elements of a linguistic description of a language will merely enable the student to learn about the language, and knowing about a language is quite different from knowing the language itself.

All languages are systematic. When we learn a language, we are learning a system—creating an internal grammar. This was discussed in the two preceding chapters with reference to children's native language acquisition. There it was observed that by studying the utterances children produce, we can learn much about how they acquire their language. The same is true of foreign language learning.

True language learning is a process that necessarily involves errors. As children and adults are exposed to samples of a language, they form hypotheses about the language. Frequently, the initial hypotheses are inadequate, failing to recognize the limits of a particular rule or the exceptions to the rule. One result of this is the kind of overgeneralization revealed so often in the speech of children. The study of errors made by foreign language learners reveals much about the process of language learning and the factors that affect this process. One of the chief contributions of linguistics to the field of foreign language learning, therefore, is the area of **error analysis.**

Errors must be distinguished from mistakes. Errors are defined here as systematic deviations from the foreign language and are due to the emerging system that the language learner is constructing (usually, but not always, in a subconscious, internalized way). In this sense, errors are reflections of the student's developing linguistic competence in the foreign language. Linguists sometimes refer to this systematic, but incomplete, emerging competence as an **approximative system** or an **interlanguage.** Both terms reflect the view that in acquiring another language, learners are constructing a system different from their native language but not yet identical to the system of the foreign language.

In contrast to errors, mistakes are random deviations, unrelated to any system, and instead representing the same types of performance mistakes that might occur in the speech or writing of a native speaker (e.g., slips of the tongue or failure to produce correct subject-verb agreement in a long, complicated sentence).

The analysis of errors reveals several factors that play a role in foreign language learning. For adults, approximately one-third of the errors that occur are due to differences between the native language of the student (the **source language**) and the foreign language being learned (the **target language**). For example, adult native speakers of

English who are learning French often make errors in the use of certain French verb forms called subjunctives. Either they fail to use the subjunctive forms in appropriate sentences or they overgeneralize and use the subjunctive where it is not appropriate. This error occurs because English has very few subjunctive forms (the use of *were*, rather than *was*, in *If I were a millionaire* is an example of a subjunctive verb form).

Errors due to differences between the source language and the target language systems frequently can be predicted (before they actually occur) by means of a **contrastive analysis:** a comparison of the linguistic systems of the source and target languages. Consider, as an example, Figure 23.2, which presents the basic vowel systems of English and Spanish. A contrast of the two systems will predict, quite accurately, that when Spanish speakers attempt to learn English, they will encounter relatively few problems with the vowels [i, e, u, o, a] (which occur in Spanish), but the remaining vowels, [ɪ, ɛ, æ, ʊ, ɔ, ə], will provide greater difficulty. This example is a very simple one. A complete contrastive analysis of the phonological systems of Spanish and English would have to include comparison of distinctive and redundant features, suprasegmentals, intonation, and phonological rules. Furthermore, a truly complete contrast would cover word formation, the lexicon, syntax, and semantics in both languages.

Contrastive analysis generally serves as the basis for the language teaching materials and techniques of the audio-lingual method, where emphasis is placed on those potential problem areas in which the source language and the target language differ. Since the languages are considered merely as sets of habits in this approach, it seems to follow that the long-established habits of the source language will create **linguistic interference** when the student attempts to use the new habits of the target language. In other words, the old linguistic habits may interfere with the proper use of the new habits. In this view, the problem areas where such interference might occur because of differences between the two linguistic systems must be practiced extensively in order to strengthen the new responses. Of course, where source and target languages are similar in some respect, it is expected that the learner will have little difficulty with the target forms, and, therefore, extensive practice will be unnecessary. We return to this topic in the next chapter.

The remaining two-thirds of the errors made by adult foreign language learners cannot be explained as interference or predicted by contrastive analysis. For example, some errors may be due to a universally valid difficulty factor. Complex embedded sentences are more difficult to master than simple sentences, no matter what source and target languages are involved. Systematic errors also arise due to the nature of the language learning situation and the psychological strategies used by learners. Here we find

Figure 23.2

	English Vowels			Spanish Vowels	
i		u		i	u
ɪ		ʊ			
e	ə	o		e	o
ɛ		ɔ			
æ	a			a	

the overgeneralizations and incomplete rule applications noted in child language acquisition. The specific materials and teaching techniques used to present the target language may themselves be a source of errors. Students learning Spanish may encounter adjectives only in a position after nouns in their first few weeks of instruction. They may then make the error of saying *un hombre grande* rather than *un gran hombre* when they mean 'a great man'; *un hombre grande* generally means 'a big man' ('big' in size). The student has no way of knowing that a small set of Spanish adjectives occur before, not after, the noun, usually with a difference in meaning and sometimes (as with *grande/gran*) with a difference in form. Many times, several of these factors interact and it is not possible to isolate a single cause for a particular error.

Error analysis is a relatively new approach to the understanding of foreign language learning. There are surely many causes of errors that are still unrecognized. Even at this point, however, implications for materials and methods are emerging. Foremost among these is the fact that errors in foreign language learning are not only natural but possibly may constitute necessary stages as learners progress from their partial approximative system to the complete and correct system of the target language. This does not mean that materials should be designed to lead to errors but that it may be unnatural and even harmful to the learning process if materials are so carefully structured that errors cannot occur.

MOTIVATION AND LEARNING CONTEXTS

Successful foreign language learning is dependent on many factors, and it is not surprising that most of the past approaches to teaching methods have been less than totally successful. For example, the direct method fails to take into account the systematic nature of language and therefore fails to provide the student with explicit generalizations, explanations, and discussions about the language system. Since many aspects of a linguistic system are not directly observable, students are prevented from readily comprehending the rules that constitute the system they are studying. The imitation, repetition, controlled practice, and memorization of both mimicry-memorization and the audio-lingual method may enable students to produce certain limited types of sentences or to reproduce memorized dialogues, but these classroom techniques alone do not lead to the kind of creativity we now know to be the essential characteristic of human language.

The study of linguistic competence and the realization of the abstract and complex nature of language have led linguists away from the behavioristic, stimulus-response view of man and language. Modern linguists recognize that, in order to understand the phenomenon of language acquisition, it is necessary to consider the nature of humans —that they are rational creatures equipped with powers of reasoning and with an innate capacity for language acquisition. Rather than ignoring such characteristics of people, language teaching methods might do well to utilize them. This is the goal of the cognitive approach, but, as we have noted, this is still more a theoretical view than a practical method.

Despite the weaknesses of all existing methods and approaches, almost every language class includes at least a few students who are successful. Success depends on more than teaching methods. One important factor is motivation. Extensive research studies (cited in ''Further Exploration'') have demonstrated that students are most successful when they study a foreign language because they admire the culture, like the people, and wish to become familiar with (or even part of) the society in which the language is used. This is called **integrative motivation** and is distinguished from **instrumental motivation** where the purpose of foreign language study is more utilitarian (such as meeting a graduation requirement or preparing to apply for a higher paying job). Students with instrumental motivation, not surprisingly, rarely achieve full success in foreign language classes.

The learning context for foreign language study is also important. One can study another language in a classroom setting where opportunities for use of the language are limited to that situation. Or, another language can be studied in a broader environment where it is used in the society at large, as well as in the classroom. In the former case, the language is a **foreign language,** foreign not only to the learner but also to the context. It is sometimes useful to refer to the latter situation as **second language** learning, since the language actually can be used for normal purposes of communication outside of the classroom. The level of achievement in second language learning situations is usually much greater than that attained in foreign language contexts. Second language situations, of course, permit greater contact with the language, and this extensive exposure may be a primary factor necessary for success.

Frequently, integrative motivation, a second language situation, and extensive language contact occur together, while instrumental motivation is more commonly found in the foreign language context, associated with limited language contact. For example, a person willing to spend the time and money for a term or a year away from home, studying and using a language in the country where it is spoken, is likely to have integrative motivation. Instrumental motivation, however, generally is not sufficiently compelling to lead an individual beyond the readily available foreign language classroom. Type of motivation appears to be a more significant factor than context in successful language learning. Students with integrative motivation can achieve success in a foreign language situation, whereas those with instrumental motivation may learn little even in a second language context. Of course, amount of exposure is also crucial; no one can acquire a language without sufficient exposure.

The most successful language programs are designed to promote or utilize all three of the factors considered here: integrative motivation, extensive exposure to the language, and a second language context. Thus, summer language programs overseas or junior-year-abroad programs provide to the student with integrative motivation the opportunity to learn the language in a setting where it serves as the chief means of communication for the society and, therefore, opportunities to use the language are frequent. Even intensive courses in a foreign language context present good results since they permit substantial exposure to the language and attract students with integrative motivation.

RELATION TO NATIVE LANGUAGE ACQUISITION

The relation of foreign (or second) language learning to child language acquisition constitutes an interesting and important issue. If the two are essentially similar, then it must be concluded that foreign language learning, like native language acquisition, is a natural process, one that cannot be taught as such but rather that will occur, under the right circumstances. On the other hand, if there are fundamental differences between acquiring a first language and learning a second, then perhaps teaching is possible and methods should take such differences into account.

There are a number of indications pointing to a close relationship between foreign language learning and native language acquisition. We have just observed that the most successful foreign language learning occurs under the conditions of extensive exposure to a language in a context where the language serves as the primary means of communication and when learners possess integrative motivation. All of these factors are present, so far as can be determined, for children acquiring their native language. Furthermore, error analysis reveals that many of the errors made by foreign language learners, as they utilize their approximative systems, are similar to errors made by children. Overgeneralization, incomplete rule application, universal difficulty factors—all play a role in both native and foreign language acquisition.

Despite the undisputed fact that many adults fail to master another language, it must be noted that some adults do succeed, even under less than ideal circumstances. This indicates that children's basic capacity for language acquisition is not lost as they mature. Perhaps the capacity is more difficult to activate, or maybe it is simply more difficult for adults to attain the necessary environment to activate their capacities. In any case, foreign language learning is possible for adults.

There are several factors by which adult language learners differ from children, including the following:

1. Adults have already mastered one language and therefore they know a large number of linguistic forms and rules.

2. Adults' nervous systems and the muscles of their vocal tracts are accustomed to transmitting and carrying out instructions for particular sets of phonetic features.

3. Adults have acquired certain strategies for learning new materials (they rely more on explicit explanations than does the child and may be somewhat less capable of induction, that is, of reaching generalizations on the basis of particular data).

4. There is some evidence that adults can make changes in their native language system (dialect changes, for example) only by adding extra rules; it is possible that this limitation affects foreign language learning.

5. Adults know a great deal about properties of meaning and the world.

None of these factors exists in children learning their native language. For the adult, foreign language learning is both easier and more difficult than native language learning is for the child. It is easier in that adults are knowledgeable about the world and about language, and this prior knowledge may permit concentration on the task of language learning; children must divide their attention, mastering not only language but other types of knowledge as well. Thus, under the proper conditions, adults can succeed in becoming rather fluent speakers of a foreign language in a year or two; no child attains equivalent linguistic control of his or her native language in such a short period of time. But language acquisition is more difficult for an adult, for many adults have an accent even after prolonged contact with and use of the foreign language. Each of the factors listed above as characteristics shared by adults but lacking in young children contributes to the adult's success or failure in learning a foreign language.

Before proceeding to the next chapter and a discussion of the various aspects of language that must be learned, let us first consider another possible cause for the adult's difficulty in mastering foreign languages in the classroom. Neurophysiological research has demonstrated that an individual's brain reaches a mature, adult state at approximately the age of puberty, that is, at roughly twelve years of age. It is precisely at this point in life that many people begin to experience increased difficulty in learning a foreign language, and it is not unreasonable to ask whether the maturation of the brain is somehow directly related to language learning ability. There is no firm answer to this question at the current time; too little is known about the brain and how it functions. Whatever the relationship between the brain and the ability to acquire a foreign language, it is clear that brain maturation does not cause loss of that ability. If it did, no one would ever be able to learn a foreign language after the age of twelve or thirteen.

Some readers may have observed in the text a distinction between *acquisition* and *learning*. Children are described as acquiring their native language, whereas adults are said to learn a foreign language. This distinction is a common one. Acquisition is viewed as a natural, unconscious, untaught, and probably unteachable process, while learning is somewhat artificial, usually conscious, and possibly dependent on instruction and study. The distinction has been preserved in this discussion since there is relatively little conclusive evidence that foreign languages can be acquired naturally by adults, but such evidence is increasing as research proceeds. Soon, linguists and language specialists may refer to foreign language acquisition, just as today they discuss child language acquisition.

SUMMARY

The basic approaches to foreign language instruction are the grammar-translation method, the direct method, the audio-lingual approach, and the cognitive approach. All suffer from inadequacies due to a failure to observe either the nature of language or the nonlinguistic factors that affect language learning. The learning situation, the amount of exposure to the language, and the type of motivation possessed by the learner are all crucial factors in the success of foreign language learning. Indeed, given the right combination of such factors, it is possible that foreign language learning may be accomplished naturally, without instruction, much as a native language is acquired.

FURTHER EXPLORATION

25 Centuries of Language Teaching by L. G. Kelly presents an account of language teaching methods from 500 b.c. to the present. More specifically, Chapter 5, "Principles of Language Teaching,'' in Robert Lado's book *Language Teaching*, provides an uncritical summary of the audio-lingual approach; although somewhat out of date, the discussion may interest readers who have studied a foreign language under this method. A critical discussion of the inadequacies of the audio-lingual method is presented clearly and briefly by Sol Saporta in the article ''Applied Linguistics and Generative Grammar'' (Valdman 1966). Both the audio-lingual and cognitive approaches to foreign language teaching are discussed at length by Kenneth Chastain in *The Development of Modern-Language Skills: Theory to Practice*. *Toward a Cognitive Approach to Second-Language Acquisition*, edited by Robert C. Lugton and Charles H. Heinle, contains a number of articles on cognitive theory and practice.

Robert J. Di Pietro offers many examples of contrastive analysis involving syntax, semantics, phonology, and the lexicon in *Language Structures in Contrast*. Eleven articles on error analysis and approximative systems (and interlanguage) are collected in *Error Analysis: Perspectives on Second Language Acquisition*, edited by Jack C. Richards; included are three studies of second language acquisition by children, as well as three analyses of adult second language errors.

Integrative and instrumental motivation are discussed fully by Robert C. Gardner and Wallace E. Lambert in *Attitudes and Motivation in Second-Language Learning*, a detailed report of research on this topic over a period of twelve years. A short summary of the most significant results is presented by Lambert in the article ''Psychological Aspects of Motivation in Language Learning,'' reprinted in *Language, Psychology, and Culture: Essays by Wallace E. Lambert*.

''Necessity and Sufficiency in Language Learning'' by Leonard Newmark and David A. Reibel (Lester 1973) examines the arguments for and against the view that native and foreign language acquisition are similar. In ''Implications of Recent Psycholinguistic Developments for the Teaching of a Second Language'' (Lester 1973), Leon Jakobovits discusses the rationalist theory of native language acquisition in reference to selected aspects of foreign language learning. Noam Chomsky discusses native and foreign language learning, as well as a number of other topics of interest to psychologists and philosophers, in the article ''Linguistics and Philosophy'' in his book *Language and Mind*.

1. Examine the following simplified chart of the fricative sounds in English and German. [ç] represents a voiceless fricative made by the body of the tongue at the palate, slightly behind the position of articulation of [š]; [x] is a voiceless fricative articulated at the velum, with the same position of articulation as [k].

	English					German			
f	θ	s	š		f	s	š	ç	x
v	ð	z	ž		v	z	ž		

(a) Based on the principles of contrastive analysis, which sounds would cause difficulty for a speaker of German learning English? Which would be problems for a speaker of English learning German?

(b) Before language learners master the production of a new sound, they usually will substitute a sound from their native language that has a position of articulation similar to that of the new foreign language sound; this represents a type of linguistic interference. What substitutions would you expect the speaker of German to make for the new English sounds? What substitutions might the speaker of English make for the new German sounds? (*Hint*. Consider the stops, as well as the fricatives on the chart, as possible substitutions; German has the same series of stops as English, [p, b, t, d, k, g].)

2. Obtain a short sample of the written work of a student in a beginning foreign language class (your own work would be most interesting). If the errors have not been indicated, have a teacher or native speaker of the language mark them and write in the correct form. First, try to eliminate any errors that are probably just mistakes (accidental slips of the pen, typing mistakes, etc.). Then, perform an error analysis: attempt to decide for each error whether it was caused by differences in the source and target language, inherent difficulty, overgeneralization, incomplete rule application, the form in which the material was taught, a combination of these factors, or perhaps some other factor not discussed in the text.

3. Explore the effects on language learning success of integrative and instrumental motivation, foreign language and second language contexts, and amount of exposure. Consider your own foreign language experiences, if any, in these terms. Survey the attitudes of students in a language class and determine whether there is a positive relationship between integrative motivation and success (as measured, perhaps, by grades).

4. Explain the following in terms of the factors affecting success in foreign (or second) language learning.

(a) Following a ten-week training period, including five hours per day of instruction in Spanish, at an American university, a Peace Corps volunteer was assigned to a village with a population of 250 people in rural Bolivia. Most of the people there spoke Spanish, but they also used Aymara (an Indian language); no one knew English. Within six months in Bolivia, the volunteer spoke excellent Spanish and could even understand and use Aymara in simple conversations.

(b) At the age of twenty, a young couple immigrated to the United States from Poland. They moved into a small apartment house owned by the woman's uncle, who himself had come from Poland several years before. Since they did not speak English, the couple found their friends among other Polish-speaking people and obtained employment in the ethnic restaurant managed by the uncle. Thirty years later, the couple still had a Polish accent in their English pronunciation and, in fact, knew only enough English to communicate about simple needs.

(c) An American student went to Paris for a summer. He lived in a dormitory for foreign students and took special courses taught in English at the university. On weekends, he went to London to visit friends. When he returned to the United States, he discovered that he had learned less French during three months in Paris than his roommate had in an intensive course offered at a college in New Jersey.

CHAPTER 24242424242424242424242424242

FOREIGN LANGUAGE LEARNING: MASTERING THE SYSTEM

No matter what approach is used or what factors are present, foreign language learners must master at least the fundamental aspects of the linguistic system of the language they are studying. In this chapter, we present concrete examples of the material that must be acquired, with descriptions and explanations of the problems that a foreign language learner may encounter.

PHONOLOGY

Students of a foreign language, if they are concerned with learning to speak and listen, as well as to read and write, must master the phonological system of the language. As we saw in Part 3, this system consists of the phonemic and phonetic representations of morphemes and a set of redundancy and phonological rules. Like children acquiring their native language, adults can observe directly only the phonetic forms in a language. From these they must determine the more abstract rules and underlying forms possessed by fluent, native speakers of the language.

One of the main obstacles in learning the phonological system of a foreign language involves the interrelationship between the phonetic properties of sound segments and the physiological characteristics of adult human beings. When listening to words in a foreign language they do not know, adults do not "hear" all of the sounds that are actually produced. Instead, they interpret the sounds in terms of the phonological system of their native language. In those cases where some sound occurs in both the foreign and the native language, it is identified correctly. For example, the Spanish words *ley* 'law', *gana* 'desire', and *vaca* 'cow' contain only sound segments that also occur in English; phonetically these words may be represented as [ley], [gána], [báka], respectively. Speakers of English can identify the sounds correctly if they hear these words, and can pronounce them correctly without difficulty. On the other hand, when speakers of English hear the Spanish word *lago* 'lake', they will normally interpret this as [lágow]; however, the word is pronounced [láɣo]. When speakers of English encounter the unfamiliar sound [ɣ] (a voiced velar fricative), they identify it with the closest sound segment they know—[g] (a voiced velar stop). Similarly, in English, when the sound segment [o] occurs at the end of a word, it is always followed by a [w] glide; such gliding does not occur automatically in Spanish. Thus, we interpret what we hear in terms of the sound system of our native language. In the case just described, it should be apparent that, if students incorrectly identify the sounds they hear, they certainly will not produce those sounds correctly. In fact, a beginning student of Spanish normally will pronounce a word such as 'lake' as [lágow]—a pronunciation that speakers of Spanish would identify as reflecting a foreign accent.

In teaching pronunciation, it is usually not enough to simply instruct students to repeat words containing unfamiliar sounds. Students first must learn to recognize these sounds when they hear them. Only then can they proceed to the problem of trying to articulate them. In both cases, a brief description of the phonetic features of the sound in question is helpful in calling the students' attention to the differences between the phonological system they are learning and the one they already know.

Even after sufficient exposure and discussion enable students to correctly identify new sounds and even when they know how they should be articulated, it is often difficult for them to actually produce sounds that do not occur in their native language. This problem is nonexistent for children learning a foreign language, but it becomes progressively greater with age. At issue here is the fact that the articulation of sounds involves the coordination of a variety of muscles in the vocal tract. As we saw in Part 3, each sound requires careful control of a number of independent activities in the vocal tract. That is, each sound segment consists of a particular combination of phonetic features. In English, for example, the phonetic features [+ consonantal, − anterior, − coronal] are always converted into a sound that is also [− continuant], that is, [k], [g], or [ŋ]. English speakers automatically block the air stream in the oral cavity for velar consonants; their neurophysiological system is conditioned to carry out the instructions [+ consonantal, − anterior, − coronal, − continuant] as a set. In terms of a formal linguistic description of English, we can say that speakers of the language know a redundancy rule that predicts the feature [− continuant] for sounds which are [+ consonantal, − anterior, − coronal]. To attempt to change just one of these features without changing the others is like trying to break a habit, yet this is exactly what must be done if a speaker of English is to learn how to produce [ɣ], which is [+ consonantal, − anterior, − coronal, + continuant]. The longer people have carried out one particular set of instructions, the more difficult it will be for them to change one feature in the set. Therefore, older people generally have more trouble in mastering pronunciation of new sounds than do young people.

The same type of problem occurs with sounds in unfamiliar sequences. For example, in Russian, words may begin with consonant clusters such as [kt] in the word *кто* 'who' and [št] in the word *что* 'what' ([št] is the normal pronunciation of the consonant cluster in *что;* there is also a spelling pronunciation that involves the cluster [čt]). Although the sounds [k], [t], and [š] occur in English and although they occur in clusters, as at the end of the words *baked* and *cashed,* these clusters never appear at the beginning of an English word. In fact, as we saw in Chapter 9, for every word-initial sequence of two [− vocalic, + consonantal] sounds in English, the first is always [s]. The rules of English include this fact, and the automatic consequence of this restriction on initial consonant clusters is that native speakers of English will often interpret the Russian sequences [kt] and [št], not as consonant clusters at the beginning of a word, but as if a vowel appeared between the consonants. When English speakers initially attempt to say [kto] *кто,* they will usually say [kətó], and the result is a foreign accent.

Since all human beings are equipped with the same type of vocal tract and nervous system, it is possible for anyone to learn to produce sounds involving new combinations of phonetic features or new sequences of sounds. The amount of practice required to condition the vocal tract to carry out such new sets of instructions, however, is often very great. People vary in their ability to master new vocal tract activities quickly, just as they vary in the amount of time it takes them to master other activities involving muscular control. For many, the goal of nativelike pronunciation in a foreign language is simply not worth the amount of time needed for practicing articulation. An accent in a foreign language does not always interfere with communication. A Spanish speaker will recognize [lágow] as the word for 'lake' in spite of the two mispronunciations involved because 'lake' is the only word in Spanish with a phonetic representation similar to this. Likewise, English speakers would be understood if they pronounced the word *casa* 'house' as [kʰása] (i.e., with aspiration accompanying the first sound). In so doing, they would be using the English rule that voiceless stops are aspirated word-initially; this rule does not exist in Spanish, where all stops are [− aspiration]. But if Americans were to use the

English rule inserting a [y] glide after word-final [e], they would pronounce the Spanish word *le* 'him' as [ley]. The Spanish pronunciation of *le* is [le]; [ley] is another Spanish word meaning 'law'. Thus, in learning a foreign language, there are cases in which failure to learn certain aspects of the sound system will lead to failure in communication.

In addition to mastering new combinations of features, new sequences of sounds, and learning to avoid certain rules of their native language, foreign language students must also learn some of the phonological rules that determine the correct phonetic forms of morphemes in the language they are studying—for example, the phonological processes discussed in Chapter 10 involving rules of umlauting for certain plurals in German, vowel harmony for the possessive suffix in Turkish, and nasalization of vowels in some masculine adjectives in French. If one is ever to speak a foreign language fluently—without conscious effort directed toward HOW something should be said—it is necessary that he or she learn such general rules. It is not enough to be able to pronounce a nasalized vowel in French; one must also know that for adjectives ending in a vowel followed by a [+ nasal] consonant there is a rule that nasalizes the vowel and deletes the consonant when the adjective refers to a masculine noun, but not when a feminine noun is involved. Thus, rather than memorizing two different phonetic forms for each adjective (such as [bɔn] and [bɔ̃] 'good'), the learner has only to memorize a single underlying representation for each morpheme and one or two rules that produce the correct phonetic forms in all cases.

To summarize, the teaching of the phonological system of a foreign language can be greatly facilitated if the nature of speech sounds and how they are organized into a system is kept in mind. The competent, successful foreign language teacher is not merely a fluent speaker of the language; he or she must also possess a background in the linguistic description of the language being taught. For example, a brief description of the phonetic features involved in the production of individual sounds serves to call the student's attention to the necessary vocal tract movements. Furthermore, if students are ever to become fluent speakers of the language, they must acquire the phonological rules, or generalizations, that constitute a major part of the linguistic system. Since these generalizations are not always immediately obvious from the phonetic facts, it is helpful if the teacher, or the textbook, presents them explicitly. Care must be taken to avoid excessive use of formal rules to the exclusion of actual exposure to and practice in the language itself. Learning about such phonological facts is not equivalent to acquiring them in a way that results in actual language performance, but for most adults it is a helpful step.

In the preparation and organization of teaching materials, the most important fact about phonology is the following: language is a system and the phonology of every language is systematic. Rather than concentrating on the production of one sound at a time, it is far more effective and efficient to utilize the system itself. For example, in Bengali, a language spoken in the northeastern region of the Indian subcontinent, all stops, whether voiced or voiceless, occur word-initially both with and without aspiration. Thus, there are contrasts in meaning for the words listed in Figure 24.1. For speakers of English, it is difficult to learn to produce word-initial voiceless stops without aspiration since, in English, such sound segments in this position are almost always aspirated. Even

Figure 24.1

Meaning	Example	Phonetic Features
'flower'	[pʰul]	$\begin{bmatrix} - \text{ voice} \\ + \text{ aspiration} \end{bmatrix}$
'bridge'	[pul]	$\begin{bmatrix} - \text{ voice} \\ - \text{ aspiration} \end{bmatrix}$
'food'	[ban]	$\begin{bmatrix} + \text{ voice} \\ - \text{ aspiration} \end{bmatrix}$
'pretence'	[bʰan]	$\begin{bmatrix} + \text{ voice} \\ + \text{ aspiration} \end{bmatrix}$

more difficult, however, are the aspirated voiced stops which never occur in English in any position. Since the problem occurs for all stops in Bengali, it would be highly inefficient for a teacher to instruct students in producing [p] and [bʰ] without also treating [t], [k], [dʰ], and [gʰ]. The instruction can be divided into two parts, one concentrating on all of the word-initial, unaspirated voiceless stops, the other on all of the aspirated voiced stops.

Knowledge of the system underlying the pronunciation patterns of a language also enables a teacher to understand why students are having difficulty with particular sound segments. In fact, such knowledge will enable a teacher to predict just where many pronunciation difficulties will occur., For example, a teacher of English as a foreign language may have students who are native speakers of Spanish. If the teacher is unaware of the sound system of Spanish, he or she may think that the students are being perverse when they pronounce the word *daddy* as [dæði], *deduce* as [dəðus], and *dodder* as [daðər] (since the vowels are not under discussion, they are represented as English speakers normally pronounce them, but the Spanish speaker would also have difficulties with them). A teacher who is uninformed about the phonological system of Spanish cannot understand why the students can pronounce [d] correctly at times, but at other times use [ð] instead. As we noted in Chapter 10, if a sound segment in Spanish is [+ voice, − continuant, − nasal], it will remain [− continuant] at the beginning of a word, but between vowels it undergoes an assimilation rule and becomes [+ continuant]. Thus, Spanish speakers learning English will automatically produce [d] correctly in word-initial position, but intervocalically they will make use of their native phonological rule and produce the corresponding [+ continuant] sound [ð]. As indicated earlier, the same knowledge of linguistics that would assist the teacher in understanding why the students have this pronunciation problem can also help him or her to teach them how to overcome it.

WRITING SYSTEMS

Pronunciation difficulties in a foreign language sometimes result not from differences between the students' native language and the language they are learning but rather from certain aspects of the writing system of the foreign language. It is partly for this reason that some language teaching specialists recommend that students not be introduced to the writing system of a language until they have mastered the phonology. The chief problems arise when the language being learned has an alphabetic writing system. If one is studying Chinese, with a logographic writing system, it is difficult to learn the symbols, but the nature of this type of writing system precludes any pronunciation problems due to the writing itself. The syllabic writing system of Japanese seldom causes pronunciation problems, primarily because students have generally mastered the phonology before they encounter the written symbols. The situation is different, however, for the more commonly taught languages, such as French, German, Russian, and Spanish, all of which utilize alphabetic writing systems.

As discussed in Chapter 11, no language has a phonetic writing system. The symbols of alphabetic systems basically reflect the phonemic representation of the morphemes of the language. This fact immediately poses problems for foreign language learners since, at the beginning stage of their study, they do not yet know such phonemic representations, nor do they know the phonological rules of the language that convert phonemic to phonetic representations. Thus, when they encounter a word written with familiar letters, they will pronounce the word by assigning to the letters the same sounds they normally represent in their native language. To use a familiar example, an English speaker who knows no Spanish would read the word *dado* 'gave' and probably pronounce it [dǽdow]. In English, the letter *d* is almost always pronounced [d], and the letter *a* often represents the sound [æ] (as in the English words *pat, daddy, patch, action*). In Spanish, however, *d* represents the phonemic segment that is [d] word-initially but [ð] intervocalically; *a* in Spanish always represents the sound [a] ([æ] never occurs in Spanish). Any speaker of English can correctly pronounce the Spanish word *dado* without difficulty (with the possible exception of the last sound segment, which in English, but not Spanish, would be followed by a [w] glide). Therefore, the problem is not purely a phonological one, but is due to the writing system.

Figure 24.2 illustrates other problems associated with alphabetic writing systems. The examples are taken from Russian and divided into three sets. The letters in set I present no difficulty for English speakers since they are almost identical in form to letters in English that represent similar sound segments. On the other hand, the letters in set III are the most difficult for speakers of English to master since they look like familiar English letters but have totally different sound correspondences. Set II represents an intermediate stage of difficulty. The sound segments represented by these letters are familiar but the form of the letters is quite different from any letter found in the English alphabet. This order of difficulty is parallel to that which occurs in learning a new phonological system. Sounds that are identical in the native and foreign language present no problem, and sounds involving a completely new phonetic feature are usually easier to

Figure 24.2

	Russian Letter	Sound	Common Corresponding English Letter(s)
I.	м	[m]	m (mill)
	к	[k]	k, c (key, call)
	а	[a]	a, o (father, pot)
II.	д	[d]	d (do)
	ж	[ž]	s, z (pleasure, azure)
	ф	[f]	f (find)
III.	в	[v]	v (very)
	н	[n]	n (now)
	р	[r]	r (rose)

master than sounds consisting of unfamiliar combinations of familiar features or unfamiliar sequences of familiar sounds.

One argument in support of the recommendation that foreign language students learn the phonological system of a language prior to learning the writing system is again related to the fact that alphabetic systems reflect phonemic rather than phonetic representations. It is rarely sufficient to learn that a particular letter corresponds to a particular sound, for, frequently, a letter will have several sound correspondences, depending on the phonological rules of the language. We have already seen one instance of this in Spanish, and there are examples from other languages. The Russian letter *o* generally represents the sound [o], but, following the general phonological rule of Russian that converts [o] to [a] in unstressed position, a Russian word like *kopóba* 'cow' is pronounced [karóva]. The French letter *n* often represents the nasal consonant [n], but following the phonological processes described in Chapter 10, the French word *plan* 'level' (as an adjective modifying a masculine noun) is pronounced [plã]. The German letters *b, d,* and *g* normally represent the sounds [b], [d], and [g], but in word-final position, according to the German rule discussed in Chapter 10 as an example of assimilation, these letters represent the sounds [p], [t], and [k], respectively. Thus, the word spelled *Tag* 'day' is pronounced [tak]. It is clear that only with some knowledge of the phonological rules of a language can a student determine the pronunciation of a word on the basis of its spelling.

One can also argue that, by withholding exposure to the writing system until after the student has mastered the phonology, a teacher or textbook is depriving the student of an aid in determining the phonological system of a language. How words are spelled is very often a reflection of their underlying phonemic representation, as is the case for the languages and words discussed in the preceding paragraph. Since foreign language learners cannot directly observe the phonemic representations or the phonological rules of a language from the phonetic forms they hear, it seems only reasonable to assist them in determining this information by allowing them to see how words are spelled. Of course, it is important that they be made aware of the fact that spelling reflects not pronunciation but the phonemic representations underlying pronunciation.

SYNTAX

Only during the last two decades have linguists concentrated their research efforts on the study of syntax. Since there is almost always a substantial time lag between research results and the application of these results to practical matters such as the teaching and learning of foreign languages, it is not surprising that linguists have less to contribute regarding the teaching of syntax than they have about phonology. Nevertheless, certain facts are known. We can be reasonably confident that some assumptions about syntax are valid, and the directions for future development are beginning to become clear.

The audio-lingual approach to foreign language teaching, based as it was on a type of linguistics primarily concerned with the diversity that exists among the surface structures of languages, failed to make use of the universal properties that we now know exist. Modern linguistic research strongly indicates that the basic, deep structure level of all human languages is very similar. Furthermore, the languages that have been investigated in detail all make use of the same basic transformational processes in converting deep structures to surface structures. Thus, foreign language learners know a great deal about the nature of the language they are learning. Since they are human beings and already know one human language, they assume that they will find certain properties in the language they are studying. More often than not, their assumptions are correct. They certainly expect to find ways of converting concepts into speech. They know that the language will have possibilities for paraphrase, that they will be able to ask questions, make requests, and produce statements, and that there will be some way of negating such sentences. They also expect to be able to combine simple sentences in order to produce more complex ones, and they know the processes that will probably be used to convert deep structures to surface structures—processes such as deletion, addition, and substitution. The fact that these assumptions, expectations, and knowledge are usually not conscious does not mean that language learners cannot make use of them in carrying out their task. None of these things ever has to be taught, and, for that reason, language teaching specialists often overlook the great contribution that the students themselves make to the task of foreign language learning.

Given the fact that certain aspects of language are universal and others are common to many languages, it would seem that a certain amount of translating from one language to another might be useful in helping students to see both the similarities and the differences in how the two languages express concepts. But translation is not at all popular in most modern foreign language classrooms. This is, in part, a leftover reaction to the old grammar-translation method of teaching in which translation was the only use to which the foreign language was put. But the modern lack of interest in translation is also due to the audio-lingual method's emphasis on the diversity among languages. It was widely believed that languages could differ from one another in innumerable ways and that translation would somehow prevent the student from mastering the new language because he would be continually confusing it with his native language. Most modern linguists believe that these views are not correct. They maintain that there are definite limits to the ways in which languages can differ from one another, limits established by linguistic universals that have already been discovered or have not yet been investigated. It is not unlikely that, in the future, language teachers will once again examine the effectiveness of translation, although, of course, under no circumstances should translation replace normal use of the language.

The existence of language universals does not deny the presence of substantial diversity among languages. This diversity occurs primarily at the surface level of language, in phonetics and in syntactic surface structure. Since surface structure is the only directly observable aspect of syntax, foreign language learners must begin by memorizing those aspects of surface structure that differ from their native language—for example, whether objects generally come after the verb, as they do in English, or before the verb, as happens in some types of German sentences. The learning of principles of word order can be facilitated by techniques such as the pattern practices discussed in Chapter 23. Such exercises, while useful as an aid to eventual memorization, are limited in terms of teaching actual use of the language. Pattern practices are highly controlled exercises in which emphasis is placed on a particular structure, as illustrated by the exercise in Figure 23.1. Normal use of language rarely, if ever, consists of sequences of sentences all of which are identical except for one word.

Normal language use consists, in part, of creativity—the ability to produce and understand utterances never before encountered. In a native speaker of a language, this ability is reflected in the recognition of paraphrases, related sentences, ambiguous sentences, grammatical as opposed to ungrammatical sentences, and so on. All of these aspects of language are related to the deep and surface structures of sentences and the transformations that link them. Thus, if people wish to become fluent speakers of another language, they must in some way acquire knowledge of such structures and the transformations of the language. But it must be recalled that linguists are not yet confident that they fully understand the nature and form of transformations, either in general or for any language in particular. Furthermore, although a transformational grammar is intended to be an accurate account of the knowledge that native speakers have about their language, it does not necessarily reflect processes, or the application of rules, that speakers actually use to understand what they hear or read or to produce what they say or write. It is, therefore, both premature and basically irrelevant to present the formal transformational rules of a grammar directly to students in a foreign language classroom. On the other hand, informal discussion of the syntactic generalizations of a language is useful in helping the student to arrive at the kind of internalized linguistic knowledge possessed by native speakers.

People sometimes confuse the ability to cite rules of grammar with knowledge of a language. Clearly, the two are not equivalent, for a large majority of the native speakers of any language are unable to verbalize more than a few of the great number of rules they know unconsciously. Furthermore, adults, as well as children acquiring their native language, can learn a language perfectly without ever hearing a discussion of grammar. The use of grammatical discussion in the foreign language classroom is merely one way of compensating for the lack of the best environment for learning, that is, a situation in which the learner is continually exposed to the language.

A related matter is the treatment of exceptions. A language is a system, but it is never a perfect system. Nevertheless, the fact that exceptions to generalizations exist does not invalidate the generalizations, which may be valid 99 percent of the time. In many foreign language textbooks, however, generalizations are presented in one or two lines of print and thereafter ignored in favor of long lists of exceptions to the rule. Presented with both the generalization and its exceptions at the same time, many students learn neither. Since beginning language students have a great deal to learn, it would seem reasonable to present them first with the most productive aspects of the language, provide them with the opportunity to master them, and only then to consider the exceptions. As we have seen, this is essentially what children do in acquiring their native language.

In addition to creativity, normal language use involves appropriateness. For example, if two strangers are discussing politics at a party and have been doing so for the last hour, one of them, upon seeing a dog, may say "I see a dog" but not "I see the dog." Both sentences are grammatical, but only the former is normally appropriate in a context in which the individuals involved have not been talking about dogs. Pattern practice exercises may be helpful in learning basic syntactic structures in a language, but, since they involve concentration on one structural pattern at a time, they cannot serve as examples of appropriate use of language in context. The dialogues used in mimicry-memorization and the audio-lingual approach do illustrate normal use of language, but the length and number of dialogues a student can learn for a foreign language course is limited. For people who are studying a language independently in the country where it is spoken, learning which sentences are appropriate in which situations is a relatively simple matter, for they are constantly surrounded by the examples of native speakers of the language. In the foreign language classroom, however, the problem is acute. There is not enough time to provide the student with sufficient exposure to actual language use. Few people, including language teachers, are able to describe explicitly the conditions under which some linguistic forms are appropriate but others are not. With matters of grammar, one can turn to a linguistic description of the language for an account of grammatical rules, but few descriptions currently exist for matters of appropriateness in actual usage. While research in this area develops, language teachers can at least attempt to provide their students with as many samples as possible of actual language use, pointing out the known generalizations and otherwise relying on the students' innate ability to induce such generalizations from the samples of language use they encounter.

The concept of linguistic interference, mentioned in Chapter 23, is found so frequently in materials on foreign language acquisition that it should be examined more closely. There appears to be some validity to this concept insofar as the acquisition of phonology is concerned, for, as we saw earlier, the muscles of the vocal tract must become accustomed to carrying out new instructions in the production of unfamiliar sounds or sequences of sounds. In syntax, however, the concept is less valuable. If students do not know the position of adjectives with respect to nouns, they naturally will use the same order as in their native language. But this is not interference in any normal sense of the word; rather, it is lack of knowledge. Very few, if any, adult students of Spanish, for example, have difficulty placing adjectives after nouns once they observe, or are informed, that this is the normal order in Spanish. If there were actual interference from their native language, they should go through a substantial period of time incorrectly using English word order in the foreign language.

LEXICON

Since the entries in the lexicon of a language consist of the unpredictable properties of morphemes, foreign language learners have no choice but to memorize such information. At the beginning stages of study, they normally do not know enough about the language to recognize the morpheme structure of words, and, therefore, they start by memorizing entire words. Gradually, however, the students will observe that certain elements recur in a number of words. They will begin to recognize the morphemes of the language and arrive at some idea of how they are combined to form words. Once students reach this point, they have learned some of the generalizations involved in word formation and no longer need to memorize each new word they encounter. They can memorize new morphemes and then utilize the rules they already know in order to combine morphemes to produce words. One example of this was presented in Chapter 4. A foreign language teacher or textbook can facilitate this process by pointing out generalizations the student can use. For example, students learning English as a foreign language can be told that the third person singular present tense of verbs is almost always formed by adding the suffix *s* to the basic verb form. This is certainly more efficient than offering no such generalization and waiting for the students to discover the fact for themselves. The students will need substantial practice in using this rule before they will consistently and correctly produce verb forms when they speak or write, for word formation involves not only the combination of morphemes but also the phonological processes that occur when morphemes are combined (the processes involved for the *s* suffix were discussed in Chapter 9).

Whether one is memorizing morphemes or entire words, the task is easiest when the written or phonological form of the item is similar in the native and foreign language. Students have no difficulty learning the Russian words *телефон* ([tɪlɪfón]) 'telephone' or *штат* ([štat]) 'state'. The Spanish words *grave* ([gráβe]) 'grave/serious', *característico* ([karakterístiko]) 'characteristic', and *resulta* ([resúlta]) 'result' are also never a problem, except for those difficulties resulting from general aspects of the phonological and writing systems, as discussed above. On the other hand, there are very definite problems when a word in the foreign language looks or sounds very much like a native language word and yet the meaning is different in the two languages. Such words are often called "false friends." Examples include: Spanish *actual* 'present/current' not 'actual', *gracioso* 'funny/witty' not 'gracious', *cargo* 'position/job' not 'cargo'; German *also* 'therefore' not 'also', *bald* 'soon' not 'bald', *hell* 'bright' not 'hell'; and French *chair* 'flesh' not 'chair', *four* 'furnace/oven' not 'four', *lecture* 'reading' not 'lecture'.

SUMMARY

The language learner must master at least the basic properties of the linguistic system of the foreign language. Aspects of phonology, syntax, lexicon, and the writing system must be learned. All present particular problems when the target language differs substantially from the student's native language, but the difficulties can be anticipated, understood, and overcome when both teacher and learner are aware of the systematic nature of human languages.

FURTHER EXPLORATION

The *Contrastive Structure Series,* edited by Charles A. Ferguson, includes volumes comparing the phonological and syntactic systems of English and several commonly taught languages, including German, Italian, and Spanish. Emphasis is on the difficulties that speakers of English encounter, and most of the volumes offer suggestions to aid the teacher and learner. There are many books available for methods of teaching specific languages. One series has been produced by Robert Politzer and contains volumes on the teaching of French, German, and Spanish (complete references are given in the bibliography at the end of the text).

In Part II of *The Development of Modern-Language Skills: Theory to Practice,* Kenneth Chastain discusses foreign language learning from the point of view of the linguistic goals involved: mastering the ability to understand spoken language, to speak, to read, and to write. Also of general interest are two articles printed in Lester (1973): "How Not to Interfere with Language Learning" by Leonard Newmark discusses the importance of providing students with adequate exposure to language use in real contexts; Robin Lakoff, in "Transformational Grammar and Language Teaching," discusses the necessity of presenting foreign language students with linguistically valid information about language without excessive use of formal rules. Particularly interesting is another article by Robin Lakoff, "Language in Context." A large number of journals publish practical and theoretical articles devoted to issues in foreign language teaching; included among these journals are *International Review of Applied Linguistics, Language Learning, Modern Language Journal,* and *TESOL Quarterly* (the last journal devoted to issues in the teaching of English to speakers of other languages).

1. English-speaking students of languages in which the sound [ŋ] occurs word-initially often have difficulty with words such as [ŋo]. Why? How might this be pronounced by a native speaker of English? (There are several possibilities.) With practice, anyone can produce [ŋ] at the beginning of a word. Try to do this and then check your response to the above question by producing [ŋo] for another speaker of English and ask him or her to repeat what you said. How does the person respond? Is the response one of those you had predicted?

2. Native speakers of English, when first encountering the following German words, occasionally make the error of producing the initial consonant as [s] rather than [š]. What two aspects of German, as compared to English, cause this error?

Stadt	[štat]	'city'
Spiel	[špil]	'game'
Speck	[špɛk]	'bacon'
stecken	[štɛkən]	'to put'

3. The following pairs consist of grammatical sentences in English. Assume that you are a teacher of English to speakers of other languages. How would you explain the difference in meaning within each pair? In what circumstances would each sentence be appropriate? (If you have difficulty responding, read the articles by Robin Lakoff mentioned above.) How would these sentences be expressed in some other language with which you are familiar?

(a) (i) I need a book about syntax.
    (ii) I need the book about syntax.

(b) (i) Susan saw George once a week for a year.
    (ii) Susan has seen George once a week for a year.

(c) (i) May John do that?
    (ii) Can John do that?

(d) (i) Michael has left, hasn't he?
    (ii) Has Michael left?

PART 9999999999999999

LANGUAGE, LINGUISTICS, AND TEACHERS

From the nursery school through the university, a substantial segment of education in our society is devoted to language. In the early years, emphasis is placed on reading and writing; later, attention shifts to English "grammar" classes and eventually to the use of language in literature and poetry. Although all of these areas of instruction are sometimes labeled *language,* very few of them actually deserve such a heading. As we have seen in the preceding sections, language is a system of knowledge and ability that, in large part, is possessed by every child at the time he enters kindergarten. No one is taught his native language; a linguistic system is acquired through innate capabilities and exposure in ways that are, as yet, not fully understood. It is possible to teach students ABOUT their language, to provide them with skills of language use, and even to aid them in acquiring certain minor dialect variations, but no one really teaches language. What is of direct concern to the teacher, therefore, is not language itself, but rather various aspects of language use.

Linguists are primarily concerned with gaining some understanding of language competence, the nature of language in general, and the properties of particular languages. The teaching of reading to five-year-old children or the analysis of Cummings' poetry are far removed from these concerns and yet related to them in ways that are of great importance to the educator. While the linguist can provide no "method" for teaching reading or for analyzing poetry, his insights about and understanding of language constitute essential contributions for the eventual development of sound educational methodologies in areas related to language and language use.

CHAPTER 2525252525252525252525252

THE EARLY
SCHOOL YEARS

The teacher of young children spends a substantial amount of time dealing with areas of instruction commonly known as the "language arts," including the teaching of reading and writing. Elementary school teachers are also often responsible for determining which students should be tested for speech problems and for providing instruction in standard English to those students who speak nonstandard dialects. To be carried out effectively, each of these tasks requires a certain degree of linguistic knowledge on the part of the teacher. Teachers should understand the nature of language in general, and they must have at their disposal valid information about such specific areas as the relationship between speech and writing, the facts of dialect variation, and the process of native language acquisition in the normal child. Almost every topic discussed in this book is relevant to both the theory and the practices of elementary school teaching. In this chapter, then, we will return to many matters that were covered earlier, emphasizing their role in the area of elementary education.

Children enter school knowing their native language. While they may not yet have acquired some of the phonological segments and complex syntactic patterns, the only great difference between their knowledge of English (or Spanish, or whatever) and that of adults lies in the area of vocabulary acquisition, an area open to learning throughout a lifetime. The teacher must be aware of the great body of linguistic knowledge that every child brings to the tasks of learning to read and to write. Children know their language and are able to carry out the major types of language performance, speaking and listening. Reading and writing are simply other types of performance, and although they differ in some respects from speaking and listening, they make use of much of the same linguistic knowledge that underlies the abilities already possessed by the child.

THE READING PROCESS

Before we can discuss the teaching and learning of reading, it is necessary to understand what reading is. For literate adults, who already know how to read, reading is an active interaction of adults' knowledge of their language with the material, printed or written, that they perceive visually. The purpose of reading is to comprehend meaning. For young children, just beginning to deal with printed material, reading can become just what it is for the adult. But, before children can read for meaning, they must first recognize that the squiggles on a page are related in some way to knowledge that they already possess (their language) and to a performance that they are already capable of accomplishing (listening). It is important to note that reading is related only indirectly to speech. Reading is a comprehension process, as is listening, while speech, like writing, is a production process.

Despite the fact that reading and listening are both comprehension activities, there are very definite differences between them. The most obvious difference, of course, is the medium of expression—written symbols as opposed to sounds. With an alphabetic writing system, the written symbols are related to phonological units, as we observed in Chapter 11, but it should be recalled that alphabetic symbols correspond to phonemic representations (including morphophonemic properties) and not to speech sounds. Even so, true reading is possible even without detailed knowledge of the phonological system of a language. Many graduate students, for example, learn to comprehend written French or German in order to meet university requirements for advanced degrees, but these students are often unfamiliar with the phonological systems of these languages and may be unable to pronounce the title of the work they are reading. Similarly, in other countries, students may be able to read English but not to pronounce it. Furthermore, people who are mute and/or deaf do learn to read (although their progress is frequently slow).

It is also important to examine the concept that reading is a comprehension process. The relation between written symbols and phonological units certainly exists for languages like English (although it is, at most, indirect for Chinese), but knowledge of this relationship is not sufficient to produce comprehension. Language consists of more than just sounds. To comprehend any concrete expression of language, such as speech or writing, it is necessary to identify the morphemes with their associated meanings and also to understand the meaning conveyed by the syntactic structure of sentences. A person can learn to "read" aloud material in another language, but be unable to understand anything of what he or she has "read." This ability is not uncommon in students of singing, who may learn the writing system and diction of a foreign language so that they can sing Italian art songs or German lieder. Similarly, children can learn to produce written material orally, but if comprehension is lacking, it is not correct to characterize their performance as reading. The converse of this situation is also true. It is possible to read with comprehension and yet bypass sounds. Several examples were cited in the preceding paragraph. Again let us consider children. When asked to read aloud, children may produce many deviations from the printed page, yet if they comprehend the material (generally the case when the deviations do not substantially change meaning), it is still reasonable to assert that such children can read.

Although some reading specialists maintain that all reading is accompanied by **subvocalization** ("silent speech"), in which the reader is said to initiate vocal tract movements but not carry them through to the production of actual speech, subvocalization apparently is not a necessary component of the reading process. There are people who subvocalize when they read, but, in general, such people read more slowly than those who do not subvocalize. This is not surprising since the physical activities that constitute subvocalization require extra time not needed if one can progress directly from the written material to meaning (without utilizing sound as an intermediate step). "Speed reading" is probably possible only in the absence of subvocalization. The emphasis on reading aloud in the early stages of reading instruction indicates a lack of awareness that true reading and the ability to read aloud are somewhat different tasks. Very little valid research has been done on this matter, but it would certainly be interesting to determine whether reading aloud in elementary classrooms encourages subvocalization, which must later be unlearned if the student is to become a rapid reader.

Although activation of the vocal tract, as in subvocalization, appears to be unnecessary for reading, reading is an active process. Readers must interact with the written material; they cannot simply absorb what is placed before them. This interaction occurs on at least three levels: visual processing, linguistic processing, and content processing.

In visual processing, the eyes must perceive and transmit the written material to the brain before any further progress can be made. Experimental studies have demonstrated that visual processing in reading is not normally a letter-by-letter, or even a word-by-word, procedure. Instead, the competent reader, who is reading in the normal silent manner in an attempt to understand meaning, may process an entire phrase at one time.

Next, readers must utilize their internalized linguistic knowledge of the language in order to comprehend the basic meaning of what they have seen. This linguistic processing is not simply a matter of identifying letters or words; syntax contributes to the meaning of sentences, and syntax involves more than the surface structure order of words that is reflected by the printed page. From the overt, visible material, readers, if they are to understand what they are reading, must determine the deep structure of the sentences, as well as their linguistic relationship to one another. Meaning is essentially dependent on deep structure, yet deep structure is not directly observable. Therefore, the reader must process the observable surface structure into the deep structure that represents the meaning. Recall also that some aspects of surface structure do not play any major role in conveying meaning. Sentences (1) and (2) convey the same meaning; a reader can ignore the presence of *that* in sentence (2) and still understand.

(1) I know John is coming this evening.

(2) I know that John is coming this evening.

Indeed, this is frequently the case. It is not necessary to process each and every word in order to read with comprehension.

Content processing reflects the fact that reading is partly a process of relating new knowledge to old knowledge. The content and context of a written passage provide readers with clues toward understanding that passage in relation to knowledge that they already possess about the subject matter. It is not possible to read with full comprehension material that involves topics or concepts that are totally unfamiliar to us. What we read must be related to our previous knowledge of the world; certainly, reading matter can contain new information, but that new information must refer to information we already possess. (To test this, one need only pick up a book or article on an advanced topic in some unfamiliar field or subject.) As a consequence of the fact that readers already know something about the subject of what they are reading, it is not necessary to process every word, or even every sentence, in order to understand a passage. This is readily demonstrated by considering the differences in reading speed related to differences in type of reading material. Most people read substantially faster when reading for pleasure than when reading to master subject matter.

Research on the PROCESS of reading has engaged the attention of educators, psychologists, and linguists only within the past decade. Earlier work focused almost exclusively on the TEACHING of reading, and, therefore, it tended to stress methods and materials but to ignore readers themselves. The situation bears striking parallels to the state of work and the emphases found in the field of foreign language learning, discussed in the preceding two chapters. And so, in reading, as in foreign language learning and even in studies of native language acquisition, there are two distinct theoretical orientations, each with different practical implications. The cognitive view of reading emphasizes the process of reading and the knowledge brought by the child to the task of learning to read; reading is viewed as an active process involving factors such as those discussed above. The behavioral view of reading concentrates on the development of response patterns and habits, with focus on such observable matters as eye movements, converting print into sound (reading aloud, for example), and error-free performance. Both approaches have found some support from linguists. In the older, structural linguistic framework, with its behavioristic orientation and concentration on phonology and word formation, reading specialists discovered parallels to methods such as phonics or the whole-word approach to teaching reading (defined and discussed below). The more recent transformational linguistic framework, with its rationalist orientation and study of syntax and semantics, as well as phonology and word formation, tends to lend support to the cognitive view of reading, where the child's natural capacity for the acquisition and understanding of language play a central role.

TEACHING AND LEARNING READING

Perhaps the best-known methods for teaching reading are those that utilize ''sounding out'' principles, frequently referred to as **phonics.** The approach emphasizes the association of letters with sounds, and each letter is claimed to "say" a certain sound. Certain aspects of phonics are valid from the linguistic point of view. For example, many consonant letters do consistently represent particular sounds. But this is not the case for all letters. Some are pronounced in many different ways, depending on factors such as the position of stress in a word, surrounding sounds, and, from the written point of view, other letters. The letter *a* is pronounced [e] in *agent,* [a] in *father,* [æ] in *pad,* and [ə] in *above.* The assumption that each letter "says" a sound leads to false comments on the relationship between sounds and letters. Even some recent books on phonics contain statements such as: "When the letters *sh* occur together, the resulting sound is a blend of *s* and *h.*" There is no way in which this is true for English. The sequence of letters *sh* generally represents the sound [š], which is not at all the same as the sequence of sounds [sh], a sequence that does not even occur in the English language.

In Chapter 11, we provided some evidence that English spelling reflects the underlying phonemic representations of morphemes and not their surface phonetic forms. To the extent that phonemic and phonetic representations are similar, the phonics-oriented approach to the teaching of reading may be successful. But, in those cases where phonetic form differs substantially from the underlying representation reflected by writing, it is not clear how phonics can succeed. A purely phonic method will encounter difficulties in sets of words like *nation/national, telegraph/telegraphy, democrat/democracy,* where the vowel sounds in each member of a pair are phonetically different. Research in reading instruction rarely deals with such problems. Usually, by the time children encounter such words in print, their teachers assume that they can read. In other words, many children are taught that English spelling is "phonetic" and, in some unknown way, later discover for themselves that it is actually phonemic. It is possible that some people who fail to become competent readers have never made this discovery.

Phonics approaches are inadequate in other ways. One of the chief difficulties in any method utilizing "sounding out" is that speech is a continuum. When we pronounce a word, we do not produce a series of separate sounds but, instead, a complex set of vocal tract movements, many of which overlap. In the word *quick,* for example, often represented in phonetic symbols as [kwɪk], the lips are rounded for the [w] as the initial [k] is being produced. Similarly, for many speakers, the velum has already opened for [n] during the production of the vowel in the word *man.* Compare the position of the lips for the first two consonants in *strudel* and *straddle.* In the former, the lips protrude even during the production of [s], in anticipation of the lip rounding for [u], while, in the latter, no such lip rounding occurs since the vowel [æ] is not rounded. Thus, in pronunciation, aspects of one sound may be present in the production of an earlier sound. In writing, however, the symbols are discrete; a following vowel has no effect on how the letter *s* is printed. By "sounding out" a letter in isolation from the sounds represented by other letters in a word, beginning readers often so distort the actual pronunciation that they fail to recognize the series of independent sounds they have produced as constituting words that are familiar in their normal spoken form. Furthermore, certain sounds cannot be produced in isolation; they must be accompanied by a vowel. This is the case for stops, such as [p] and [t]. To produce [p] you must either block the air stream at the lips and hold it, in which case no sound at all will be produced, or you must then release the lips, in which case the [p] will be followed by a vowel similar to [ə]. The situation is similar for other stops. It is not surprising that children often have difficulty recognizing even such simple words as *pat* when they use a "sounding out" approach. Rather than producing [pæt], this method usually results in the distorted pronunciation [pəætə]. Hearing [pəætə], most adults would fail to realize that the word was *pat,* too. Some children learn, on their own, to ignore the distortions introduced by "sounding out." Attempting to eliminate the distortion by having students "say the sounds more quickly" is rarely successful since it ignores the continuous nature of speech and retains the concept that each sound can be pronounced in isolation.

From a practical standpoint, a phonics approach to the teaching, and the learning, of reading is difficult to justify. In order to learn the assumed relation between letters and sounds (and remember that letters actually correspond to phonemic representations, not to sounds), children must master rules called phonic generalizations. Consider, as an example, one rule for vowels: "When two vowels go walking, the first one does the talking" (or, stated less childishly, "when two vowel letters occur in sequence, the first is usually pronounced while the second is silent"). The sounds referred to are the names of the alphabet letters, so that the sound of *e* is [iy]. The rule holds for many words, such as *bead, pie, boat,* and *speak.* However, there are a larger number of exceptions; at least one study (cited in "Further Exploration") found more words that disobey the rule than that follow it. Consider: *chief, view, sound, quick, build, said,* and *friend.* In order to provide for the exceptions, new phonic generalizations can be composed and taught to children: "When the letters *ie* occur together, the *i* is usually silent and the *e* is pronounced." This new rule will account for the pronunciation of *chief,* but it does not work for *pie.* Children now have two overlapping and partially contradictory rules. How can this help when they encounter a new word, such as *field?* If children know and recognize the word, they will be able to pronounce it without recourse to their phonic generalizations. If they do not know or recognize the word, the phonic generalizations will not help them since they won't know which one is applicable. Thus, phonics is in the position of adding more and more rules to take care of exceptions, and each added rule is itself subject to exceptions. The result is between 100 and 200 phonics rules, most of which lead from spelling to the wrong pronunciation in one out of four applications.

The fundamental problem with phonic generalizations is not that the generalizations are the wrong ones. If that were the case, it would merely be necessary for reading specialists to find the right generalizations. The basic problem with phonics is that it is inherently wrong. The phonics approach is based on an incorrect view of the nature of an alphabetic writing system. Phonics implies that our writing system is phonetic, with symbols corresponding to sounds. We have discovered, however, that English spelling is phonemic (eliminating redundant features) and, more importantly, morphophonemic (providing a single spelling for a morpheme, no matter what that morpheme's various pronunciations might be).

From the point of view of the child learning to read, phonics poses yet another difficulty. As was observed in the chapters on native language acquisition, some children are not able to isolate the individual sounds in words until AFTER they are able to read. Without this linguistic ability, any method that tries to teach reading through the identification of letters with individual sounds is certain to fail. And, of course, the reading process involves much more than the identification of sounds. Even for children who are able to isolate sounds and who can overcome the distortions resulting from sounding out words, and even if phonic generalizations could be revised, phonics would remain basically incomplete as a method of learning to read. It ignores the fact that reading with comprehension involves words and sentence structures.

Some readers may be puzzled at the amount of space we have devoted to the inadequacies of phonics, especially since many reading specialists and teachers are aware of the problems discussed here. The situation in the schools, unfortunately, is frequently one that promotes phonics as the primary method for reading instruction. In some cases, pressures from parents, recalling phonics lessons in their childhood, prompt school officials to implement a phonics approach. In other cases, the teachers and administrators responsible for selecting materials were trained at a time when the phonics approach had not been investigated scientifically and was accepted without question. It is not at all uncommon to find elementary schools investing large amounts of money in the purchase of phonics-oriented reading materials and exercises that are used, not only for beginning readers, but up to the fourth grade level, long after students have learned to read. The preliterate child, who has no knowledge of reading, may benefit from some initial instruction in the relation between sounds and letters. This information can serve as the key that opens the door to reading. But once children are aware that writing is related to the language they already know, they may be able to activate their linguistic knowledge and language acquisition capacities and apply them to the task of learning to read. At this point, learning to read is accomplished by reading, not by "circling the words that have the long vowel sound of *e*."

Another common method of teaching reading, the **whole-word** approach (sometimes referred to as **look-and-say**), seeks to avoid the problems involved in phonics and to bypass the apparent irregularities of English spelling by attempting to have children recognize whole words, rather than sound them out. This method fails to utilize the great number of regularities in English spelling, regularities that are undoubtedly important in converting a nonreading child into a literate person. It seems likely that a whole-word approach, when it succeeds, does so because of the child and not because of the method. Just as children make a great many generalizations from very restricted samples in learning to speak their native language before they enter school, so they may very well continue to make similar generalizations about reading no matter how they are taught.

While the whole-word method does avoid some of the problems inherent in phonics, it, too, is basically incomplete for many of the same reasons. Children learn to recognize words in this approach through the use of various clues, such as the overall shape and configuration of words, making sense through context, identifying roots and affixes, and so on. These skills are certainly useful to a reader, yet they alone do not constitute true reading. As has been noted, full comprehension depends on interpreting the surface structure of a text and then utilizing one's internalized knowledge of syntax and semantics to comprehend the meaning that underlies what is visible. In actual classroom practice, it is unusual for children to be instructed beyond the point where they can recognize words. From that point, they are more or less on their own. Fortunately, the knowledge about syntax and semantics required to read with comprehension already constitutes part of the child's linguistic competence by virtue of the fact that he or she knows the native language. Therefore, given a start in the classroom, children normally teach themselves to comprehend the meaning of phrases, sentences, paragraphs, and books.

Since there are clear indications that children learn many aspects of reading without being overtly taught, it is reasonable to at least consider the possibility that learning to read is a natural process, just as learning to speak is a natural process. Once the child has recognized that writing is a way of representing language, the process of reading may develop naturally in most children, dependent only on a sufficient amount of exposure to written material, a particular level of physical and mental development (normally achieved by the age of seven years), and the type of positive attitude and motivation that have been found essential for successful foreign language learning. There are societies in which children are not taught to read in school; rather, they are not even permitted to begin school until they have learned to read (this situation has been reported for Iceland). It should also be noted that even in those cases where the teaching of reading occurs, the learning of reading may be independent. That is, just because a teacher has utilized a phonics, whole-word, or some other method in an attempt to teach reading and, then, at the end of several months, the teacher's students have learned to read, it cannot be concluded that the children learned to read BECAUSE OF the teacher's methods. They might have learned to read in spite of those methods. All that can be said with assurance is that the teaching and the learning occurred during the same period of time; we cannot be sure that it was the teaching that produced the learning.

At the current time, the cognitive view of reading is receiving increasing support from the research efforts of educators, linguists, and psychologists. There is a de-emphasis on detailed, structured methods of teaching and a new orientation toward the child's contribution to the learning process, as well as the teacher's role in facilitating that process. As talented teachers have always realized, the teacher must select and provide reading materials that interest and motivate children and that are suitable in terms of content and degree of difficulty. Furthermore, the teacher has the obligation to determine the children's progress in learning to read and to offer special assistance to those who require it.

Frequently, the diagnosis of reading progress is accomplished through tests in which the child is required to read aloud. This is necessary since true reading, which is done silently, is not observable directly, but it must be recognized that the ability to read with comprehension and the ability to read aloud without errors are not equivalent. All readers make errors in that they deviate at times from the printed page. Such deviations are the natural consequence of the reader's active involvement in the reading process, and, indeed, they may be necessary for rapid reading. The deviations are most obvious in reading aloud, but they are not harmful unless they interfere with comprehension. A reader who says *somebody* when the text is *someone* does not have a reading problem, even if he or she makes such substitutions often. The substitution does not interfere with comprehension; in fact, it demonstrates comprehension by showing that the reader has understood the text. Simply counting up the number of mistakes made by a child who reads aloud will not reveal very much about any problems that the child may have. One must consider the types of errors that are made, for, as with native and foreign language acquisition, the analysis of errors reveals the knowledge that underlies the observed performance. Some errors may be natural and harmless, such as the type mentioned above, while others may be simple performance mistakes, occurring randomly and without affecting comprehension. Other errors may be symptomatic of true reading difficulties, as when a child frequently reverses the order of letters in words (reading *was* as *saw* and *but* as *tub*), or when the child reads very slowly, word-by-word, without comprehension, or in cases where the reader omits many words or phrases from the text and thus misses significant portions of the meaning. Still other errors may reflect the child's own dialect, a matter discussed in the next chapter. In any case, the teacher cannot provide effective assistance unless he or she understands the reading process and the basis for any problems that may require attention.

Our discussion has concentrated on only a few aspects of reading. Many other factors lie outside of the domain of the linguist's knowledge, and it is for this reason that linguists should not propose methods for the teaching of reading. The content of reading materials, for example, must be determined by the reading specialist who is familiar with the findings of a variety of disciplines, including psychology and linguistics. Whether or not beginning reading books should include illustrations is not an issue to which linguistics can contribute. Some aspects of the question of content, however, may become better understood if reading instructors are informed about the nature of language and the linguistic abilities of children. Studies of child language acquisition, for example, show quite clearly that children's speech is usually far more sophisticated than the written material which they are given to read. Children spontaneously produce long, complex sentences, and yet most beginning readers contain short, simple sentences. There may be psychological advantages, in terms of learning, to the use of such simple sentences, but the matter has never been investigated fully because many educators in the past have merely assumed, incorrectly, that children do not use more complex syntactic structures in their speech. Such issues deserve careful study, but the study must be based on a valid view of language.

There are many other aspects of the reading process and the teaching and learning of reading that have not been mentioned here. "Further Exploration" offers a number of additional resources, but the entire issue is of such great complexity that no single scholar or field of study can hope to encompass all aspects.

WRITING

Writing involves at least three separate tasks: the formation of letters; spelling and the rules of punctuation, capitalization, and syllabification; and the creative aspects of communicating on paper. The first task involves motor skills and is unrelated to matters of language. The second involves the relationship between the writing system and the sound system of a language, and the third is so complex that no real method has ever been devised to cope with the task.

Many of the comments made above about the teaching of reading are relevant to matters of spelling. Certainly, any method that teaches spelling by the converse of the "sounding out" approach to reading will encounter the same advantages and disadvantages. To the extent that letters do represent sounds in a consistent way, the student will be able to determine the spelling of a word by carefully observing its pronunciation. But, in general, this works only with simple words like *pad, bag, sad, mad,* and *glad.* A child who attempts to use pronunciation as the basis for determining the spelling of *photograph* (pronounced [fótəgræf]) or of *sophomore* (pronounced [sáfmɔr]) is bound to encounter difficulties. If the child has been told explicitly that spelling reflects pronunciation, he or she can either believe the teacher and spell poorly or decide that the teacher is wrong and try to determine independently how the system works.

The teaching of spelling must involve concentration on the regularities in the writing system of English. Consider the words in Figure 25.1. In the first column, the letters *oo* represent the sound [ʊ]; in the second column, *oo* represents the sound [u]. There is a system at work here; generally, *oo* represents [ʊ] before *k* and [u] elsewhere. There are exceptions to this generalization, such as *flood,* but, in teaching spelling, it is more helpful to the child to organize materials in such a way that they reflect the generalization. For example, one spelling lesson might include the words from column I, and the next lesson could then deal with those in column II. The child is more likely to see the pattern than he would if each lesson included some words from both columns. In order to organize material in this way, the teacher must be aware of how words sound and not just how they are spelled. The children are aware of pronunciation, and they often try to make use of it in their spelling. Children who spell *everything* as *evrithin* are coming as close as they can to spelling the word in the way they may normally pronounce it. In addition to mastering generalizations about sounds and spelling, children must also learn that this relationship is not always consistent.

At a later stage in spelling, children, and even adults, encounter difficulties relating to the morphophonemic properties of our writing system. Is the word pronounced [kánfədəns] spelled *confidance* or *confidence*? No rule relating sound and spelling will help in a case like this one because the vowel sound [ə] can be represented by the letter *a,* the letter *e,* or, for that matter, by other vowel letters as well. If the speller is aware of the morphophonemic aspect of English spelling, he or she can use a strategy of searching for

Figure 25.1

Column I	Column II
book	room
shook	soon
took	tooth
cook	smooth
look	loose
hook	boot
nook	bloom

words related to the word in question. Consider, for example, the words *confide, confident,* and *confidential.* Knowing the spelling of any one of these words provides a clue as to the correct vowel letter for use in the final syllable of the problem word. The best clue comes from the word *confidential;* even if a person were not certain of the spelling, the vowel in question occurs here under stress in speech, and stressed vowels have the most direct relation to spelling. Thus, the sophisticated speller, aware of the morphophonemic nature of English spelling and able to compare words sharing particular morphemes, can resolve questions of spelling. For the question raised above, of course, the answer is that the correct spelling is *confidence.*

Punctuation and syllabification are also related to speech, but, as with spelling, the relationship is often indirect. The use of a period at the end of a written sentence may correspond to a slight pause and/or drop in the pitch of the voice for a similar spoken sentence, but this is not always the case. Furthermore, one of the main problems in punctuation, the use of commas, is more closely related to the syntactic structure of a sentence than to the location of pauses in speech. This relationship can be utilized in teaching punctuation, but its use requires that the teacher be aware of syntactic structure and understand the structures of English. Rules for breaking words into syllables are often said to be based on pronunciation, but, when these rules are examined, one finds that they are usually based on the morpheme structure of words. Thus, the word *longer* is pronounced [lɔŋ-gər] in many dialects (the hyphen indicates syllable division), but since *er* represents a suffix, the word is divided as *long-er* in print.

An understanding of the differences between speech and aspects of writing such as spelling, punctuation, and syllabification can be valuable in helping a teacher to understand the reason for certain common errors in children's writing. As a final example, consider the problem many children have when learning to use the apostrophe correctly. It is not uncommon to find children writing *girls* when in fact they should use *girl's*. The reason is quite simple: the two words sound exactly the same so the child writes them in the same way. Furthermore, the apostrophe has no phonetic content; that is, the apostrophe itself does not represent a sound. Therefore, the spoken form of a word contains no indication of whether or not an apostrophe should be used in writing it.

When we turn our attention to more complicated aspects of writing, linguistic facts about syntax and child language acquisition play an important role. The passages children write for a teacher are often monotonous repetitions of simple sentences, as in the following excerpt from a writing assignment completed by a second-grade student:

> Mother was baking a cake. She wanted some milk. Billy said "I will go to the store." Mother gave Billy some money. He put on his coat. At the corner, he met a friend. The friend had a new bike.

The child who wrote this passage produces far more complex, and interesting, sentences in his everyday speech, as the following samples indicate.

(3)   I saw a long train which was being pulled by three locomotives.

(4)   That boy in the red jacket is the one who lives in the apartment across the hall from ours.

Both of these sentences involve the use of the syntactic process of embedding. Notice, for example, the presence of clauses with the relative pronouns *which* and *who*. The child obviously knows how to use such sentences, and yet he avoided them in his writing. He could have written sentence (5):

(5)   At the corner, he met a friend who had a new bike.

What accounts for this discrepancy between speech and writing? It is impossible to answer the question at the present time, for the matter has not been investigated. Yet two points may be relevant. The first involves a common practice on the part of writing teachers, that is, a tendency to correct every error of spelling and punctuation children make when they write. Although spelling and punctuation must be taught, it is not clear that constant attention to such matters is desirable. A child who is constantly corrected for errors in the placement of commas may avoid writing the complex sentences in which commas may be needed. The second relevant factor is the kind of written material to which a child has been exposed. We noted earlier that children's readers often contain simple sentences, and, in the case of the child who wrote the passage quoted above, one of the readers he had used contained the following passage.

John and Billy went to a movie. The picture was about a horse. He was brown and had white spots. His name was Spotty.

A child who uses such a reader may learn something that no one intends to teach—that written material should consist of awkward sequences of simple sentences. In fact, the situation is somewhat the reverse, for written material usually is syntactically more complex than speech.

People's ability to make use of their linguistic competence is often improved when they encounter written material. For example, native speakers of English would seldom say a sentence like (6):

(6)   The book that the girl who is in the class I teach bought is pornographic.

If you were to hear sentence (6), your first reaction might be that it is ungrammatical. Yet, when you see it in writing, (6) makes perfect sense. You know what it means, and you can determine that it does follow the rules of sentence embedding in English. You might reject the sentence as being bad style, but the point is that, when it is written, you can understand it, whereas in its spoken form it might be incomprehensible. Although sentence (6) is an extreme example, it illustrates the fact that writing can, and does, make use of language in a way that differs from speech. Written material can be reread if the reader misses some aspect of meaning. Writers themselves can revise and refine what they have written. The beginning writer, as well as the beginning reader, must learn that there are differences between speech and writing and that, in order to write well, one cannot merely set down on paper the same sentences he or she might use in conversation. It is unfortunate that the practices of many textbooks and teachers encourage some children to write sentences that are less complex than those they use in speech. The opposite should hold true if the children are to eventually acquire an adequate, mature written style.

Although we have discussed the teaching of spelling and writing here, it is entirely possible that these aspects of language are learned naturally, in much the same manner proposed above for reading. From exposure to a substantial amount of written material, the child may be able to internalize the principles of spelling, punctuation, organization of written material, and so on, that constitute acceptable written work. Extensive reading, coupled with extensive opportunities to write, may be more effective in ultimately producing a competent writer than particular skills exercises that focus attention on spelling problems, the identification of paragraphs, or the use of the apostrophe. Indeed, such exercises usually are testing, rather than teaching, devices. For example, when we give children a list of unpunctuated statements and questions and ask them to place periods after the statements and interrogation marks after the questions, we are merely determining whether or not they have learned to do this. The exercise itself provides practice in the task, but it does not teach the knowledge required to perform the task.

PROBLEMS IN LANGUAGE DEVELOPMENT

The great majority of children in the early school years require no special training in language acquisition, but there are, of course, some who are in need of assistance from speech therapists. The identification of those children who actually require speech therapy is not as straightforward as it might seem. Some aspects of language normally are not acquired until after the age of five or six; these should not be confused with problems in acquisition. Similarly, dialect differences must be distinguished from actual articulation problems. Those who are responsible for the identification and treatment of language acquisition problems must be well informed about normal language acquisition and about regional and social dialect variations. In a survey of language and linguistics, it is not possible to include a detailed description of common language development difficulties, but at least a few basic comments are necessary.

Many children enter kindergarten lacking the full set of sound segments in English. It is, for example, not uncommon for five year olds to have difficulty articulating [r]. The child's [r] often sounds like [w] to the adult although, upon close observation, the so-called [w] children substitute for [r] is usually articulated differently from the [w] they use in words where adults also produce [w]. Thus, the child's articulation of *red* may sound like [wɛd], *wed,* to the adult, but it is actually different from the child's production of *wed* itself. Difficulties with [r], as well as with segments such as [l] and [s], at this early age do not require speech therapy, for they are usually overcome within a year. If such problems persist up to the age of seven, however, investigation of the child's language development is called for.

More serious speech problems usually can be identified by the age of five, although it is not always easy to determine how such problems might be treated. Treatment methods lie within the domain of the speech therapist, but a few basic principles from the linguistic research on phonology are relevant. First, the use of the abbreviatory phonetic symbols by therapists should not obscure the fact that every sound segment consists of a combination of phonetic features. Many sounds share a number of features in common and differ from one another by only one or two vocal tract activities. This fact can be useful in speech therapy since it may lead to a more efficient and effective means of articulation training. Thus, the child who produces [m], [n], and [ŋ] as [b], [d], and [g], respectively, does not need to be taught three separate sounds. The problem sound segments all share the feature [+ nasal], which is the primary vocal tract activity that distinguishes them from [b], [d], and [g]. The therapist, therefore, need work only with the vocal tract activity of lowering the velum. Once the child is able to control that action, his difficulty with all three [+ nasal] sound segments will be overcome more or less simultaneously.

Another linguistic concept of use to the speech therapist is the basic distinction between linguistic competence and linguistic performance. Even those children with severe speech disorders often possess a fully developed linguistic competence in that they know the sound system of their language. However, their performance may fail to reflect this knowledge because of some physiological, neurophysiological, or psychological problem. For example, children with some physical disorder in the blade of the tongue may not be able to articulate [+ coronal] consonants correctly, but they may still be able to understand the difference between someone else's production of *pea* and *tea* (where [p] is [− coronal], [t] is [+ coronal], and this feature constitutes the essential distinction between the two segments). Such children know the distinction even though they are physically incapable of producing it themselves. Recognition of this fact will enable the therapist to concentrate on the articulation problem itself, rather than wasting time and effort in instructing such children about the nature of the distinction—a matter that they already know.

Those working with articulation problems should also keep in mind the continuous nature of normal speech. In the past, it was common practice for many therapists to work on isolated sound segments rather than on sounds in the context of normal words. Thus, if a child had difficulty with the feature of [abrupt release] and therefore with the stops [p, b, t, d, k, g], therapists would attempt to have children produce these sounds, failing to recognize that any attempt to produce them in isolation normally results in a distortion that involves the occurrence of a vowel along with the consonant. In the case of children who are suspected of having hearing problems that affect their speech development, tests have been administered in which the child is asked to respond to isolated sound segments or to tape-recorded words that are combinations of sound segments originally produced in isolation. When children fail to respond with a correct identification of the sound or word, it is then assumed that they have a hearing problem. In fact, it may be that the sound or word has been so distorted by the manner in which it is produced that not even a child with normal hearing would recognize it. Consider the word *sun* (or its homonym *son*), normally pronounced [sən]. If one pronounces the word "sound-by-sound," the result is very likely to be [sə]–[ʔə]–[nə]. The phonetic symbol [ʔ] represents a glottal stop, produced by a temporary blockage of the air stream at the vocal cords. This sound occurs frequently in English when speakers attempt to produce a vowel, starting from the prespeech position discussed in Part 3. The glottal stop commonly occurs between the vowels, and sometimes initially, in the negative expression often spelled *uhuh*, [ʔə̃ʔə̃]. In some dialects of English, a glottal stop is occasionally used in place of a [t], as in the pronunciation [baʔəl] for *bottle*. Thus, children who hear [ʔ] in a word may interpret it as [t]. In the case of [sə]–[ʔə]–[nə], they may identify the word as *stun* rather than *sun*. There is no hearing problem involved here; the "incorrect" identification is due to a distorted stimulus to which the children have been asked to respond.

Since our primary concern in this chapter, and throughout this book, is with normal language development and properties of language shared by the majority of speakers, we will say no more about problems in development. Nevertheless, many aspects of the linguistic study of language are essential for an understanding of nonnormal language development and the preparation of methods for treating language development problems.

SUMMARY

Linguistics offers no particular method for the teaching of reading or writing to young children. Nevertheless, every teacher should possess a valid understanding of the nature of language, the relationship between speech and writing, and the facts of child language acquisition. Only in this way can teachers detect and thereby avoid the inadequacies of existing methods and practices in reading and writing instruction. Many of the facts and hypotheses of modern linguistics call into question some of the most basic assumptions in the field of elementary school education insofar as this area deals with language and language use. Educators, linguists, psychologists, and others who are concerned about children, learning, and language must join together in research on the reading process, the learning of reading and writing, and the possible development of materials and techniques that will effectively assist teachers to facilitate learning in children. Similarly, the identification and treatment of language development problems in children requires a basic understanding of the properties of language and the characteristics of normal language development.

FURTHER EXPLORATION

The literature available on the teaching and learning of reading is overwhelmingly extensive, and it is impossible to provide a truly representative sampling with just a few titles. One major work of special significance due to the depth and scope of coverage is *The Psychology of Reading* by Eleanor J. Gibson and Harry Levin; in over 500 pages of text, the authors discuss the psychological, linguistic, developmental, and practical aspects of the reading process and the teaching and learning of reading. A number of perspectives are offered in the articles contained in *Language by Ear and by Eye,* edited by James F. Kavanagh and Ignatius G. Mattingly, and *Basic Studies on Reading,* edited by Harry Levin and Joanna P. Williams. *Psycholinguistics and Reading,* by Frank Smith, presents a cognitive view of the reading process; the main themes are summarized in the final chapter, ''Twelve Easy Ways to Make Learning to Read Difficult.'' A more behavioral approach is offered by Jeanne S. Chall in *Learning to Read: The Great Debate.* A short article by Theodore Clymer examines ''The Utility of Phonic Generalizations in the Primary Grades'' and concludes that many are of limited value (in the anthology *Reading Instruction: Dimensions and Issues,* edited by William K. Durr). A detailed and practical approach for the analysis of readers' errors is offered by Yetta M. Goodman and Carolyn L. Burke in *Reading Miscue Inventory Manual: Procedure for Diagnosis and Evaluation.*

The relationship between letters and phonology, relevant to both reading and writing, is examined in depth by Richard L. Venezky in *The Structure of English Orthography.*

Martin Joos, in "Language and the School Child" (in Emig et al. 1966), provides a number of suggestions as to how the teacher can use the child's knowledge of his language in his own compositions. Reading and writing, as well as other topics involving language in the elementary school, are discussed clearly, with many examples, by Bradford Arthur in *Teaching English to Speakers of English*.

Many studies of problems in language development presuppose substantial technical background in speech therapy. One widely-used introductory text is *Speech Correction: Principles and Methods* by Charles Van Riper; see especially Chapter 4, "Delayed Speech and Language." More linguistically oriented is *Principles of Childhood Language Disabilities*, edited by John V. Irwin and Michael Marge. Of particular interest to those with a basic background in linguistics is the article "Children with Language Problems: What's the Problem?" by Paula Menyuk (in Dato 1975).

1. A person untrained in proofreading will often fail to note errors of the following types when reading a manuscript: omitted letters (*consitution,* rather than *constitution*), transposed letters (*belnog,* rather than *belong*), omitted words (*people tend believe,* rather than *people tend to believe*), repeated words (*Harry is is angry*), and even entire repeated lines. (The last two occur most frequently at the end of one page and the beginning of the next or, in the case of omitted or repeated words, at the end of one line and the beginning of the next.) Explain this in terms of the reading process as discussed in this chapter.

2. The following examples of phonic generalizations are the type studied by Theodore Clymer. For each, two examples are given; the first is a word that follows the generalization; the second is an exception. Cite three additional words (or more) of each type for each of the generalizations.

(a) If a word has only one vowel letter and that letter is word-final, the letter usually will be pronounced like its alphabet name (for example, *a* is [ey], *e* is [iy], *o* is [ow]).

she   do

(b) When a word has two vowel letters, one of which is final *e*, the final *e* is silent and the other vowel letter generally is pronounced like its alphabet name.

made   some

(c) The sequence of letters *ow* normally is pronounced [ow].

low   cow

(d) The letter *g* usually is pronounced [ǰ] before the letter *i* or *e*.

gin   give

3. The following spellings come from the work of a second-grade girl and a seventh-grade girl. The correct spellings are given in parentheses.

Second Grade		*Seventh Grade*	
capten	(captain)	benefitiary	(beneficiary)
choklet	(chocolate)	numberous	(numerous)
meny	(many)	pronounciation	(pronunciation)
minits	(minutes)	repeatition	(repetition)

There is a fundamental difference between the kind of errors made by the second grader and those made by the seventh grader. Characterize this difference in terms of the relationships between written symbols, sounds, and phonemic representations.

CHAPTER 2626262626262626262626262626(

SOCIAL DIALECTS AND THE SCHOOLS

One of the central issues in education today involves the topic of nonstandard dialects. Many children, in all parts of the country, enter school as speakers of dialects that differ from the regional standard dialect of their area. Educators, school administrators, and parents are all confronted with a major question: should schools attempt to teach such students a standard dialect? There is no ready answer to this question, for the matter involves complex social issues, as well as linguistic factors. Our purpose in this chapter is not to propose a solution to the problems presented by social dialects, but to outline some basic, relevant linguistic considerations that must be taken into account in dealing with the topic in an informed manner.

BASIC ISSUES

The question of whether or not speakers of nonstandard dialects should be exposed in school to instruction in a standard dialect is basically a nonlinguistic matter. From the point of view of linguistic science, all dialects of a language are equally systematic, complete, productive, and useful as a means of communication among the people who know them. Furthermore, there is no linguistic necessity for everyone in a society to speak the same dialect. In fact, within our own society, there is widespread general acceptance of regional dialect variations. This objective perspective, along with societal concern for the rights of minorities, children, and others, has led recently to several statements from educational organizations in support of children's right to use their own dialect or language. While entirely valid linguistically, this position may overlook important nonlinguistic factors relevant to the issues of social dialects.

Any dialect, whether it is considered standard or nonstandard, is fully appropriate for use among other speakers of the same dialect. The difficulty arises in situations of intercommunication among speakers of two different social dialects, for it is in such cases that popular, emotional attitudes about dialects may affect the situation. Those who use some variety of nonstandard English in the classroom may receive low grades from a teacher who speaks a standard dialect. Similarly, adults who apply for a job involving contact with speakers of a standard dialect may be rejected if their own dialect is nonstandard. Therefore, the ability to use a standard dialect of English is often socially advantageous to those who encounter speakers of such standard dialects. In the education of young children, one argument for teaching a variety of standard English is that this knowledge may better prepare them for situations they may encounter later in life. Ideally, one should work to remove the linguistic and social prejudices that lead to this conclusion. At the present time, however, such prejudices do exist, and one immediate, practical means of coping with them is for speakers of nonstandard English to learn a standard dialect.

If the parents and educators of a school system decide that speakers of nonstandard dialects should acquire a standard dialect of English, two other basic questions must be answered. First, it must be determined what role the standard dialect is to play in relation to the nonstandard dialect already known and used by the children. Should the standard dialect be used to replace the nonstandard? Or, should the standard dialect serve as a supplement to the nonstandard dialect? No matter which role is assigned to the standard dialect, it is also necessary to investigate those factors that will affect the success of children in achieving the established dialect goal.

The replacement approach to standard dialects ignores the fact that the reason children learn a nonstandard dialect in the first place is because their family, friends, and neighbors use that dialect rather than the local standard variety of English. Thus, any attempt to eliminate children's nonstandard dialect is probably doomed from the start. No matter what they are taught in school, children will continue to use their original dialect in those situations where it is accepted and used by others. The replacement approach to standard and nonstandard dialects is not feasible in such situations.

Mastering the standard dialect as a supplement to the nonstandard dialect is a more

LANGUAGE, LINGUISTICS, AND TEACHERS

attainable goal. In its most complete form, this approach would lead to **functional bidialectism,** a situation in which speakers know two dialects (one standard and the other nonstandard) and use each in the appropriate situations. For example, the original dialect may be used at home, on the playground, among other speakers of the dialect, and perhaps even in the classroom for informal discussion, but, at the same time, the students use a standard dialect with those people and in those contexts that require it. With functional bidialectism, the individual is able to participate effectively in a linguistically complex society. However, in most cases, functional bidialectism is almost as difficult to achieve as total replacement of the nonstandard dialect because people learn and use the dialect spoken in their environment. If children encounter standard English only during part of the time they are at school, they have little opportunity to learn and use this second dialect. Their own nonstandard dialect will remain dominant. Functional bidialectism describes an ideal situation, one that can be attained only rarely and with difficulty. But there are many degrees of bidialectism. A speaker of nonstandard English can become partially bidialectal by learning to avoid certain nonstandard features in situations where standard English is more appropriate. In the author's native dialect, for example, *bring* and *take* are synonyms in certain cases; this is considered nonstandard by many people. In order to avoid negative reactions, the author uses sentences like (1) only in the company of close friends and speakers of the same dialect.

> (1)   Sally, bring this book to Marcia's office.

In other situations, (2) is used instead.

> (2)   Sally, take this book to Marcia's office.

Whatever degree of mastery of a standard dialect is desirable in a particular case, it should be noted that the teaching of standard English as a supplement to a nonstandard dialect reflects the situation of linguistic and social prejudice discussed above. People rarely suggest that all children become even partially bidialectal in standard and nonstandard English. Only those whose native dialect is considered nonstandard are asked to master a second dialect. Children who speak standard English are not expected to learn a nonstandard dialect of the language, in spite of the fact that they, too, may encounter situations in which their native dialect is not appropriate.

All children are capable of mastering a second language or a second dialect, regardless of their social class, race, economic background, or any other factor except severe physical or psychological problems. It would seem that learning a second dialect should be a simple task for children, especially since standard and nonstandard dialects of English share many forms and rules in common. Although the observers of an unfamiliar dialect notice numerous differences from their own speech, the great similarities are not noted. Given the fact that these similarities do exist, learning a second dialect is less difficult than learning a second language in which the differences are much greater. Yet, despite the child's natural ability and the small number of new facts to be acquired, many children fail to learn standard English no matter what method is used for instruction. The problem is due to those factors discussed in Chapter 23 regarding successful foreign language learning: motivation, learning context, and degree of contact.

While most research on integrative and instrumental language learning has dealt with foreign language instruction, it is not unreasonable to hypothesize that motivation is also a primary factor in successful acquisition of a new dialect. For learning to occur, there must be some positive motivation, even if this motivation is merely instrumental. This poses a serious problem for elementary school children whose native dialect is considered non-standard. Until they entered school, no one questioned their ability to use their language. They communicated successfully with the people they knew. Suddenly, they may find their teacher trying to get them to speak differently—to use an unfamiliar dialect that they rarely encounter outside of the classroom (except perhaps when they watch television). Since they have no need to speak standard English, why should they learn it? Indeed, as mentioned above, the reasons are largely utilitarian and grounded in the attitudes of a large segment of our society that is basically uninformed about language and thus biased in regard to dialect variation. But young children are not aware of the fact that people judge one another according to how they talk. Studies have shown that even many teenagers do not yet realize the social implications of language. Lacking even instrumental motivation to learn a standard dialect of English, children will fail to do so.

Instrumental motivation is a problem for young children who speak nonstandard dialects, and yet, as we have seen in the discussion of foreign language learning, integrative motivation seems to be the key to success. In the case of social dialects, integrative motivation may be particularly difficult to achieve. In some minority communities, there are strong pressures against cultural or linguistic integration. For example, those minority groups who feel that the dominant, white middle class is attempting to eradicate their native language or dialect, as well as their cultural heritage, sometimes propose active resistance to this eradication by refusing to learn or use standard English. This attitude is conveyed to the children of the community, who may then come to consider success in learning standard English as a denial of their ethnic, racial, or social background. Clearly, this is contrary to the attitude that underlies integrative motivation. On the other hand, however, there are minority groups for whom cultural and linguistic integration are positive goals. In such cases, the acquisition of a socially standard dialect is more likely to occur, as indeed has happened for thousands of European immigrants to the United States, as well as for many other people from various racial, ethnic, and social backgrounds.

The context in which the language or dialect to be learned occurs is also a factor important for successful acquisition. As noted earlier with regard to functional bidialectism, it is difficult to acquire a standard dialect if contact with that dialect is limited to the speech of teachers at school. In such cases, parallel to the distinction between foreign and second language, we might best describe the standard dialect as a foreign dialect. For the standard dialect to be a second dialect, the situation must be such that this dialect is used quite widely throughout the learner's community. Then, the learner will have extensive opportunities to utilize the dialect in the natural communication situations that promote dialect acquisition.

TEACHERS

Whether or not a school system has a policy of actually teaching a standard dialect of English, teachers must be informed about any nonstandard dialects used by their students.

Both the nature of social dialect variation and the linguistic properties of particular dialects must be understood for a teacher to be effective and able to relate to students in a positive manner.

Perhaps the most common, and also the most damaging, pitfall for teachers in dealing with nonstandard dialects is that of attitude. Even inadvertently, it is easy for the teacher whose own dialect is standard to convey an impression that the students' native dialect is not only nonstandard but somehow "bad." Young children may interpret such an attitude to mean that they themselves, or their families, are bad, and, as a result, they may become hostile toward the teacher, or the children's self-image and pride may suffer. Neither situation provides a desirable atmosphere for learning. Teachers should understand, and be able to express to their students, that dialect variation is normal, that all dialects are linguistically equal and "good," and that dialects may vary in appropriateness according to variations in context and situation. It will also be helpful for the teacher to become informed about the attitudes on dialects of the local community, for these, of course, will affect student motivation and contact with standard dialects of English.

Related to attitude is a particularly disturbing, but rather common, misconception about the relationship between dialect and mental ability. In the past, some educators who were uninformed about social dialects maintained that children who spoke nonstandard English were mentally deficient and unable to think or to reason. There is absolutely no truth in this position, and yet there have been documented cases in several states of children being placed in special classes or schools for the mentally retarded—solely because their native dialect was not standard English. There can be no excuse for the ignorance that led to such actions, and it would be comforting to believe that similar cases do not occur today. Unfortunately, there are still those in our school systems who maintain that children "have no language" unless they speak standard English and that, therefore, such children cannot think, learn, or be taught.

All of these attitude problems and misconceptions are avoidable, particularly when the teacher knows the linguistic properties of the students' nonstandard dialect, and more so when the teacher actually knows and can use the dialect. In situations where teacher and student speak quite different native social dialects, bidialectism is even more important for the teacher than it is for the students.

While many of the features distinguishing a particular nonstandard dialect from a standard dialect are relatively minor, some differences can lead to failure in communication. A teacher must be able to "translate" such material, both to understand what the students say and to enable the students to understand the teacher. Some examples from Black English:

(3) He be getting down. ('He performs well.')
(4) Henry, he greased.   ('Henry ate a lot of food
                           quickly and he looks like he
                           really enjoyed it.')

Knowledge of both standard and nonstandard dialects of English is of enormous practical value to the teacher, particularly in schools where policy demands that students learn and use a standard dialect. With such knowledge, the teacher can predict those aspects of standard English that will be especially difficult for the children and will know which aspects of standard English are shared by the nonstandard dialect and need not be taught. In addition, by knowing the nonstandard dialect, the teacher can distinguish between differences in pronunciation that are due to the dialect and differences that may reflect true speech development problems. A child who says [tif] and [wɪf] rather than [tiθ] and [wɪθ] may have a speech problem, but if the use of [f] for [θ] in all but very formal speech is part of his or her native dialect, there is no reason to conclude that this is anything except a dialect difference. The same point holds true for regional dialect differences, and teachers should be aware of these facts as well. For example, in much of the midwestern section of the country, people pronounce the words *merry, marry,* and *Mary* in exactly the same way, and there is no reason why they should not do so. English contains many homonyms, and, although these three words are distinct from one another in some dialects, it is probably a waste of valuable classroom time for a teacher to insist that children learn to distinguish the words in a region where even the most educated speakers do not do so. Similarly, the use of [w] rather than [hw] in words like *when, which, where,* and *why* is a regional characteristic, and neither pronunciation is more "correct" than the other. It is true that our writing system distinguishes *which* from *witch,* for example, but that does not mean that there must be a difference in pronunciation, as demonstrated by many pairs of homonyms that are spelled differently, such as *plane/plain, fare/fair, eye/I, cite/sight,* and *knot/not.*

As with native language acquisition, and possibly for foreign languages, it is not clear that a second dialect can actually be taught. Instead, under the ideal conditions of integrative motivation and extensive contact, children may acquire a second dialect naturally, without special instruction. Conditions in schools, however, are usually less than ideal, and teachers may be required to provide instruction in standard English even in the absence of student motivation or opportunities for contact with and use of the standard dialect. There is no "linguistic teaching method" for such situations, but to some extent, teachers may be able to adapt techniques from foreign language instruction. Some of the principles and methods of the audio-lingual and cognitive approaches could be useful in teaching a standard dialect of English to speakers of other dialects. But there are aspects of the dialect situation that are quite different from that of foreign language teaching. It should be recalled from Part 8 that most discussions of foreign language instruction are concerned with teaching a language to adults, or to young people who are past the age of puberty. Yet, it is very often in the elementary school that the dialect issue is raised, and it may be that young children learn language best in ways that differ from those which succeed with older students. Thus, while foreign language teaching methods may be useful in teaching some aspects of standard English to high school students, some totally different approach may be required for a successful elementary school program. It is not surprising that different methods may be desirable for different age groups, especially if one keeps in mind the apparently greater difficulty teenagers and adults have in learning a foreign language, as compared to the relative ease with which many children accomplish the task. In fact, the ease with which children learn foreign languages indicates that instruction in a standard dialect of English, if it is to be carried out at all, should begin as early as possible, thereby utilizing this natural ability.

LANGUAGE AND DIALECT MAINTENANCE

Children who speak nonstandard dialects are not the only ones affected by the matters discussed above. There are a number of linguistic minorities in the United States who constantly confront a society that, as a whole, is intolerant of language, as well as dialect, differences. Consider the situation of children from a low socioeconomic background whose native language is Spanish. Their educational position is a difficult one. They may not speak English at all, and, if they do, it may not be a standard dialect. Thus, in many school systems, they will be required to learn either a second dialect of English or English as a foreign language. Most school systems confronted with large numbers of children who are not native speakers of English have special programs in English as a foreign language. But children are often asked not only to learn English but also to abandon their native language. Spanish-speaking children may not be permitted to use Spanish in the classroom; in fact, their teacher may not even know the language. Similarly, in many of the boarding schools administered by the federal government for American Indian children, the teachers do not know the language of the students, and, thus, directly or indirectly, these students are discouraged from using Navaho, Hopi, or whatever their native language might be. The entire situation with regard to such matters is somewhat paradoxical. Millions of dollars are spent by school districts throughout the country to teach foreign languages to native speakers of English, and knowledge of a second language is generally considered to be a worthwhile educational goal, particularly for high school students. Yet, there are students who already know another language that conditions in their schools prohibit them from using.

In recent years, a number of progressive school systems have adopted a policy of **language maintenance,** in which continued use of the native language is encouraged. For the child who speaks Spanish, the school would provide some experiences in which Spanish is the language of instruction and communication. Such an approach requires bilingual teachers, but the demands placed on the teacher with respect to language are no greater than those placed on students. Language maintenance programs are now required by law for school systems in which there are children whose native language is not English.

It is clear that a parallel exists betweeen language maintenance programs and a possible dialect maintenance program for speakers of nonstandard English. In fact, such a program could be an integral part of any approach that teaches a standard dialect as a supplement to, rather than a replacement for, a nonstandard dialect. A policy of language or dialect maintenance, in which it is clear that the standard dialect of English is not intended as a replacement for the native language or dialect, presents children with the opportunity to learn and use a standard dialect without abandoning their own.

READING AND WRITING

Children who speak a nonstandard dialect of English or who are not native speakers of English encounter special difficulties in learning to read and write. In the early school years, they are presented with written material in an unfamiliar dialect and are expected to master the equally unfamiliar task of reading in the same way as would someone who speaks the standard dialect. The difficulty is compounded by the almost universal practice in our schools of evaluating ability to read by having children read aloud. Teachers often confuse the ability to comprehend the meaning of a written passage with the ability to pronounce it according to the patterns of standard English. Learning to read is sometimes a difficult undertaking for children; likewise, learning a second dialect is not an easy task. The child who is expected to accomplish both simultaneously is bound to do poorly in both.

Teachers of reading must take great care to differentiate between errors in reading and dialect differences in pronunciation, grammar, and vocabulary. Children who read aloud and pronounce *pen* as *pin* are not necessarily having difficulty distinguishing the letters *e* and *i*. It may be the case that, in their dialect (whether regional or social), only [ɪ] occurs before a nasal. The children know that the word is *pen,* and they know the meaning involved, but they are pronouncing it according to the phonological rules they possess. Children as well as adults use their knowledge of language in reading, and their primary goal is to understand the meaning of what is written. The particular surface form they produce in reading aloud is irrelevant so long as they succeed in understanding. Consider, for example, the following pairs of sentences:

(5) a. I looked for you last night.

  b. I look fo you las night.

(6) a. Sally is at the library every day.

  b. Sally be at the library every day.

In each case, children who speak a nonstandard dialect might read sentence (a) aloud in the form (b), and the teacher would be inclined to correct them. But both (5b) and (6b) merely reflect features of nonstandard dialects of English. Thus, in (5b), the children's native dialect may be one in which word-final consonant clusters are not produced in all but highly formal speech and [r] is lacking after a vowel. The absence of the past tense indicator [t] on the verb *look* does not necessarily mean that the child has misunderstood the meaning and interpreted the sentence as present tense. There is no reason to assume a failure to read correctly in this case. Similarly, in (6b), the children's substitution of *be* for the written word *is* actually demonstrates that they fully understand the sentence, for it is precisely in the case of habitual action, as described by (6a), that the children themselves would use *be*. Correcting them for (5b) and (6b) is almost certain to confuse the children as to the task at hand. This does not mean that a teacher cannot teach standard English at some other time, but reading difficulties and dialect differences must be recognized as separate areas of concern.

In an attempt to separate reading from dialect variation, some researchers in the fields of education and sociolinguistics have proposed that special reading materials be developed for those children who speak nonstandard dialects that differ substantially from standard English. Such materials would make use of regular English spelling but would contain sentences in the grammatical structures of the nonstandard dialect. For example, the materials for Black English would include sentences like (3), (4), and (6b), as well as double negatives and other grammatical structures used in Black English but not in a standard dialect. Thus, students and teachers could concentrate on actual reading, leaving the acquisition of standard English for another time. Later, the students would be able to apply their knowledge of reading to reading the standard English they learn as a second dialect. The proposal for such special dialect readers is relatively new and certainly controversial. Efforts to implement experimental reading programs using such readers frequently have encountered substantial resistance, not only from teachers and school officials, but also from the parents of children who would be exposed to the materials. Parents who want their children to learn a standard dialect of English sometimes view nonstandard dialect reading material as an attempt by the "establishment" to prevent their children from acquiring standard English. While this is not the intention of those who advocate dialect readers, they find it difficult to convince parents that children may learn to read more easily in this manner and, at a later time, be able to master a standard dialect.

Not all specialists in social dialects and reading support the proposal for nonstandard dialect readers. In fact, some argue that such readers are unnecessary and probably impossible to design and use effectively. Since there are many similarities among all dialects of English, much of what appears in traditional reading materials designed for children will be comprehensible to those who speak nonstandard dialects, as well as to those who speak standard dialects. In those areas of divergence, there are a number of possible reactions to traditional materials for children whose dialect is nonstandard. First, the children may miss some nuances of meaning, but probably these are of relatively little importance for overall comprehension. Second, the children may comprehend standard written English even though they do not speak it (many speakers of nonstandard dialects are able to understand spoken standard dialects). Third, if asked to read aloud, the children may "translate" the standard dialect of the text into their own dialect, as illustrated in (5) and (6) above. Thus, the necessity of special reading materials in nonstandard dialects is open to question, and until there is a substantial body of experimental research to support the need for such materials, it is unlikely that they will be developed and utilized in large quantities. Furthermore, the proper content of such materials is difficult to determine. In the case of Black English, for example, there are varieties of this dialect, differing from group to group. Not all children who speak Black English do so in exactly the same way or to the same extent. Therefore, the writer of a Black English dialect reader must make a decision, perhaps arbitrarily, as to which Black English features to incorporate into the reader. Such readers also require teachers who are sufficiently familiar with the dialect in question; this is not always the case. Whether or not special reading materials are used, both research and classroom experience indicate that children learn to read best when the task of reading is kept clearly distinct from any efforts on the teacher's part to teach a standard dialect to those whose native dialect is nonstandard.

Just as reading and dialect should be kept distinct if the student is to become proficient in the former, so writing and dialect must also be distinguished. Encouraging children to write in their native dialect does not involve the abandonment of correct spelling, punctuation, capitalization, or paragraph formation, for the principles governing these matters apply equally well to nonstandard dialects as to standard dialects. It is unreasonable to expect young students to use standard English grammatical forms in their writing if they have not yet learned them in speech. If standard English is taught at the same time or after writing begins, writing lessons and assignments can be specified as either standard English or the students' native dialect. The important thing is to make clear what is desired.

Creative writing was once a subject reserved for secondary school students, but modern elementary curricula often include it as well. For certain areas of creative writing, the goal is to convey to the reader a sense of realism and involvement. The functional bidialectism discussed earlier can be utilized in meeting this goal by offering students, whether in elementary or high school, the opportunity to make use of both dialects in a writing assignment. For example, a short story may contain descriptive passages in standard English, but the dialogue could be in nonstandard English if appropriate for the characters. Similarly, children who are bilingual could be assigned writing tasks in which they are free to use both English and their other language. In addition to dialogues in stories, poetry and plays offer valuable opportunities for the utilization of standard and nonstandard dialects, as well as other languages. Experienced teachers can readily devise other possibilities.

Reading and writing at the secondary school level may involve many of the factors discussed above for the elementary school level. In addition, however, it should be noted that as children advance in age and reading ability, they are normally exposed to literature that includes the representation of a variety of social and regional dialects (such as the writings of John Steinbeck, Mark Twain, and James Baldwin). Through our educational system, we expect students to be able to comprehend dialects other than their own in written form. In the student's own writing, then, it is only reasonable to permit, and even encourage, the representation of the student's native nonstandard dialect. However, it is also the case that students are expected to master the style of formal written standard English. In teaching this, nonstandard dialects may be utilized indirectly to aid students in increasing their awareness of the differences between dialects and the situations in which each is appropriate. A teacher could, for example, use a kind of "translation" approach in which material is first written with emphasis on content, rather than form or style, and then revised to eliminate any nonstandard forms. Discussion of the dialect and style differences might constitute part of the revision process.

SUMMARY

Those involved with the education of children whose native dialect is nonstandard must determine whether some variety of standard English should be taught, toward what goal, and in what way. Although these issues involve matters well beyond the areas of professional concern to the linguist, certain fundamental linguistic concepts must be understood if the issues are to be discussed and resolved in an informed manner.

A child's use of nonstandard English must not be confused with a speech development problem, for the child has usually acquired his or her native dialect in a complete and normal manner. This dialect, however, may present special problems in reading and writing, particularly if teachers fail to separate their efforts to teach standard English from the teaching of these language-related skills.

Both *The Study of Social Dialects in American English* by Walt Wolfram and Ralph W. Fasold and *Black English: Its History and Usage in the United States* by J. L. Dillard contain a chapter devoted to nonstandard dialects and education. A number of articles relevant to the topic are included in *Language and Poverty: Perspectives on a Theme,* edited by Frederick Williams. Nonstandard urban dialects, especially those of black children, form the focus of *Teaching Standard English in the Inner City,* edited by Ralph W. Fasold and Roger W. Shuy; the articles in this collection deal with methods, as well as basic issues, from a linguistic and sociolinguistic point of view. The third section of *Contemporary English: Change and Variation,* edited by David L. Shores, contains ten articles on problems, methods, and issues of teaching standard English. A particularly valuable article is "The Logic of Nonstandard English" by William Labov (available in Labov 1972a *Language in the Inner City,* as well as in Lester 1973 and Stoller 1975).

Most collections of articles on nonstandard dialects include material on the teaching of reading; one work dealing exclusively with this topic is *Teaching Black Children to Read,* edited by Joan C. Baratz and Roger W. Shuy. Three reading selections using Black English in literature are offered in Part 3 of the book *Black American English: Its Background and Its Usage in the Schools and in Literature,* edited by Paul Stoller.

1. The following letter was written to the author by a thirteen-year-old girl whose native language is Navaho. She has learned English in the local school on a Navaho reservation in New Mexico. At home, she speaks only Navaho since her parents and grandmother do not know English. Consider the letter in terms of your capacity to read material representing a dialect of English different from your own. Do the differences in spelling and syntax have any substantial effect on your comprehension? What conclusions can you draw about the situation of a child whose native dialect is nonstandard but who attempts to read material representing a standard dialect?

> Dear frend.
> I would like to writing you a letter to you. My grandmom is find. She is very very old now and I have no grand farther he died long time ago when I was little girl. My sister is makeing clothe. The Bus driver is to lazy and the Bus always have a flat tire. Our little goat are big now. The weather over here is hat and rain. Have a nice day to all you family. Mary christmas happy New Year. I forget one more to say. Have a nice vacation.

2. Ask a speaker of standard English who has not seen the above letter to read it aloud at a normal rate and with an effort to understand the content. Record the reading. Note any deviations between the printed page and what the reader says. Do the deviations reflect the reader's own dialect? What does this reveal about the reading process?

3. Informally, apply the concept of error analysis (discussed in Chapter 23) to the above letter and list at least six aspects of standard English pronunciation and syntax that present difficulties for a Navaho speaker and that may not occur in the Navaho language.

SOCIAL DIALECTS AND THE SCHOOLS

CHAPTER 272727272727272727272727

THE LATER SCHOOL YEARS

In the later school years, language-related education generally shifts from basic reading, writing, and spelling to more sophisticated aspects of language. Junior and senior high school students, as well as those in colleges, frequently are exposed to some kind of English "grammar" course and to the aesthetically creative use of language in prose and in poetry. Teachers involved in each of these areas can benefit from a knowledge of the basic concepts of linguistics and from an understanding of language in general and English in particular. As with elementary education, not all of this knowledge is appropriate for actual presentation to students, but it is important that teachers themselves are informed about language.

THE LANGUAGE CLASS

In this book, we have surveyed many aspects of the English language, ranging from processes involved in the formation of words to regional and social dialect variation. We have described the grammar of a language as a set of rules and forms that relate the meaning of sentences to pronunciation, and we have noted that this system of rules and forms is extremely complex and abstract. Language becomes an object of wonder to those who realize its complexity, and the fact that human beings are capable of mastering their native language during childhood reflects the enormous powers of the human mind. Yet, for many years, the typical English language course has ignored the most interesting aspects of language in favor of a very narrow, prescriptive view of both English and grammar. Students in "grammar" classes generally learn almost nothing about the set of rules that reflect the principles of sentence formation in English, nor are they taught about the consequences of these rules, such as ambiguity and paraphrase. Instead, the emphasis in such courses is focused on the "correct" usage of isolated vocabulary items. Thus, the differences between *can* and *may, shall* and *will,* and *who* and *whom* become the center of attention, despite the fact that these distinctions exist primarily in textbooks and only rarely in speech. When attention is directed to syntax, it usually involves only the most superficial account of the surface structure of a limited number of sentences. The labels for parts of speech and the dissecting of sample sentences by some form of diagraming do not even scratch the surface of grammar. Yet, because this may be all that they study about English grammar, many students fail to realize what a complex system of communication they know and use, and, quite naturally, they find little of interest or value in the study of language.

In recent years, this situation has been changing, although the change remains gradual. Many teacher training programs now require that all teacher candidates enroll for at least one course in linguistics, and the result is that young teachers often possess a more detailed, valid, and sophisticated understanding of English than their older colleagues. Certainly, a single course or a single introductory text does not provide sufficient preparation for secondary school classes devoted to the study of language. But the initial introduction to linguistics does provide the prospective teacher with a basis on which to build. Without a beginning awareness of the true nature of language, no teacher can even hope to overcome the apathy his or her students may display toward the study of the English language.

It is not immediately obvious to students that their native language is worth studying, and it is important that English teachers recognize this fact. There are a number of valid reasons for investigating English in the high school, but, unless these reasons are pointed out by the teacher, most students will not grasp them on their own.

One assumption underlying much of modern educational philosophy is that students, through their formal education, should develop the kind of self-understanding that leads to the realization of their full potential as human beings. A student can be guided in the development of his potential in a number of ways. Independent study projects, opportunities for self-expression, and formal courses in disciplines directly related to man and his mind are all valuable. Of all topics related to man, none reveals more about the

LANGUAGE, LINGUISTICS, AND TEACHERS

complexity of the mind than the study of language. Individuals who know about language and the abstract forms and extensive system of rules that constitute language know something about themselves.

The humanistic goal of self-awareness is, by itself, worthy of pursuit, but there are also practical reasons for studying language that can be brought to the attention of students.

It was noted in the preceding chapter that even teenagers are often unaware of the role language plays in terms of the judgments that people make of one another. Recognition of the facts of social dialect variation is important to those who may someday wish to function effectively in our linguistically heterogeneous society. Even for the student still in high school, an understanding of language variations can be of practical value. To cite only one example, it is a well-known fact among educators that the verbal individual who makes use of standard English almost always scores higher in tests, class participation, and other academic achievement measures than does the equally intelligent but less talkative student who may speak a nonstandard dialect. From an objective, purely linguistic point of view, this situation may be unfair, but since it does exist, students should be prepared to deal with it.

For the most part, our use of language is an automatic activity, involving little conscious attention to how something is said. But there are times in everyone's life when control of language is important. In writing, for example, it is not enough to put down on paper the same words and sentence structures one would use in speech. Written language is usually more formal than speech, involving more learned vocabulary and more complex syntactic structures. Students who are unaware of these differences may receive poor grades on compositions and term papers, not because their ideas are inadequate, but because they are expressed in an inappropriate manner. A well-designed course on the English language should include discussion of the differences between written and spoken English. Knowledge of these differences can then lead the students to change their style of writing.

Awareness of language has other practical consequences. Consider, for example, the phenomenon of ambiguity. In speech, the context and the rapid flow of conversation often serve to camouflage ambiguous sentences, and listeners fail to notice them. In writing, however, where the reader has the time to consider each sentence carefully, ambiguity is far more obvious and must be avoided. All speakers of English are capable of detecting ambiguity by virtue of their knowledge of the language. But, unless one is consciously aware that ambiguity exists, it is easy to overlook when writing, as well as when speaking. Students who have studied ambiguity as one aspect of language, no matter how informally, are more likely to note any ambiguous sentences in their own writing and to rephrase such sentences before submitting their papers.

An explicit knowledge of the paraphrase relationships in language can also be helpful in the development of a good written style. A passage in which all sentences consist of the same syntactic structures is monotonous. A student who, in the study of language, has been exposed to the possibilities of conjoining, embedding, and optional transformations can revise an uninteresting sequence of sentences by making use of these syntactic processes.

It is important to note the absence of concrete evidence that the study of formal grammar automatically leads to improved writing ability. Linguists do not suggest that high school or college writing courses include a detailed study of the rules and forms represented in the formal, explicit grammar of English. The point of the discussion above is that students who are aware of general aspects of language, such as ambiguity and paraphrase, will be likely to utilize such information in revising their written work. Their initial written work may not improve, but their added sensitivity to certain aspects of language may contribute to their ability to detect inadequacies in what they have written.

There are, then, a number of practical reasons for the study of language. But the language class need not be a dull means to a useful end. The detailed, explicit, formal rules provided by the linguist in a description of English are not always appropriate for the high school classroom. While the teacher should understand the deep structures and the rules that ultimately may yield an ambiguous sentence like (1), the students can investigate ambiguity more informally by paraphrasing the different interpretations of the sentence.

(1)   Biting dogs can become tiresome.

Rather than emphasizing the formal rules of a grammar, English language teachers can make very effective use of the fact that language is all around us. Students do not need a special laboratory to investigate language, nor are special textbooks required. Simply by paying attention to how people talk one can learn a great deal about English.

The observation and analysis of language in use can be based on a variety of sources accessible to most people in this society. Consider television commercials. Students who are given an assignment to watch television for an evening invariably return to class the next day with examples of ambiguity, puns, nonstandard dialects, and other interesting observations about language. For example, a chain of motels adopted the slogan in (2), almost certainly because of the ambiguity involved in the word *accommodating,* which can be interpreted either as 'obliging and pleasant' or as 'providing accommodations'.

(2)   We are the most accommodating people in the world.

The advertising writers for a low-calorie breakfast cereal provided the linguistically aware members of their audience with a series of commercials involving ambiguity before they finally expressed their point unambiguously. The commercials involved a mother and daughter who were both slender and who looked very similar. The daughter's boyfriend would mistake mother for daughter and then apologize, at which point the mother would say:

(3)   Oh, that's all right; we're often mistaken.

or

(4)   Oh, that's all right; we're often confused.

Subsequently, the commercials were refilmed with a sentence like (5), which did not improve matters very much:

(5)   Oh, that's all right; people often confuse us.

To anyone aware of ambiguity, it is difficult to see how a professional copywriter could produce such sentences inadvertently. Whether or not the ambiguity was intentional, (3), (4), and (5) eventually were replaced with the less interesting, but unambiguous, phrases (6) and (7):

(6) Oh, that's all right; we're often mistaken for one another.

(7) Oh, that's all right; we do look alike.

An almost forgotten controversy involving language and advertising occurred some years ago when a cigarette company initially adopted the phrase in (8):

(8) Winston tastes good like a cigarette should.

Many listeners, having been subjected to lengthy instruction in school on the differences in "correct" usage for *like* and *as,* responded that the phrase was "ungrammatical," and some people even stopped buying the brand of cigarettes in protest. However, the use of *like* in (8) reflected the normal usage of the majority of Americans at the time, and the company developed a highly successful advertising campaign that retained the slogan in spite of the fact that some people considered it nonstandard English.

As with any subject, if the study of language is presented in an interesting manner, it will be more effective. The old approach to English grammar classes, with its emphasis on minor points of usage and on labeling parts of speech and diagraming sentences, was both boring for the students and almost totally ineffective in bringing about changes in usage. People continue to use *who* in sentences where their teachers insisted on *whom*. A more modern, descriptive, and objective approach to the subject, such as that offered in this book, will not result in great changes in usage. However, it usually does lead to greater awareness of language, increased tolerance for dialect variation, and recognition of fundamental issues in such practical areas as foreign language learning.

THE LITERATURE CLASS

In any study of prose or poetry, two matters must be investigated: what authors are saying and how they are saying it. The former involves the content of a literary work; the latter concerns its form. The two are interrelated, and one can neither understand nor appreciate any work of literature without considering both the ideas involved and the way in which these ideas are expressed through language. English, as well as every other human language, provides its speakers with a variety of sentence structures that may be used for the expression of a given meaning. In other words, all languages contain numerous possibilities for paraphrase. The selection of one of these possibilities by an author is the basis of literary style. Students in a literature class cannot be expected to carry out any type of stylistic analysis unless they have been exposed to the possibilities of expression present in their language. Consider the following sentences:

(9) The book that is red looks interesting.

(10) The red book looks interesting.

Both (9) and (10) are ordinary sentences, and both share the same deep structure and meaning. Yet, the effect is different. (10) is somehow more forceful than (9). The presence of a full relative clause in the surface structure of (9) creates a separation between *book* and *interesting,* whereas in (10) the simple adjective, occurring before the noun, reduces the emphasis on the color of the book and focuses attention on *interesting*. If readers encounter one of these sentences in a book, they may comprehend the basic meaning and move on. But a full appreciation of what the author intends can be attained only if the reader is aware of the alternatives the author did not select. Thus, any significant discussion of style in a literary work must take into account not only the actual form of expression but also those possibilities that could have been used. An understanding and awareness of language plays a vital role in the study of literature.

Many scholars from the field of linguistics have made contributions to literary analysis and criticism. Indeed, these areas of study have been interrelated for centuries; recall from Chapter 1 the concerns of the ancient Greek Alexandrians. Modern linguists have proposed three approaches to the analysis of literary style.

Literary language often appears distinct from normal, everyday usage in that it employs vocabulary items, syntactic structures, and phonological sequences that are quite different from those one might encounter in conversation. This is particularly true of poetry. Thus, one approach to the linguistic study of literary style contrasts the literary use of language with more ordinary use.

A second conception of the linguist's contribution to stylistic analysis arises from the fact that the paraphrase possibilities of language provide writers with a choice of how they will express their ideas. Careful studies of several authors and poets indicate that some writers show preferences for certain grammatical patterns or phonological sequences. This partially accounts for the ability of well-read people to recognize the author of a particular passage from his or her style alone.

A third means of analyzing literature is restricted to the study of a particular poem or prose selection. Here one can investigate the internal structure of the literary work, noting the recurrence of linguistic units. For example, rhyming and alliteration in poetry consist of the repetition of sound segments or sequences, and metrical patterns, such as iambic pentameter, require a certain pattern of syllables per line, with a particular arrangement of stressed syllables. In prose, patterns of syntactic structures may be noted, such as the use of conjoining in a passage that contrasts two opposing ideas.

Although somewhat different in emphasis, each of these approaches makes use of the fact that the language in which authors are writing allows them options, while, at the same time, imposing certain restrictions on what they can do. If a poem or a prose selection is to be intelligible to its readers, it must be expressed in a form corresponding to the basic linguistic system shared by author and reader. Thus, if a poem is written in iambic pentameter, there is a general metrical requirement that the even syllables be stressed. Poets who have selected this metrical form must then select their lexical items in such a way that the stresses within words fit the metrical pattern. If the metrical pattern requires a word with stress on the first syllable, poets are free to select any word of the pattern *lóvely, sínful, lústy, sólemn* that suits the concept they wish to express. They are constrained by the stress patterns of English, however, from selecting a word like *adóred, unkínd, undecíded,* or *flambóyant*.

Language in literature plays a special role in dialect writing, where authors attempt to convey to their readers a particular regional or social dialect used by the characters in a story or play. In order to analyze the accuracy and effectiveness of dialect representation, the readers must be familiar with the facts about dialect variation in their language. A number of contemporary authors are themselves native speakers of the dialects they attempt to represent; thus, their representations are more accurate than those of writers in the past, some of whom had only impressions, but little factual knowledge, of nonstandard dialects or of regional dialects other than their own. A common practice in earlier dialect literature was the use of **eye dialect,** providing words with spellings different from the ordinary written form whether or not these special spellings actually reflected pronunciation differences. As an example, consider the spelling *sez* for *says*. Certainly, *sez* is about as close as one can come with the letters of our alphabet to reflecting the actual, normal, standard pronunciation [sɛz]. But an author who writes *sez* usually is attempting to convey to the reader the idea that the character involved speaks a nonstandard dialect. Readers who are unaware of actual pronunciation may even be led to believe that the eye dialect representation is an accurate indication of pronunciation differences. The reader who is conscious of English phonology, however, can recognize eye dialect as a purely stylistic device unrelated to actual pronunciation.

Some writers, who are otherwise highly reliable in representing dialect variations, also distort actual speech by presenting phonological or syntactic features in their characters' speech as invariant when these features are actually used only under certain conditions or to a limited extent. For example, an author may have a character of the lower socioeconomic class always use [n] in place of standard [ŋ], so that we find the spellings *somethin, goin,* and *interestin,* rather than *something, going,* and *interesting*. While it is true that [n] does occur in such words in many nonstandard dialects, it is not the case that this happens 100 percent of the time. Speakers of such dialects utilize [ŋ] in informal speech, to some extent, and almost always in more formal situations. The author's representation of the character's speech is thus linguistically inaccurate, although it should be noted that it may still be stylistically effective.

The study of language in literature need not be restricted to the traditional "good" literature of the normal high school English class. Many of the same principles and insights about literary usage can be obtained from other sources of written English. Newspaper and magazine articles, press releases from industry or government, and advertising can all be surveyed for the techniques of language usage that are particularly effective in the expression of concepts. For example, press releases by the U.S. Department of Defense are often characterized by the use of a special set of lexical items and particular syntactic structures (a style sometimes referred to as *governmentese*), in a way similar to the lexical items and syntactic structures that characterize certain types of poetry and literary prose. As with the study of language itself, the study of language in literature can be closely related to real life and the situations students encounter every day.

SUMMARY

Traditional high school language classes concentrated on superficial, and sometimes outdated, descriptions of language forms and usage. This narrow view of the subject ignored the most fascinating and valuable aspects of language that can be investigated in the schools. One of the high school teacher's chief responsibilities is to design a course in such a way that students understand the practical applications, as well as the more general benefits, of the study of their native language. By discussing such topics as ambiguity, paraphrase, social dialects, written and spoken language use, and the complexity of a linguistic system, a language course can contribute to students' general intellectual development, possibly improve their writing skills, and add to their awareness and appreciation of everyday language usage.

The study of literary style can be greatly enhanced by a knowledge about language. Readers can appreciate the particular style authors have selected to express their ideas only if they are aware of the other possible linguistic forms the authors could have used. An evaluation of the accuracy and effectiveness of dialect literature is possible only if readers have at their disposal facts about actual dialect variation.

FURTHER EXPLORATION

An overview of transformational linguistics and its relevance to English language classes is given by Noam Chomsky in "The Current Scene in Linguistics: Present Directions" (Reibel and Schane 1969). More specifically directed toward the teacher is Chapter 8, "Teaching about Language," in *Teaching English to Speakers of English* by Bradford Arthur. Composition and literature are discussed in Part 2, "The Application of Transformational Grammar to English Teaching," of the anthology *Readings in Applied Transformational Grammar,* edited by Mark Lester. Roderick A. Jacobs and Peter S. Rosenbaum also deal with these topics in *Transformations, Style, and Meaning.* More technical studies on linguistics and the study of literature appear in the collection *Linguistics and Literary Style,* edited by Donald C. Freeman; the introductory chapter, written by the editor, provides a clear survey of the basic issues. A short, nontechnical article for those interested in poetry is Paul Kiparsky's "The Role of Linguistics in a Theory of Poetry" (Bloomfield and Haugen 1974); primarily concerned with poetic language and syntax is "The Application of Transformational Grammar to Literary Analysis," Chapter 11 of *Guide to Transformational Grammar: History, Theory, Practice* by John T. Grinder and Suzette Haden Elgin.

1. A major concern of contemporary American educators is the apparent decrease in reading and writing abilities of high school graduates and college students. Many diverse factors have contributed to this phenomenon, but educational authorities have yet to agree on which factors are most significant. Use your knowledge of linguistics, language, and language learning to discuss the possible effects of the following on reading and writing ability. What other factors might be involved in this situation?

(a) Absence of required traditional English grammar courses in high school.
(b) Increased television viewing.
(c) Decreased reading and writing experiences in high school.

(d) Increase in the number of students graduating from high school and going on to college who are native speakers of nonstandard dialects of English.

(e) Shifts in language use throughout society from formal to informal style.

2. Devise a lesson on regional or social dialects for presentation to a group of high school students. If possible, obtain permission from the administration of a local high school and conduct the lesson.

3. Select a short work of poetry (no more than fourteen lines) and prepare an analysis by listing (1) the instances in which the poet has deviated from normal, conversational language usage and (2) any syntactic structures that the poet uses several times (for example, sequences of adjectives, conjoined phrases, inverted word order, multiple negatives). Rewrite the poem as a prose selection.

EPILOGUE

The work carried out by American linguists during the first half of this century consisted largely of the collection of data about the directly observable aspects of language. In the past twenty years, modern linguistic research has made significant progress in explaining language, as well as in describing it. In this book, we have surveyed many of the basic assumptions, research results, and applications of contemporary linguistics, but, as with all surveys, much has been omitted or mentioned only in passing. None of the topics discussed here has been treated in depth. The reader who wishes to achieve a more complete understanding of language must now go on to more advanced books, articles, and courses.

Linguists, too, will go on with their work, for the more that is learned about language, the more questions arise. We are only beginning to understand just how abstract and complex human languages are. Since only the most superficial aspects of a linguistic system are directly observable, the study of language is a difficult, challenging, and rewarding undertaking. To those who work within the field of linguistics, the insights achieved in the past are exciting, and many important discoveries about the nature of language have been made. But there are undoubtedly many aspects of language as yet unknown, unexplained, and even unsuspected. For example, there is still much to be learned about underlying syntactic structures and the relationship between syntax and semantics. Even in phonology, the linguists' work is not over. The universal system of phonetic features must be tested and refined, and the phonological systems of a great number of languages must be investigated and their universal properties determined.

An even greater challenge for the future of linguistic studies arises from an increasing awareness of the interaction of linguistic and nonlinguistic factors in speakers' knowledge and performance. The areas of linguistics, psycholinguistics, and sociolinguistics are beginning to merge as each approach considers factors previously left to others for investigation. The study of pragmatics and the theory of generative semantics, both mentioned in Chapter 17, demonstrate this trend. In another ten years, the topics of central concern to linguists may be quite different from those stressed today. Students sometimes find this prospect disturbing, but actually it is an exciting indication of progress in our understanding of human language.

As our understanding of language and language use increases, linguists and specialists in other, related fields must reevaluate theories, methods, and techniques in such practical areas as foreign language instruction, the teaching of reading and writing, and the stylistic analysis of poetry and prose. Only by means of such efforts will the results of linguistic investigations have effects for all of those in our society who might benefit from future developments.

Throughout the course of history, one of the greatest challenges to scholars has been the study of man himself. Man is unique among the creatures of earth in possessing language. The study of language reveals properties of the human mind, and thereby contributes to our understanding of man. Linguistics is a science, searching for generalizations and explanations of language, emphasizing objectivity and the explicit formalization and testing of hypotheses, but linguistics is also a humanistic discipline, investigating the most valuable, unique, and universal possession of man—language.

BIBLIOGRAPHY

Akmajian, Adrian, and Heny, Frank. 1975. *An Introduction to the Principles of Transformational Syntax*. Cambridge, Mass.: MIT Press.

Anderson, Wallace L., and Stageberg, Norman C., eds. 1975. *Introductory Readings on Language*. 4th ed. New York: Holt, Rinehart and Winston.

Anttila, Raimo. 1972. *An Introduction to Historical and Comparative Linguistics*. New York: Macmillan.

Arlotto, Anthony. 1972. *Introduction to Historical Linguistics*. Boston: Houghton Mifflin.

Arthur, Bradford. 1973. *Teaching English to Speakers of English*. New York: Harcourt Brace Jovanovich.

Atwood, E. Bagby. 1962. *The Regional Vocabulary of Texas*. Austin: University of Texas Press.

Bach, Emmon, and Harms, Robert T., eds. 1968. *Universals in Linguistic Theory*. New York: Holt, Rinehart and Winston.

Bar-Adon, Aaron, and Leopold, Werner F., eds. 1971. *Child Language: A Book of Readings*. Englewood Cliffs, N. J.: Prentice-Hall.

Baratz, Joan C., and Shuy, Roger W., eds. 1969. *Teaching Black Children to Read*. Washington, D.C.: Center for Applied Linguistics.

Bloom, Lois, Hood, Lois, and Lightbown, Patsy. 1974. "Imitation in Language Development: If, When, and Why." *Cognitive Psychology,* 6:380–420.

Bloomfield, Morton, and Haugen, Einar, eds. 1974. *Language as a Human Problem*. New York: W. W. Norton.

Brown, Roger. 1973. *A First Language: The Early Stages*. Cambridge, Mass.: Harvard University Press.

Burt, Marina K. 1971. *From Deep to Surface Structure: An Introduction to Transformational Syntax*. New York: Harper & Row.

Cattell, N. R. 1969. *The New English Grammar: A Descriptive Introduction*. Cambridge, Mass.: MIT Press.

Chall, Jeanne S. 1967. *Learning to Read: The Great Debate*. New York: McGraw-Hill.

Chastain, Kenneth. 1971. *The Development of Modern-Language Skills: Theory to Practice*. Philadelphia: Center for Curriculum Development.

Chomsky, Carol. 1969. *The Acquisition of Syntax in Children from 5 to 10*. MIT Press Research Monograph Series, No. 57. Cambridge, Mass.

Chomsky, Noam. 1957. *Syntactic Structures*. The Hague: Mouton.

————. 1965. *Aspects of the Theory of Syntax*. Cambridge, Mass.: MIT Press.

————. 1972a. *Language and Mind*. Enlarged ed. New York: Harcourt Brace Jovanovich.

————. 1972b. *Studies on Semantics in Generative Grammar*. The Hague: Mouton.

————. 1975. "Questions of Form and Interpretation." *Linguistic Analysis*, 1:75–109.

————. 1976. *Reflections on Language*. New York: Pantheon Books.

————, and Halle, Morris. 1965. "Some Controversial Questions in Phonological Theory." *Journal of Linguistics*, 1:97–138.

————. 1968. *The Sound Pattern of English*. New York: Harper & Row.

Cole, Peter, and Morgan, Jerry L., eds. 1975. *Syntax and Semantics, Volume 3: Speech Acts*. New York: Academic Press.

Dale, Philip S. 1976. *Language Development: Structure and Function*. 2nd ed. New York: Holt, Rinehart and Winston.

Dato, Daniel P., ed. 1975. *Georgetown University Round Table on Languages and Linguistics 1975: Developmental Psycholinguistics: Theory and Applications*. Washington, D.C.: Georgetown University Press.

Dillard, J. L. 1972. *Black English: Its History and Usage in the United States*. New York: Random House.

————. 1976. *American Talk: Where Our Words Come From*. New York: Random House.

Dillon, George L. 1977. *Introduction to Contemporary Linguistic Semantics*. Englewood Cliffs, N. J.: Prentice-Hall.

Dingwall, William Orr, ed. 1971. *A Survey of Linguistic Science*. College Park: Linguistics Program/University of Maryland.

Dinneen, Francis P. 1967. *An Introduction to General Linguistics*. New York: Holt, Rinehart and Winston.

Di Pietro, Robert J. 1971. *Language Structures in Contrast*. Rowley, Mass.: Newbury House.

Durr, William K., ed. 1967. *Reading Instruction: Dimensions and Issues*. New York: Houghton Mifflin.

Emery, Donald W. 1973. *Variant Spellings in Modern American Dictionaries*. Rev. ed. Urbana, Ill.: National Council of Teachers of English.

Emig, Janet A., Fleming, James T., and Popp, Helen M., eds. 1966. *Language and Learning*. New York: Harcourt, Brace & World.

Fasold, Ralph W., and Shuy, Roger W., eds. 1970. *Teaching Standard English in the Inner City*. Washington, D.C.: Center for Applied Linguistics.

Ferguson, Charles A., gen. ed. 1962—. *Contrastive Structure Series*. Chicago: University of Chicago Press.

————, and Slobin, Dan Isaac, eds. 1973. *Studies of Child Language Development*. New York: Holt, Rinehart and Winston.

Fishman, Joshua A. 1972. *The Sociology of Language: An Interdisciplinary Social Science Approach to Language in Society*. Rowley, Mass.: Newbury House.

Fodor, Jerry A., Bever, Thomas G., and Garrett, Merrill F. 1974. *The Psychology of Language*. New York: McGraw-Hill.

Fodor, Jerry A., and Katz, Jerrold J., eds. 1964. *The Structure of Language: Readings in the Philosophy of Language*. Englewood Cliffs, N. J.: Prentice-Hall.

Freeman, Donald C., ed. 1970. *Linguistics and Literary Style*. New York: Holt, Rinehart and Winston.

Gardner, R. Allen, and Gardner, Beatrice. 1969. "Teaching Sign Language to a Chimpanzee." *Science,* 165:664–672.

Gardner, Robert C., and Lambert, Wallace E. 1972. *Attitudes and Motivation in Second-Language Learning*. Rowley, Mass.: Newbury House.

Gelb, I. J. 1963. *A Study of Writing*. Rev. ed. Chicago: University of Chicago Press.

Gibson, Eleanor J., and Levin, Harry. 1975. *The Psychology of Reading*. Cambridge, Mass.: MIT Press.

Gleason, H.A., Jr. 1961. *An Introduction to Descriptive Linguistics*. Rev. ed. New York: Holt, Rinehart and Winston.

Goodman, Yetta M., and Burke, Carolyn L. 1972. *Reading Miscue Inventory Manual: Procedure for Diagnosis and Evaluation*. New York: Macmillan.

Greenberg, Joseph H., ed. 1966. *Universals of Language*. 2nd ed. Cambridge, Mass.: MIT Press.

Grinder, John T., and Elgin, Suzette Haden. 1973. *Guide to Transformational Grammar: History, Theory, Practice*. New York: Holt, Rinehart and Winston.

Halle, Morris, and Keyser, Samuel Jay. 1971. *English Stress: Its Form, Its Growth, and Its Role in Verse*. New York: Harper & Row.

Harris, James W. 1969. *Spanish Phonology*. MIT Press Research Monograph Series, No. 54. Cambridge, Mass.

Hernandez-Chavez, Eduardo, Cohen, Andrew D., and Beltramo, Anthony F., eds. 1975. *El Lenguaje de los Chicanos: Regional and Social Characteristics of Language Use by Mexican-Americans*. Arlington, Va.: Center for Applied Linguistics.

Householder, F. W. 1965. "On Some Recent Claims in Phonological Theory." *Journal of Linguistics,* 1:13–34.

Hyman, Larry M. 1975. *Phonology: Theory and Analysis*. New York: Holt, Rinehart and Winston.

Irwin, John V., and Marge, Michael, eds. 1972. *Principles of Childhood Language Disabilities*. New York: Appleton-Century-Crofts.

Jacobs, Roderick A., and Rosenbaum, Peter S. 1968. *English Transformational Grammar*. Lexington, Mass.: Xerox College Publishing.

―――. 1971. *Transformations, Style, and Meaning.* Lexington, Mass.: Xerox College Publishing.

Jakobovits, Leon A., and Miron, Murray S., eds. 1967. *Readings in the Psychology of Language.* Englewood Cliffs, N. J.: Prentice-Hall.

Jakobson, Roman. 1968. *Child Language, Aphasia, and Phonological Universals.* Translated by Allan R. Keiler. The Hague: Mouton.

Katz, Jerrold J., and Postal, Paul M. 1964. *An Integrated Theory of Linguistic Descriptions.* MIT Press Research Monograph Series, No. 26. Cambridge, Mass.

Kavanagh, James F., and Mattingly, Ignatius G., eds. 1972. *Language by Ear and by Eye: The Relationships between Speech and Reading.* Cambridge, Mass.: MIT Press.

Kelly, Louis G. 1969. *25 Centuries of Language Teaching.* Rowley, Mass.: Newbury House.

Kerr, Elizabeth M., and Aderman, Ralph M., eds. 1971. *Aspects of American English.* 2nd ed. New York: Harcourt Brace Jovanovich.

Keyser, Samuel Jay, and Postal, Paul M. 1976. *Beginning English Grammar.* New York: Harper & Row.

King, Robert D. 1969. *Historical Linguistics and Generative Grammar.* Englewood Cliffs, N. J.: Prentice-Hall.

Kornfeld, J. R. 1971. "Theoretical Issues in Child Phonology." In *Papers from the Seventh Regional Meeting, Chicago Linguistic Society, April 16-18, 1971.* Chicago: Chicago Linguistic Society.

Kurath, Hans. 1949. *A Word Geography of the Eastern United States.* Ann Arbor: University of Michigan Press.

―――, and McDavid, Raven I., Jr. 1961. *The Pronunciation of English in the Atlantic States.* Ann Arbor: University of Michigan Press.

Labov, William. 1970. *The Study of Nonstandard English.* Urbana, Ill.: National Council of Teachers of English.

―――. 1972a. *Language in the Inner City: Studies in the Black English Vernacular.* Philadelphia: University of Pennsylvania Press.

―――. 1972b. *Sociolinguistic Patterns.* Philadelphia: University of Pennsylvania Press.

Ladefoged, Peter. 1962. *Elements of Acoustic Phonetics.* Chicago: University of Chicago Press.

―――. 1975. *A Course in Phonetics.* New York: Harcourt Brace Jovanovich.

Lado, Robert. 1964. *Language Teaching: A Scientific Approach.* New York: McGraw-Hill.

Lakoff, Robin. 1972. "Language in Context." *Language,* 48:907–927.

―――. 1975. *Language and Woman's Place.* New York: Harper & Row.

Lambert, Wallace E. 1972. *Language, Psychology, and Culture: Essays by Wallace E. Lambert.* Selected and introduced by Anwar S. Dil. Stanford, California: Stanford University Press.

Langacker, Ronald W. 1972. *Fundamentals of Linguistic Analysis.* New York: Harcourt Brace Jovanovich.

Langendoen, D. Terence. 1969. *The Study of Syntax: The Generative-Transformational*

Approach to the Structure of American English. New York: Holt, Rinehart and Winston.

Lees, Robert B. 1966. *The Grammar of English Nominalizations*. 4th printing. Bloomington, Ind.: Indiana University/The Hague: Mouton.

Lehmann, Winfred P. 1973. *Historical Linguistics: An Introduction*. 2nd ed. New York: Holt, Rinehart and Winston.

————, ed. 1975. *Language and Linguistics in the People's Republic of China*. Austin: University of Texas Press.

Lenneberg, Eric H. 1967. *Biological Foundations of Language*. New York: Wiley.

Lester, Mark, ed. 1973. *Readings in Applied Transformational Grammar*. 2nd ed. New York: Holt, Rinehart and Winston.

Levin, Harry, and Williams, Joanna P., eds. 1970. *Basic Studies on Reading*. New York: Basic Books.

Liles, Bruce L. 1975. *An Introduction to Linguistics*. Englewood Cliffs, N. J.: Prentice-Hall.

Lugton, Robert C., and Heinle, Charles H., eds. 1971. *Toward a Cognitive Approach to Second-Language Acquisition*. Philadelphia: Center for Curriculum Development.

Lyons, John. 1968. *Introduction to Theoretical Linguistics*. Cambridge: Cambridge University Press.

————. 1970. *Noam Chomsky*. New York: Viking Press.

Marchand, Hans. 1969. *The Categories and Types of Present-Day English Word-Formation*. 2nd ed. Munich: C. H. Beck.

McCawley, James D. 1968. *The Phonological Component of a Grammar of Japanese*. The Hague: Mouton.

McNeill, David. 1970. *The Acquisition of Language: The Study of Developmental Psycholinguistics*. New York: Harper & Row.

Moore, Timothy E., ed. 1973. *Cognitive Development and the Acquisition of Language*. New York: Academic Press.

Morris, William, and Morris, Mary. 1975. *Harper Dictionary of Contemporary Usage*. New York: Harper & Row.

Moulton, William G. 1962. *The Sounds of English and German*. Chicago: University of Chicago Press.

Nida, Eugene A. 1949. *Morphology: The Descriptive Analysis of Words*. 2nd ed. Ann Arbor: University of Michigan Press.

Nilsen, Don L. F., and Nilsen, Alleen Pace. 1975. *Semantic Theory: A Linguistic Perspective*. Rowley, Mass.: Newbury House.

Oxford English Dictionary. Oxford University Press, 1933.

Palermo, David S., and Molfese, Dennis L. 1972. "Language Acquisition from Age Five Onward." *Psychological Bulletin,* 78:409–428.

Palmer, F. R. 1976. *Semantics: A New Outline*. New York: Cambridge University Press.

Parret, Herman, ed. 1974. *Discussing Language*. The Hague: Mouton.

Partridge, Eric. 1966. *Origins: A Short Etymological Dictionary of Modern English*. 4th ed. London: Routledge and Kegan Paul.

BIBLIOGRAPHY

431

Penfield, Wilder, and Roberts, Lamar. 1959. *Speech and Brain-Mechanisms*. Princeton, N. J.: Princeton University Press.

Pike, Kenneth L. 1947. *Phonemics: A Technique for Reducing Languages to Writing*. Ann Arbor: University of Michigan Press.

Politzer, Robert L. 1965. *Teaching French: An Introduction to Applied Linguistics*. 2nd ed. New York: Blaisdell.

———. 1968. *Teaching German: A Linguistic Orientation*. Waltham, Mass.: Blaisdell.

———, and Staubach, Charles N. 1965. *Teaching Spanish: A Linguistic Orientation*. Rev. ed. New York: Blaisdell.

Postal, Paul. 1964. *Constituent Structure: A Study of Contemporary Models of Syntactic Description*. The Hague: Mouton.

Premack, David. 1970. "The Education of S*A*R*A*H: A Chimp Learns the Language." *Psychology Today,* 4:54–58.

———. 1971. "Language in Chimpanzee?" *Science,* 172:808-822.

Pyles, Thomas. 1971. *The Origins and Development of the English Language*. 2nd ed. New York: Harcourt Brace Jovanovich.

Quirk, Randolph. 1962. *The Use of English*. London: Longmans, Green.

Reed, Carroll E. 1977. *Dialects of American English*. Rev. ed. Amherst: University of Massachusetts Press.

Reibel, David A., and Schane, Sanford A., eds. 1969. *Modern Studies in English: Readings in Transformational Grammar*. Englewood Cliffs, N. J.: Prentice-Hall.

Richards, Jack C., ed. 1974. *Error Analysis: Perspectives on Second Language Acquisition*. London: Longman.

Robins, R. H. 1967. *A Short History of Linguistics*. Bloomington: Indiana University Press.

Sadock, Jerrold M. 1974. *Toward a Linguistic Theory of Speech Acts*. New York: Academic Press.

Schane, Sanford A. 1968. *French Phonology and Morphology*. MIT Press Research Monograph Series, No. 45. Cambridge, Mass.

———. 1973. *Generative Phonology*. Englewood Cliffs, N. J.: Prentice-Hall.

Schrier, Allan M., and Stollnitz, Fred, eds. 1971. *Behavior of Nonhuman Primates, Vol. 4*. New York: Academic Press.

Searle, John R. 1969. *Speech Acts: An Essay in the Philosophy of Language*. New York: Cambridge University Press.

Sebeok, Thomas A., and Ramsay, Alexandra, eds. 1969. *Approaches to Animal Communication*. The Hague: Mouton.

Shores, David L., ed. 1972. *Contemporary English: Change and Variation*. Philadelphia: J. B. Lippincott.

Shuy, Roger W. 1967. *Discovering American Dialects*. Urbana, Ill.: National Council of Teachers of English.

Sledd, James, and Ebbitt, Wilma R., eds. 1962. *Dictionaries and THAT Dictionary*. Glenview, Ill.: Scott, Foresman.

Sloat, Clarence, Taylor, Sharon Henderson, and Hoard, James E. 1978. *Introduction to Phonology*. Englewood Cliffs, N. J.: Prentice-Hall.

Slobin, Dan I. 1971. *Psycholinguistics*. Glenview, Ill.: Scott, Foresman.

Smith, Frank. 1973. *Psycholinguistics and Reading*. New York: Holt, Rinehart and Winston.

Steinberg, Danny D., and Jakobovits, Leon A., eds. 1971. *Semantics: An Interdisciplinary Reader in Philosophy, Linguistics, and Psychology*. New York: Cambridge University Press.

Stockwell, Robert P. 1977. *Foundations of Syntactic Theory*. Englewood Cliffs, N. J.: Prentice-Hall.

Stoller, Paul, ed. 1975. *Black American English: Its Background and Its Usage in the Schools and in Literature*. New York: Dell Publishing.

Teschner, Richard V., Bills, Garland, and Craddock, Jerry, eds. 1975. *Spanish and English of United States Hispanos*. Arlington, Va.: Center for Applied Linguistics.

Traugott, Elizabeth Closs. 1972. *A History of English Syntax*. New York: Holt, Rinehart and Winston.

Trudgill, Peter. 1974. *Sociolinguistics: An Introduction*. Baltimore, Maryland: Penguin.

Valdman, Albert, ed. 1966. *Trends in Language Teaching*. New York: McGraw-Hill.

Van Riper, Charles. 1972. *Speech Correction: Principles and Methods*. 5th ed. Englewood Cliffs, N. J.: Prentice-Hall.

Venezky, Richard L. 1970. *The Structure of English Orthography*. The Hague: Mouton.

Webster's Third New International Dictionary of the English Language, Unabridged. Springfield, Mass.: G. & C. Merriam, 1961.

Wentworth, Harold, and Flexner, Stuart Berg, comps. 1975. *Dictionary of American Slang*. 2nd supplemented ed. New York: Thomas Y. Crowell.

Williams, Frederick, ed. 1970. *Language and Poverty: Perspectives on a Theme*. Chicago: Markham Publishing.

Wilson, Graham, ed. 1967. *A Linguistics Reader*. New York: Harper & Row.

Wolfram, Walt, and Fasold, Ralph W. 1974. *The Study of Social Dialects in American English*. Englewood Cliffs, N. J.: Prentice-Hall.

SUBJECT INDEX

BRITISH SPELLING, 162
BROAD TRANSCRIPTION, 86–87

CALQUE, 56
CASE GRAMMAR, 263, 274
CASE RELATIONS, 262–263, 275. *See also* semantic relations
CAWDREY, ROBERT, 72
[CENTRAL], 97
CHEST PULSE, 105
CHILD LANGUAGE ACQUISITION. *See* native language acquisition
CHOMSKY, NOAM, 11. *See also* "Author Index"
CLASSES OF SOUNDS, 89–90, 95–96, 128–129
CLICHÉS, 65
COGNITION, 5
COGNITIVE APPROACH, TO FOREIGN LANGUAGE TEACHING, 358, 362, 365–366, 408
COGNITIVE DEVELOPMENT, 330, 345–346, 350–351, 353
COGNITIVE VIEW, OF READING, 388, 392, 399
COINING, 59–62, 65
COLLOQUIAL. *See* style, colloquial
COMMAND. *See* imperatives
COMPARATIVE METHOD, 282–284, 290–291
COMPETENCE, 14–17, 21–22, 151–152, 269–270, 299, 396
    and foreign language learning, 358–359
    and meaning, 261, 263–270
    and native language acquisition, 318, 334, 339, 398
    and phonology, 80, 120
    and syntax, 170, 216–217
    and word formation, 28, 31, 41–42
COMPLEMENTIZER, 235–236
COMPLEMENTS, 221–226, 231–232, 234, 236, 256
COMPOSITION, 5, 418, 422. *See also* writing
COMPOUNDING, 42–48, 57, 61–62
CONJOINING, 217–219, 231, 234, 236–237, 334

CONJUNCTIONS, 217, 234
[CONSONANTAL], 91–93
CONSONANT CLUSTERS, 133, 144–145, 157–158, 271, 306, 312, 323–324
CONSONANTS, 91–93, 96–98, 101–102
CONSTITUENT, 178–181
CONSTITUENT STRUCTURE, 178–192
CONSTITUENT STRUCTURE RULES
    in a complete grammar, 196, 245, 248, 250, 256
    for deep structure, 196, 219, 229–237, 273
    for surface structure, 185–190, 196, 199, 220, 229, 234
    and universals, 273
CONSTITUENT TYPES, 182–185
CONSTITUTIVE RULES, 17–19, 21–22, 167
CONSTRUCTION, 178–181
CONTENT WORDS. *See* lexical morphemes
CONTEXTUAL GENERALIZATION, 342–344, 350–351
[CONTINUANT], 93, 271
CONTOUR TONE LANGUAGES, 106
CONTRASTIVE ANALYSIS, 361, 366–367, 380
CONVERSATIONAL PRINCIPLES, 266–267, 274–276
COOING, 319
[CORONAL], 98–102, 128–129
CORTEX, 346
[COVERED], 101, 271
CREATIVITY, 17, 36, 42, 49, 377. *See also* infinite number of sentences; productivity
CREOLE LANGUAGE, 310
CRYING, 319
CUMMINGS, E. E., 35, 40–41, 47, 383

DARWIN, 10
DEEP STRUCTURE, 195–237, 245, 248, 250, 256–257, 273
    in generative semantics, 263, 265, 268–269, 273–274
    properties of, 204–206
    syntactic evidence for, 206–210, 236–237
    and universals, 270–273

LANGUAGE INDEX

AUTHOR INDEX

Shuy, Roger W., 300, 413
Skinner, B. F., 350
Sledd, James, 74
Sloat, Clarence, 86, 107
Slobin, Dan Isaac, 275, 335, 351
Smith, Frank, 399
Stageberg, Norman C., 61
Steinberg, Danny D., 257
Stockwell, Robert P., 234
Stoller, Paul, 413
Stollnitz, Fred, 351

Taylor, Sharon Henderson, 86, 107
Teschner, Richard V., 313

Traugott, Elizabeth Closs, 290–291
Trudgill, Peter, 275

Valdman, Albert, 366
Van Riper, Charles, 400
Venezky, Richard L., 399

Weksel, W., 351
Wentworth, Harold, 74
Whitaker, Harry A., 351
Williams, Frederick, 413
Williams, Joanna P., 399
Wilson, Graham, 175
Wolfram, Walt, 313, 413